The Choices of Power

Marc J. Roberts and Jeremy S. Bluhm

With the assistance of Margaret Gerteis

The Choices of Power

Utilities Face the Environmental Challenge

HARVARD UNIVERSITY PRESS

CAMBRIDGE, MASSACHUSETTS, AND LONDON, ENGLAND   1981

Library of Congress Cataloging in Publication Data

Roberts, Marc J
    The choices of power.

    Includes bibliographical references and index.
    1.   Electric utilities — Environmental aspects —
United States — Case studies.   2.   Electric utilities —
Environmental aspects — Ontario — Case studies.
I.   Bluhm, Jeremy S., joint author.   II.   Title.
HD9685.U5R63   363.7'31   80-20729
ISBN 0-674-12780-3

Preface

The last two decades have been very demanding ones for American institutions. The struggle for civil rights, the development of the so-called counterculture, the rise of the consumer and environmental protection movements, the agitation over the Vietnam war, Watergate, and the growth of the women's movement have all made it necessary for business and government to display greater flexibility, sensitivity, imagination, and responsibility. Meeting these demands has not been easy. Those who have challenged particular organizations have often found that institutional power, inertia, and ambition thwart efforts to achieve social change. At the same time, many within these organizations have felt that they were being pressed to do the impossible.

Despite these difficulties, many social changes have taken place, which indicates that change is indeed possible. Government and economic policies can incorporate new ideas, and institutions can adapt. The record of the last twenty years shows much that is encouraging. Yet the forces that determine the success or failure of efforts to alter political and economic institutions still seem confusing and often beyond control. Policies and politics appear to be determined for the most part by large, impersonal bureaucracies whose operations seem to offer little opportunity for individual thought, action, or responsibility, either for people inside or outside the organizations.

This book illuminates the process of organizational change, as shown by an inside view of six electric utilities. It is designed to help individuals understand and more effectively influence such large organizations, whether they work within them, interact with them, or both. In a sense, it represents an attempt to contribute to the revival of an older school of economic analysis, now largely displaced by formal mathematical theorizing based on the assumption of consistent profit maximization and on statistical investigation. Its intellectual traditions go back to Max Weber, Thorstein Veblen, and Joseph Schumpeter, continue through a classic work by Adolph Berle and Gardiner Means, and find current expression in the work of writers as diverse as John Kenneth Galbraith, Alfred D. Chandler, Jr., and Herbert Simon. Although we appreciate the power and rigor of formal methods, we believe that this older methodological tradition of nonquantitative theorizing and detailed case study evidence can contribute greatly to the understanding of social and economic processes. It emphasizes the diversity of managerial motivation, and thus facilitates the empirical study of specific, complex decisions that are inexplicable in terms of simpler models and assumptions.

Our decision to study electric utilities was prompted in part by a comment made to Marc Roberts by Aubrey Wagner, then chairman of the board of the Tennessee Valley Authority, at a conference on energy and the environment held in 1972 at Johnson State College in Johnson, Vermont. The conference was sponsored by the Sierra Club, and those present included scholars, government officials, representatives of environmental organizations, and utility executives. During one of the many animated conversations that took place among the participants, Wagner extended a friendly invitation. "Young man," he said to Roberts, "you should come down to TVA and see how we do things—see what the problems of responding to environmental regulations are really like." Ultimately we did visit TVA, Roberts having first formulated a research plan and obtained support for the project. Then a member of the Department of Economics at Harvard, he submitted a proposal to the Ford Foundation, whose subsequent generosity made possible the first two years of fieldwork and writing.

A major goal of Roberts' research was the reexamination of the apparently oversimplified motivational and behavioral assumptions underlying traditional economic theories of the firm. An extensive field study of six utilities would not only provide data for such a reevaluation, but would shed light on social policy issues such as environmental decision making and would explore ways of judging economic outcomes other than the traditional criterion of short-run economic efficiency. The study was designed instead to focus on the longer-run, dynamic question of how institutions respond to external change. The conceptual framework that Roberts developed to guide the study (see Chapter 2) in its earliest versions predates the empirical work done as part of this project—although it was refined and developed in the course of our work.

In mid-1973, at the time the study began, Jeremy Bluhm was a Harvard undergraduate concentrating in government but also taking a number of economics courses, including several taught by Roberts. He shared Roberts' interest in the way in which organizational and political factors influence economic decisions, and, as a former member of Ralph Nader's staff, he wanted to learn more about the reasons for the ineffectiveness of much environmental and consumer regulation. Starting as a research assistant with the project, he soon became a full partner in the research and writing.

The Choices of Power does not try to evaluate particular organizations or decisions as either "good" or "bad." Our intent was to learn about the social and organizational processes that lay behind these decisions. Certainly, we have personal views about what course of action is best. On the most general level, we favor giving the environment more careful protection than it has received in the past. On the issue of nuclear power, we have conflicting opinions. Jeremy Bluhm feels that the inherent risks and inevitable operational problems associated with nuclear power argue against any expanded dependence on this form of electricity generation. Marc Roberts feels that, given the environmental risks of using fossil fuels, nuclear power may well be the lesser evil, particularly if plants are located far from population centers and perhaps built underground.

Organizational decisions that affect the environment are never easy to make. This book explores the many factors that influence such decisions, and suggests ways in which organizations can be encouraged to make choices that are more responsive to the environment and to society at large.

During the seven years we worked on this project, we received assistance from many people. Margaret Gerteis did follow-up research, participated in revisions of two of the case studies, and helped reformulate the structure and argument of the book. Lane McIntosh made a substantial contribution to the research on the two California companies. Others who contributed to the research effort were Nancy Boxer, Susan Catler, Joan Youngman, Emily Tipermas, and Wanda Beard.

The comments of many readers were extremely valuable in helping us define what we wanted to say and in our efforts to refine particular points. These sources of support and advice included: John Kenneth Galbraith, Richard Neustadt, Richard Caves, James Duesenberry, Richard Stewart, Samuel Beer, Thomas Schelling, John Dunlop, Graham Allison, Donald Price,

Kenneth Johnson, Jonathan Brown, Kenneth Dryden, William Beckett, Wilfred Roberts, and Seymour Bluhm. They are not responsible for the use we made of their advice, or for any errors that may remain in the text.

This book has gone through many, many revisions over the years, and the burden of typing and retyping them fell on a valiant crew: Lois Hager, Karla Kelly, Laurie Auerbach, Marian Miele, Mark Slawson, Barbara Donnelly, and Mary Schaefer. All have the authors' profoundest appreciation for this work and for help with many administrative details.

Maria Kawecki did a masterful job of pruning and refining our prose. For her skill, energy, tolerance, and attention to detail, she has our admiration and thanks.

The help and encouragement of Marshall Robinson, former vice-president of the Ford Foundation, and of the foundation itself, are gratefully acknowledged. The Harvard School of Public Health supported our work out of funds provided by a series of grants and contracts for curriculum development and research. Without the financial, organizational, and personal aid provided by the school and by its dean, Howard Hiatt, this project never would have been brought to completion. The support of the Department of Health, Education, and Welfare during various stages of the work is also gratefully noted.

We would particularly like to thank the managers and staff members of the six utilities for the time and energy they devoted to our study and for patiently awaiting its outcome. It was a great privilege for us to have had the opportunity to share in their work and to learn about what they did and thought. They may not agree with everything we say here, and they certainly bear no responsibility for it. We hope that they will find the study fruitful, nevertheless.

Of those who are or were with the Tennessee Valley Authority, we wish especially to thank Aubrey Wagner, who not only was generous with his own time but made every effort to facilitate our work. Two of his staff people, Paul Evans and Pete Stewart, were gracious and effective in making arrangements for us. Among those we interviewed, we imposed particularly on the time of Frank Gartrell and Larry Montgomery and we much appreciate their cooperation. At the closing stages of our work, the new chairman of the board of TVA, David Freeman, continued the cooperative relationship. Others who helped us greatly include: Robert Betts, John Bynon, Roy Dunham, James Durrell, E. C. Hill, Albert Hudson, Nat Hughes, George Kimmons, Gerald

McGlamery, John Oliver, Jack Rozek, Lynn Seeber, Lee Shep-
peard, Frank Smith, H. N. Stroud, Fred Thomas, Louis Van
Mol, Lewis Wallace, Grahm Wallis, and G. O. Wessenauer.

At Pacific Gas and Electric, our initial contact was through
Frederick Searls, at that time general council. Our initial guide
through the organization was William Johns. We are grateful to
them and to the top management of the company for their help
and assistance in making our study possible. Many other people
gave willingly of their time, including Walter Allen, Clint Ash-
wood, Larry Barrett, John Bonner, Ralph Brooks, John Cooper,
Phillip Damask, Owen Davis, Kenneth Diercks, Malcolm Fur-
bush, William Gallavan, Robert Gerdes, John Gibson, Elmer
Hall, Glen Hessler, Elmer Johnson, Sharaz Kadarali, Ellis Langley, Jr., John LaRue, Ralph Longaker, Paul Matthews, Ferdinand Mautz, Eugene Meyers, Frederick Mielke, Jr., Richard
Miller, John Morrisey, James O'Keefe, Ray Perry, Richard Peterson, Bart Shackelford, Stanley Skinner, Gordon Smith, John
Sproul, and Harold Williamson.

Among those at the Los Angeles Department of Water and
Power we wish to thank former general manager Robert Phillips,
current general manager Louis Winnard, and chief electrical
engineer James Mulloy for cooperating with our study and for
allowing us to interview widely throughout the Department. Special thanks are also due to the staff of the Office of Environmental Coordination for directing us to appropriate personnel,
setting up interviews, and assisting us willingly with many details.
To them and to the many engineers and other staff people in the
Department who gave so freely of their time, we are most grateful.

At Ontario Hydro we are indebted to Harold A. Smith for
facilitating our study, and to Pat Campbell for his assistance in
arranging our interviews. During the interview process, Arthur
Hill and Wes James were particularly helpful. In addition, we are
pleased to acknowledge the help of C. H. Clark, George Gather-
cole, D. K. Gillies, Douglas Gordon, Douglas Harrison, Barry
Havelock, Edwin Holdup, William Killough, Loren McConnell,
William Morison, Milan Nastich, William Polson, W. E. Raney,
Harold P. Smith, Michael Spence, Robert Swift, J. H. Weghorne,
Bruce Wilson, and W. H. Winter.

Our research at the Southern Company was facilitated by the
cooperation of Clyde Lilly, William Harrison, and William Reed,
and by the willingness of Alvin Vogtle to make his own time, and
the time of these and other members of his organization, available to us. We appreciate as well the time and aid provided us by

Eason Balch, Alan Barton, Roger Boudet, Thomas Byerley, John Craig, George Campbell, John Farley, Joseph Farley, E. C. Gaston, R. L. Harris, Robert Hart, Roy Krotzer, William Lalor, Sherwood Lawrence, James Ludwig, Loren Pitts, Gayle Riley, Robert Scherer, Henry Strozier, Dwayne Summar, Jerry Vandergrift, John Vezeau, Charles Whitmore, and Ed Williamson.

Perhaps because Boston Edison was easily accessible to us, we asked repeatedly for help from the utility's staff, who were unfailing in their cooperation. The president, Thomas Galligan, was generous with his time and offered many valuable insights. William Irving and Frank Lee served as our guides and aids during our fieldwork and have our thanks for their efforts. Among those we interviewed, we would like to thank Charles Avila, Andrew Corry, Bruce Damrell, John Desmond, Charles Dolloff, John Falvy, Maurice Feldmann, Frank Gottlich, Edward Howard, James Lydon, Daniel May, Robert Parry, Charles Quigley, Warren Roche, John Rock, M. J. Ryan, Frank Staszesky, Dale Stoodley, Steven Sweeney, and Joseph Tyrrell.

Many people from regulatory agencies, advocacy groups, and the media in the regions where these utilities are located were generous with their time and effort. We are grateful for their assistance.

Finally, Marc Roberts wishes to thank his wife, Ann, and their children, Jennifer, Justine, Clement, and Zachary, for their patience and tolerance during the years of work this book has required.

Contents

Figures

The Choices of Power

1

Statement of the Problem

As you drive west on Interstate 75 from Knoxville, Tennessee, the steep green foothills of the Cumberland Mountains raise the road up toward the bright blue sky. As you come over one particular ridge, you can see in the valley to your right the smokestacks of the Kingston Plant of the Tennessee Valley Authority. This was the largest coal-burning electric power plant in the world when it was completed in 1953. For many years, when the plant was operating, a long plume of gray-brown smoke poured from these stacks and spread out over the pine forests. In contrast, drive north over a much smaller road in California, black asphalt instead of white concrete, from Castroville to Watsonville along the flat blue Pacific shoreline of Monterey Bay. Towering above the artichoke fields are the stacks of the Moss Landing plant of the Pacific Gas and Electric Company. The air above these stacks is usually so clear that it is difficult to tell whether or not the plant is operating.

What explains such variations in environmental performance? Is it simply a question of different laws, or are other kinds of social and political pressures involved? Do outside forces alone matter, or do various features of the organizations themselves—like the views of their members and the kinds of internal incentives that are offered—also make a difference? How do we explain the fact that the Tennessee Valley Authority, a public agency, has dirtier smokestacks than Pacific Gas and Electric, a private company?

First and most obviously, this book is about the process by which electric utilities have come to terms with growing environmental pressures. Doing business has become more difficult and more costly because of new environmental regulations and expectations. Although many managers resent these new demands and question their ultimate value, they have had to comply to some extent. This book provides a close look at the way in which six utilities have coped with this challenge. Our aim is not to pass judgment on these utilities — to distinguish between "good" companies and "bad" companies — but rather to learn more about the forces, both inside and outside an organization, that account for that organization's particular response to the changing problems it confronts.

What we can learn from this investigation goes well beyond utilities and environmental protection. Rising social expectations and organized citizen action have initiated governmental regulation in many areas: streams must be made cleaner, products safer, workplaces more healthful, employment less discriminatory. Organizations of all kinds face these requirements, and they respond in a variety of ways. Some resist to the death, others are passive, a few react effectively and rapidly. How and why do such variations come about, and what can be done to encourage more responsive behavior?

Our case studies allow us to make some generalizations about these larger issues, and doing so is the second purpose of our study. Such a discussion should be of interest both to managers who want to improve the capacity of their organizations to cope with "outside" changes, and to those "outside" an organization who would like to change — or simply understand — the organization's behavior.

Our third goal is to explain the systematic framework we have developed for analyzing organizational behavior, and to show how to use this tool by employing it in six different case studies. The framework identifies a wide variety of factors, external and internal to an organization, that affect the decision-making process, and it provides a basis for constructing generalizations about how these factors affect behavior in a wide variety of cases. It can be used to understand all kinds of organizations, not just utilities, and decisions of many sorts, not just responses to external regulation. Apart from its academic value, anyone who works in a large organization — a considerable proportion of the working population — could find this framework useful in understanding his or her own place of work.

Our framework includes, but is not limited to, the external circumstances confronting an organization; these determine the consequences of various actions. In some cases, the range of choices that will bring success may be very narrow. Yet outside the most competitive economic markets, most organizations have significant discretion; they can follow more than one strategy and still survive and grow. Often the organization's managers find it hard to determine the most successful way to behave. In this context of discretion plus ignorance, features of the organization itself—the beliefs of its members, their incentives, their relative power, and so on—have a significant impact, and our framework calls attention to these as well. Differences in the construction of automobiles lead to variations in the way in which they perform and handle, just as do differences in the roads they are driven on. Similarly, we should expect that variations in the structure of organizations will be reflected in variations in their performance —even allowing for the fact that the larger world they encounter (that is, the road) also influences what occurs.

Our conceptual scheme is modest in its limited specificity, since it is intended instead as a guide for conducting specific studies; it focuses attention on the various features of an organization and on the external circumstances that might help to explain particular actions. The scheme is ambitious, however, in the breadth of its intended applicability: it can be used to analyze a very wide variety of organizations (public, private, nonprofit). In a sense, theories about the behavior of business firms, hospitals, or government agencies can all be seen as special cases within this more general set of ideas. By examining various specific organizations in terms of these categories, researchers will be better able systematically to propose and evaluate alternative generalizations about what determines organizational behavior.

The Central Empirical Issue

Going through the cases, the reader will no doubt be struck, as we were, by the broad differences in environmental outcomes; the air in some cities is much cleaner than in others. Such variations result partly from basic physical and economic factors like climate, topography, and the location of fuel deposits. But some are also caused by variations in the way companies have reacted to environmental regulations. Although an organization's reaction is not perfectly consistent from issue to issue, some patterns do emerge in the long run.

The members of an organization can only deal with the present by relying on what they have learned in the past. The membership of an organization and the mechanisms it uses to reach and implement decisions change very slowly. Having successfully solved a problem in one way, the members of an organization tend thereafter to solve apparently similar problems in the same fashion. Hence the observable consistency. At the same time, the processes by which individuals and groups within the organization interact to determine its behavior do not operate with unchanging precision. Some variation in behavior from problem to problem is thus equally inevitable, and also must be dealt with by those who would understand, predict, or control such organizations.

Society has a great deal at stake in whether or not organizations follow the strategy of acting sooner or more energetically than external social coercion would demand. In order to call attention to this phenomenon, and to our related discussion and explanation, we have chosen to distinguish it by the term "positive responsiveness."[1]

Since we invented the term, we could define it in any way we pleased. Our definition, however, is not arbitrary but has been shaped by our studies. We intend "positive responsiveness" to refer to a set of organizational behavior patterns that observation suggests tend to coexist — a syndrome, if you like. Such a behavior pattern includes taking the initiative and proposing new government rules and regulations (to which the initiating company will be subject) for dealing with emerging problems. It also includes cases in which the organization alters its behavior sooner, or more extensively, than formal requirements and the threat of external coercion would indicate, and cases in which the organization makes serious efforts to overcome technological or organizational barriers to regulatory compliance, even when such barriers might provide a ready excuse for doing less than what is required. (On occasion, where the context is clear, we will simply use the word "responsiveness" to refer to such behavior.)

Organizations that adapt themselves to public expectations can be of great social value. Coercing a large organization to alter its behavior through the political and regulatory process can be costly and time-consuming. Determined opposition from vested interests delays the passage of new laws. Once laws are passed and regulations written, enforcement is expensive and imperfect, at best. It may be difficult to detect violations of the rules, and cumbersome processes are often needed to impose penalties on offenders. Successful regulation, therefore, typically is only possible at acceptable cost if the majority comply more or less voluntarily. If enforcement resources are limited and noncompliance is widespread, the probability that violators will be caught becomes so low that there is no effective deterrence. On the other hand, vigorous enforcement in the face of opposition means that both sides will use up significant amounts of resources in ways that are ultimately not very productive.[2]

In theory, society could have too much "positive responsiveness"; large organizations could become overly sensitive to social demands. As the cases below illustrate, once focused on a problem the American political system tends to demand rapid and far-reaching action. But priorities are not stable; crisis replaces crisis in a pattern that Downs has called the "issue attention cycle."[3] Often the result is a series of sweeping, unspecific pieces of legislation creating new programs with ambiguous or impossible missions, and with insufficient time or resources to carry them out. Under such circumstances, by overreacting to short-run fads, an organization could do more than would later seem appropriate once popular opinion had swung back the other way. However, given existing levels of institutional inertia, the United States today seems far from the point where too much positive responsiveness would be a problem. Furthermore, taking into consideration cognitive patterns (discussed in the next chapter) and organizational limitations, organizations cannot be expected to overly refine their responses to social pressures. Their behavior will be both patterned and imperfectly adjusted. Because society's ability to compel organizations to change their behavior is limited, there is reason—as a matter of broad social policy—to prefer organizations that exhibit the particular kind of imperfect behavior we have focused on.

Another objection to organizational flexibility should be noted: a person with certain values might prefer particular organizations to defend those values consistently, rather than to respond to changing social attitudes. A dedicated environmentalist, for example, might favor an electric utility committed to environmental protection, even if popular sentiment were to change in an antienvironmental direction.

Our response to such concerns is that designing our organizations to be positively responsive represents a long-run social strategy. In some ways it is similar to establishing a constitutional rule such as "one man, one vote." The decision to follow a broad maxim can be defended only by arguing that, over time, the society will be better off by consistently following the particular principle, rather than by following any other principle or by trying to custom-tailor each response. Here we can do no more than sketch the kind of argument we would make on this point. It would begin with the assertion that the process of human self-discovery and self-definition through participation in collective political activities is itself valuable and likely to continue. Some continuing change in social policy is, then, desirable and probable. Hence, we would argue that the capacity to implement that change in creative ways is also desirable. Finally, we would suggest that change is so much harder to bring about than continuity that increasing the capacity for change in our social and economic system is a wise way to proceed.

Although concerned with the environmental implications of many decisions involving the production of electricity, this book does not attempt to answer the question "How should electricity best be produced?" Our focus is on social organization, not technological options. The choices involved in producing electricity in an environmentally acceptable manner are not easy, as we will see in Chapter 3. Nuclear plants involve the risk of improbable but potentially catastrophic accidents, and pose radioactive waste disposal problems. Fossil fuels mean air pollution, land disruption from coal mining or oil drilling, tanker accidents, hazards to miners, and the international complications of oil imports. There is great need for a better understanding of energy conservation and the development of clean, economically feasible energy sources, though it is clear that none of these could make a major contribution for at least ten and perhaps not for twenty years. Naturally, we have opinions as to the best course to follow. But this book is not intended to prove or disprove the various possible positions on such issues. It is about how and why organizations function as they do — knowledge that should be useful regardless of the choices we as a nation make in the energy policy area.

Study Design

There are a variety of methodological traditions in social science. Many classic works in sociology and political science have been based on detailed case studies. There is also a strong tradition of statistical investigation, especially in economics, which is becoming steadily more influential in other disciplines. Theoretical work in economics places strong emphasis on expressing arguments in the form of mathematical models. Yet there is also a long history of nonquantitative theorizing, both in economics and in other social sciences.

Which of these methods should we use in obtaining answers to the questions we have raised? What kind of study should we undertake and what concepts should we construct to guide that study? We need to clarify the rationale for our study design and for the kind of analysis that we have employed — namely, looking in an exploratory way at a series of detailed cases, using a non-mathematical theory to guide the work.

Our choice of theory and methods reflects our views about what "good" science in general should try to do and about the nature of our subject matter. Briefly, we believe that science does, can, and should try to serve three distinguishable functions: explanation, prediction, and control. Although the second and third terms are relatively clear, the first is less so. In our view, a "good" explanation is simply a particular kind of description — an account of what happened that makes it plausible that events should have occurred as they did.[4]

Although the three functions are distinguishable,[5] they lead to a similar view of what "good" science is like: "good" science is based on understanding the "structure" of the process that generates the phenomena we are interested in. By "structure," we mean the physically less aggregate component parts of a system, and the ways in which they interconnect and interact. Thus, for example, when we explain why a glass window breaks when hit by a rock whereas a steel panel does not, we do so in terms of how their respective molecules are formed, connected with each other, and so on. Similarly, we explain how muscles work by talking about their cellular structure, and how organizations function by examining their human structure. Such an approach has virtues with regard to all three of our objectives. Structural insights and accounts allow us to make better predictions and to devise more effective control approaches. They also provide aesthetically satisfying explanations.[6]

Focusing on structure involves accepting the view that where the structures of objects or processes are similar, we can expect their behavior to be similar also. This assumption is widely and appropriately made: structure does in fact determine behavior.[7] We are not advocating the simple reductionist view that the behavior of a system is "nothing but" the behavior of its component parts. Instead, if the interaction of various components leads to outcomes that could not have been foreseen by looking at the component parts in isolation, that is something about the structure we wish to understand.

Our view of what we can expect to learn about organizations has been shaped not only by our view of science, but also by our research. Because organizations vary widely in structure, we should expect them to vary widely in behavior. The mere fact that a word ("organization") has been devised to denote a set of objects does not mean that they will turn out to be homogeneous for scientific purposes or that they will act the same in a given set of circumstances. Real phenomena do not obligingly sort themselves into well-defined classes and categories that automatically match whatever arbitrary linguistic distinctions we happen to make.

Organizations are, in fact, linguistic fictions. We talk of how "the Gotham Electric Company" planned to do this or that, but only people can plan or think or decide. In the case of an organization, then, a "structural" view means understanding how its behavior arises out of the choices and actions of its members.

We believe that the only way to gain information at the level of detail such structural accounts require (at this point in the development of theory) is to look at a few cases and explore these with great thoroughness. As a result, we have not studied enough cases to employ statistical analysis or to establish any of our insights or proposed generalizations with high reliability.[8] Our project should be viewed as an exploratory study *intended to generate new ideas and hypotheses.*

In part for these reasons, we have chosen not merely to present general conclusions but also to review each of the case studies in some detail. We believe that there is a "feel" for organizational behavior, which can be enhanced by carefully exploring specific situations with all their complexities, exceptions, and loose ends. Such an exercise gives a sense of the imperfect relationship of particular cases to larger patterns and generalizations. It also provides a set of analogies, suggestions, questions, intuitions, and warnings that are potentially helpful in other studies and that cannot be reduced to the brief compass of a systematic generalization.

Case studies do, however, benefit greatly from a theoretical framework that provides a way to organize data, generate questions, and focus attention. Such a framework can supply a context within which specific hypotheses about the relationship between an organization's structure and its behavior can be elaborated and interconnected. It can also help clarify the relationships among various case studies. By presenting such a framework, we hope to do more than contribute to the already extensive series of investigations that describe this or that interesting feature of some particular situation, and that do not add up to a systematic program of comparative analysis.

Our "theory" is thus designed to be used as a checklist to guide empirical research, to enhance comparability among particular

studies, and to call attention to possible alternative or complementary interpretations of particular events. Given our
"structural" view, we want a "theory" that allows us to describe
systematically differences in the structures and situations of organizations, and to analyze how these differences in turn account
for differences in the organizations' behavior. This is quite different from making a case that behavior will develop in the same
way in all organizations (or even in a class of organizations), regardless of their internal features.[9]

Our approach allows us to avoid having to base our study on a
particular model, either of how people think or of how organizations act. Instead, various images, models, and theories become
alternative possible descriptions whose applicability in each case
is a factual matter. For example, we do not have to choose between the hierarchical image of organizations, in which subordinates accept and carry out the instructions of their superiors, and
the more collegial model, which views power in the organization
as distributed among various groups and individuals.[10] We con-
cede from the outset that there is a (probably multidimensional)
continuum of possible organizational structures; what we seek is
the image that best captures the particular organization being
studied, and the way in which this image explains the outcomes
we are concerned with. As a second example, our approach allows us to accept the economist's view that self-interest and incentives determine much of organizational behavior, without ignor-
ing the sociologist's emphasis on the role of those experiences that
transform the way in which people respond to their incentives.[11]
We ask: What in fact was decision making like in this organization? To what extent did self-interest, politics, rational analysis,
emotion, or bureaucratic routines have an impact on what occurred?[12]

Given this approach, we have to be ready to borrow from the
concepts of a number of intersecting lines of analysis within economics, political science, sociology, and management. In so doing we run the risk that our results will seem incomplete, unrigor-
ous, and almost certainly unorthodox to practitioners in all of
these disciplines. This risk seems worth taking, however, if it enables us to provide better ways of explaining, predicting, and
controlling organizational behavior, which is the goal that provoked our research in the first place.

Reduced to its essentials, the point is that we have *not* set out to
discover simple, categorical generalizations about organizations
of the form "All *A* are *B*." Such rules are the sort of "laws of na-

ture" philosophers seem to prefer when constructing examples about scientific reasoning—laws that resemble the first element of the famous Platonic syllogism, "All men are mortal; Socrates is a man; therefore, Socrates is mortal."[13] In practice, there are few scientific generalizations of this form. More usual is a rule or formula that relates variations in one set of circumstances ("independent variables") to variations in specific outcomes or consequences ("dependent variables"). Such rules can be written as mathematical functions, like many well-known generalizations in the physical sciences.

But even such functions are too simple and restrictive to capture what occurs in most social-science contexts. Iron atoms are all very similar; organizations are not. Because the underlying structure of organizations varies from case to case, the nature of the relationships we are trying to determine will also vary.[14] In physics we can write $E = mc^2$ and believe that it will in all circumstances be true. In social contexts, *any generalization will involve many more variables and will itself vary with the situation.*

This observation suggests that the *form* of any generalizations about organizations will be complex: a pattern of patterns, a rule about the changing form of rules. We will be trying to discover not simply the relationship of certain features of an organization to its behavior, but how that relationship itself changes as a result of still other aspects of the situation.[15] And even then we can expect any generalizations we discover to be inexact, qualitative, and frequently inaccurate in specific cases.

We have described the kind of mathematical relationships one might look for, but we have *not* tried to express our theory in mathematical terms. We know very little about the exact form of the relationships, or about the best way to formulate key concepts so as to make them numerically measurable. Hence, expressing our conclusions symbolically, while easy enough to do, would add little or nothing to the argument at this stage.

Although, as we have stated, our case-study approach precluded a large sample, we still had to examine enough cases to avoid being misled by the idiosyncratic features of any one situation. Also, we wanted to study a set of organizations that were similar in many respects yet potentially very different in internal organization, and ones that had recently made important decisions in a rapidly changing regulatory context.

We chose to study environmental decisions in electric utilities for a number of reasons. The industry includes both public and private firms and greatly varied forms of organization; this allowed us to make a comparative analysis of a number of potentially relevant internal characteristics. Furthermore, because they are regulated monopolies, utilities typically have more discretion, more room to maneuver, than companies in a highly competitive market; thus, the influence of internal structural variations should be more noticeable.[16] Utilities are also regionally specific, potentially revealing the effects of variations in political and cultural context from one part of the country to another in a way that would not be possible with, say, automobile manufacturers. Their product is relatively standardized, which simplifies the interaction between environmental protection decisions and other kinds of business choices precisely because the companies' choices themselves are simplified. Finally, decisions by utilities often have an important environmental impact, making these decisions worthy of study in their own right, apart from any more general theoretical insights.

As a compromise between available resources and the value of broader efforts, we ultimately focused on six companies:

The Tennessee Valley Authority
The Pacific Gas and Electric Company
Ontario Hydro
The Southern Company
The Los Angeles Department of Water and Power
Boston Edison

Three are publicly owned and three are private. One of the public companies is federally owned, one is a municipal utility, and the third serves a province in Canada. The private companies, like the public ones, vary substantially in size. One is also a gas company and another a multistate holding company. This gives us the sort of internal variation that our general perspective suggested was important. Further, to clarify public-private differences and allow us to distinguish their impact from other causes, we paired the companies—choosing one of each type from each of three regions. We expected that this would make it easier to understand the role of interregional economic and political variations. The service areas of the six utilities are shown in Figure 1.

In each company, we focused on a small number of illustrative environmental choices, which we studied in some detail. Who first noticed a particular "problem"? Who performed the staff work that defined the organization's options? Who had final authority to choose a course of action and how was this authority exercised? Once chosen, how was a particular policy imple-

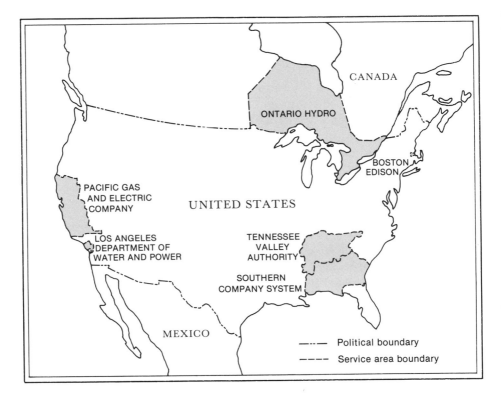

Figure 1. The service areas of the six utilities. Based on information supplied by the companies.

mented? Such explorations were intended to expose the real and not merely the formal patterns of organizational functioning. We also reviewed the history of each company, both generally and with regard to environmental decisions, in order to understand its evolution—the process by which its internal features had developed in response to earlier external challenges and as a function of prior internal characteristics.

Given the scarcity of written sources, we had to rely on interviews to acquire much of the relevant data. The fieldwork consisted of over two hundred interviews conducted over a four-year period with people from a wide variety of positions both within and outside each of the participating companies. We talked to low-level engineers and chief executives, vice-presidents and middle-level supervisors, newspaper reporters and state regulatory officials. We talked to engineers, lawyers, biologists, and financial managers. We examined all the published material we could obtain—books, annual reports, pamphlets, and so forth.

Most conversations lasted between one and two hours and took place in the office of the person being interviewed. In about half the cases, we talked to more than one person at a time—for example, a department manager and one of his key technical assistants. Most interviews were conducted by two people, who alternately took notes and asked questions as the discussion proceeded. No tape recordings were made. In many instances, we made follow-up telephone conversations. Some people were interviewed only by phone.

Such data, of course, must be used very carefully. An individual's information and perspective are influenced by his particular situation. Some used the occasion of our interviews to try to establish their own wisdom and virtue. Many expressed what they acknowledged to be long-held opinions, theories, or complaints. Some, for corporate or personal reasons, concealed or distorted information. More frequently, people made what later seemed to be honest mistakes—hard to avoid when discussing events that may have occurred five or six years earlier and that were no longer clearly in mind. Many were eager to be helpful and went into their files to verify specific dates and factual details. On the whole, those we interviewed appeared candid and interested, in part because many people obviously like to discuss their work.

Selected state and federal regulatory personnel, environmental activists, and reporters for local newspapers were also interviewed. By cross-checking, calling sources back to verify specifics, and so on, we were able to establish reasonably accurate accounts of what occurred in each case. In some instances we were forced to speculate, but we have tried to note such instances when they occur.

The interviews employed two kinds of questions. First, we tried to illuminate how each company functioned. We explored the structure of authority, the incentives, the division of tasks among various units and individuals. Who does what in your area? How is your unit organized? How are budgets and promotions handled? What qualities seem necessary for success within the organization? The second set of questions focused on specific decisions and examples.

It was agreed that each organization would have the right to review published materials for confidentiality and accuracy. Interviews were treated as off-the-record and subject to specific clearance before attribution. We believe that this requirement, although time-consuming, has not introduced any significant inaccuracy of tone or detail into the results. There is an element of nonverbal art or craft in the process of discovering what has occurred in an organization. We hope that we have learned this craft well enough so that our case studies will illuminate both the process and the companies concerned, and also provide a basis for the general conclusions we offer at the end of the volume.

2

A Framework for Explaining
the Behavior of Organizations

Organizations do not make decisions or take actions; their members do. These people act and decide within a context that is provided most immediately by the organization in which they work, and more distantly by the organization's physical and social setting. Our conceptual framework is designed to reveal how such individual decisions are made and how they are combined within an organization, so that we can then explain the behavior of an organization as a whole.[1] The basic concepts involved, refined in the course of our research, have guided our work from the beginning.[2] They have served both as a checklist to guide the case studies and as a theoretical basis for the development of more general hypotheses.

We use the term "organization" in a perfectly ordinary way, referring to a group of people and the arrangements by which they assume specified responsibilities for jointly performing certain tasks. Given such a definition, there is no clear line between what is and what is not an organization. Organizations vary enormously in size, scope, structure, formality, stability, membership, and decision processes; but such ambiguity is not unusual in social science, nor is it a serious difficulty.[3] The less a particular set of social arrangements resembles an organization, the less likely it is to behave like one. We will attempt to clarify how and why those entities that are clearly "organizations" behave as they do.

One way to approach the problem is to ask why societies create organizations in the first place. What are the advantages of a more or less stable system of relationships for coordinating the joint action of a number of individuals? The answer is relatively straightforward.

It takes time to acquire information, skills, methods, concepts, and experience, but people do not live forever. This limits how much a person *can* learn, and limits even more sharply how much

15

it *pays* anyone to learn. At some point, added time devoted to study is too costly because it diminishes the time available to use capacities already acquired. Thus, people suffer from *qualitative* (that is, skill) limits as problem solvers: each of us can only do certain kinds of things. There are also *quantitative* limits on the rate at which we can use whatever skills we have acquired: people cannot think very quickly, or think about very much at any one time.[4]

Organizations can circumvent these limits. They operate by dividing large problems into sets of smaller problems. This makes it possible for a number of people to work on each problem simultaneously and to employ people with different skills and training.

If such joint action is to function successfully, certain tasks must be accomplished. Various individuals with various skills have to be recruited. Tasks must be assigned and compensation decided upon. Given their diverse backgrounds and perspectives, these people are not likely to agree spontaneously on what should be done. Mechanisms for resolving disagreements and eliciting consistent behavior must be created — that is, incentive systems and patterns of interpersonal influence must be put into place. It is also desirable to have the participants commit themselves to common goals and to cooperative patterns of action so that they do not behave toward each other in the impersonal, even mutually suspicious manner of "arm's length" buyers and sellers in a marketplace.[5]

It requires too much effort to create such arrangements each time there is a complex task to be done. The gains of constantly renegotiated relationships are not worth their costs, and insofar as psychological forces are at work, it may not be possible to readjust them quickly or often.[6] Not only is joint action therefore at least potentially in everyone's interest, but so is the creation of stable relationships that minimize the costs of such coordination. One way to do this is to designate some people to specialize in the tasks of operating these arrangements and of readjusting them over time. The result is an organization, and in many cases one that embodies important elements of authority and specialization.[7]

The virtues of an organization, however, are also the source of its deficiencies. It is a relatively stable mechanism for solving problems — but problems are not all alike. Some will not match its set of skills and methods of proceeding. The process of subdividing problems can also cause difficulties. Large problems can be broken down into smaller ones in many different ways, but it may be difficult to find a satisfactory division if the various aspects of the larger problem are closely interrelated.[8] For example, engineering decisions regarding the construction of a particular type of power plant will determine how much pollution the plant generates, which in turn will affect the likely response of public and regulatory agencies. In such a case it can be foolish to have engineering, legal, and public-relations planning proceed independently. On the other hand, in order to obtain the advantages of cooperative specialization, tasks must be divided up somehow. But how is that to be done in a way that does not create as many problems as it solves?

A number of basic facts about an organization must be understood. What kind of members does it have? Who is given what tasks? What decisions do members make in light of the circumstances they face? Our framework follows the basic form of most models of decision making. It represents the situation in terms of two components: the options available to the decision maker and the decision maker's response to those options. The analysis must also be conducted on two levels: that of the organization as a whole and that of its individual members. We will therefore focus on four major components:

1. the external conditions that organizations face
2. how the internal structure and operating practices transmit these pressures into decision problems facing organization members
3. the attitudes, preferences, and beliefs that influence the way in which members solve these problems
4. how the structure of the organization aggregates these individual decisions into a pattern of organizational action

We would also like to understand why an organization and its members have the characteristics they do. This means studying the past. A recursive process is at work in shaping the organization's strategy and its structure (which itself represents an implicit strategy for solving problems). Such a perspective may allow us to avoid the frequent interpretive errors that plague this kind of study. Because successful organizations adapt to external circumstances, it is tempting to conclude that such circumstances have *always* "caused" whatever has occurred. Such arguments ignore the fact that the organization could have made any one of a number of choices and still survived, so that the context cannot be said to have forced it to adopt the particular behavior it did. Conversely, it is just as much of an error to assume that outcomes are always the result of *internal* features of the organization. Such arguments fail to consider how and why the internal features of an organization have developed as they have and the extent to which these have evolved in response to external pressures. Only a historical perspective on the origins and development of the organization can help us account for its current form and behavior.

Our views about the determinants of organizational behavior are grounded in our views about the fundamental nature of human experience and about the way in which people modify their behavior in light of that experience. The consequences to an individual (or an organization) for taking any action have certain typical characteristics. The first is their *multidimensionality*. Any given decision generally has a variety of results that are of interest to the decision maker. When an electric utility designs a power plant, it is affecting its costs and profits, the probability of power outages to its customers, the job descriptions of many members, a series of aesthetic and environmental conditions, its public image, the tax bases of various communities, and the likelihood of a whole range of bureaucratic responses. And these are only some of the more obvious ramifications. The consequences of any one decision are so numerous and their ramifications so complex, that selective attention is necessary. Individuals and organizations seem myopic in their dealings with the world partly because they have to be: the full range of conceivable relevant consequences of most decisions is simply too much to think about.

A second feature of the world is what Herbert Simon in a slightly different context has called *continuity*.[9] Small changes in circumstances or behavior usually result in small changes in outcomes; if a little bit of something produces a little result, more of that something is likely to produce a bit more of the same result. This feature of reality makes it possible to extrapolate from previous experience to novel situations. It explains the fact that most experience is not surprising—even if we haven't been in exactly that situation before. Most social and physical systems do not produce large responses to small changes in their environment.

Reality is also *unpredictable:* most actions do not have exactly foreseeable consequences. This reflects two different phenomena. First, the behavior of social and natural systems involves important elements of *randomness*. There is no fully determined relationship, for example, between the current circumstances confronting a businessman and his competitors and the precise advertisements a competing business will run next season. Second, our *ignorance* of the world increases its apparent unpredictability. Often we simply don't know what will take place. (From the viewpoint of modern decision theory, interestingly enough, these two sources of uncertainty should be treated identically by a decision maker.)[10]

Another critical feature—especially of social and economic reality—is *novelty*. Human institutions and activities cannot easily be sorted into stable and homogeneous classes of objects. The structure and behavior of the entities we include under the label "political parties" or "business firms" or "families" often change with disconcerting rapidity.[11] Even when we learn something about our society, this knowledge can become obsolete over time.

Finally, our experience is *ambiguous*. People and organizations often choose (or are forced by circumstances) to perform poor experiments. They typically change several aspects of their behavior at the same time. The larger world does not cooperate by standing still while these changes are made. A company that introduces a new product usually gives it a new name and new packaging and promotes it by a new advertising campaign. Meanwhile the economy, the national mood, fashion, and competing products are also changing. Even if the new product succeeds, how can anyone be sure what produced the results? Was it something the company did, and if so, what? Was it some change in the larger world? Or was it simply an accident, a matter of luck? Answering such questions is often complicated by the fact that results take a long time to be apparent, so that it is impossible to learn from them rapidly or to know which prior actions were causally important.

Thus, the decisions that individuals (and organizations) face are often complex. There are many consequences to consider and many options to explore. It is usually difficult to learn enough about the world to be able to predict the consequences of alternative courses of action. Experiments are often time-consuming, costly, impractical, and uninformative. Furthermore, any understanding that one does acquire (experimentally or otherwise) may well become obsolete before it can be used. Other people may learn enough about your strategy to change their own reactions to it—making your policies ineffective.[12]

Our view of the way in which individuals make decisions in light of such circumstances owes much to writers who have emphasized that decision making is an art as much as it is a science.[13] Since resources are scarce, it is possible to spend too much time thinking and analyzing instead of doing. Deciding how much time to spend thinking, and what simplifications to make, is itself a problem that is usually too complicated to solve easily. Human beings, in response, have developed a mode of problem solving that relies heavily on the continuity of experience and conserves the limited resources available for serious thinking. People typically use well-established, previously developed, routine responses as long as these produce acceptable answers, and they only think hard about something when these fail. Most people, for example, usually stop when they see a red light, and they do so without making an elaborate calculation of the costs and benefits of alternative actions. They do not estimate the value of the time saved, the probability of being caught, the fine they would pay, or the harm to society of lawbreaking.

When routine responses fail, or seem likely to prove inadequate before the fact, a decision maker typically relies on familiar strategies and approaches for solving problems. Existing mental equipment defines and simplifies the problem, suggests where to look for solutions, provides "truth" criteria for testing ideas, and so on.[14] Even when individuals apparently are most "rational" — that is, engaged in scientific inquiry — conceptual structures of this sort play a central role,[15] just as their less formal counterparts do in other circumstances.[16] Thus, a complex system of norms and beliefs, of moral commitments and professional predilections, must be studied in order to understand how individuals both inside and outside organizations respond to the decision problems they face. How can we describe such ideas?

Although it is a highly simplified and stylized view of reality, we can think of individuals as subscribing to certain broad, imperfectly rationalized, more or less conscious ethical premises. To use these as a guide to action in any real situation would require a complex and subtle argument about the likely consequences of various actions and how good or bad these consequences would be in terms of basic values. In practice, such arguments are seldom made; they are too time-consuming and difficult. Instead, people rely on derivative and specific maxims and decision rules that tell them what to do in certain kinds of situations. Such rules can be thought of as embedded in a hierarchy of increasingly specific norms. Insofar as this intellectual system is consistent, the more specific maxims can be derived from the more general ones by relying on descriptive views of how the world works, which are needed to *predict* consequences, and on fundamental ethical premises, which serve to *evaluate* those consequences. For example, a fundamental value like "Human self-fulfillment is a good thing" could be used to justify a derived principle like "Democratic government is a good thing." But justifying that principle in terms of the more basic value requires a complex empirical and normative argument. A belief in the value of democratic government, by a similar sort of argument, can lead to a maxim like "Vote regularly." This derivative and unexamined behavioral rule may then provoke a relatively unanalyzed decision to leave work early in order to vote.

Alongside this normative set of concepts, individuals have a set of descriptive views which are distinct but interdependent, and similar in structure. To learn anything, one needs some basic assumptions about the way in which to obtain knowledge. Not everyone shares such premises — as the differences between faith healers and neurosurgeons suggest. Given some basic assumptions, however, we can create and judge substantive hypotheses and models.[17] Like the system of normative rules, the system of descriptive generalizations can be seen as beginning with general theories and concepts which form a basis for more specific factual conclusions.

The self-consciousness and elaborateness of a person's system of descriptive models and normative rules vary enormously. In religion, politics, and academic pursuits we can find people with very complex and elaborate structures that link broad sets of facts, theories, and models into a well-integrated "world view." For most people, however, such intellectual structures are more unconscious than conscious. People seldom formalize the arguments that support the various maxims they rely upon, or even verbalize the maxims to themselves. Their norms and rules are often filled with unrealized or unresolved conflicts. Similarly, descriptive beliefs about the way in which the world works can easily be wrong or inconsistent, and cannot always be clearly distinguished from normative rules.[18] Imperfect as they are, such intellectual structures are the unavoidable basis for all thinking about specific problems.

The role of norms, rules, ideas, and injunctions in individual action is in turn reflected in certain organizational phenomena. Differences in concepts among individuals can easily lead to mutual incomprehension, misunderstanding, and disagreement which the participants may find it difficult to resolve or even to understand. Unaware of how they think, people are often deceived about the impartiality of their views. Their own assumptions and beliefs typically function either as unconscious predispositions or are accepted as obvious truths about the world. Conflicts may also be exacerbated by the fact that individuals often become emotionally committed to their own ideas and way of thinking. The perspectives and methods they have been trained to use professionally may well acquire symbolic meaning, and may become a critical part of an individual's self-image. As we will see, such problems can occur not only between organization members and outsiders but among organization members themselves.

Disagreements among individuals with different conceptual systems can be difficult or easy to reconcile, depending on the intellectual commitments at stake.[19] If these people share enough common assumptions, one of them might be able to construct an argument that the other will find compelling. If they do not even agree on how one obtains relevant data, dialogue will be more difficult. How can a neurosurgeon convince a mystic that the latter is "wrong" about the sources of psychic energy, or vice versa? Even where conceptual and epistemological disagreements are few and minor, the complexity, uncertainty, ambiguity, and novelty of experience can make it very difficult to construct mutually acceptable definitive arguments. As a result, individuals with very different views might each find it easy to continue to defend their ideas.

The External Context

These features of the way in which people think and act influence all four of our categories for explaining organizational behavior, including the external context of the organization. In the vast literature on organization behavior (in at least three disciplines) this context is characterized by a wide variety of terms, such as "constraints," "pressures," and "opportunities". All such terms are actually ways of talking about the *consequences* to an organization, and to its members, of various actions. Saying that an action is ruled out by a legal constraint means that if people try to do it, they would be more or less likely to be fined, go to jail, or suffer guilt or social disapproval as a result. Even the question of what is technologically possible is likely to be ambiguous on the technical frontier.

How do the various kinds of external consequences that an organization faces relate to its behavior? As a set of people and relationships for accomplishing certain tasks, an organization can be thought of as acquiring certain "inputs" (to use economic terminology), processing them in certain ways, and generating various "outputs."[20] The conditions under which the organization can engage in these activities are determined both by the physical world and by a bewildering variety of collective social, cultural, and economic arrangements. The processes that an organization uses to transform inputs into outputs are governed by its own internal structure and the technology it employs. The physical and social consequences of acquisition and disposal can trigger social processes that generate responses directed at the organization and its members. These responses may alter the terms on which the organization can operate, or even force a change in the organization itself. The effects can be mutual, however: sometimes an organization can affect social attitudes and the institutions that are trying to influence it.

Typically, the link between what an organization does and the consequences it suffers involves actions by outsiders. In a few cases, there may be direct physical feedback, as when a utility finds its generating plants corroding due to its own air pollution. More often, such pollution is significant because of its political and economic consequences. The people who participate in these external social processes behave just like anyone else—that is, in ways that are imperfectly rational and that are conditioned by prior expectations and concepts.

With these conceptual points as prologue, we can now provide a checklist of features of the external world that are potentially relevant to explaining the behavior of any particular organization. For expositional purposes we will divide such factors into three categories—natural, social, and technological—recognizing that in a sense the last is the product of the first two.

The Natural World. The world of natural phenomena and processes will not be equally important to all organizations. It is, however, quite important to electric utilities. Two different aspects of such systems are worth distinguishing:

Resources. The costs of acquiring physical inputs will, for many organizations, be heavily influenced by the nature and distribution of the known stock of resources.

Physical and biochemical systems. The natural world is also an important determinant of the consequences of an organization's output decisions. Various physical and biochemical systems (including various organisms) transform, disperse, and are affected by these outputs.

The Social World. Natural phenomena also have an impact through the reactions generated by various social institutions and processes. The immediate social and economic effects of the organization's actions are also processed and mediated by outside social and economic institutions. Although many classifications of these phenomena are possible, one way to sort them is as follows:[21]

Attitudes. The response to an organization's actions will be heavily influenced by the attitudes, ideas, and expectations of those on the outside. These are not fixed, however. Larger social forces and, in some cases, the organization itself can influence them.

Arrangements for acquiring inputs. Any organization needs resources to accomplish its tasks. The terms on which it can acquire these are often critical to determining the consequences of various actions. Whether the organization needs labor, capital, or materials or whether it relies on a market, a government, or voluntary gifts, its actions may be greatly influenced by these features of its environment.

Arrangements for disposing of outputs. Most organizations have to arrange for someone to notice, buy, or accept their outputs. The kind and quantity of outputs produced are often linked to the organization's ability to acquire inputs. It may have to make profits in order to pay costs or acquire added capital. Or it may have to provide service to win government appropriations. In any case, conditions for output disposal are a key feature in shaping the consequences of various actions.

Arrangements for imposing conditions on the organization. Outsiders trying to influence an organization typically try to tie certain aspects of its behavior to rewards and punishments. The structure of regulatory institutions and the kinds of problems and opportunities they pose to would-be outside influencers, can greatly affect the context confronting an organization.

Specific requirements. Outside attitudes and institutions at any one time will have produced a set of particular requirements — together with a set of consequences for noncompliance. These include both consequences for the organization as a whole (monetary penalties, for example) as well as those that directly affect individual members (such as social disapproval or criminal sanctions).

Technology. The set of possible combinations of inputs and outputs at any one time is part of the range of opportunities available to an organization. Yet in a sense only the *possible* technologies are external, since organizations vary in their knowledge of these options and in their willingness to run technical risks. What is possible technologically is often poorly defined.[22] This is especially clear when we think of "technology" in the social as well as the physical sense — that is, as including the available techniques for organizing people and coordinating their activities.

In sum, the consequences to an organization of its actions are filtered through a series of uncertain and unpredictable social, natural, and technical systems. The resulting constraints on organizations are typically not well defined. For example, small violations of air quality rules usually produce only a complaining letter from the state, and sometimes not even that. A series of such violations extending over several years might lead to strict enforcement or tighter controls, and even could seriously threaten current management.[23] Then again they might not. In what sense are such violations either "allowed" or "not allowed"? The way in which consequences vary according to the particular action, their multiplicity and uncertainty, our ignorance of them, the difficulties of inference, and our limited ability to think — all these contribute to the lack of well-defined constraints. Except in spy novels and crime movies, society seldom imposes prohibitive penalties on an organization or its members for even the slightest violation of the rules. We do not shoot the chairman of the board for major crimes committed by his company, still less for small violations of environmental regulations. Courts and administrative agencies merely impose "reasonable" sanctions according to the seriousness of the violation. The regulatory process involves a good deal of bargaining and leaves room for substantial maneuvering.[24]

Within the range of behavior compatible with the survival and growth of an organization, there is usually no one strategy that can easily be shown to be "best." This view contrasts sharply with the economist's model of the firm in a purely competitive industry, where any departure from the one profit-maximizing path means bankruptcy as consumers switch to the firm's competitors. Few real markets are so competitive; few real consumers are so perfectly informed. If a firm sets prices higher or lower; if a university admits more or fewer students; if an auto manufacturer produces cars with a slightly higher or lower rate of defects — the change in consequences may well be very small. The organization in question may well not even realize that it has made a mistake or perceive a need for corrective action.

The preceding arguments can be put in mathematical terms by considering what we can call the "payoff function," which describes the consequences to the organizations of taking various actions.[25] Generally, these consequences are not certain. Each possible action by the organization gives rise to a probability distribution of outcomes, which in turn is imperfectly known to the organization. Most of these "payoffs" have more than one aspect so that, for each action, an organization confronts a multidimensional probability distribution that describes the likelihood of various sets of consequences.

The function in question usually will have a relatively "flat" maximum. That is, assuming we can find a way to value multidimensional, uncertain outcomes, many choices will look equally promising. There are likely to be a number of local maximums, each representing very different strategic choices. Such functions seldom will be "step functions" of the sort that imply that drastic changes in consequences result from infinitesimal changes in behavior. Constraints on the organization are represented by regions in which the probability of some serious adverse consequence increases relatively rapidly. This is not a precise definition, but real constraints are seldom precisely definable.

There is no way to determine what is a more or less desirable outcome without invoking some values. In order to rank multidimensional uncertain outcomes, we need some "valuation function" that reflects a willingness to trade increased gain on some dimensions against decreased gains on others.[26] In this sense, too, the external world is only imperfectly coercive and behavior depends on the values that shape organizational decision making.

Before an organization's behavior can provoke a regulatory response, outsiders first have to notice the behavior in question. Given imperfect information, limited knowledge, and rule-based decision making, whether they notice depends only partially on the "objective" magnitude of the effects in question. What else determines which actions are noticed? What physical, social, and institutional forces are at work and how do they operate in various circumstances?

Once an organization's actions are noticed, outsiders are faced with the need to alter the consequences that the organization confronts for behaving as it does. Our view of human decision making suggests that the easier it is for outsiders to impose such sanctions and the more serious the issue appears to them, the more likely they are to try to influence the organization in question. But what determines perceived seriousness? Are the forces at work the same as those that determine what is noticed in the first place? What determines the perceived costs of such action to outsiders? What role is played by the objective costs of manipulating a target organization's environment, and what determines these costs? What else is important here?

The last question leads to still another issue. For various out-siders, the probability of successfully altering an organization's behavior is the product of two probabilities. First, given various levels of effort on the part of the outsiders, how likely is it that they will be able to impose certain consequences on an organiza-tion? Second, if they succeed in that first effort, how likely is it that the target organization will then alter its behavior in the de-sired direction? Our theoretical perspective suggests that the tar-get organization will be influenced by the costs of compliance — as determined by the technology being used, the penalties that the organization confronts, and so forth. These externally im-posed consequences, however, are unlikely to coerce the organiza-tion into taking specific actions, especially since it will be difficult for the organization to determine the costs of various responses in advance. What is it about the external context that influences an organization's perceptions of these costs and its overall decision making? We believe that our case studies shed light on all these matters.

External circumstances are only one class of influences on or-ganizational behavior. The very fact that it is so hard for an organization to discover what it "must" or even "should" do means that those with different perspectives within an organiza-tion will argue for different decisions — and there will be no easy way, analytically, to resolve these disagreements. What an organ-ization actually does, therefore, will depend in part upon how it goes about deciding what to do. Understanding that process means understanding the choices of individual members and the way in which these choices are aggregated into a pattern of joint action.

Individual Decision Problems

Each member of an organization has certain tasks to perform and controls certain resources. Managers may determine the deploy-ment of many individuals and much equipment, but even the lowest-ranking members apportion their own time, effort, and influence. Organization members face consequences as a result of such choices — consequences to themselves, to the organization, and to the larger world.

To the extent that members care about the latter two sorts of consequences, external physical and social systems may directly determine their opportunities. For example, engineers personally concerned about water quality in a particular river confront con-sequences for their actions that are in part determined by the hydrology of that river. From the point of view of organizational design, however, the more interesting question is how the organization's structure links the engineers' design decisions to the rewards and punishments that the organization itself dispenses. Two features of the organization, in particular, shape the problems confronting its members: its mechanisms for assigning tasks and its incentive systems.

Members' tasks depend largely, but not entirely, on their position within the organization's *structure*.[27] By this we mean the various subunits that are established, the division of work among them, their size and professional composition, the mechanisms for transmitting reports and instructions, and the arrangements for laterally coordinating their work. (Some of these features would be captured by an accurate organizational chart.) For example, the project manager in a civil engineering group that is designing a new pumping station has to allocate the time of various employees—as well as his own—to accomplish this task.

One common solution to this problem is a hierarchical structure in which superiors successively subdivide tasks for their subordinates, leaving certain coordination, supervision, and substantive functions for themselves. Even in the most formal system of this sort, however, actual task assignments do not always proceed in the way the formal structure appears to indicate.[28]

In practice, task assignments are subject to a decision process that combines both "rational" and "political" aspects. There are many possibilities in any specific organization. Not only can the structure be altered *ad hoc* (for example, a special task force can be created to solve a special problem) but, within a given set of formalized arrangements, there is often considerable room for negotiation over tasks and resources. *The actual process of task assignment is very important because it determines what kinds of people and, hence, what kinds of assumptions and beliefs are deployed in solving the organization's problems.*

A hierarchical system has potential advantages for facilitating coordination. Top management can set up mechanisms to assign tasks, monitor performance, assess penalties, distribute rewards, recruit compatible people, and exercise leadership to promote unified, conscientious action. At least in theory, most members then confront manageably small tasks within their relevant field of expertise and need spend only limited time on communication and decision making. It is not necessary that everyone know everything, or talk to everyone else. Most members do not have to make the effort that would be required to become broadly informed, and hence useful participants in top-level decision making.

Hierarchy also has clear deficiencies. Decisions made by those without first-hand knowledge can lead to serious problems. No one person or small group has enough time or mental capacity to learn everything that is occurring throughout a large organization; this is partly why the organization exists to begin with. Information must be synthesized, focused, and digested so that those doing the coordinating and planning can more easily master and use it. As a result, those at the top learn about reality primarily from subordinates. But each subordinate has only limited information, which has been processed through a particular set of inaccurate conceptual lenses whose distorting qualities neither they nor top management may fully understand.

The diversity and specialization that are the advantages of an organization thus create their own problems. How are top managers, as specialists in broad policy, to evaluate the various divergent reports and suggestions that are continually being advanced?[29] Their mental capacities, too, are limited, so that they cannot take a "neutral" or "universal" view — especially in a crisis, when their time is very scarce.[30] To the extent that the problems are not easily divisible into tasks that can be performed in isolation, difficulties with coordination and communication can multiply. Even where tasks are divisible a manager is forced to rely on incentive schemes, which are highly imperfect, to provide signals to his subordinates as to how to behave.

Given these limits on hierarchy as an organizational tool, we should expect to find great variations among organizations in the extent and nature of their hierarchical relationships, the degree of centralization of authority, and so on. Our analysis should describe such variations and develop their implications for the decision processes of the organization as a whole.

In order to comprehend members' actions we must understand the consequences to them of their various actions. These, in turn, depend on a large and complex set of mechanisms that determine promotion and compensation, impose penalties, alter the distribution of other rewards (for example, status), handle grievances, and so forth. We use the terms *control system* or *incentive system* more or less interchangeably to denote this set of processes and arrangements.[31]

From the viewpoint of top management, the purpose of a control system is to give members a reason to make one decision rather than another. An ideal system would reward and punish

individuals according to their contribution to the achievement of
the goals set by top management. In a sense, a chief executive
would like to motivate his subordinates to decide as he would
decide, if he had all the information, expertise, and time that is
available to them.

The difficulties of monitoring performance and of attributing
results to individuals mean that *real control systems are always
less than perfect*. In particular, they often respond to what individuals *do* rather than to the *consequences* of their choices.
Choices are often easier to monitor and to assign responsibility for
than outcomes.[32] And the uncertainty of the world may make it
difficult to judge the excellence of a manager's decisions from his
or her results. This is especially so when evaluations must be
made before those results — which may take years to occur — are
fully evident.

Those who assign rewards on the basis of decisions instead of
on the basis of outcomes must assume that they can determine
what the right decision would have been in each situation. This,
however, is generally difficult or impossible. Supervisors typically
don't have the time or the knowledge to rethink all their subordinates' decisions; if they did, they wouldn't need subordinates.
This tends to lead to simple rules for evaluating a subordinate's
decision. These rules often call for evaluating the decision process, and not even the decision itself.

Rewards based on whether or not a manager "follows regulations" or "goes by the book" are characteristic of control systems
that evaluate decisions (not outcomes), and often evaluate them
by process standards. Indeed, the distribution of rewards can be
based in whole or in part on individual characteristics — like race,
sex, school background, or age — instead of on performance.[33]

Rewards based on the consequences of decisions still may not
be oriented toward *relevant* outcomes, given the organization's
objectives. It may be very difficult for a manager to collect data
that are inexpensive and have the right incentive effects. Suppose, for example, that a utility rewards those engineers who keep
down the capital cost of new generating capacity — an easily observable outcome. This could encourage them to build plants for
which fuel and operating costs are so high that, even though capital costs may be low, overall the plants are more expensive than
necessary.[34]

The difficulties and imperfections in all such arrangements
mean that a person within an organization tends to confront uncertain consequences for any given action. Nevertheless, a *strong*

control system is one that, on the average, presents members with different consequences if they take different actions. It is also one in which the consequences of any given action are fairly certain.[35] Conversely, a *weak* system leads to similar outcomes no matter what the person chooses. In this case, ironically, organization members must resort either to actions designed to provoke rewards from outsiders or to some nonselfish basis for making decisions — to their professional and social values, for example — unless, of course, they seek simply to minimize their own efforts. If controls are weak, the organization itself is providing no reason for members to make one particular choice rather than any other.

Decision making within an organization is also influenced by where in the hierarchy incentives are manipulated. Suppose that a person can be influenced by his immediate superior but that this superior is not controlled by his superior in turn; the initial person, then, cannot be controlled by the top. We have to ask how *deep* the control system is — how far down any one executive, particularly the chief executive, can shape individual rewards and punishments.[36]

In Figure 2 we present one possible schematic view of the operation of the control system. As illustrated, the consequences that decision makers care about may depend on their actions, the organization's actions, the consequences for the organization, and the consequences for the larger world: these either affect the individuals directly or are mediated by the control system. Furthermore, the various outcomes are not determined by the actions of any one person; other decision makers, both internal and external, play a role.

Given these limits on formal control systems, managers resort to influence and leadership, which often are important determinants of organizational behavior. Such informal mechanisms may operate quite selectively in an organization. For example, a top manager's ability to influence a subordinate tends to be greater if they can understand each other easily. Shared experience can facilitate this; company presidents with a background in marketing typically find it easier to communicate with, influence, and evaluate the vice-president for marketing than they do the head of production. Feelings of personal loyalty, too, may make a subordinate more cooperative.

Top management may have limited ability to provide incentives to some members if these members care about consequences outside the organization's control, such as social justice or professional status as determined by an outside group. People whose

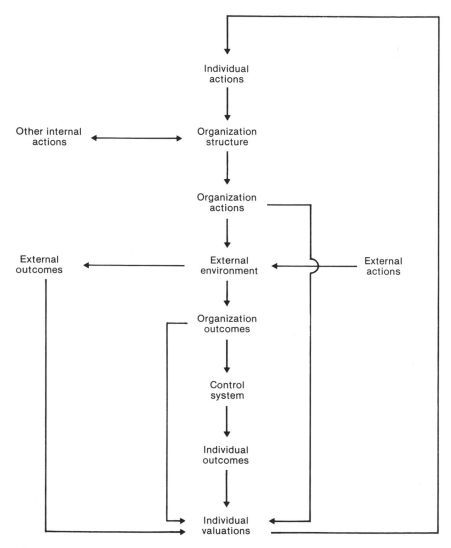

Figure 2. The structure of an individual organization member's decision problems.

careers are likely to span several organizations may care more about how their actions will be judged by future employers than about the incentives the current organization has to offer.[37]

A manager's power to shape a subordinate's incentives is also limited by the subordinate's ability to resign. It can be time-consuming and expensive to find and train a person with equivalent skills and knowledge. Poor performance by the new person and a decline in morale are added risks. A manager thus may not find it advantageous to replace an uncooperative subordinate, especially if the disagreement is temporary or limited in scope, and this may expand the discretion of subordinates who know they will be hard to replace. When the conflict is not of major importance, some managers avoid overruling or offending a powerful subordinate for fear of losing their cooperation on other issues.

The division of tasks and the control system influence one another. The possibility of changes in task assignments creates incentives that are distinct from, and potentially in conflict with, those offered by the control system. A given unit's size, budget, current tasks, and the promotion opportunities it offers can all change as a result of changes in its function. Consequently, the members of a unit may have good reason to try to ensure its survival and growth, especially if their own long-run careers are closely tied to its fate. Such incentives can be so strong that members of an organization may openly oppose a superior and risk giving up the immediate rewards he can offer. Where the control system is weak and where individuals know they would be difficult to replace, this tactic is particularly attractive.

The pattern of task assignments can also influence the strength and relevance of the control system by making it easier or harder to assign responsibility for outcomes to particular units or individuals. In recent years many businesses have therefore moved to a "profit center" system, in which systems managers make most or all decisions related to specific products and are then held responsible for their products' subsequent performance. Another response has been to create project or matrix organizations, with responsibility for getting a well-defined task done focused clearly on a project manager or activity manager who supervises a multidisciplinary team. In either case the objective is to assign tasks in a way that makes it easier to distribute rewards and punishments on the basis of performance.

Focusing responsibility for a task or operation on a specific manager does not eliminate the problem of measuring the manager's performance, especially if it is impossible to measure the "profits" generated by the operation. Even where profit measures are possible, they can have distorting effects. For example, a manager whose performance is evaluated on the basis of short-run profits may avoid investing in worthwhile longer-run projects because they will not provide enough immediate return.[38] Middle managers in such a system have little incentive to comply with top management directives on social responsibility issues, such as pollution control or minority opportunities, because such compliance will not contribute to the profit measure by which they will be judged.[39]

The flaws in the control system mean that poor decisions may not adversely affect the rewards and punishments of the individuals who were responsible. Consequently, an organization's response to changes in its circumstances will be imperfect and not fully predictable. Most organizations are simply too loose and flexible to expect anything else. They are best thought of as highly varied collections of highly limited animals — not as implacable, all-powerful computing machines.

What can we say about the likely influence of variations in the control system on organizational behavior? Insofar as top management has a strong, deep, relevant control system that accurately and effectively transmits management priorities, the views of these managers are likely to be more influential. In contrast, weak control systems leave members free to pursue their particular private, social, and professional agendas. Discussion at this level, however, does not tell us very much about what, operationally, makes for a strong control system. Only if we can identify these characteristics (as we do in our case studies) can we form some useful generalizations about the relationship between these internal features of an organization and its behavior.

Regardless of the control/incentive system, substantial declines in the fortunes of an organization tend to have an adverse effect on all members, except perhaps those who can leave easily. Promotions come more slowly and financial rewards are less generous. Most organizations thus usually try to survive and grow, because members will orient their individual decisions toward this end.[40] Our analysis suggests that outsiders trying to coerce an organization, especially one with a weak control system, may have to threaten its very survival if their external pressure is to be effectively transmitted to individual decision makers.

Members of an organization react to problems on the basis of their beliefs, concepts, values, and ideas. What is it about an organization that determines these aspects of the mental equipment of its various members?

To some extent this is a matter of *self-selection*. People join and remain in organizations whose activities and policies are compatible with their own views and skills. But the organization is not passive in these matters: *recruitment* and *advancement* practices greatly affect the placement of people with certain viewpoints in certain roles.[41]

Such policies may take into account the *cultural background* and the specific *professional training* of potential members. One well-known study describes how differences in the socioeconomic backgrounds of police officers affect the style and performance of various police departments.[42] Another describes the key role of education in inculcating professional norms.[43]

Professional training may be especially important because of its impact on people's mental processes. There is some justice to the popular impression that lawyers "think like lawyers" and that engineers "think like engineers." Legal training emphasizes the need for general rules, which are nevertheless ambiguous when applied to specific cases.[44] It is based on the legitimacy of divergent interests, which in turn legitimates bargaining and compromise as ways of settling disputes—especially in light of ambiguously applicable principles and different goals. Engineering, in contrast, focuses on the need to reduce problems to numerical form; the existence of "right" (or at least "best") answers to problems thus defined; the importance of a nonrhetorical, objective approach; and the importance of vigorously implementing the "right" answer. Thus, organizations whose personnel practices tend to put lawyers in top management jobs may act quite differently from those whose recruitment and advancement systems turn key tasks over to engineers.

The beliefs and concepts of an organization's members are also, to an extent, a product of their experiences within the organization. Formal training programs, conversations with fellow members, instructions from superiors, and general participation in the organization's ongoing activities all play a role in such socialization.[45]

Our analysis of human thought processes provides a way of thinking about these changes. People's basic values, derived norms, and operational decision rules are rarely conscious or consistent. This makes it possible to reshape the way in which they approach problems and to alter the rules and norms they perceive as relevant to particular situations. Since most people are aware of the limits of their own ideas, they can also be convinced that they previously did not understand the facts of a situation or were mistaken about what would happen under certain circumstances. Indeed, people can pick up new, quite basic ideas and norms as a result of their experience within an organization.[46]

In summary, one can use a number of different methods to "teach people what to think" about a problem. The members of an organization tend to bear the marks of common experiences that will have had that result, if not that purpose. The resulting effects can be substantial. Basic and powerful psychological forces are at work within the process we label "leadership" or "peer pressure" or "identification."

The widely discussed notion of "organizational strategy" is especially relevant to our analysis.[47] It has been used in the literature either to refer to a collection of more or less conscious norms, rules, and ideas about the way in which the organization should act, or to refer to the actual pattern of organizational behavior, apart from what anyone says or claims to believe. The first of these notions—strategy as a set of conscious beliefs—has itself been used in varied ways. Sometimes it denotes the particular views of the top managers in a hierarchical structure; on other occasions it has been used to refer to norms and premises widely accepted throughout an organization.

According to our views on individual cognitive processes, such a shared strategy usually will not be entirely explicit. There are forces that encourage common perceptions within an organization: common experience, mutual socialization, a shared interest in the organization's survival, the need to deal with the world's complexity, and the ability of management to change people's ideas. Still, it is unlikely that an absolute consensus will exist regarding "strategy" within the organization. Various individuals and groups typically advance conflicting views that reflect their particular backgrounds and interests. Indeed, such disagreements can develop between top management and the rest of the organization; this is likely when top management is new, when its control is limited, and when there are strong and explicit organizational traditions.

For all these reasons, there may be a great difference between what people say their organization does and should do, and what it actually does.[48] Ideas may change more slowly than behavior. Perhaps what is said is (unconsciously) more flattering to the organization than what in fact occurs. Perhaps top management has been able to alter policy more readily than it has been able to reshape ideology. Given these and other possibilities, an examination of members' views about how the organization functions is not always sufficient to either describe or explain what actually goes on — although such ideas may be quite important. The situation in any particular organization is a factual question. Organizational strategy — meaning either the ideas of top management or widespread organizational norms and notions — thus may or may not help explain an organization's operational strategy — meaning its actual behavior.[49]

As an added complication, a person may have different, if interdependent, notions about how to pursue various objectives. A manager can have a plan of action for advancing the organization's interests, a personal strategy for advancing his own career, and ideas about how to advance certain substantive or ideological ends.[50] These strategies might be complementary, or they might imply conflicting maxims and decision rules. In such situations it becomes all the more apparent that people's behavior can depend on the way in which they see the problem at hand. Is it perceived in personal, organizational, or social terms?

One of the most powerful mechanisms shaping ideas and attitudes within an organization is the bureaucratic group to which a member belongs. By "group" we generally mean a set of individuals with common perspectives and activities and some sense of mutual awareness. The members of a given functional unit — for example, the mechanical engineering section or the legal department — often satisfy this definition, since they will have common skills, experience, and interests.

The congruence between formal units and bureaucratic groups is not perfect.[51] People transferred to other units may retain important loyalties to, or identification with, earlier associations. This is likely if their training or background differs from that of their new colleagues, or if they have been in the new unit only a short time. Common background, long service, personal friendship, and extensive internal mobility can produce groups whose members are widely dispersed throughout the organization.

Members of a group frequently advocate similar policies that are compatible with their common interests. They tend to favor actions that allow them to exercise their technical skills, more easily perform their tasks, and increase their collective responsibility. To an extent, this may reflect learned professional norms, which reinforce the claims and role of each profession. But conscious self-interest may also be at work. Transmission engineers find reasons to build new power lines; research units argue that larger budgets for research will solve a company's environmental problems; power plant operators favor expenditures that will make generating plants easier to operate.

The strategies that a group's members have learned as part of their professional education can lead the group to advocate different approaches to different situations. Lawyers, for example, sometimes urge negotiation and sometimes litigation. Even if a group's approach is well defined, it may offer recommendations with different substantive implications in different contexts. Public-relations people, for example, who are concerned with responding to outside pressures, may change their spending recommendations according to shifts in public opinion.

Flexibility can be useful to a group if it is to keep its role in an organization in the face of changing circumstances. Groups have to be concerned with whether or not their strategies will help the organization survive and prosper. To get them adopted they must convince others, and plausibility certainly facilitates this. Everyone in an organization, particularly the policy's advocates, may suffer when a policy leads to failure. Apart from its own biases and interests, therefore, a group has every reason to make its suggestions and activities compatible with the organization's situation.

A group's response to a particular situation is not perfectly predictable. Individual temperament, especially of group leaders, may play a role. So, too, will a group's composition. When members come from varied and unusual backgrounds they are more likely to seek new ways to respond and new roles for their unit.

In studying organizations the notion of groups can be a helpful simplification methodologically and practically. Members of an organization cannot always remember exactly who did or said what at various times. Within groups, distinctions in viewpoint and responsibility can be blurred. Furthermore, it is often groups (through their leaders) and not individual members who participate in the policy-making process. Insofar as the members of a group act in a unified manner, we can use the group as the basic unit of analysis. But the applicability of this simplification is an *empirical* matter. In any given situation, an adequate understanding of what has occurred may require some or all of the discussion to proceed at the individual level.

How, then, does a member of an organization decide what to advocate or how to act? How can the substance of the problem and the personal consequences of various decisions — as conveyed by the control system — be taken into account? Those who encounter familiar problems, which they were trained professionally to solve, may have a well-developed method for reaching an answer. In other cases, a person will have to rely on more generalized problem-solving strategies. Learned and developed over the years, such strategies have many often unrecognized assumptions and decision rules built into them. Peer pressure, professional pride, and personal values may come into play. Career interests may or may not be strongly at stake. Perhaps a supervisor has specific ideas and pleasing him will help you advance. Or perhaps performance will have little influence on your career—which, being lazy, is why you joined the organization to begin with. All of these considerations will reach varying levels of consciousness and consume varying amounts of time and energy. Such imprecise and partly unconscious individual decision processes contain much of whatever there is that is systematic about the behavior of organizations.

In summary, if we are to understand individual decisions, we have to understand how and why the members of an organization think as they do. We have to look at the ideas they have in their heads—at objectives, beliefs, maxims to guide decisions, and problem-solving strategies—and how these ideas got there. We need to explore how culture, background, professional education, selective recruitment and self-selection, training and socialization within the organization, job exposure and experience, group structure, and promotion patterns contribute to these results. Having done all this, however, we next have to understand how individual decisions are aggregated into a collective response.

Organizational Decision Processes and Their Evolution

Organizational decision making does not occur in the form of continuously fine-tuned optimization of the sort depicted in economic models. Attention is limited and analysis is costly; action is episodic and problem-oriented. At any one time only a limited set of adjustments and responses can be considered. To understand how various groups and individuals influence such decisions it is useful to distinguish four stages in the process by which organizational behavior is formulated and carried out.

Notice. To initiate the decision cycle, an organization must first notice (that is, define) a problem. Often such problems arise in the context of changes in the larger world which make existing behavior no longer satisfactory. Problems also can be anticipated.[52] Not every change in outcomes will be seen as a problem; the change in consequences must be adverse in terms of the values of at least some members.

Plan. Once a problem is noticed, the organization has to develop a response. This can be characterized as a planning phase. When the problem is familiar the planning may be very brief, since the organization will already have a well-developed rule for such situations. Otherwise, it can be among the most difficult tasks facing an organization. It is here, in developing options and in formulating possible strategies, that the ideas and concepts of an organization's members are likely to be the most influential and the most restrictive.

Decide. The actual decision-making process may vary greatly in formality and explicitness; however, unless the planning phase has produced a variety of options, the importance of decision making can be easily overstated. Indeed, until the problem has been noticed, the machinery of planning and deciding will not be set in motion.

Implement. In this phase the actual behavior of the organization is specified and implemented. Here again, the results of decision making can be undermined if those who execute an idea do not do so faithfully—whether out of incompetence, divergent interests, or contrary conviction.

There are two ways in which a group or individual can affect what occurs at each of these stages. The first is to *do the work*, so that ideas and preferences are directly embodied in the product. But no one works in a vacuum; others can affect outcomes by *influencing those who do the work*, whether up, down, or across the organization's structure.

These two mechanisms do not operate independently. Doing the work at any one stage enables a person to influence those who function later in the process. Conversely, because task assignments are not immutable, those who can affect the decision process often use their influence to determine who does what work. Some of the most interesting and highly contested decisions discussed in our case studies are task-allocation issues.

The second of these two mechanisms—namely influence— itself operates through two different, simultaneously interacting processes: *rational arguments* concerning the best way to proceed, and a *political process* in which power and influence are both inputs and outputs.[53] In the first, expertise matters; in the second, it is more a question of who can impose costs on whom. How and why do these activities occur side by side?

In most organizations, at least some rational argument is possible. Most members, despite their professional differences, share a great deal in the way of objectives and assumptions. If they share a joint interest in the survival and growth of the organization, they will probably agree, in the broadest sense, about what they are trying to accomplish; this provides part of the basis for considering competing suggestions "on their merits." Similarly, the differences in assumptions and world views within most organizations, when it comes to questions of logic and evidence, are typically not very divergent; a utility lawyer and a utility engineer, for example, usually share enough ideas, attitudes, and expertise to make it possible for them to have meaningful discussions and arguments.[54]

The members of an organization may also try to strike deals, line up support, call upon old debts, and so forth to resolve some particular question. Such political processes develop in part because rational arguments alone do not always resolve disagreements: often evidence is too slight and the problem too difficult. In such situations, "politics" (that is, influence, compromise, and so forth) may be the only means for making the decision.

Members with a substantial stake in an organization's decisions may have every reason to engage in political action to influence what occurs. Why not try to influence decisions even (or especially) when one fears one will lose "on the merits"? In addition to opportunity and incentive, the members of an organization normally have the resources to behave in a political manner. Even when top management is strong, subordinates do have some capacity to impose costs on superiors (not to mention on each other) by refusing to cooperate.

Matters of policy aside, politics can be especially important when the organization has to distribute individual gains and losses. The lack of quantitative performance measures, the element of luck, the length of time before results are clear, and the difficulties in deciding who is responsible all can make the rational allocation of rewards difficult, and the operation of the control system consequently can become quite "political."

What characteristics of groups and individuals are likely to influence task assignment, insofar as this is a rational process? Our analysis of human decision making indicates that historic routines and rules will play a major role, especially in familiar tasks. Ask a senior manager why he gave task X to group Y and he will often give the deceptively simple answer: "That is how we assign such jobs around here." Organizations exist in part because, by having such routines, they economize on the resources used in dividing up problems among specialists.

When the task-assignment decision is more novel, a manager

faces a question without a standard answer. Trying to decide rationally who should do what job involves balancing the availability of various groups, the relevance of their training and experience, and their ability and reliability. Such suggestions, however, are very general and will need refining in the course of our case studies. What kinds of groups tend to have responsibility for various tasks in an organization's decision-action cycle? What do differences in this regard imply for organizational performance?

In studying any particular organization we also have to inquire into the politics of organizational decisions, regarding both substantive policy and task assignments. To some extent, the influence of a group will depend on the personal influence of its members over key decision makers; factors such as past contact, similar viewpoints, charisma, and mutual need will all play a role. Given the imperfection of information processing and everyone's limited time and attention, *access* to critical decision makers should also affect a group's influence. How long and how encumbered are various communication channels? Who reports through whom, both in theory and in practice?

What is it that gives a group leverage in internal bargaining processes? Groups with greater internal cohesion and with more at stake are more likely to influence what occurs. But what brings about such cohesion and provides such incentives? Again, we look to our empirical studies to suggest more detailed and specific hypotheses on these points.

The ability of the top to manage the overall process, and hence to determine the behavior of the organization, depends on its ability to control what occurs at each stage of the notice-plan-decide-implement cycle. A strong control system obviously will help, and so will having middle managers who are personally loyal. To the extent that planners and implementers agree with top management, there will be less need to resort to rewards and punishments.[55] Control is also enhanced if it is easy to monitor the behavior of various groups in terms of objective magnitudes.[56] Having to rely on interpretive reports, particularly if the groups in question report on themselves, may make evaluation difficult. Finally, a manager's ability to achieve his objectives depends on whether or not he is pursuing a well-designed and efficacious course of action to begin with.[57]

Understanding how and why organizations act as they do thus requires us to answer the interrelated questions of who does the work and who has influence; this means knowing about the relative size and apparent sphere of expertise of various groups, as well as their perspectives, values, and modes of problem solving. We must understand the interpersonal dynamics between top management and the leaders and members of various groups; explore formal and informal communication channels; determine which groups are in a position to "demand" influence as the price of continuing cooperation; and study the way in which the control system affects implementation. This may seem like a lot to have to learn, but there is no other way to understand a phenomenon as complex as organizational behavior.

The very process of solving day-to-day problems can lead to changes in an organization's structure and in the strategic ideas of its key managers. Such changes, however, impose costs both on those making them and on those subject to them. Rather than occurring spontaneously, they originate with someone's perception that the organization is not coping as well as it should with external stresses or opportunities.[58] Given our concern with responsiveness, we will pay some attention in our studies to this process of change. How large a crisis is required, and what kinds of responses result? Are they small adjustments in policy, major changes in personnel, new structural arrangements? If some groups rise or fall in the process, what determines how and why this occurs? To what extent is new management needed to accomplish major changes, and how does this occur?[59]

We should not expect that a crisis will necessarily produce change. In a crisis, time is short; this can produce an *increased* reliance on traditional habits of mind and rules of thumb, for both cognitive and psychodynamic reasons.[60] Structural change may occur only after the acute phase has passed.

In terms of our conceptual framework, changes in the structure and behavior of organizations will range along a continuum from trivial to profound. Some will involve alteration of fundamental practices and decision rules; others will touch only middle-level strategic principles; still others will affect only superficial tactics and unimportant procedures. Thus, we would blur the distinction suggested by Argyris and Schön, who see only two kinds of change (that is, "learning") occurring in organizations: that which *does* and that which *does not* call into question accepted premises.[61] We suggest that *all* change/learning involves some modification or rejection of earlier views, as well as continued adherence to others. The question is one of the degree of the change involved.

Our view here is parallel to our dissent from Kuhn's suggestion that scientific change either does or does not involve a revolution-ary shift in "paradigms" — that is, in world views. Given our hier-archical view of cognitive structures, we can account for and por-tray partial and intermediary events. It is possible to have changes in middle-level principles that leave some fundamentals intact.[62] "Learning," in the sense of progress toward a goal, is possible only if some assumptions (by which this progress is defined) do persist.

We have not distinguished between behavioral and structural changes, yet their interrelationship is an issue that has been de-bated at length in the management literature. Some writers have suggested that structure determines strategy, through its impact on the decision-making process.[63] Others have emphasized the extent to which structure has been and should be designed to be compatible with a chosen strategy.[64] Our framework, in contrast, suggests that in an organization both relationships are possible — even likely — at any one time. We have discussed how, in the short run, structural features are likely to affect the "aggregation pro-cess" that combines group perspectives. We have also noted how, in the longer run, that structure itself is open to continual evolu-tion — in part due to accident or current structural influences and in part as a result of conscious decisions to change structure so as to achieve different behavioral results.

The relationship between strategy and structure seems notice-ably elastic. Given the potential impact of individual views and personal skills, any given structure is capable of generating a vari-ety of behavioral patterns, depending on the particular people involved. For the same reason, we should expect that any given strategy could be supported by a number of different structural arrangements.

Our view of the process of organizational change is an evolu-tionary one, in which new strategies and new structures adapt over time to the changing social niche into which an organization fits. The process is unlike biological evolution, where some ran-dom mutations survive because of greater reproductive success: organizational change is in part conscious, and success means the survival and growth of the original entity.

Not all successful organizational change is the result of accu-rate analysis and intentional action. A strategy or structure that is adapted to the environment may not have derived from conscious calculation.[65] Effective approaches and arrangements could have been arrived at accidentally and then continued. Maladaptive ones would have been modified, or the organizations that employed them would disappear. Looking backward, therefore, all that we may see are organizations that are well adjusted structurally and strategically. This makes it tempting to attribute more foresight and wisdom to the process of organizational design than may actually have been present.

Organizations do have discretion. Structural and strategic developments are not perfectly coerced by external circumstances. Thus, to see why any particular organization is what it is today, we have to understand its internal development. We must look back, perhaps to its inception, to seek the roots of its current character. At least some of what occurs is not systematic from the viewpoint of larger social processes. We must explore the impact of particular events and individuals on the organization's development. The past leaves its mark on organizations, even as it does on the anatomy of animal species.

3

A Primer on Electric
Utility Operations

Electricity is not a primary source of energy; some other form of energy must be used to produce it.[1] Electric current is created when a wire with the necessary properties is moved through a magnetic field. A modern generator has many turns of wire wrapped around a rotor that spins at high speed within a very strong magnetic field. This creates a large amount of current, but the power to turn the generator must come from somewhere else. And once produced, the electricity must be made accessible to users. Thus, a utility must decide what sizes and types of generating plants to build, where to build these plants, what kinds of transmission and distribution lines are needed, and along what routes the lines should be constructed.

These decisions involve various environmental problems.[2] There are land-use and aesthetic issues raised by the mere existence of generation and transmission facilities; and there are the waste products that the generating plants emit into the surrounding ecosystem (heat, dust, radioactivity, and so forth). These residuals, in turn, have an impact on many physical and biological systems, including man. The physical magnitude and social impact of adverse effects will vary, depending on the types of generating technology and fuels that are used, the safeguards and controls installed, and the location of the plant.

Utilities currently rely on three main types of technology for generating power: hydroelectric, fossil-fuel, and nuclear. At hydroelectric plants, the potential energy in water backed up behind a dam is stored in a reservoir. The water is then allowed to fall so that it passes through a turbine, turning a shaft with blades attached to it. The turbines, in turn, drive the generators.

Hydroelectric development may raise serious land-use and aesthetic issues. Dams alter the character of free-flowing rivers, destroy wildlife habitats, flood farmlands, and displace home-

46

owners. Yet hydroelectric facilities do not produce air pollution and are very inexpensive to operate because they involve no fuel cost. Since World War II, however, few hydroelectric facilities have been constructed since most of the best sites were already developed. Several of the projects that have gone forward are of the "pumped-storage" type, in which surplus power not needed during the nighttime is used to pump water back behind the dams for release during peak demand periods the following day.

In fossil-fuel or nuclear plants—now the primary sources of new capacity—the energy released by burning fossil fuels such as oil or coal or by fissioning uranium atoms in a nuclear reactor is used to boil water; the resulting steam drives the turbines, which in turn drive the generators. In order for the turbines to work properly the steam must rush through them steadily, and this requires cooling and hence condensing the steam to lower the pressure on the far side of the turbine. Water is generally used for this purpose, although there are some experimental air-cooled systems. Often this water, which has absorbed heat from the system, is simply returned to the stream, lake, or ocean it came from. The impact of this heated discharge varies. In some cases, fish have been known to thrive in the warm water around a power plant. Yet raising the temperature of the water can reduce its capacity to assimilate other wastes, and may seriously disrupt the ecological balance. Even heat discharges that attract fish may cause harm in the long run by changing normal feeding and migration patterns. And the risk of disruptions becomes more severe as more and more plants are built on a given body of water. Heavy reliance on nuclear generation enhances these risks, since for a given amount of power generated, a nuclear plant releases about one-sixth more heat to the water than a fossil-fuel plant.

There are several ways to correct the thermal pollution from such "once through" cooling systems. The returning water can be diffused widely into the receiving water body by specially engineered piping systems. Or the water can be air-cooled by using ponds, spray systems, or cooling towers. In such towers, the hot water is dribbled down over a series of baffles while fans or a large chimney-like structure draws air over the water to cool it; once cooled, the water can be returned to its original source or can be reused for cooling purposes (a "closed-cycle" cooling system).

Both nuclear and fossil-fuel plants produce thermal pollution, and have additional distinct problems of their own. Nuclear plants pose the risk of unplanned releases of radioactivity into the atmosphere. Although there is no danger of a nuclear plant ex-

ploding like an atomic bomb, it is theoretically possible that a
failure of its reactor cooling system could cause it to melt, allowing radioactivity to escape. While such a contingency is highly
unlikely, it could result in a catastrophe. There are also potential
problems in disposing of, or reprocessing, spent fuel elements
from nuclear reactors. Can they safely be buried in certain kinds
of geologic formations? If the fuel elements are reprocessed, will
terrorists be able to obtain the plutonium they contain to make
bombs? Academic and popular opinion on these issues is divided,
to say the least, although it has not had a major effect on the
cases we consider.

Of more immediate relevance is the geological stability of nuclear plant sites. In areas of geologic faults, major earth slippage
(horizontally or vertically) during earthquakes could damage a
reactor and cause a release of radioactivity. This has been an
especially vexing issue in California, where coastal sites provide
abundant cooling water, yet are close to major fault zones. The
use of coastal sites also raises significant land-use and aesthetic
problems.

Plants that burn fossil fuels produce many waste products.
Leftover ash must be disposed of in a landfill. And pollutants
such as particulate matter, oxides of sulfur, and oxides of nitrogen (NO_x) are released from the smokestacks. The amount of
particulate matter and sulfur oxides released depends largely on
the composition of the specific fuel, on how much sulfur and ash
it contains. NO_x emissions, on the other hand, depend more on
combustion temperatures inside the boiler.

Once discharged into the air, the impact of these pollutants is a
function of the way in which they are dispersed, since plants, animals, and people react not to how much comes out of the smokestack, but on what is called the ambient concentration — the level
of pollution in the air they breathe. For example, when a smoke
plume is trapped by the thermal layers in the atmosphere (an inversion), it can produce very high concentrations where it strikes
the ground. The topography in the vicinity of the plant, the wind
conditions, the location of the people, and the height of the stack
will all influence the damage that results from any given level of
emissions.[3] The impact can also depend on how rapidly pollutants are chemically transformed in the atmosphere, into what
they are transformed, and how long they tend to remain. NO_x,
for example, combined with hydrocarbons and strong sunlight, is
a major cause of smog. Among sulfur compounds, sulfur dioxide

(SO_2) tends to be washed out relatively quickly; other sulfur compounds (written as SO_x and referred to as "sulfates") may be more persistent and hence may travel longer distances. When they do, they can affect the environment as much as five hundred to eight hundred miles downwind, falling out as "acid rain" which inhibits plant growth and alters the chemistry of receiving water bodies.

Generally the air pollutants produced by fossil-fuel power plants do not have noticeable health effects at usual ground level concentrations. However, unusual weather conditions have led to some severe air pollution incidents, during which the normal death rate has noticeably increased. There are also longer-term effects from continued lower-level exposures—on plants, property, and people. And some air pollutants may have direct visibility effects as well. The exact magnitude of these effects and the levels at which they occur is still much in dispute. Federal primary air quality standards, which are designed to protect human health, restrict both short-term and longer-term exposures. Expressed either in micrograms per cubic meter ($\mu g/m^3$) or parts per million (ppm), the SO_2 standard is 365 $\mu g/m^3$ or .14 ppm for any 24 hours and 80 $\mu g/m^3$ or .03 ppm on an annual average. For particulates the numbers are 260 $\mu g/m^3$ for 24 hours and 75 $\mu g/m^3$ on an annual basis. NO_x, on the other hand, is restricted only on an annual basis—at 100 $\mu g/m^3$. In general, at concentrations that are three to six times as high as the 24-hour levels, death rates rise among the already ill and even healthy people begin showing some symptoms.[4]

The production and transportation of fossil fuels (coal mining, oil refining and transport, and so forth) may have serious environmental consequences even before these fuels arrive at the power plant. There has been continuing dispute at the national level about what risks to tolerate and what cleanup costs to bear. One might have thought that a fossil-fuel user would not be directly involved in such matters, but as we will see in our first case study, these issues, too, have become a focus of utility decision making.[5]

Beyond these technological alternatives are a variety of other energy sources that have recently been discussed—sources such as solar energy, ocean tides, geothermal power, windmills, and nuclear fusion. For a utility that needs large amounts of low-cost, reliable power in the short run, all or most of these potential sources are too expensive or uncertain to be alternatives, although they may prove fruitful in the future. The utilities in our study for the most part have not yet seriously considered these alternatives.[6]

Planning and Constructing Facilities

Even before the choice of technology is made, a utility must decide how much capacity to build. Resolving this issue is not easy because forecasts of future developments are an essential part of the process. Since new plants can take from three to twelve years to construct, demand must be forecast that far in advance in order to ensure that capacity will be available when customers want to use it. Until recently, demand for electricity grew at a very stable pace, averaging 7 percent a year nationally. But due to the "energy crisis," rising fuel costs, the resulting sharp rise in electric rates, and a weak economy, growth in demand has fallen off since about 1973. Nationally, sales actually decreased between 1973 and 1974, and in the five years since the growth rate has varied noticeably, from less than 3 percent to more than 6 percent.[7] This variability has made future planning all the more difficult.

The question of how much capacity to build is further complicated by the fact that the company needs to provide some reserves for unanticipated contingencies.[8] All generators break down occasionally (an event called a "forced outage"). The less reserve, the more likely it becomes that the utility will not be able to meet demand; in this case it will have to try to purchase power from neighboring systems or else try to stretch its own capacity further (that is, lower the voltage and cause a "brownout"). In extreme circumstances, it will simply cut some customers off altogether (impose a "blackout"). Customers also lose service when the transmission and distribution system fails. Since perfectly reliable supplies are impossible, a utility in order to decide how much generating capacity to build, must choose how reliable to try to make the system. This involves comparing the costs and benefits of various levels of reliability, which implies forecasting not only demand but also the likely rate of equipment failures, the likelihood and cost of obtaining electricity from other systems, and the costs of additional or more reliable equipment.

The electric demand on any one system varies considerably with the time of day, season of the year, temperature, and so on. Hence, a company does not build all its plants alike. Some are "base-load" plants, designed to run all the time. Others, intermediate or cycling units, are turned on and off each day. Still others are "peaking" units, operating only a few hours a day. It is usually more cost-effective to build a plant that costs more but uses less fuel in the case of a heavily used base-load plant rather than a peaking unit. The more a plant is used, the more benefit is derived from the fuel-saving features. Thus, in deciding what capacity to build, a system must forecast its load curve—that is, the pattern of expected demand—and ask how much of each kind of capacity it requires.

Other utility decisions also require making forecasts. The attractiveness of alternative plant designs will depend, among other things, on the relative prices of various fuels over the life of the plant, which must therefore be predicted. Given constant progress in the technology of generation and transmission, firms must also decide how likely it is that equipment suppliers will be able to live up to claims of improved performance when new equipment is actually delivered.

Each facility gives rise to thousands of interdependent and potentially important decisions. For a generating station, for example, specifying fuel, size, and location provides only the broadest context for innumerable choices about boiler design, generator configuration, pump sizes and types, smokestack heights, fuel handling equipment, pollution control equipment, and so on. The engineers who make these decisions often cannot predict precisely what will happen if the machinery is a little bit bigger or faster or hotter than previous models. Forecasting the costs and workability of alternative approaches to a design problem involves uncertainty and uses resources; a certain number of engineering mistakes are inevitable, since there are limits on how much it pays to spend on problem solving. As a result, the question of what margin to allow for possible errors in the analysis is pervasive and fundamental.

In making such decisions, a regulated private company motivated by profit theoretically has some incentive to make extra investments, even in pollution controls.[9] By law the regulatory agency is supposed to allow the utility a specified "rate of return" on its "rate base"—that is, on the total amount of capital it has invested in the business. Rates are supposed to be determined so that a utility's total revenue will cover its operating costs and provide such a return. In practice, however, there are a number of political and bureaucratic forces at work that reduce the advantages of making extra investments. Historically, electric costs and rates have fallen as growing use of electricity has permitted economies of scale and the use of new, more efficient designs. But since the late 1960s utilities in general have faced increasing expenditures due to sharply rising fuel costs, interest rates, and construction charges. Although utilities are supposed to be allowed rate increases that will maintain their rate of return, rate-setting commissions have been under considerable political pressure to hold down rate increases. The slowness of the regulatory process itself leads to delays in recovering costs, even when a rate commission does grant a requested increase. Hence, in practice, utilities are by no means guaranteed a return on all new investments, which can give them an incentive to avoid making expenditures on pollution control. Even when costs are declining, there is some incentive to hold costs down. Under these circumstances, regulatory lag may allow a company to hold on to cost savings until a rate reduction is imposed.[10] As we shall see, however, some public companies are free of these constraints and are able to set their own rates.

To finance their investments, both public and private utilities must raise capital. Private companies sell shares of stock and various kinds of bonds, with the proportions depending on their overall financial position. Traditionally thought of by investors as low-risk, low-profit businesses, private utilities have always relied heavily on bond financing. However, if a regulatory commission holds down rates when costs are rising, a utility could find itself unable to attract investors to buy its securities. Some public companies also sell their own bonds, while others get their capital from the government—which in turn sells its own bonds or uses tax funds to finance the utility.

Financing aside, the physical decisions are of primary interest to us here. For a fossil-fuel plant, it must first be decided what type of fuel to use.[11] Natural gas is the cleanest-burning. For many years it was cheap and available in the South and West, and hence was widely used in power plants in California. However, it is now becoming unavailable for such purposes since price controls have led to an imbalance between supply and demand; in response, the Federal Power Commission has given priority to individual homeowners.

Oil, too, can be clean-burning, provided it is low in sulfur and ash. But such fuel generally comes from Africa or Indonesia, raising many national security and international economic questions. Alternatively, low-sulfur supplies can be obtained by specially processing ("desulfurizing") less desirable oil from other areas. Such processing is often necessary because most power plants

burn not crude oil, but the heaviest fraction of the crude produced by the refining process ("residual fuel oil") which contains
in concentrated form all the impurities from the original crude.

Coal as a fuel is even more heterogeneous than oil. It varies
greatly in heating value, sulfur and ash content, and other chemical properties. There are broad variations in coal obtained from
different coalfields, and even from different parts of the same
coalfield or different parts of the same mine. Of all the fossil
fuels, coal tends to have the highest pollution levels and raises a
number of other serious environmental difficulties. Hence, a
coal-burning company must determine what kind of coal to burn
and, if low-sulfur coal is available, how much extra it is worth
paying for such supplies.

Coal can be processed *before* combusion to reduce its environmental side effects, but such processes are not yet routinely available on a commercial basis.[12] Several of the companies in our
study have been working on developing them. And some manufacturers, drawing on European experience, are prepared to offer
equipment for coal gasification, which removes pollutants as part
of the process.

A number of other aspects of the design of fossil-fuel plants
tend to have less immediate environmental impact, but shed considerable light on company functioning. One such question is
unit size. The capacity of a generating unit is measured in thousands of watts (kilowatts) or more recently in millions of watts, or
megawatts (MW), of power output. To measure the energy actually produced or used by an electric system we multiply the power
output by the hours of operation to get a number labeled in terms
of kilowatt-hours. Ten kilowatts used for one hour gives us the
same energy use as 20 kilowatts for half an hour. In the late 1940s
units of 100-200 MW were common. But to increase efficiency
and lower costs, plant sizes have increased steadily; units of 700-
1200 MW are now typical. Larger sizes imply both greater savings
and greater risks of unreliability, so a company's choices on this
question reveal something of its overall engineering philosophy.[13]
To put trends in generating-unit size in perspective, it must be
realized that a one-megawatt plant can light up 10,000 light
bulbs of 100 watts each. At the time of our study, the entire national generating system was only about 500,000 MW — for industrial and commercial as well as residential purposes. Hence a
1,000 MW unit is a large plant indeed, producing a trillion watts
of power at any one time.

Each plant usually contains more than one generating unit.

One site may have five to eight units of several different sizes and ages that have been added at different times — a procedure that allows the utility to avoid the costs and difficulties of acquiring new locations. On the other hand, it can result in the concentration of so much capacity in a single place that emissions can lead to unacceptably poor air quality in the vicinity of the facility.

Units also vary in steam temperature and pressure. Since World War II the trend has been toward hotter and higher-pressure steam conditions because units are able to save fuel by improving thermal efficiency. At the same time, in the last few years there has been some pullback from very high temperatures and pressures because of adverse operating experience. Units also use different methods for drawing air into the boiler: pulling in by "induced draft" fans, pushing in by "forced draft," or both pushing and pulling in a "balanced draft" design. Some boilers have been designed so that the combustion chamber is under positive air pressure, to improve fuel-burning. Other design choices concern the amount of effort made to recover heat from the smokestack gases, the way in which the burners are placed in the boilers, and so on. On many of these issues, there are tradeoffs between capital costs and operating costs that can be made differently, depending on how often the unit will be operating and on the concerns and perspectives of the company in question.

In the design of nuclear plants, similar choices must be made. In our case studies, however, we focus less on such details and more on plant location and choice of technology. Ontario Hydro, for example, has helped develop a distinct Canadian nuclear reactor design, and this is of interest because of what it reveals about corporate strategy. While American reactors are housed in one large "pressure vessel," whose disruption could lead to a large radioactive release, the Canadian approach permits the use of many small "pressure tubes," making the likelihood of a large-scale accident more remote. Additionally, Canadian reactors use unrefined uranium, which eliminates the need to send the fuel to the United States for preprocessing.[14] Their decision to develop this sytem, rather than use American technology, is one we will look at carefully.

Even before the technology of a plant has been specified, the location must be chosen. Rationally, these decisions should be interdependent. Technology influences siting; fossil plants, for example, need to be on transport routes appropriate for conveying fuel supplies. Conversely, the site shapes design; the kind of cooling system to be used, for example, depends on water availability, climate, and the nature of the receiving ecosystem. Many considerations must be balanced simultaneously: land use, ecological impact, construction costs, impact and cost of transmission lines, the electrical characteristics of the company's entire system, and so on. Often in recent years the companies we studied have had great difficulty in finding acceptable locations.

Public controversy over plant location can be substantial, arising in part because this is an obvious and dramatic issue, easily grasped by the layman. Local residents usually find it easy to organize opposition, since they pay the pollution and aesthetic costs yet do not receive most of the benefits. Of course, some communities solicit plants for the jobs and tax base they can provide, although this has become less common in recent years. Instead, many companies are facing greatly increased pressure to open up their planning processes to local and outside participation because these would-be participants want to avoid new facilities in their own areas.

Once a generating station has produced power, the power has to be delivered to consumers. Although some public companies (for example, the Tennessee Valley Authority) are primarily wholesalers, most systems maintain not only high-voltage transmission lines for shifting major blocks of power to load centers, but also lower-voltage distribution systems for delivering power to individual customers. Such a system includes a series of substations from which the distribution circuits radiate. Comprising areas of a few hundred or a few thousand square feet, substations contain transformers and other electrical equipment that switch the high-voltage power to lower voltages and send it out over the individual distribution lines.

Transmission and distribution lines are characterized by different voltages. Voltage is the pressure beind the current—the work being done to force each unit of current through the line. Normal household current is at 115-230 volts. High-voltage transmission lines operate at 60 to 400 thousand volts or kilovolts, or even higher. Distribution systems run at perhaps 20 kilovolts. Most household electricity—and most of that sent through the distribution and transmission system—is alternating current ("AC"), which reverses direction regularly, in the United States at a rate of 60 times, or cycles, per second. Yet for complex engineering reasons, some high-voltage transmission lines are direct current ("DC")—that is, current flows all in one direction.

The major environmental issues raised by transmission systems are those of location and land use. Often very visible, transmission lines have been a target of increasing public complaint in recent years. To soften local objections, some companies have made special efforts to landscape their rights-of-way or make them available for park development. Others have tried to use visually less offensive tower designs—for example, graceful steel poles instead of the traditional latticework structures. Such changes are expensive. In some areas, there has been considerable public pressure to put transmission lines underground, but the utilities argue that this is less reliable and vastly more expensive than overhead transmission. As a result, relatively few transmission lines, none of the very highest voltages, have been put underground. Public calls for outside participation in such decisions—as well as for undergrounding, rerouting, different towers, and so on—are increasing steadily.

Undergrounding distribution lines, because of the lower voltages involved, is technically much easier and has been routinely done in downtown areas of large cities for forty years. Many companies, however, are now being asked for aesthetic reasons to provide underground lines in suburban and residential areas. Similar pressures arise for landscaping, building walls around, and limiting the noise from substations—which ideally should be located close to concentrations of power users. Deciding how and where to spend company money on landscaping and undergrounding, and determining how to respond to pressures for "open planning," are policy questions that arise several times in our study.

Pollution Control and Environmental Regulation

Every utility must make decisions regarding the provision of pollution control devices. We have already mentioned the cooling towers that reduce thermal pollution. Measures must also be taken to control stack gas emissions. One option is to use "clean fuels," either naturally clean or specifically processed. Another is to add stack gas cleaning equipment.

Until the late 1950s, both mechanical collectors and electrostatic precipitators were installed on coal-fired plants to control particulate emissions.[15] In the 1960s precipitators, which are more efficient than mechanical collectors, became the rule on new plants.

Precipitators function by setting up a strong electrostatic field through which the exhaust gases pass. The dust particles in the gas become electrically charged and migrate to one of the metal plates or wires generating the field. By periodically agitating this structure, the dust can be dislodged and collected in hoppers at the bottom. Mechanical collectors work by imparting a rotating motion to the exhaust gases. The dust moves toward the walls due to centrifugal force.

Such machines are quite sensitive to operating and maintenance practices and to margins for error built into the design. The hoppers must be emptied regularly, the electrical circuits kept intact, mechanical breakages repaired, and so on. Size and sectionalization are critical in precipitator design. Building multiple sections lowers the risks of poor performance when one unit fails. Larger sizes provide more collector area and hence better performance. The problem is that precipitator performance varies with the chemical composition of the coal. A large plant uses a lot of coal—about 9,000 tons a day, a whole trainload, for a 1,000 MW unit. This often comes from various mines that produce coal of various qualities. Even in coal that comes from a single mine there may be noticeable differences from day to day. Thus it is not easy to decide exactly what conditions to design for.

The most important characteristic is the sulfur content of the coal. Unfortunately, the relationship between precipitator efficiency and fuel sulfur content is perverse. Ash from low-sulfur coal is harder to collect. A precipitator that removed better than 99 percent of the particulates from 3 percent sulfur coal might do no better than 95 percent on 2 percent sulfur coal and less than 90 percent on 1 percent sulfur coal. Designing for average conditions will lead to substandard performance half the time. Should there be enough equipment to handle 70 percent, or 80 percent, or 90 percent of the situations that are likely to arise? One option is to put the stack gases through a "hotside" precipitator. This means treating them before they have been cooled by the heat exchanger, which is used in most power plants to transfer heat from the stack gases to the new air coming into the furnace. Such hotside units are less sensitive to coal characteristics, but must be larger (and hence are more costly to construct) because the stack gases occupy a larger volume when they are warmer.

Particulate matter collection levels of 95 percent or higher have been possible since the early 1960s, provided the equipment was well maintained. Current designs, however, usually aim for 99 percent or even 99.5 percent. (Note that a 98 percent unit allows four times as much particulate matter to escape as one operating at 99.5 percent.) Although largely used on coal-fired units, precipitators have been used on a few oil-fired plants as well in the last few years. Oil units tend to have low emissions in terms of pounds, but the ash particles they emit are small and hence have a greater effect on light scattering; thus, the plumes from oil-fired plants are usually more visible than plumes from coal plants, even with less material coming out of the stack. Such small particulates—which in general are the hardest to collect whatever the fuel—also appear to have the largest health effects because they can get so far into the respiratory system. Some utilities have experimented with "bag houses" to increase control of such emissions. These devices are essentially large filters that trap the particulates. Though used in some chemical plants, the technology has been unattractive to utilities for several technical reasons, including the fact that a good deal of energy must be used to push the gases through the cleaning system.

Although precipitators can control particulate emissions quite effectively, they have no impact on sulfur dioxide emissions. Much work has been done in recent years on a variety of stack gas "scrubbing" systems designed to remove sulfur, and sometimes particulates as well, from the gas stream.[16] Early experimental units were plagued by problems, like many engineering prototypes, but these were usually matters of detailed design, resolved in later units so that scrubber reliability has been improving steadily. Many utilities insist that they are not a "proven" option, while other companies are installing them; the United States Environmental Protection Agency (EPA) says they can and should be used where required. There is still much debate about the appropriate role for such systems, even assuming they are effective in controlling SO_2 emissions.

Most scrubbers work by getting the sulfur compounds in the exhaust gases to react chemically with, and hence become trapped by, some material that they are exposed to. There are two kinds of systems; "throwaway" systems where the material containing the captured sulfur is disposed of as waste, and "regenerable" systems where this material is processed further to recover the sulfur as a by-product and is itself reused. The most popular throwaway systems use large quantities of lime or limestone and produce substantial solid-waste disposal problems. Regenerable systems yield sulfur (or sulfuric acid) as a potentially profitable by-product but also tend to be more expensive because of the additional processing involved.

The oldest form of SO_2 control is the use of tall smokestacks to diffuse emissions over a wide area and thus lower their impact on air quality at any one ground-level point. This approach can be supplemented by keeping some low-sulfur fuel on hand for use when weather conditions could lead to poor dispersion and increased pollution concentrations. Another alternative is to reduce generation—and hence emissions—during such weather conditions. Many utilities defend these approaches as an alternative to expensive and (they claim) unproven stack gas scrubbing systems, or reliance on low-sulfur fuel. But in order for fuel switching and generation cutbacks to work, a sophisticated system of air quality monitoring and weather forecasting is required. Since it is not clear whether the companies will conscientiously operate such a system, the attitude of regulatory agencies to such schemes has often been skeptical. This skepticism has been reinforced in recent years by concern over the long-distance transport of sulfates and acid rain. Recent court decisions support the Environmental Protection Agency's current position that tall stacks and intermittent controls are not "emission limitations" within the meaning of this term as used in the Clean Air Act. Even supposing that states were to take stack height into account informally and implicitly in setting emissions limits, and ambient standards were met, it is not clear whether or not this would violate the current interpretation.[17]

Fuel changes and control devices are more relevant to SO_2 and particulate control than to NO_x problems, although different broad fuel types do have different NO_x emissions levels. Dealing with the NO_x issue, however, usually means working on the boiler design itself and how it is operated. It is desirable to lower combustion temperatures and lessen the oxygen available for combustion in high-temperature locations, since NO_x is formed in high-temperature environments where a great deal of oxygen is present. Thus, control measures include relocating fuel burners in the boiler, changing how much and at what point air is added to the system, and perhaps recirculating fuel gases (which are low in oxygen) through the boiler.

Companies are almost never free to make design, construction, and equipment decisions on their own authority. Their choices are constrained by a maze of local, state, and federal regulation which has grown and changed considerably in recent years.

With regard to location and land use, companies often must get local government permits to extend lines across streets or to erect certain kinds of facilities. The state's department of public utilities or some other agency often must approve a new transmission line or generating unit. And in the process, permits or approvals may also be required from other state agencies, such as those in charge of pollution control, fish and game regulation, and state planning.

The construction and operation of all hydroelectric units and all nuclear power plants must be licensed, respectively, by the Federal Power Commission and the Nuclear Regulatory Commission (formerly the Atomic Energy Commission). There is no federal licensing for fossil-fuel plants. However, many proposed coal-burning plants in the Southwest have been either on federal land or required federal water rights, again involving a federal agency. The need for a federal decision is important because then the agency must prepare and circulate an environmental impact statement, in keeping with the provisions of the National Environmental Policy Act (NEPA) of 1969.[18] Such statements must include a report on certain salient features of the project, including irreversible resource commitments, environmental impact, and alternatives. Under current procedures, they are circulated for public and agency comment in draft form before being reworked for final approval. Since it is the companies who typically prepare such reports, this places yet another demand on the internal structure of the utility organization. Serious work is required to prepare these reports, given the readiness of the federal courts to hold up projects when draft statements are challenged by environmental groups. Many states now require such reports when state action is involved. In at least one case, an environmental impact statement acceptable at the federal level was turned back by a state agency for further work. Since the need to produce environmental impact statements was thrust upon the companies quite suddenly, the companies' different responses to this need, and their expertise in dealing with it, offer an interesting special case of organizational responsiveness.

Although utilities in the Los Angeles area were subject to stringent air pollution regulations as early as the 1950s, prior to 1966 most North American utilities faced no air pollution regulations other than some local ordinances prohibiting dark smoke emissions. In 1966 the United States government issued emissions guidelines for federal agencies, and federal legislation the following year provided a framework for stronger state action. In the next several years a number of states (and, independently, the province of Ontario) adopted standards for ambient air quality and emissions regulations to meet those standards, and did so for a number of air pollutants. This was not done statewide, but in selected regions called Air Quality Control Regions. After Congress enacted the Clean Air Act Amendments of 1970, all states had to adopt plans designed to bring air quality throughout the state up to nationally uniform ambient standards, as set by the EPA. These "state implementation plans" must limit the emissions of various pollutants such as SO_2, NO_x, and particulates from power plants and other industrial facilities, and must be approved, along with any changes or variances, by the EPA. While the states are supposed to enforce the regulations they issue, the EPA is empowered to take over these enforcement responsibilities if the states fail to perform them. In comparison to earlier approaches, this represents a significant centralization and an elimination of state and local discretion.[19]

The states were given only nine months to develop their original plans. Their limited technical capabilities, and a national mood favoring strict environmental regulations, led many of them to settle quickly on a few quite stringent standards. The SO_2 standards adopted by many states were particularly troublesome from the utilities' viewpoint, since implicitly they often required the use of scrubbers or extremely low-sulfur fuel. Such standards were expressed either as limits on the percentage of sulfur in fuel, or in terms of pounds of sulfur emitted per million Btu's (British thermal units) of heat released in combustion. Subsequently, states began to review their plans on a region-by-region basis. With public enthusiasm for strict and expensive standards declining, many states have revised their plans to the extent that in some cases utilities are now permitted to emit about as much SO_2 as they did formerly at existing plants. In contrast, new plants are governed by strict national "new source" performance standards. Although these used to specify an allowable emissions rate based on coal heat content, since congressional action in 1977 they have required the use of control technology — that is, scrubbers or precombustion processing — on all new coal-fired plants.[20] Furthermore, if a utility tried to build a plant in an area not in compliance with federal ambient standards, it would have to arrange for some existing sources to reduce their pollution by as much as, or more than, the new emissions. This would be required by the so-called "trade-off policy" enforced by the EPA.[21]

Often the utilities have played an important role in the process of reviewing and revising state standards. At the federal level, many have lobbied against the emissions standards approach, arguing for permission to rely on tall stacks and operational controls (such as fuel switching) instead. In the discussions that follow, we will be interested not only in whether and when utilities will be meeting the emissions limits prescribed, but also what role they played in plan development and revision.

With regard to water pollution the situation is slightly different. Until the 1970s the legislation governing water pollution control allowed states to set source-by-source discharge limits. Then in 1971 the Nixon administration, prodded by environmentalists, revived the Refuse Control Act of 1899 which required federal permits for any discharge into a navigable waterway. This permit system was then incorporated in the Clean Water Act of 1972, which specifies that the "best available technology" for control (as defined by the EPA) must be used by 1977, and the "best practicable technology economically achieveable" by 1983. In effect, this led to national emissions standards for each class of facilities. As a result, most new plants must install cooling towers or similar equipment to control thermal pollution. But the law gave the EPA considerable discretion in defining standards. And in response to an aggressive utility campaign opposing the generalized use of cooling towers, EPA issued guidelines which in fact exempted most older, smaller units from retrofit obligations.

Many other federal agencies can get involved in utility decision making on specific issues. If federal water rights are being used, the approval of the Department of the Interior is required. If research is being done on coal processing, the Department of Energy may be involved. If an environmental impact statement is circulated, diverse agencies and private groups could offer comments or criticisms. A large project, all told, can easily involve a company with dozens of state and federal agencies and authorities in the effort to obtain approvals and permits. The need simultaneously to deal with these requirements, make the many technical judgments outlined above, and achieve economic and other objectives creates difficult decision problems which the companies in our case studies must confront every day. The way in which they have dealt with these problems will be the focus of our work.

4

The Tennessee Valley Authority

The Tennessee Valley Authority (TVA) is the oldest and largest federally owned utility in the country. Born in the midst of great controversy and New Deal hopes for massive social and economic reform, the agency has been both acclaimed for the benefits it has brought to the Tennessee Valley and condemned as a threat to "free enterprise," although these attacks have subsided in recent years. Environmentally, TVA's behavior is paradoxical. One of the first companies to study smoke plumes from generating plants, it built tall smokestacks to alleviate air pollution at a time when there was little external pressure to do so. Yet during the 1970s it strenuously refused to meet state regulations limiting sulfur dioxide emissions, and in the past sought to minimize its environmental expenditures on many occasions.

Despite the agency's broad responsibility for conservation and regional development, most of its engineering decisions have reflected a continuing attempt to minimize the cost of power. This pattern reflects the complex interaction among internal and external features of the organization and their evolution over time. Politically and legally TVA has been relatively insulated from external pressures, except for a certain amount of concern about regional economic development. Thus, TVA has often been able to make its own judgments regarding the wisdom of environmental expenditures.

In recent years, TVA's traditional emphasis on low costs and regional industrial development seems to have undergone a substantial modification. In 1978 S. David Freeman, a long-time critic of TVA's environmental practices, became the utility's chairman, replacing Aubrey J. Wagner, who retired after a total of forty-four years of TVA service. Simultaneously, William Jenkins resigned from the board of directors, citing environmental requirements which he felt had robbed the board of discretion.

Freeman, who clashed openly with Wagner and Jenkins following his appointment to the board in 1977, wants TVA to expand
its conservation efforts, to explore new, cleaner energy technologies (particularly as alternatives to nuclear generation), and to
reduce its air pollution. Even before Freeman became chairman,
other forces were pushing TVA in the direction of greater environmental spending. After years of litigation, the agency was beginning to accept state and federal pollution control requirements that it previously had found unthinkable. In the future, it
may adopt a new role—demonstrating how "clean" electricity
can be produced economically. In the past, however, low costs
have often overridden environmental quality as a goal of the
agency's power program.

TVA's concern with the cost of power is rooted in its early attempts to prove its value and to survive in a hostile environment.
This concern was perpetuated by the agency's internal structure
—a structure Freeman will confront as he seeks to put TVA on a
new course. The agency is substantially decentralized (which limits the role of the general manager and the board), and its pattern of recruitment, socialization, and advancement reinforces
this perspective. Where positive responsiveness to external pressures has suited various competing internal groups, they have on
occasion been able to bring TVA to pursue such programs. But,
in general, the agency has only gradually and imperfectly shifted
away from the objective of low-cost power and the rules of behavior this strategy implies. As is apparent from TVA's record, the
fact that a utility is publicly owned is no indication that it will be
particularly open to accommodating changing public priorities.

Background and Context

From its earliest days, TVA has been responsible for a wide variety of functions. Besides power production, it also undertakes
flood control, navigation improvement, fertilizer production,
agricultural assistance, forestry, and recreation development.
Power activities have become by far the most important component. In 1975 the power program budget was $971 million com-
pared to a little over $35 million for all other activities.[1]

With nearly 30 million kilowatts of capacity, TVA's power system is the largest in the nation, providing electricity to about 2.5
million customers in parts of seven states in the southeastern
United States. Although the agency sells power directly to a few
large industrial users, most of its power is sold wholesale to 160

local municipal and cooperative electric systems. Formerly, its major power sources were its large multipurpose dams (also used for flood control and to foster navigation). But in the late 1940s TVA began to rely increasingly on coal-fired steam plants, especially to meet new demands from the Atomic Energy Commission's nuclear facilities. These coal-fired plants — located in Alabama, Kentucky, and Tennessee — now constitute about two-thirds of TVA's capacity. A large nuclear plant accounts for another 10 percent, and TVA has chosen nuclear power for all of the new baseload generating stations now in the construction or planning stage.[2] Figure 3 shows the location of TVA's steam plants.

By maintaining rates far below the national average, TVA has been able to facilitate the growth of considerable new industry in the relatively poor region it serves — a fact that accounts for a major part of TVA's political popularity. Its large and efficient steam plants, considerable hydro capacity, low fuel costs and interest rates, and tax advantages have all contributed to its ability to provide low-cost power; in 1966 its average residential rate was less than half the national average. Although TVA's rates — and dissatisfaction among its customers — have been rising rapidly since 1967, in 1975 its average residential rate was still only 65 percent of the national average.[3]

TVA is well-established today, but its survival and growth have not always been assured. The history of the agency, reflected in and reinforced by the organization's strategy and structure, continues to influence its decisions. As recently as the late 1950s, the future of TVA was a matter of substantial national controversy. For complex historical reasons, the United States has generally been hostile to public enterprise. The creation of an entity like TVA required some particular justification. The agency is actually a product of the controversy over how the government should dispose of Wilson Dam and its associated power and fertilizer facilities, which had been built with federal funds at Muscle Shoals, Alabama, during World War I. In the 1920s hostile Republican presidents twice vetoed bills which would have established a public corporation to operate these facilities. Only at the height of the New Deal, with the support of Franklin D. Roosevelt, was TVA created and given a broad spectrum of responsibilities for "multipurpose" development of the Tennessee Valley's resources.[4]

The ambiguity of TVA's founding legislation meant that it remained for the first board of directors to define the course that

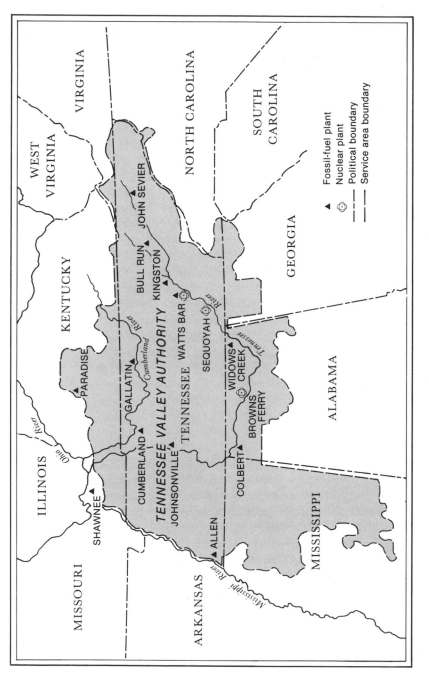

Figure 3. Tennessee Valley Authority: service area and major generating stations. Based on annual reports of the Tennessee Valley Authority.

the agency would take. Advocates of public ownership at Muscle Shoals envisaged creating a low-cost/low-rate yardstick by which to measure and discipline private utilities. Roosevelt himself had argued for this during his campaign. But how was this yardstick function to be carried out? How large a service area would TVA take over, and on what terms, from the existing private owners? How were the needs of the power program to be fitted in with navigation, agriculture, and social and economic reform?

The views of the original three board members differed significantly.[5] Arthur E. Morgan, the first chairman, was not enthusiastic about competing on a wide scale with private utilities. He envisioned TVA as a regional social and economic planning and development agency, setting aside large areas as national forests — even coining money, if that was necessary to stimulate economic activity. This vision was opposed, however, by the other two members of the board; they shared Morgan's view that TVA should foster regional development, but they had different ideas about its primary focus and methods of operation.

One of these was David Lilienthal, fresh from the Wisconsin Public Service Commission. He was eager to expand power production and take on the private utility interests, provided this was done in a way that maintained TVA's low-cost/low-rate position. His enthusiasm for the power program was shared by Franklin Roosevelt. Arthur Morgan, in contrast, thought that a fight with the utilities would jeopardize TVA's social-planning activities; he favored making an early settlement with neighboring power companies. Harcourt Morgan, the third director, was mainly interested in providing agricultural assistance by working with and through the local agencies in the Valley — particularly the Extension Service and the land-grant colleges. Ultimately, Lilienthal and Harcourt Morgan succeeded in defining the direction of the agency. They formulated a policy based as much on expediency as on logic: TVA would avoid social planning and play essentially a supporting role in the agricultural development of the region, while carrying out an aggressive power program. "From 1936 on," a disappointed Rexford Tugwell wrote, "the TVA should have been called the Tennessee Valley Power Production and Flood Control Corporation" — a charge that contemporary critics continue to echo.[6]

Although TVA's power program has indeed overshadowed its other functions, the agency's behavior still in part reflects its multipurpose character. TVA includes groups with such concerns as public health, forestry, and fertilizer development.

These groups have had some impact on TVA's power policy, but their various objectives have never been able to compete with low costs as the primary aim of all power-related activities.

In explaining this commitment to low-cost power, TVA's managers often cite both legal and moral obligations. The agency's legal obligations are set out in the Tennessee Valley Act of 1934, which has been amended over the years. The statute requires that rates should be sufficient to cover costs, including payments in lieu of taxes, debt service, repayments to the United States Treasury, reserve funds, and so forth. It concludes by saying that decisions about rates should be made "having due regard for the primary objectives of the Act, including the objective that power shall be sold at rates as low as are feasible."[7]

Given that more than one objective is explicitly invoked, this is hardly restrictive language. TVA is also charged with the agricultural development of the region. Thus, raising rates to pay for pollution control equipment to prevent vegetation damage or to finance the reclamation of strip-mined land would certainly seem well within the requirements of this provision. It is perhaps not too much to say that the emphasis on legal obligation in the power area amounts to putting a gun to one's own head and pleading helplessness in the face of such coercion. Indeed, the board has not objected to bending other provisions of the law when it suited its purpose — for example, it chose to locate its headquarters in Knoxville, Tennessee, rather than in Muscle Shoals, Alabama, as required by the statute.[8]

The moral obligation cited by TVA in support of low rates is that this policy is, in fact, the best way to develop the region. As Aubrey Wagner put it, "What we really are doing is trying to help the people of this region mobilize their resources so that they get more satisfaction from living. We're in the utility business only because electricity is one of the tools to help these people develop the region."[9] Obviously, when TVA decides not to invest in some called-for pollution controls, it is not doing so in the interests of profits. And from the viewpoint of TVA's managers, such a decision is justified because of the social benefits of low rates.

TVA's historical experience gives this view considerable legitimacy. Particularly in TVA's earliest days, low rates had an obvious and compelling social value. They enabled TVA to bring electricity within reach of many for the first time, in a region that was severely affected by the Depression. The plentiful, low-cost electricity that TVA provided also helped promote an influx of industry, providing many new jobs in an area that had previously been poor and isolated. Low rates have contributed not only to the Valley's economic health, but to TVA's political health as well.

Throughout TVA's early existence, the agency's low rates garnered national political support and helped protect the power program against recurring attacks. From its inception, the private utility industry, led by Wendell Willkie of the Commonwealth and Southern Company, attacked TVA both in the courts and in the political arena. The question of its survival was in doubt until, in two major decisions (*Ashwander* v. *TVA* and *Tennessee Electric Power Company* v. *TVA*), the Supreme Court upheld TVA's constitutionality. Roosevelt continued to stand behind TVA politically, and so the program began to flourish. Congress appropriated money for additional dam construction and permitted the issuance of bonds to finance the purchase of private utility properties. In one town after another, the owners of the existing distribution systems were convinced to sell out to the municipality—which then signed up for TVA power. The strategy was to threaten to give the city federal public-works loans to enable it to duplicate the existing private distribution system. After a heated battle of this sort in Chattanooga, Willkie agreed to sell TVA the entire Tennessee Electric Power Company. Along with pieces of other neighboring systems that TVA bought, this gave the agency its basic service area.[10]

Defense requirements connected with World War II and the Cold War fostered a rapid expansion of TVA's generating capacity and eased TVA's initial move into the use of steam, rather than hydroelectric, power plants. This transition was fraught with political tensions for a number of reasons. Steam plant construction would end, once and for all, the deliberately ambiguous status of the TVA power program as an offshoot of the agency's flood control and navigation activities; it would allow TVA's territory to extend beyond transmission-line distance from the Tennessee River. Thus, the move to steam plants reawakened fears among private utilities that TVA would expand into their territory. From TVA's perspective, on the other hand, expansion into steam generation was vital if it were to continue to serve even the needs of consumers within its existing territory.[11]

Initially, TVA's steam plant construction program was defended on the basis of national security. TVA argued that the power was needed to supply the massive needs of the AEC's nuclear facilities in the Tennessee Valley, as well as the demands of other defense-related industries like aluminum. This argument helped TVA to overcome initial opposition to construction of the Johnsonville steam plant and to justify the construction of six more steam plants during the period 1948-1953.

But the public-private issue came to a head when TVA attempted to persuade Congress to finance the construction of a steam plant in western Tennessee to serve the needs of the city of Memphis, a long-time TVA customer. (Until 1959, each plant was subject to the congressional appropriations process, even though retained earnings provided a substantial portion of the capital.) The problem, the agency said, was that it could not otherwise meet the increasing demand of both Memphis and the AEC. Yet the request coincided with the advent of a Republican administration hostile to TVA's power program and to the agency as a whole. Dwight Eisenhower, the new president, apparently would have liked to dismantle the agency altogether. That already seemed impossible, but he did refuse to support TVA's request for construction funds.

Instead, the administration and the AEC developed an elaborate alternative. Two neighboring private utilities signed a contract with the AEC. Under this so-called "Dixon-Yates" agreement they would build a special plant to provide Memphis with the power it needed, thus "replacing" some of TVA's power so that it could serve the AEC. This arrangement was widely perceived as an attempt by the administration and the private utilities to roll back the borders of the TVA service area. It rapidly grew into a continuing, acrimonious, and highly symbolic public controversy, rather like the prewar debate over Muscle Shoals. After hearings, investigations, and filibusters, the citizens of Memphis voted to construct their own independent municipal steam plant (which TVA later took over on a long-term lease basis).[12]

Throughout the rest of the 1950s, Eisenhower and the Congress stuck by their refusal to provide appropriations to TVA for the construction of new steam plants. TVA had to finance new units entirely through the earnings of the power program and was limited to adding them at existing plant sites, since it had no authorization to build a completely new plant. Funding for nonpower programs was cut back, and Gordon Clapp, former general manager of the agency and long-time TVA employee, was replaced as chairman of the board. Eisenhower appointed Herbert Vogel, a retired general in the Army Corps of Engineers, an agency traditionally in competition with TVA; Vogel was unsympathetic to much of what TVA represented. (Although his criticisms of TVA were almost the opposite of David Freeman's, Vogel's experience as a chairman ideologically opposed to the TVA staff has some parallels to Freeman's situation.) Vogel disapproved of the agency's social-welfare orientation and of its public financing of power system expansion. He was, however, impressed with the technical efficiency and low cost of the power program, and in time this led him to become a strong supporter of the agency.[13] The conversion of Vogel was not a one-way affair: his own point of view, which emphasized the production of low-cost power, became more dominant in the agency. Initially, his views often came into conflict with those of the other two board members — a conflict that was openly displayed on occasion before the congressional committees that were considering TVA's appropriations. But gradually the orientation of the entire TVA board changed, as others who shared Vogel's attitudes were appointed.[14]

In 1959 the TVA Revenue Act terminated TVA's need for congressional appropriations to finance new power plant construction; the agency was given authority to issue its own revenue bonds up to a certain ceiling set by Congress. Some old-timers opposed the move, saying that it would prevent TVA from continuing to build plants ahead of demand growth in order to foster regional development. The bond market, they claimed, would limit the unique and progressive features of TVA's program by forcing it to operate on a "pay-as-you-go" basis. The new board, however, concurred with the changes. At the same time, TVA's neighboring private utilities were protected by a clause limiting the territory served by TVA power to existing geographical boundaries. (In practice, most of the boundaries between TVA and adjacent systems had been worked out informally years earlier.) Additionally, a program was instituted for TVA's repayment, with interest, of appropriations it had received in the past for the power program. This somewhat ingenious compromise managed to satisfy both those who supported TVA's low-rate power program and those who opposed any increase in federally financed competition with private enterprise.[15]

The TVA Revenue Act reflected and fostered a transformation of TVA's political circumstances. It resolved previous controversy firmly on the side of a permanent but limited role for the agency. In giving up its authority to control the pace of TVA's expansion on an annual basis, Congress in effect made the growth of TVA's power program into a nonpolitical issue. It transformed TVA's capital market to one based on economic, rather than political, criteria.

Furthermore, Congress declined to impose detailed controls on how borrowed money was spent. From the start, it had appropriated funds for TVA in a lump sum without restricting them to specific functions or to use within the current fiscal year. (It was understood, however, that TVA would depart from its budget only for special reasons.) The subcommittees charged with reviewing TVA's nonpower appropriations could still insist, as a matter of courtesy, that TVA present its power program budget to them each year, and, in fact, have recently questioned TVA officials closely about rising rates. But under existing legislation no congressional approval is required for TVA's power expenditures.[16]

With less controversy today over its power program, low rates might no longer appear as vital to TVA's survival as they were in the past. TVA still balances environmental goals against the need to hold down costs, however, in part because even today the Tennessee Valley is still relatively rural and relatively poor. Many TVA managers believe that the "low rates attract industry" argument is still compelling. A caption in TVA's 1972 Annual Report summarized this viewpoint: "Poverty remains the chief environmental ugliness in the Nation."[17]

Despite the obvious benefits that the low-rate strategy brought in the past, the relative value of low rates has diminished as the years have passed, creating in theory the possibility of more emphasis on such values as environmental protection. Few homes in the Valley remain to be won over to electricity, pressure on young people to leave the Valley to find jobs has diminished, and the industries that have come to the Valley are not going to leave en masse if TVA's relatively low rates rise in relation to those of other utilities. With TVA's political survival no longer based on low rates, we might expect that there has been some change in the organization's thinking.

The organization's persistent allegiance to the low-rate policy illustrates how a strategy can maintain its hold even after the circumstances that brought it into being have changed. The TVA low-rate experiment succeeded so well that it became very difficult to alter the original formula.

Added to the inevitable difficulty of changing people's ideas was the fact that the costs of producing power began rising rapidly in the 1960s, just when other changes in TVA's circumstances might have led to a change in the agency's basic strategy. This situation naturally reinforced the concern of TVA's managers for cost control; indeed, given their traditional commitment to low rates, the rising costs were profoundly disturbing to long-time agency members. Although TVA could have altered its strategy and placed greater emphasis on goals other than low rates, many in the Valley shared TVA's continuing belief in the value of low rates. They agreed that the agency should spend only what was clearly and obviously necessary for environmental protection. Representatives of many of TVA's municipal and industrial customers in Alabama appeared before the state's Air Pollution Control Commission in 1973 to support TVA's position that stack gas sulfur scrubbers were prohibitively expensive and should not be required.[18]

To be sure, TVA has not totally escaped local criticism of its environmental policies. A court challenge to TVA's Tellico Dam project—which culminated in the Supreme Court's 1978 "snail darter" decision—is one significant example of local protest. And the states of Kentucky and Alabama began court action several years ago to compel TVA to comply with state air pollution standards; in 1977 they were joined by citizen groups from the Valley in this effort. Yet in general, and especially until very recently, citizen support for environmental protection efforts has been less vociferous in this region than in others.

Nor does TVA welcome such protest when it occurs. Many middle-level executives in the organization are conscious of the paternalism that colors its sense of mission. As one said, "We believe we are the guys in white hats come to save this Valley." Another, in discussing the opposition of local governors to TVA's Tellico Dam project, said that the agency had viewed the reaction with shock and outrage: "It was seen around here like a child turning on his father."[19]

Not surprisingly, some of the earliest and most significant objections to TVA's environmental policies have come from outside its own service area. This is especially noticeable with regard to strip mining, where TVA's policies have inspired considerable criticism in Congress, and even a suit filed by three national environmental groups in 1971, for TVA's failure to prepare environmental impact statements on its coal purchase policies. Perhaps because the damage from unregulated strip mining is both evident and acute for those in the immediate area, this issue has produced some protests even within the region. The strongest protest has come from eastern Kentucky, an area whose geological characteristics are such that strip mining damage is particularly severe but which also lies outside the agency's service area—a fact that TVA's eastern Kentucky critics frequently point to with bitterness. In comparison, public concern over strip mining in Tennessee has been noticeably less vigorous.[20]

There is a striking contrast between the local situation confronting TVA, and that confronting some of the other systems we are studying. Although Pacific Gas and Electric has had difficulty finding sites for enough new capacity to meet anticipated load growth, TVA's plans to build a new plant are often greeted with enthusiasm by the community in which the plant will be located. With time and economic growth, environmental concerns may take on greater importance to citizens of the region and hence may constitute an increasing restraint. At least until the mid-1970s, however, regional impetus to control TVA's environmental practices was limited. In the absence of federal legislation requiring the states to set standards, it is unclear how aggressively the state governments of the Valley would have moved to regulate TVA's activities in this area.

Even when Valley citizens and agencies have tried to act, TVA's institutional situation has limited its vulnerability to outside control. As a federal agency, TVA claims constitutional immunity from state regulation. It sets its own rates without state review, for example. During the last several years, TVA and the states have clashed over the agency's obligations with regard to state environmental quality requirements. For five years TVA refused to comply with SO_2 emission standards, claiming that scrubber technology is not sufficiently developed for general use. The agency contended that wholesale use of scrubbers would add $200 million a year to system costs, whereas tall stacks and occasional use of low-sulfur coal and generating cutbacks would adequately protect ground-level air quality at one-tenth the cost; it therefore proposed to go ahead with the latter approach. In taking this position, TVA became an industry leader in fighting federal and state air pollution control laws.

The states of Alabama and Kentucky sued, seeking TVA's compliance with their SO_2 regulations, but were rebuffed by a Supreme Court decision that declared TVA's independence of state regulatory procedures.[21] However, another court decision in 1976 rejected intermittent controls as a permissible control strategy, and this led TVA to begin seeking low-sulfur coal and planning SO_2 control facilities at a number of its plants. Negotiations continued between TVA and federal and state authorities, concerning control plans at other plants.

Unhappy with the progress of these negotiations, the states of Alabama and Kentucky, plus a coalition of environmental groups from all three states with TVA power plants, began a new suit against TVA under the "citizen suit" provision of the Clean Air Act. Congress, too, made it clear that federal agencies like TVA were subject to state plans promulgated under the act.[22] As a result, under agreements worked out with the active participation of board chairman David Freeman, TVA developed plans to comply with SO_2 standards through the combined use of low-sulfur coal, coal washing, and the installation of scrubbers at four of its plants.

As a federal agency, TVA has sometimes been more sensitive to national opinion than it might have been if otherwise organized. In response to the 1971 suit filed under the National Environmental Policy Act, it provided a short draft environmental impact statement on its coal purchasing policies and circulated it to other agencies for comment, as required by federal procedures. TVA received critical responses from several agencies. When issuing its final impact statement, TVA announced that it was strengthening the reclamation provisions in its coal contracts.[23] Legally, TVA was not forced to act on the comments it received, but the fact that it was required to seek them and include them along with the impact statement clearly encouraged the agency to take outside opinion into account. TVA, after all, does have some concern for its public reputation. And there was always the possibility that, in the absence of stronger voluntary action by the agency, the president or Congress might have restricted its discretion.

Such restriction is not very likely, however, especially in day-to-day matters. TVA was designed intentionally to operate with greater flexibility than an ordinary government agency. Originally placed outside any of the regular government departments, it has managed to stay outside them despite a move in the late 1930s to place it within the Department of the Interior. Legislation located its headquarters outside Washington, D.C., and its directors serve nine-year overlapping terms to insulate them from presidential pressure. Only a series of historical accidents has allowed President Carter to name *three* new directors—David Freeman and two others—to the TVA board within a period of two years.

The agency was also exempted from the federal civil service system and was effectively freed from the purchasing procedures required by the General Services Administration and the General Accounting Office. TVA has always been able to spend its power revenues as it sees fit on power activities, and, as noted, has traditionally had considerable discretion over the spending of appropriated funds.[24] All these features make outside interference sufficiently costly to insulate TVA from routine control by the federal government.

The ultimate guarantee of TVA's independence, however, is

its political position, both regionally and nationally. Operating in a small area of the country, its activities become a national issue only when strong local complaints, or some other process, bring them to national attention. TVA's very existence as a public enterprise has on occasion been just such an issue. Its purchases of strip-mined coal have also threatened to attract national attention. But most aspects of TVA's behavior, including its environmental policies, have not been issues of this sort, at least until recently.

Congress, by requiring TVA to obey state air standards, and President Carter, by appointing David Freeman to the TVA board, signaled an intention in 1977 to steer TVA in a more environmentally responsive direction. Freeman, former head of the Ford Foundation Energy Policy Project, has been an outspoken critic of TVA's environmental and conservation policies. But during the 1960s and most of the 1970s, Congress and the executive branch faced a pattern of incentives and pressures that led them not to exercise their latent authority to change TVA's behavior.

Illustrative of these circumstances is a well-known series of incidents in which John F. Kennedy tried to convince the Authority to locate a new power plant in the Appalachian region of Kentucky. In response to the urging of Senator John Sherman Cooper of Kentucky, the president (who was then very interested in the problem of Appalachian development) wrote to TVA asking it to locate a facility, then in the planning stages, in that region. The board, under Vogel, refused on the grounds that its analysis showed that the chosen site in Tennessee was marginally cheaper, and cited its legislative obligation to keep costs down. According to one account, Kennedy was furious and wrote a second letter. But there was little he could do without trying to force resignations from the board majority. The plant was built in Tennessee.[25]

While Kennedy might have tried to change the composition of the board in order to achieve his ends, the costs and risks of doing so and the absence of compensating gains made such intervention politically unprofitable. Eisenhower had sought to alter agency policy by appointing Vogel, but he had had a vacant position to fill and had acted with strong support from a national, antipublic power constituency.

In this context, the Environmental Protection Agency has until recently found it difficult to force TVA to observe state environmental standards, given the lack of public — and presidential —

interest in this problem. As one former federal air pollution official observed:

> If you're in an organization charged with enforcing regula-
> tions against a sister agency, you don't want to make too
> many waves, or you may be out looking for a new job . . .
> Politically, TVA is much stronger than EPA. They have
> 30,000 employees; EPA has 6,000. And they have more poli-
> tical savvy and a lot more experience. They have not only
> political support but public support. I've seen pictures of the
> Tennessee River flooding out Chattanooga. TVA built
> dams, controlled floods, and brought cheap electricity
> which led to new industry. Clean air's not that important in
> comparison. The citizens of the Valley would rather have a
> job, meat on the table, than a few pine trees.[26]

Understandably, then, EPA has moved gingerly in responding
to TVA's refusal to comply with state SO_2 emissions standards.
EPA objected when Kentucky and Tennessee proposed to allow
large sources like TVA to use high stacks, fuel switching, and
generation cutbacks — rather than emissions controls — to protect
ground-level air quality. In 1974 it forced TVA to install precipitators to meet state particulate standards, but for several more
years it delayed enforcement of state SO_2 emission requirements.
In the interim, officials from EPA and TVA met, discussed their
differences — and left them unresolved. The burden thus fell on
the states. Finally they were joined by EPA, and in late 1977 congressional action resolved the issue.[27] Clearly, until recently, the
environmental "constraints" that TVA confronted were neither
restrictive nor well defined.

Where it has encountered regulatory constraints with severe
penalties, TVA has been more compliant. For example, it has
agreed to install what it contends are unnecessary cooling towers
at two nuclear plants in order to comply with state thermal standards. But it had very little choice in the matter; the agency refused to install cooling towers at a number of coal-fired plants
where state thermal standards were being violated, but it was
forced to comply in these two cases in order to obtain plant operating licenses from the Atomic Energy Commission. Litigation
and delay were unattractive alternatives, given the costs of having
the nearly completed plants idle and the low probability of winning a challenge to the AEC in the courts.[28]

As a coal-burning utility, TVA has faced higher air pollution
control costs than utilities that burn oil or natural gas. On the
other hand, TVA's air pollution problems will be eased somewhat

in the future because, on cost grounds, TVA is concentrating all its new expansion for major units on nuclear generation, supplementing this base-load capacity with pumped storage and gas turbine peak-load units. Nevertheless, its continued reliance on coal at existing plants means that the agency remains faced with significant air pollution difficulties. And TVA's expanding nuclear program carries with it its own environmental and safety problems. Indeed, TVA has been criticized by a Nuclear Regulatory Commission investigation for lax quality-control procedures which contributed to a near-disastrous fire at the agency's Browns Ferry plant, and some local groups have criticized TVA's nuclear program on safety grounds.[29] But finding sites for and constructing nuclear plants has not been as difficult for TVA as for many other utilities, particularly those in California.

In summary, although the agency faces external constraints and pressures, it has had significant discretion, especially in view of its relative structural and fiscal autonomy. If power rates had been higher than they were as a result of the costs of better environmental protection, surely the pressures on TVA for low rates would not have had a significantly different impact on the agency during the last ten or fifteen years. TVA's continued loyalty to the goal of low-cost power and the way in which it has chosen to use its discretion can only be understood by examining its internal structural features, which have both reflected and perpetuated this strategy in most phases of the organization's decision making.

Internal Organization

TVA provides a clear example of the interdependence between strategy and structure. Over the agency's lifetime, its internal structure has evolved in a way that has reinforced the "low-cost power" strategy. Its divisional arrangements and its control and incentive system have provided top management with relatively weak control over the agency, and have allowed considerable influence to internal groups opposing environmental expenditures. Looking at the way in which these features have evolved, and at the way in which they have been shaped by key individuals within the TVA organization, can help us understand the agency's response to changing external circumstances.

In 1979 the TVA board made some changes in agency organization that may counteract some of the structural obstacles to top management control that we perceived. Since the changes were made after our research was essentially complete, we cannot say what impact these changes have had on the traditional balance of power within the agency. We presume that the changes have given top management more control. In this section, we will be reporting primarily on TVA as it has operated over the decades prior to these changes. We will close with a brief look at the new developments.

TVA includes a large number of organizational units that perform a variety of functional tasks — power generation, engineering, fertilizer development, forestry and wildlife management, and so on (see Figure 4). Traditionally, all of these units (thirteen Divisions, plus three Offices each containing more than one Division) reported directly to the general manager.[30] The general manager has three assistants, a small budget and planning staff, and direct authority over TVA's Public Information and Washington offices. His ability to supervise effectively all of TVA's activities has clearly been limited.

TVA's weak general manager structure reflected its early development. Initially, TVA lacked a general manager, and Arthur Morgan, the first chairman of the board, had administrative responsibility. Early policy disagreements soon led to a three-way division of authority. For a time, TVA ran almost as if it were three separate agencies: Arthur Morgan was in charge of engineering and dam construction, Harcourt Morgan supervised agricultural assistance, and David Lilienthal took control of the power program. Continued friction led Lilienthal and Harcourt Morgan in 1936 to force the appointment of a general manager, who was responsible primarily for facilitating project coordination, budget preparation, organization of reports to the board, and so on. But the new structure also limited Arthur Morgan's direct control of engineering activities. Outraged, he made unsubstantiated accusations of malfeasance against his colleagues, and was ultimately removed by Roosevelt. The tradition of strong divisions continued, and no dominant central office was created.[31]

The continuity of principal officers helped preserve these arrangements. Harcourt Morgan succeeded Arthur Morgan as chairman and served until September 1941, to be succeeded by Lilienthal until November 1946, who was in turn succeeded by a former general manager, Gordon Clapp. Vogel, an outsider, served as chairman from 1954 to 1962, but from 1962 until 1978 Aubrey Wagner, another former general manager who joined TVA as a young engineer in 1934, was chairman of the board. David Freeman, TVA's new chief executive, is only the second

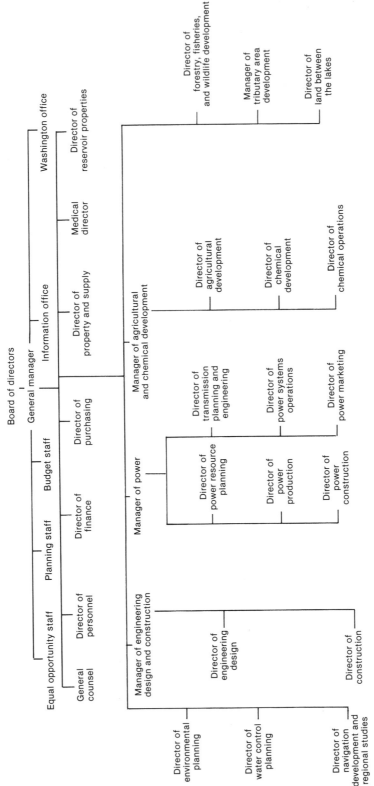

Figure 4. Organization of TVA in early 1973. Notice that the general manager has more than twenty people reporting directly to him. From Tennessee Valley Authority, *Organizational Bulletin*, January 1973.

"outsider" chairman in TVA's history, although he did work for the organization early in his career.[32]

Of necessity, much of the technical and operational responsibility for TVA activities had to be left with the managers of the various Divisions and Offices, or, since they too have limited staffs, with the Branches and their chiefs, one level further down. The job of the general manager in such an organization has been largely one of coordination — facilitating bargaining among functional divisions where their responsibilities overlap. The general manager also acted as a channel between the board of directors and the organization, transmitting for board ratification the agreements he has helped to construct. He also had to exercise some leadership in the negotiation/policy-making process in order to move outcomes in the direction he and the board desire; among other things, he identified the issues that the Offices and Divisions must address. He sometimes could pay special attention to the weaker voices among the Divisions when he felt these were not receiving an adequate hearing. But the written literature on the agency seems to agree with our observations that the general manager has not — and could not — run TVA, but has largely played a mediating role.[33]

Given TVA's divisionalization, its range of activities, and the small scope of the general manager's office, the TVA board has had only a limited capacity to set a direction for the agency. What the Divisions argue for on "technical" grounds has usually been done. Former board chairman Aubrey Wagner described the problem of overseeing the agency: "You have to ask the right questions and sometimes go into the matter in some detail in order to get the right answer. The board reads a great deal of material, including some very thick reports, and time doesn't always permit complete, careful reading."[34]

Lacking its own analytical staff to review the decisions made by the Division experts, the board faced a tremendous burden if it sought on its own to verify the choices being recommended. In general, it has had to try to ask enough questions to assure that the groups making recommendations have done their homework adequately.

For similar reasons, once a policy has been established, members of the board or the general manager have not been able to supervise its implementation in detail, especially since they have usually been dependent on the Divisions for reports on Division activities. To some extent, the top executives must create and manage a certain amount of conflict among Divisions in order to gain information and preserve an independent role in decision making for themselves. The Division of Environmental Planning was explicitly designed, for example, to act as an internal policeman on pollution issues. While discussing the problems at the agency's Kingston plant that led to the installation of precipitators there in 1959, Wagner commented on this role: "When we first had the controversies over Kingston, we would ask for reports on just what the quality of the air was. This was in the days when there were no standards, no EPA. You would have two different groups looking at the situation and get different reports. That's when we decided to strengthen the Environmental Division by employing the best professional experts we could find, and hiring them as permanent staff."[35] By this means TVA's top management hoped to get some independent perspective on the air quality problem.

Such relatively nondirective general management did not allow for rapid and effective implementation of changing strategy choices. It did not even guarantee that a coherent policy would be followed, although, as at TVA, consistency was possible if one internal group dominated the process. Such an organizational structure could only flourish in a relatively stable situation, in which the tasks and strategy of the organization, once defined, did not have to be rapidly readjusted.

Given this low level of control from above, Division directors at TVA have felt some incentive to work out agreements among themselves without involving the board or the general manager. In part this tradition began with the need to work out operating rules for multipurpose reservoirs, which compromised among power, transport, flood control, and malaria control objectives. Like the reservoir problem, policy issues at TVA frequently involve complex questions of scientific fact or engineering judgment which the general manager and board members have not always felt competent to resolve. Indeed, the volume of issues arising in TVA is so large that the board can adjudicate only the most significant.[36]

The tradition of "self-coordination" has also served the interests of the Division directors: it has helped keep the general manager and the board out of their affairs. Furthermore, this practice both reinforces and is congruent with the view that TVA's task is a technical one that can best be done in a nonpolitical way. Such a view is, after all, implicit in the design of the institution— in its independence of political process and in the weakness of its internal top-level "policy-making" apparatus.

For the last two decades or so, this process of internal bargaining has brought consistent attempts to keep down rates and costs, which in turn has reflected a particular internal balance of power in the organization. The Office of Power, which is responsible for all aspects of power production and sales, has been that dominant force. In part this is because it directly performs many key tasks, and thus determines how they are performed.

The nature of the bargaining process at TVA also gives advantage to strong personalities and dedicated individuals, especially if they have well-defined goals. G. O. Wessenauer and R. H. Kampmeier, who led the Office of Power during the 1950s and 1960s, were by all reports among the toughest and smartest individuals in the entire organization.[37] Given their dedication to the relatively clear-cut aim of low-cost power, they had a major impact on organizational policy and on the activities of other Divisions—more so than would have been the case with a different organizational system.

TVA's structure, and the process of choosing policy through negotiation, interacted with the substantive implications of the low-rate objective to strengthen the position of the Office of Power. In the context of internal negotiations, past success has given the status quo a presumptive validity that innovators must overcome. Furthermore, by emphasizing the scarcity of resources, the strategy has made growth difficult for any group advocating conflicting objectives—a development that would, over time, lessen the relative influence of the Office of Power.

Fred Thomas, former chief of the Air Quality Branch, tells a story that shows the difficulties faced by advocates of relatively unestablished perspectives. In the early 1950s, when only a section head, he and his boss went to see the chief construction engineer to try to get the stacks on a plant under design raised from 250 to 500 feet. "In a brief exchange, we were rather unceremoniously hooted at and almost booted out of his office," Thomas recalled.[38] (Yet Thomas' group was able to get the height of plant smokestacks raised in the late 1950s, after it had demonstrated some skill and expertise in constructing mathematical models of the effects on air quality of such discharges.)

Rather than engage in the internal conflict that limited resources could produce, groups have found it advantageous to advocate policies that complement the goals of other (especially stronger) groups. In this way, a group increased the likelihood that it would participate in the winning "coalition" that emerged from the bargaining process. The strategy reinforced the orienta-

tion toward low cost, since the Office of Power, the leading expo-
nent of this perspective, is the unit that others in TVA have had
to negotiate with most often.

For example, the Division of Environmental Planning has pioneered in the development of "operational" methods of controlling sulfur dioxide emissions. This has expanded its own role, and
yet has been attractive to Power because it is much cheaper than
using low-sulfur fuel or stack gas scrubbers. Similarly, the Office
of Engineering Design and Construction pioneered in building
very large steam plants — a policy that tended to reduce capital
costs (per kilowatt) on new plants and appeared to offer operating economies. Indeed, in its wish to "fit in," the Design Division
may well have underdesigned some units, achieving cost savings
not worth the increased unreliability that resulted. Meanwhile,
the Division of Forestry, Fisheries, and Wildlife Development,
whose program is principally supported by appropriations, has
avoided taking a strong position on TVA's strip-mine reclamation responsibilities. Why antagonize proponents of low-cost
power inside and outside the agency who in turn might endanger
the Division's own program?[39]

The agency's financial structure also allowed the Office of
Power an important say in what power-related activities were
conducted by other Divisions. Such activities were often financed
by power revenues and revenue bond funds which the Office of
Power tended to view as "their" money (not TVA's). In their efforts to keep down rates and to control expenditures of "power
money" by other Divisions, the management of the Office of
Power has not always called attention to the fact that the board
alone has formal budgetary authority. The structure of task assignments reflected and reinforced this situation. While there is a
post on the general manager's staff for a "power finance officer,"
until the last few years this job has been filled by the manager of
power.

To enforce the low-rate strategy on the rest of the organization,
the Office of Power also used a bargaining technique that
Thomas Schelling has described.[40] The Office denied its own discretion in order to limit the concessions that could be reasonably
expected of it. Thus, in response to some expenditure suggestion,
someone from the Office of Power was sure to argue, "If you do
that you will raise the rates, hurt poor farmers, and drive out industry, so that, while it would be nice, it is not really possible or
even responsible."

Cost consciousness also limited the perceived discretion of top management; it has implied, after all, that there are no "discretionary resources" available for disposition.

Thus, in TVA the limited strength of top management has permitted groups within the organization to play a key role in defining and maintaining a consistent strategy. Furthermore, beginning with Arthur Morgan, all board chairmen (except Vogel and Freeman) have been "inside" men with considerable loyalty to the organization and to its existing strategy and structure.[41] Vogel shared the belief in low-cost power, so that there has been no radical departure from this policy. This internal balance could only survive, however, because it produced results that were not inconsistent with the demands of external conditions.

Appointing insiders to the board has limited the extent to which the directors can, or will try, to represent the perspectives and concerns of the outside world to the organization. The board member who took the strongest proenvironmental position on strip mining was Frank Smith, an "outsider" and a former congressman from Mississippi who was defeated in the 1962 primary because of his support for John Kennedy.[42] TVA's last chairman, Aubrey Wagner, was an exception—an "insider" (forty-four years with the agency) who took a strong interest in improving TVA's particulate controls and who pushed the agency staff to do more in this area.[43] However, even when the board has wanted to take stronger steps to protect the environment, it has had to overcome considerable inertia in the ranks.

Part of this inertia is due to very strong loyalties within TVA subunits. A person's identification with his group and his socialization to its perspectives operate especially strongly in TVA because each person can expect to spend his career in the Division or Office in which he started. Horizontal or diagonal mobility, although slightly on the increase, has been relatively rare.[44] Most people have limited sympathetic exposure to the viewpoints of other Divisions.

Since TVA employees typically moved up in a direct vertical line, they often advanced only when their superiors either moved or retired.[45] This made mobility painfully slow at times, especially because once TVA employees reach the managerial level, they rarely leave to join other organizations. Thus, Frank Gartrell served for seventeen years as assistant director of the Division of Environmental Planning; becoming director when his predecessor retired, he served for less than two years in that post before he himself retired. Promotion has in effect been tied to length of service. A young man could expect rapid advancement only when his Division was expanding, taking on new tasks, and creating new management positions.

As a consequence, members have had a strong interest in the well-being of their particular Division. Everyone has a reason to favor, even fight for, policies consistent with their group's growth. One TVA staff member, for example, noted that the Division of Power Resource Planning has regularly come into conflict with the Division of Environmental Planning over who would undertake certain environmental responsibilities connected with the power program.

> There's been a constant dogfight at the working level between [the two Divisions], primarily in the area of air quality. They are interested in the same things, in terms of monitoring and studies of future sites. There are fights over who should buy monitoring equipment and whose business it is to be doing this or that. The Division of Power Resource Planning says, "Really, we don't need Division X doing this, we can handle it." The Division of Environmental Planning says, "But the board's given us the role of policeman. Sure, you can handle it, but we're not sure you have the right attitude."[46]

This rivalry among Divisions can be strong enough to create a sense that members of one group are working against (as well as with) other parts of the organization. As another staff member put it, "lots of people feel they work more for a Division than they do for TVA. It seems like interservice rivalry . . . sometimes it's really anarchy. Well, not anarchy exactly, but you know what I mean."[47]

One consequence is that TVA has tried to do as much as possible in-house, which maximizes the number of internal opportunities. When new functions or problems arise, the groups involved typically try to perform any additional tasks themselves, using consultants sparingly to help in the transition process. This tendency reinforces TVA's sense of its own technical competence. As Aubrey Wagner put it, "We don't want to hire consultants who are the best experts. We want our *staff* to be the best experts available."[48]

Becoming "the best experts" is not always easy. Almost all hiring in TVA is at the lowest grades (although, in the last several years, rapid growth in the organization has led to some hiring at higher levels).[49] This tends to slow the rate at which TVA can adopt new techniques and technology. Even if no one in the organization is skilled in the new area, experienced people may still not be picked from outside. Possible ill effects are, however, ameliorated to some extent by an effort to facilitate advanced training for promising younger people, who thereby can provide technical skills that the organization might otherwise lack.

The low level of interdivisional mobility is partly a result of tendencies present in all technical organizations, and found in some degree in all the utilities we have studied. Given the technical component of middle-management work in such companies, someone already in the area will almost inevitably seem to be the best-qualified person for any supervisory job. Moreover, a person has much more opportunity to impress his superiors within his own chain of command than those in charge of other units; managers will usually know "their own people" better than they do "outsiders."

Although there have been exceptions, the tendency toward vertical promotion — particularly in "technical" Divisions — is very strong in TVA. When diagonal mobility takes place, it tends to be into "administrative" Divisions, such as Reservoir Properties or Purchasing. But there seems to have been little or no movement among Divisions like Environmental Planning, or Design, or Power Resource Planning.[50]

This pattern is reinforced because personnel activities are decentralized. Each Division is assigned its own personnel officer, who reports to the director of that Division. This tends to limit the information available to a personnel officer about possible candidates from another part of the organization. TVA's personnel director, who is unusual in having come from outside the agency, has taken steps over the last several years to obtain and distribute information about promising employees throughout the agency. But traditional mobility patterns have been slow to change.[51]

Reinforcing these patterns is the fact that, although administrative ability is considered important at higher levels, strong emphasis has been placed on technical expertise as a criterion for advancement. "To really run his organization as it should be run," Wagner has said, "a Branch chief has to be abler than all the people reporting to him."[52] Again, this tends to make for vertical promotion, since no one else will know as much about technical matters as those already in the area.

Such personnel practices are rooted in a number of aspects of the organization's circumstances and structure. Frank Gartrell, discussing the situation in Division of Environmental Planning, explained it this way: "A guy has to be good *professionally*. Just because he can run an insurance company is no reason he can run our Division. The general manager doesn't want to know we can get office space as cheap as possible; that, in the lab, we get the most samples per man/hour. He wants to be able to depend on our scientific expertise, in case TVA comes under attack by outside experts. He doesn't want us to be wasteful, of course, but the emphasis in our Division was on the professional quality of things."[53]

Expertise has a defensive value internally as well as externally. It helps a manager negotiate effectively with other Divisions and represent his group's viewpoint creditably to top management. As John Bynon, assistant director of personnel, explained: "Heads of Offices and Divisions must have a specialized knowledge as well as detailed information on their operations. There is a board meeting every two weeks attended by the Division directors. When a board member asks a question, he expects an immediate response. Divisional directors normally take additional staff to board meetings only when they are needed to assist in formal presentations to the board."[54] For the most part, then, they must be capable of discussing the technical details of their Division's activities unassisted.

To some extent, the absence of staff at board meetings reflects logistical considerations. TVA headquarters are in Knoxville, Tennessee. Many Divisions are located 100 or 200 miles away, in Chattanooga or Muscle Shoals. It is simply not practical, given the time and cost of travel and the large numbers of people involved, for Division directors to bring many staff people to board meetings or other less formal conferences. Nor, given the physical distances involved, are the absent staff generally easily available if a question should arise.

Having the facts *when they are needed*—in the midst of a negotiation or when the board is making a decision—is important in TVA. As a consequence, the ability to be authoritative and apparently competent, even when the underlying information is ambiguous, can be an asset. One middle manager said of his former boss, "He was very effective. With limited briefing on the general subject and provision of necessary technical information, he was more persuasive and more successful than most directors I have known."[55]

This premium on technical decisiveness and authoritativeness extends well down into the organization. As one manager put it, "If a fellow wants to get ahead, he has to learn to write reports that I can send on up with minimal work, reports that don't leave any loose ends hanging out."[56] We asked another rapidly rising engineer what he would do if his boss asked him a question and requested an answer within a limited time, and on examination, the engineer found that the evidence was very conflicting. The fellow leaned back and smiled and said, "If he wanted an answer at five o'clock on Thursday, he would have an answer at five o'clock on Thursday. I'd tell him, 'Based on the available evidence, the answer is such and such.' "[57] In contrast, when we asked this same question of a respected engineer at Ontario Hydro, he answered that he would speak to his boss about the difficulties and seek additional time and guidance before answering.

The emphasis on expertise within TVA serves other functions as well. Exempted from civil service requirements, TVA was required by statute to ensure that politics did not enter into its personnel policies; this was done by the first board to protect the agency from criticism and from outside interference.[58] Despite much pressure in the early days the policy has been assiduously pursued, and there has thus been strong emphasis on using "objective" criteria for advancement. Technical ability conforms well to this test. Managerial ability, on the other hand, which involves more subtle skills such as a person's leadership qualities and the capacity to get along with others, is more difficult to evaluate and more open to abuse and arbitrary application.

Emphasis on technical expertise and decisiveness both reflects and reinforces TVA's attitude that it is "above politics"—that its judgments are "scientific" and "objective" compared to those of outside critics and regulators. This viewpoint, in turn, is implicit in the most basic features of the organization's internal structure and in its linkages (or lack thereof) to the larger political system. Thus, personnel policies that originally protected TVA against inappropriate political influences reinforce today its isolation from external concerns that conflict with its own priorities.

Internally, these same attitudes have reinforced the decentralization of authority. The Division managers and Branch chiefs are the technical experts, to whom their generalist superiors (according to this logic) should defer. Top management's control over subordinates like Division directors has been weakened further by the fact that it has only limited incentives to offer them. At Pacific Gas and Electric, with its several levels of general management, a person in charge of a functional subgroup can aspire to further advancement. At TVA the head of a major Division or Office generally could not—particularly before 1979 when some additional management slots were created. There are few, if any, attractive higher-level jobs available except that of general manager. And, as a result of internal rivalries, almost all general managers have come from staff groups.[59] On the other hand, such a manager's chance of being removed for not fully cooperating has been very low; given the information flow, mild disobedience is unlikely even to be discovered, since Divisions generally report on their own performance, and from the viewpoint of top management there is no reason to believe that the "heir apparent" will behave very differently. The limits this imposes on top-management control are obvious.

Bringing in outsiders to fill Division director positions is one way to attack these problems. Outside appointees are more likely to feel personal loyalty to the general manager who selected them, and hiring them also signals to internal candidates that they have more to lose by not pleasing top management. One re- recently retired general manager, Lynn Seeber, appointed three non-TVA men to fill Division director slots — in Personnel; Environmental Planning; and Forestry, Fisheries, and Wildlife Development. Whether this indicated a new trend and a conscious intention to increase top-management control is unclear. One middle manager observed that Seeber was seeking to be "more of an administrator and less of a coordinator" than past general managers. Seeber himself did not explain the appointments in this way, pointing out that it has always been TVA practice to appoint outsiders to high-level positions when no suitable inside candidates are available. In practice, however, this has not often happened.[60]

Given all these structural features that weaken the control of top management, what has kept TVA functioning efficiently and consistently? In some organizations with weak control systems, responses to external problems have been both inconsistent and ineffective. TVA has at least been consistent, and done what it has tried to do with some energy. Part of the explanation is the "coordination from the middle" exercised by the Office of Power, but this is not the whole story. Another part of the explanation is that, in TVA, middle managers exert considerable control over their subordinates, even though top management does not have similar control over middle managers. Since a TVA engineer can only move straight up, his immediate superiors have a great deal of influence over his fate, and he thus has considerable incentive to perform well for them. There are limits here, too: promotions are infrequent and often go to people with seniority. Indeed, it has been common to designate a manager's successor years before his retirement (although this is changing).[61] Only if one is lucky or in a growing organization are things really different. Yet controls within the Divisions are still much stronger than those that have been available at the top.

Incentives apart, TVA employees have a deeply internalized sense of their agency's mission — more so than in most organizations. This helps ensure consistent decision making without strong guidance from the top. Initially, TVA's mission was quite broad, but Arthur Morgan's departure and David Lilienthal's advocacy narrowed TVA's objectives, enabling low-cost power to gain more importance. Herbert Vogel's appointment in the 1950s cemented this approach, and during the Eisenhower administration funds for the agency's nonpower programs were seriously curtailed. The sense that TVA exists to improve social and economic conditions in the Tennessee Valley has never totally vanished. Internally, low-cost power has inevitably been characterized as a means to that end. On the other hand, even the members of Divisions such as Environmental Planning, who had objectives that conflict with low-cost power, have seen the virtue of this goal. Many of them have seemed to view themselves as a corrective influence on a policy that, in general, is still sound.

This attachment to a specific perspective reflects in part a process of mutual selection: those attracted to TVA's mission are more likely to join, remain with, and rise in the organization. Much of the movement out of TVA occurs among younger engineers, who, having found out within a year or two how things operate, decide to go elsewhere. Senior managers are quite explicit in saying that dedication to TVA's mission is a central criterion for promotion. Robert Betts, an outsider who served as TVA's director of personnel, described the results of this process: "It's one of the most dedicated bunch of people I've seen anywhere. It's spooky sometimes. It's almost evangelistic . . . I'm not sure why they stay, but after they've been here for a few years, you would have to run them off with a shotgun."[62] In the same vein, Lynn Seeber said, "Many of the current managers still have the 1933 spirit. They are still questing for the Holy Grail. And that's the kind of people we want. They make better leaders."[63]

Changing the behavior of such an organization is not easy; it involves converting the membership from one faith to another. People down the line, for the highest motives, are tempted to resist — or at least not aggressively implement — directives from above that conflict with their view of the proper functioning of the agency. With a weak control system, the tools are not avail-

Figure 5. TVA was and is proud of its accomplishments in bringing electricity to the Tennessee Valley in the 1930s. The photograph shows a crew working on a line near Concord, Tennessee. Courtesy of the Tennessee Valley Authority.

able to top management to alter this behavior by manipulating economic incentives. The alternative is to get people with different views in key positions, but this is difficult and time-consuming. It provokes the hostility of long-time insiders who resent newcomers and do not trust their loyalty. And, indeed, people brought in from outside may in fact be less "loyal," in the sense of being less committed to traditional strategies.

Top management's ability to control the organization has been further limited by accidents of personality. In TVA an ability to "pound the table" with conviction and authority could be crucial in turning the tide in an argument. People who make decisions, after all, can be swayed by others in the organization. Moreover, each member's willingness to act aggressively in conflict situations will be affected by his own personality. This brings us again to the role of Wessenauer and Kampmeier throughout the first twenty years of TVA's involvement with coal-burning plants. As Wagner commented:

> The rise and fall of Divisions depends a great deal on individual personalities. Wes and Kamp believed in arguing for their viewpoint as hard as possible. They believed in their program, and felt it was the responsibility of any other Division director at odds with Power over some issue to fight just as hard for his beliefs. They certainly weren't going to help the other guy make his case before the board. Of course, there were other Division directors who were more willing to look for the common ground, or balance point, among the multiple purposes of TVA that the board and general manager have to find.[64]

Those who can see the validity of other viewpoints are often less effective defenders of their own position. Wessenauer and Kampmeier, on the other hand, never or rarely gave up. "Wes took a dim view of some of these environmental moves," Wagner commented. "Watson [his successor as manager of Power] is different. He will fight like hell, but once a decision is made he will live with it more willingly."[65] Disagreeing with Wessenauer and Kampmeier was thus not an attractive prospect. This in turn increased the incentives facing a potentially competing group to develop programs, policies, and definitions of their own role that complemented rather than conflicted with those of the Office of Power.

Accidents of personality helped other units besides the Office of Power. In the late 1950s the Division of Health and Safety (part of which is now the Division of Environmental Planning) recommended the installation of precipitators at TVA's Kingston plant. Health and Safety was then headed by O. M. Derryberry, a physician with little background in the air pollution field but with considerable ability to make an argument. This was a skill he needed, given the vigorous opposition to his view from the Office of Power. A former subordinate of Derryberry's describes the confrontation this way: "We finally won it on a dramatic, quasi-professional approach. Derry had taken a picture of a lung from a medical journal with him [to the board meeting at which the recommendation was being discussed]. We weren't doing too well at the meeting. Then Derry took out the picture and started talking about emphysema and synergistic effects. He was very effective."[66]

Clearly, personality is an important factor even at the very top of an organization. David Lilienthal, for example, was able to shape TVA's program to fit his views in the power area despite considerable national opposition. Lilienthal's zeal and skill in defending the agency were very important in protecting it against the attacks of private utilities, and in warding off moves to place it within the Department of the Interior.

It is easy, in retrospect, to overestimate the role of particular individuals. One could argue that the critical people in TVA's history could not have succeeded if conditions had not been right, or that someone else might have done the same in their position. Yet this is only partly true: someone else might well have proceeded differently or less effectively. There is an element in organizational behavior, unexplained by more systematic factors of strategy and structure, which does in fact depend on the particular people involved. In TVA this factor has, on occasion, been quite significant.

Under the direction of a new board, TVA's traditional structure underwent some significant changes starting in 1979. The number of separate units reporting to the general manager was greatly reduced by consolidating the independent Divisions outside the Offices of Power, Engineering, and Agriculture into three new Offices—for Natural Resources, Community Development, and Management Services. This reduced the supervisory burden placed on the general manager and increased the stature of the nonpower activities. Conflicting authority over environmental planning was resolved by placing control over all environmental and regulatory matters in the Environmental Quality Planning Staff, part of the Office of Natural Resources. Finally, a new corporate planning system has been instituted under which several offices will work together to plan a project, so that, for instance, the Offices of Community Development, Power, and Engineering are working together to review the social and economic effects on the Valley of different power plant siting decisions.

The structural changes made by the board seem designed to deal with some of the obstacles to top management control. And with these new organizational arrangements, top management should find it easier to increase strategic emphasis on objectives other than low-cost power. Unfortunately, our research ended before these changes occurred, and thus we cannot fully evaluate the impact they have had on TVA's behavior.

Environmental Decisions

Having taken a look at the context, background, and internal structure of the organization, we are in a position to give a plausible account of TVA's environmental decision making from the late 1940s up until the end of the 1970s. Consider the evolution of TVA's air quality program—a striking example of the way in which an organization's strategy and structure shape its responses to the external world, while at the same time being shaped by external pressures. Given the prevailing emphasis on low-cost power production, advocates of environmental protection within the agency originally had little influence over power plant design. But as their expertise increased and external pressures on the agency grew, their influence grew. So, too, did their status in the organization, as reflected in structural arrangements.

Concern over TVA's air pollution impact arose initially in the agency's Division of Health and Safety, a group that historically had coordinated public-health planning related to TVA's dam-building activities. Previous to the steam plant era, its principle activity had been controlling malaria associated with TVA reservoirs and studying the effects on water quality of TVA's dam building.[67] The group was thus already involved in assessing power-related activities from a public-health perspective. This appears to have eased its transition into monitoring the air pollution impact of TVA's steam generation program. Moreover, there were certain incentives to develop a program associated with TVA's steam plants, since, with fewer dams being built, the Division faced stagnation unless it developed new activities.

Air quality first became an issue after plans for the construction of TVA's first postwar plant at Johnsonville were announced. The Division's chief environmental engineer, C. H. Clark, became concerned about possible adverse air pollution consequences. Fred Thomas, then a young engineer, was put to work on the problem. Some preliminary calculations showed that very high sulfur emissions could be expected, and given the Division's health orientation, this became its main air pollution concern. In comparison, much less attention—then and later—was given to fly-ash emissions, which were judged to be less of a health hazard.[68]

Because of the Johnsonville plant's rural location, the designers (in the Division of Engineering) chose to keep down costs and put on only mechanical dust collectors to control fly ash. These were installed mainly to reduce corrosion of the fans drawing air through the boilers. Of more concern to the air quality group was the fact that the designers also chose to install very low stacks. Built from the powerhouse roof, they extended only 170 feet above grade—despite the fact that, for its day, this was a very large plant. Six units totaling 750 MW were installed when it was fully operational in 1953. The designers realized that these choices might be in error and room was explicitly left in the layout so that electrostatic precipitators could be added later if this proved desirable. Also, the structure was designed to be strong enough so that the stacks could be raised at a later date.[69] Given the prior history of the organization, the weak organizational basis of the air pollution control efforts, and Wessenauer's views on such matters, the choice at that time to do very little about pollution control is hardly surprising. The first units at the plant began operation in 1951.

There was enough concern, however, so that monitoring of air pollution around the plant was undertaken. The work was done by a special project group within the Division of Health and Safety; it consisted of only a few people, was supervised by a multidivisional committee, and was supported by a project authorization from power revenues. This unit was to undertake TVA's air pollution work for the next several years. Funding throughout the first five or six years, although adequate by the group's standards, was insecure, and was generally awarded for periods of only a year or so at a time. As Fred Thomas commented, "There were many occasions when it seemed reasonably clear that the Office of Power would prefer to have the air quality program in the Office of Power rather than in another independent division."[70]

To justify its existence, the unit had to find evidence of air pollution problems around TVA's plants. This did not turn out to be difficult: monitoring around Johnsonville and later at TVA's giant Kingston plant did produce such evidence. (The group monitored air quality much less intensively at other early TVA steam plants. Fred Thomas and others involved in early monitoring declare that more work would have been done at these plants if major problems had existed there; even if it was necessary to monitor these plants, it is clear that the group lacked the resources and power to pursue any but the most clearly justified projects).[71] Despite the group's fieldwork, it initially found that its advice was not always heeded.

From the first, the Johnsonville monitoring program revealed very high SO_2 levels — as high as ten parts per million for thirty minutes — which even incapacitated some of the operators. (This is approximately seventy times as high as the current EPA 24-hour standard.) This obviously unacceptable situation was caused by stack downwash and finally led to the stacks being raised by 100 feet in 1955. But this was not before the first four units at the Widows Creek plant (totaling 540 MW) were built with 170-feet stacks like those initially used at Johnsonville. The ten units at Shawnee (built between 1953 and 1956) and the first four units at Kingston (which went into operation in 1954) were built with 250-foot stacks, which was not unusual for plants in other systems at that time. The air quality people thought that even this was too low, however, and called in consultants to bolster their arguments. Their protests and arguments for 500-foot stacks were ignored, but higher stacks slowly came to be accepted: 300 feet at the last four units at Kingston, and the first four at Colbert (in 1954-1955); 350 feet at John Sevier (1955-1957); 500 feet at Gallatin and three other units installed in 1958-1959.[72] (In contrast, prior to 1965 the tallest stacks of the Southern Company, to the south, were less than 200 feet.) Later TVA stacks went even higher — to 600 feet, then 800 feet, and finally to 1,000 feet, which is as high, and generally higher, than those built by any other utility in the country.

Several factors account for this development. Beginning in 1957, with research support provided by the United States Public Health Service, the air quality group began to develop recognized expertise in monitoring the process by which smoke plumes disperse. The group was the first of its kind in the nation to use mathematical models to generalize these findings and to predict ground-level SO_2 concentrations as a function of stack height, meteorological conditions, coal consumption, and so on; as a consequence, its recommendations began to carry a great deal of technical weight within the agency. In addition, complaints from the public increased, and there was some evidence of damage to vegetation in the immediate vicinity of TVA's larger plants.[73] There were also well-publicized air pollution incidents in several places around the world. The cost of higher stacks for new units was low enough so that the organizational risks and social costs of not raising the stacks were not in TVA's interest. Eventually, then, the efforts of the Division of Health and Safety did result in substantial control efforts at a time when TVA faced little external pressure on the issue.

During the same period, chemical engineers at TVA's National Fertilizer Development Center at Muscle Shoals conducted some investigations of chemical processes to remove the SO_2 from stack gases. This early scrubber research was undertaken largely to explore the possibility of using recovered by-product sulfur as an input to fertilizer production. Here, the existence of nonpower activities in TVA created the potential for developments with important consequences for the power program, but the investigations were abandoned after a few years. A decline in the world sulfur price made sulfur recovery less attractive economically, and without this incentive the fertilizer people had no reason to continue.

The Division of Health and Safety's work appeared to offer an inexpensive alternative to stack gas scrubbing. Building on their knowledge of atmospheric dispersion, the air quality group began to explore how to use generation cutbacks and fuel switching to reduce ground-level sulfur dioxide concentrations under unfavorable weather conditions. This approach, known as "operational" or "intermittent" controls, was advanced by TVA and other SO_2 sources as a prime alternative to meeting state SO_2 emissions standards.[74]

The method was first used on a limited scale in the 1950s, before such standards existed, when TVA began stockpiling low-sulfur coal at the Kingston plant to be burned in periods of air stagnation.[75] Kingston, an extremely large plant, was located in a valley, near a small town that could be "fumigated" when the atmosphere prevented the smoke plume from rising and the winds blew it toward the town. During one such incident, before the program was initiated, an asthmatic child in the town suffered an attack and TVA paid for his medical expenses.

A much more extensive operational control effort was made at the Paradise plant in the late 1960s, when a 1100 MW unit was added to the two 700 MW units already in operation, making the combined plant one of the largest in operation in the country at that time. When the third unit at Paradise was being planned, the air quality group had become sufficiently established that it was given a chance to review plans for the unit at an early stage. This gave it the opportunity to insist on some kind of controls. The group's impact may have been boosted by a 1966 Presidential Executive Order requiring federal agencies to review plans for controlling SO_2 at new facilities with the Public Health Service; TVA was thus under official pressure to develop workable SO_2 control plans before proceeding with the plant. The agency's effort was successful enough to become the basis for TVA's plan to use operational controls throughout the system.

After a number of studies the staff of the Air Quality Branch decided that, from an air pollution standpoint, Paradise was the least desirable of several possible sites. But Paradise was virtually in the middle of a large strip mine. Since fuel costs at the site would therefore be low, the location was very attractive to the Office of Power. Even considering air pollution control costs, it seemed the most inexpensive way to produce power. Negotiations ensued between the Office of Power and the Division of Health and Safety, in consultation with the Public Health Service. The result was a plan to put the new unit at Paradise, with a high-efficiency precipitator and an 800-foot stack, and to retrofit precipitators on the first two units. These had been built without any air pollution controls at all. In addition, and most importantly in this context, an elaborate air quality monitoring and meteorological network was to be installed to forecast unfavorable atmospheric conditions, so that generation, and hence emissions, could be reduced in a timely manner.[76] TVA bought up the small neighboring town of Paradise, ostensibly for added coal storage, but several officials in the agency said that this was essentially a way to compensate those most hurt by the plant, as well as a means to limit complaints about its operation.[77]

These events illustrate central features of TVA's functioning. The policy was established by negotiation at low levels, and the resulting agreement fostered the interests of all participants while remaining consistent with the dominant organizational ideology.

The Air Quality Branch's involvement in the planning and *operation* of the Paradise plant represented a major expansion of its functions. Its role, and that of operational controls, increased still further during the 1970s. TVA was trying to avoid the expense of using scrubbers or low-sulfur coal to meet state SO_2 standards; it proposed, as an alternative, to use system-wide operational controls. This in turn required additional personnel at the Air Quality Branch and a major expansion in its influence. When the program first developed, the Office of Power occasionally refused to honor the Air Quality Branch's requests to reduce generation, citing possible problems in system stability and in meeting power requirements. Later it began responding more conscientiously,[78] recognizing that if operational controls did not work, the alternatives would be vastly more expensive.

As both cause and consequence of these developments, the organizational basis of the air pollution efforts became steadily more secure. The work started as a half-time assignment for Fred Thomas, then became the responsibility of a group of about four in the Environmental Hygiene Branch, which later, with expanded staff, acquired section status in the Branch. In 1960 the section was transferred to the Occupational Health Branch, and in 1968 air pollution was given Branch status in its own right. Subsequently, in 1969, a separate Division for environmental matters was created within the newly organized Office of Health and Environmental Sciences. Finally, in 1973, a free-standing Division of Environmental Planning was formed, in which the Air Quality Management Branch played a major role.[79]

An obvious recursive process was at work. An expanded organization led to more information on air quality problems and to new proposals for dealing with them. This in turn required an expansion of the group's activities. Growth also made Air Quality a stronger bargaining force internally, which helped lead to still further growth. Clearly, however, this was not solely a matter of internal dynamics; air pollution activities grew in part because they filled a growing need. Environmental problems were becoming more serious, and increased outside pressures and stricter controls required a response from the organization.

TVA's overall response to the air pollution problem, then, was not a strictly hierarchical process in which top management modified agency strategy and structure to suit new circumstances; much of the initial concern came from groups and individuals lower in the organization. Yet the support of top management certainly helped. The development of a strong, distinct organizational basis occurred in part because chairman Wagner wanted an independent environmental advocate within the organization. Once created, the new unit not only tended to influence decisions but also provided an independent channel of information for top management. This latter function served to increase top management's control over the organization. Both Wagner and Frank Gartrell referred to the group as, to a certain extent, an "internal policeman."

The Division of Health and Safety played a crusading role in the early years of the power program. Its work on tall stacks and operational controls ultimately did allow it to fit in to the prevailing "low-cost power" strategy, because its approach to SO_2 control was a lower-cost alternative to an expensive scrubber program. At one time it had had to persuade the Office of Power and others to spend more on environmental controls; in the 1970s, however, it defended TVA against outsiders who wanted the agency to reduce total sulfur emissions.[80] As an advocate of dispersion as a method of SO_2 control, it came to enjoy wider acceptance within TVA.

Indeed, once this group became identified as TVA's experts on air pollution, the strategy it preferred (reflecting its own expertise) was pursued with little attention to other options. In the late 1960s TVA resumed the scrubber research it had dropped in the 1950s—eventually going ahead with a full-scale prototype at Widows Creek 8—but continued to maintain that tall stacks and operational controls were the only sensible solution to the SO_2 problem. The agency did no substantial work on cleaning coal before combustion (unlike the Southern Company) and, despite an expert coal-purchasing department, argued that it could obtain only minimal amounts of low-sulfur coal in the Southeast. It contended that it had tried burning low-sulfur coal from the West and had found it too low in heat content to be practical for use in TVA's boilers.[81] Yet the Southern Company, TVA's neighbor to the south, was able to obtain substantial amounts of low-sulfur coal to meet environmental requirements—from the Southeast, from overseas, and from parts of the West that TVA had not tried. Only after Congress forced TVA to comply with state standards did the agency succeed in finding substantial supplies of low-sulfur coal in the Southeast (at high prices, of course).[82]

As the last sentence suggests, recent developments have finally resolved the air pollution control controversy. Under the 1977 amendments to the Clean Air Act, TVA is required to meet state SO_2 emissions standards at its plants. Negotiations among TVA, EPA, and the states have resulted in modifications in a number of state emissions standards, so that TVA will be able to meet these standards at many of its plants without installing scrubbers or switching fuel. (In some cases it will have to wash its fuel to remove sulfur and other wastes before burning.) But at six plants, TVA will be turning to one of these two expensive alternatives. At Widows Creek 7, TVA is installing a scrubber to supplement the prototype scrubber on Widows Creek 8, and it is planning to install scrubbers at the Johnsonville, Cumberland, and Paradise plants as well. Coal washing will also be used at the last two plants. Low-sulfur coal will be burned at the Kingston and Shawnee plants. The TVA Board approved many of these measures, as a settlement strategy, while Aubrey Wagner was still chairman; however, some of the measures had to await the appointment of new directors who would support the new chairman, David Freeman. Ironically, after the new board approved the settlement, TVA distributors opposed to these environmental expenditures intervened legally and delayed the final implementation of the settlement.[83]

The decision to install these SO_2 controls means that the strategy developed by the Division of Health and Safety is being partially superseded — although the high stacks it succeeded in getting built have helped TVA obtain a compromise on emissions standards at some plants.

The Division of Health and Safety has not been equally aggressive on all fronts. Most obvious was the early decision to focus on the health effects of SO_2 rather than particulate emissions. On several occasions Fred Thomas expressed doubts about the adequacy of TVA's particulate control measures. But his superiors, O. M. Derryberry and Frank Gartrell, apparently did not voice them strongly in discussions with other Divisions. Perhaps, given the newness of their cause and the Division's relatively weak position, its leadership felt that selectivity was called for in deciding what issues to press; perhaps they realized that it would be all too easy to lose influence by pressing for "unreasonable" proposals.

This low priority on controlling particulate emissions tended to persist because, reflecting TVA career paths, some of those involved in the original decision played key roles in the Division for many years thereafter. Frank Gartrell, for instance, was assistant to the director when this emphasis was chosen in the early 1950s. He remained in the Division until 1975, when he retired as director. TVA's board, in contrast, seems to have been more concerned with controlling particulates, as a result of the greater visibility and public-relations problems of fly-ash emissions.

Reflecting the Division's strategic choice, units built before 1959 were equipped with low-efficiency mechanical collectors, with no strong dissent from Health and Safety.[84] Over time, however, complaints from nearby residents, and indications that the presence of particulates increased the health hazards of SO_2, led the Division in the late 1950s to advocate better particulate controls. This caused a pivotal battle between the Division of Health and Safety and the Office of Power over such controls at the Kingston plant. Continuing local complaints, the evidence of synergistic effects, a local child's asthmatic attack, and Derryberry's dramatic presentation using the lung picture from the medical journal persuaded the board in 1959 to approve backfitting precipitators on the plant. These events clearly were influenced by the presence of an internal environmental group oriented toward public health. But even this victory was not complete: Fred Thomas and the people in Air Quality pressed unsuccessfully to have the stacks raised also. Somehow the issue became transformed into an either/or situation.[85] Years later, in a recent round of pollution control efforts, a new, 1000-foot stack was built at the plant. See Figure 6.

The next three units built by TVA (500 MW each—Colbert 5 and Widows Creek 7 and 8) were planned or begun during the period of financial stringency when Congress refused to appropriate money, and before new bonding powers were authorized. Having agreed to retrofit precipitators at Kingston, there was some question about how effective particulate removal should be on these new units. Fred Thomas and others urged 95 percent removal as a target, but money was scarce and costs rose rapidly as efficiencies were improved. The senior staff of the Division overruled their advice and agreed with the other Division heads on a 90 percent target, at a time when many other utilities, including TVA's neighbor, Southern, were installing 98 percent efficient precipitators. They were apparently willing to settle for having established the principle, and wanted to avoid increased interdivisional controversy. Fred Thomas did not even go to the critical meeting.[86]

The precipitators that were installed worked far below their design level. The Kingston units, nominally designed to remove 95 percent of the particulates in the stack gases, functioned at 90 percent. The units at Widows Creek 8 and Colbert 5, intended to remove 90 percent, tested closer to 50 percent in the early 1970s. This poor performance, and the precipitators' unreliability, reflect the same combination of structural incentives and personalities. The design group, under pressure from the Office of Power, wanted to minimize costs and issued performance specifications that were not very rigorous. Following normal TVA prac-

Figure 6. The Kingston steam plant showing the new 1000-foot stacks and the most recent electrostatic precipitators (which fill the area between the new stacks and the now dwarfed old stacks). To appreciate the scale of the facility, note the size of the freight train to the right of the right-hand stack. Courtesy of the Tennessee Valley Authority.

tice, units were bought from the lowest bidder — an incentive to suppliers to underdesign. TVA also lacked expertise in this area, but did not bring in anyone from outside the organization to help provide more rigorous specifications. Power wanted to minimize the length of time the plants would be out of service while the units were being installed, and Construction also wanted to keep down costs. The result was a quick and imperfect job of installation.[87] Finally, the operators had little or no incentive to maintain the equipment, which was temperamental and easily malfunctioned. Is it any surprise, therefore, that the units worked poorly?

The next major particulate control issue arose over the Paradise plant, where two 700 MW units were constructed — the largest in the world at that time. Located in the midst of a coalfield, they were built to burn relatively dirty, unprepared coal direct from the mines. The units employed cyclone-fired boilers, which theoretically entrained 70-80 percent of the ash in the slag (instead of 20-40 percent in a normal unit). They were built without *any* particulate controls at all, on the grounds that emissions would be similar to those of previous designs with mechanical collectors. Intended control levels were thus significantly lowered, since previous precipitators had been aimed at 90-95 percent, and this strategy was equivalent to collection rates of 50 to 75 percent on a conventional boiler, a step justified by the isolated location of the units.

The Air Quality Branch was dubious. They succeeded in getting 600-foot stacks, but they had neither the evidence nor the influence to dispute the Office of Power's arguments. Apparently, the Division's leadership did not press the point. Aubrey Wagner does not remember any controversy about the first units, recalling only that Health and Safety concurred with the recommendation that came to the board. As soon as the plant went into operation, however, the need for particulate controls was obvious. As Frank Gartrell put it, "It was just a mess . . . Operating without collectors was for the birds." Fred Thomas remembers the emissions as "heavy particulates, large stuff. In the vicinity of the plant, you could hear it hitting your hard hat." In part, this was because the cyclone furnaces had higher emissions than initially projected. And, as noted previously, precipitators were retrofitted on these units as part of the pollution control program worked out when the third unit was being planned for Paradise.[88]

At the time this third unit was being planned, TVA came under pressure to install precipitators at some of its other plants.

The same Presidential Executive Order that had involved the Public Health Service in Paradise 3 required TVA to submit a plan for bringing the rest of the system into compliance with certain minimum particulate control standards. Also, in the early 1960s, public protests over air pollution were increasing; for example, the residents of the town of Metropolis, Illinois, complained about fallout from the neighboring Shawnee plant. In 1967 TVA began a limited program to backfit or upgrade precipitators at Shawnee and some of its other existing plants.[89] Slowly this program was expanded and strengthened—as earlier plans came to be seen as inadequate—until its aim became that of installing 99 + percent efficient precipitators at all of TVA's existing steam plants. But this process took six years, during which the board of directors played a key role. All TVA observers agree that the board and Aubrey Wagner in particular were the strongest internal advocates for spending more money on particulate controls. "Mr. Wagner was the advocate for spending the extra money, particularly when the performance of earlier precipitators turned out to be poor," Wessenauer commented. "He took a strong position, directing the staff toward better precipitator efficiencies," said Gartrell.[90]

The Division of Health and Safety, on the other hand, did not play a strong role in the precipitator upgrading program; rather than being a "watchdog," it tended to go along with the Office of Power's attempt to minimize additional expenditures on particulate controls. The board had to leave the specifics of planning and implementation to the various technical staffs. Because Health and Safety was not more aggressive, it was easier for the Office of Power to move slowly to implement the improvement program.

Under the first upgrading plans, drawn up in 1967 by the Office of Power and the Division of Health and Safety, less than half of TVA's existing units were slated for upgrading—and these to efficiencies of between 95 and 98 percent. Twenty-four units, with a combined capacity of over 3,500 MW, were to be left with mechanical collectors (removing 50-70 percent of the emissions). The justification for this proposal was that these units would soon be used for peaking purposes only, and in some years would not be used at all.[91] As it happens, some are still heavily used today. From the Division of Health and Safety's viewpoint, excluding these plants from the upgrading plans may have seemed questionable even then; but the Division had no means to challenge the Office of Power's assertions about their low anticipated use levels—even if it had wanted to.

The board, although perhaps willing to approve more vigorous efforts, deferred to the suggestions of the staff. "All of us recognized that we ought to do *something*," Wagner recalls, "but it was less clear then what you could do. The staff was trying to get them clean and at a reasonable cost."[92] By 1969, however, Wagner had decided that TVA was not going far enough to deal with the problem of dirty stacks. During that fall the board, at Wagner's initiative, concluded that the agency should install 99 percent efficient precipitators at most of TVA's remaining units, to attain the objective of "clear stacks." The board accepted the idea that recently installed precipitators attaining a few percentage points less than 99 percent efficiency need not be upgraded, but it did decide that precipitators should be installed on the old units that the Office of Power had said were due to be phased out. However, no immediate action was taken to upgrade twelve of the system's oldest units at Johnsonville and Widows Creek.[93]

In 1972 an external initiative—in the form of state particulate standards established under the Clean Air Act Amendments of 1970—forced TVA to upgrade its upgrading program yet again. Under these standards, 99 percent efficient precipitators were effectively required at all of TVA's existing stations. This meant not only installing precipitators at the old Johnsonville and Widows Creek units, but re-upgrading inadequate precipitators at Kingston and a number of other plants where precipitators had been backfitted just a few years before. In January 1973 a new program to meet these state requirements was announced by the board. Because of the large number of units involved, however, the board stated that some units would not be brought into compliance until a year or two after the 1975 deadline.[94]

The Office of Power moved sluggishly to begin the new efforts. This time, however, the system of organizational checks and balances that Wagner constructed worked to ensure that action was taken to meet environmental requirements.

Larry Montgomery, chief of the Air Quality Branch at that time, relates the story:

> During 1972 it became clear that Power and Engineering Design had a very difficult task and schedule to meet in laying plans . . . for precipitators to meet the requirements of state implementation plans. Compliance plans were due on January 1, 1973, but until late 1972 very little progress had

been made by Power and the Office of Engineering and Design Construction toward scheduling a new upgrading program. The difficult question of what to do about SO_2, which has an impact on particulate emissions, was a major factor in complicating the development of this schedule.

The Division of Law was very interested in all this. They indicated that TVA could be required to meet state sulfur dioxide emissions standards as well as state particulate emissions standards. We supported the Office of Power's position that it would be impracticable to meet the initial, very stringent, state sulfur dioxide emissions standards.

In very late 1972 there was a joint meeting involving Environmental Planning, Law, and Power. We still didn't have a schedule for meeting state SO_2 and particulate emissions standards at the meeting. We went over what was required by the state implementation plans. Several times during the meeting, Nat Hughes [then director of Power Resource Planning] indicated that he just didn't see how it could be done.[95]

But as a result of this meeting, Power and Engineering came up with the current upgrading program.

Whether or not the agency could have met the deadline if the Office of Power had been quicker to develop a schedule is problematical. TVA faced real difficulties in obtaining equipment from manufacturers and in not being able to shut down too many plants simultaneously to install the equipment. The problem would have been less severe, however, if everyone had acted more expeditiously in 1967. The board's "representatives" in ensuring compliance with legal standards — the Divisions of Law and Environmental Planning — did help to ensure that some plan was finally prepared.[96] But given its limited ability to supervise the line divisions in detail, top management was unable to eliminate foot-dragging in the ranks.

While various groups in TVA — particularly the Office of Power — evidently hoped to save money by following a go-slow policy on precipitator installation, ironically it is not clear that the organization has in fact minimized its air pollution compliance costs. The retrofitting and re-retrofitting involved in the upgrading program have been quite expensive. Construction costs have risen rapidly in recent years. And by doing everything two or three times, start-up costs, design costs, and so on have had to be incurred twice. Moreover, there is wasted effort involved in closing things up and tearing them open again. It seems doubtful that the interest costs saved by deferring these capital expenditures comes close to the added costs involved in multiple retrofitting. TVA chief engineer George Kimmons and his staff estimate that "savings of 50 to 75 percent of the installed precipitator price could have been realized had we installed 99 + percent efficient precipitators initially rather than retrofit."[97] Even if there was no *cost* penalty, TVA surely missed some potential public-relations benefits by delaying the installation of good particulate control equipment when the equipment ultimately had to be installed anyway.

The TVA staff could argue that it was impossible to foresee in 1967, or even 1969, that this equipment would eventually be required. However, other utilities acted with greater foresight. Indeed, if the organizational structure had responded more energetically to the board's desire to install good particulate controls, TVA might not have been caught so unprepared for the state standards when they were established in 1972.

Besides permitting relatively low levels of precipitator *design* efficiencies, TVA's organizational structure has also led to the installation of precipitators that failed to meet even these relatively modest targets.[98] The poor reliability of TVA's precipitators is parallel to the undesirably low reliability it has experienced on some other pieces of equipment.

The roots of this situation are to be found in the way the design function is organized. Formally, TVA's Office of Engineering Design and Construction (OEDC) is on a par with the Office of Power and TVA's other Offices and Divisions. But, in practice, given the dynamics of interdivisional bargaining, the OEDC has often been influenced by standards and objectives set by the Office of Power. For example, instead of insisting on better precipitator design with more margin for error, for a long time the Design Division followed the Office of Power's wishes and provided what turned out to be underdesigned equipment.

The leadership of the Office of Power consistently fostered this relationship. It treated Design as a hired consultant who should properly respond to the client's (that is, the Office of Power's) wishes. On more than one occasion, the management of the Office of Power threatened to go outside the agency for design services if projects were not brought in at the lowest possible costs.[99] Of course, such a choice was not formally within the authority of the Office of Power. But who could say that the board would not go along with Wessenauer if he made such a proposal? The loss of even a part of the work would have had adverse effects on advancement prospects within the design group, so this was a contingency to be assiduously avoided.

Bargaining tactics and leadership apart, the low-cost power strategy was widely perceived as both desirable and likely to enhance the organization's success. The engineers who did design work at TVA had adopted this viewpoint as their own. This was important because, in the course of any design effort, there are innumerable tradeoffs and matters of professional judgment to be resolved. A designer's implicit or explicit view of what constitutes a good job inevitably has a significant impact on the final product.

The most dramatic manifestation of this was TVA's policy on unit sizes. Given the economies of scale enjoyed by larger generating units, the OEDC quickly took to building what were the largest generating units of any utility in the world. One TVA design engineer mentioned that he once checked the records on this question. He could never find written evidence that this was an explicit policy, but, he said, it was a commonly held goal. The policy was justified in part by the fact that TVA had such a large system. It could absorb large units and still maintain a given level of system reliability, while needing less generating reserve than would have been required in a smaller system. While there was some talk of TVA's responsibilities to the rest of the industry because of its size, this designer said, "Controlling costs was a conscious policy and that's why we were trying to get to bigger units. The top of the Office of Power was especially strong on keeping down the costs. There was more or less tacit agreement between them and OEDC as to how to go. Many of these choices were not made in formal meetings but in a series of informal working groups."[100]

Once the tradition of building large-size units was established, it became something of a matter of pride to the organization. At least three senior managers characterized the policy in those terms. Such a policy does have costs. Pioneering and prototype units tend to have more problems and lower reliability, especially when they first become operational. Could the talk of "tradition," "pride," and "service to the industry" be a way of rationalizing poor performance? To what extent did such emotional commitments influence TVA's choices, in the face of uncertainties in this area? Interestingly enough, TVA took a more conservative position on operating temperatures and pressures, seldom pushing on those fronts simultaneously with size increases.

Other design choices intended to minimize the capital costs of new generating capacity have also tended to reduce plant reliability. A long-time member of the Design Division said that there was "some justice" to the complaint that TVA's designers had been too concerned with capital costs and had tended to under-design as a result. As an example, faulty and insufficient coal pulverizers and undersized boilers have plagued TVA's newest coal-fired plant at Cumberland, Tennessee. Despite expensive modifications to Unit 1, as of 1975 neither of the plant's two huge units had ever run at full power for more than short periods with-out excessive slagging of the boilers. This makes it, in effect, a very costly plant, since it is not being fully utilized.[101]

The Division of Power Production, whose members operate TVA's steam plants, has been aware of the reliability conse-quences of underdesign. For instance, when the Cumberland plant was being designed, one operator reported, "We beseeched them and beseeched them [the Division of Power Resource Plan-ning and the Design Division] to be more generous on the sizing of the boiler and the number of the pulverizers, but we were turned down."[102] Given the outlook at the top of the Office of Power, until recently the operators were not able to get much of a hearing. Well down within the Office, they had no organizational basis (unlike Health and Safety) to challenge its policies before the board. Asked why the operators had not "pounded on the table harder," one operator responded, "We never got to sit at the table." He added that the Division of Power Production had actually had some opportunities in the past to express its view-point to TVA's designers and planners, but that the operators' viewpoint was being taken much more seriously today in the wake of problems like the ones at Cumberland.[103]

As with other kinds of equipment, many of the problems in de-signing precipitators hinge on the assumptions made in setting the specifications. For example, collection efficiency tends to fall significantly when gas flows are above planned volumes. Since generators are frequently run above their conservative "name-plate" rating, should the precipitator be designed to be big enough to accommodate this practice or not? Similarly, efficien-cies often fall when the sulfur content of the coal declines. Should the unit be able to handle the average coal (so that half the time it may be too small), 75 percent of the envisaged supply, 90 per-cent, or what? At every stage, the design process depends on ap-proximations and safety margins that are largely a matter of the designer's judgments.

These complexities help explain why even some relatively re-cent TVA precipitators, designed with some margin, have not worked up to specification. The precipitators at Paradise, for instance, do not operate at designed levels, and even those at Cumberland are apparently ineffective. (One engineer told us that, even with the units there operating at less than full load, the precipitators are not operating at their design efficiencies of 99 percent.) And yet, several people during our conversations claimed to have been responsible for adding safety margins in the design of the Cumberland precipitators. This only illustrates how long it takes to change engineering "rules of thumb," especially when these reflect deep strategic commitments in the organization.

Some in TVA are determined to obtain precipitators that will work. One of these is TVA's chief precipitator designer, J. Albert Hudson, whose involvement with particulate controls dates back to the decision to install mechanical collectors at Johnsonville (but to leave space for precipitators). Hudson urged that TVA turn to more reliable "European" type precipitator designs. So, on its very latest units — for example, the re-retrofit of Kingston — the specifications have been developed to the point where the traditional "American" design approach has been effectively ruled out.[104]

Part of the problem with the precipitators no doubt lay with the manufacturers, who cut corners to win bids. But the speed with which designers in different utilities have learned about and tried to compensate for manufacturers' misinformation has been related to the pressures exerted on them from inside and outside the organization. In TVA these pressures were weak until external particulate standards were established. Little improvement in design occurred until then. Furthermore, given TVA's hiring practices, no one was taken in from outside to oversee this problem area. Instead, the agency made its own mistakes and accumulated expertise only gradually.

The commitment to low-cost power has also shown itself in other ways. TVA has been willing to purchase electrical equipment abroad (despite significant congressional criticism) in order to lower equipment costs. It also took a key role in exposing the extensive electrical equipment price-fixing conspiracy.[105]

Ironically, the policy of minimizing the capital costs of generating plants — reflected in many design decisions over the years — may not in fact have met its ultimate goal of minimizing the costs of power in the long run. By lowering reliability, the policy may force the system to build more units to meet its expected load with a given probability. It also increases maintenance costs and creates a need to replace the power which would be generated by an out-of-service plant. A properly operated power system uses first those plants with the lowest operating costs. So whether a utility generates its own replacement power, or buys it from someone else, it tends to be quite expensive — since only expensive plants are available unused. In 1975, for example, TVA was forced to increase its purchases of outside power by nearly 500 percent over 1974 to meet system demand. Much of this increase was due to a disastrous fire that forced the shutdown of TVA's first nuclear plant at Browns Ferry, but reliability problems at Cumberland no doubt contributed to these heavy purchases.[106]

The same cost concerns evident in design and air quality decisions led the organization to move slowly in the area of strip-mine reclamation, even when there was board support for a more aggressive policy. Here, a potential internal "watchdog" — in this case, the Division of Forestry, Fisheries, and Wildlife Development — shied away from recommending strong corrective action. Compared to Health and Safety's role on SO_2 control, it was quite passive. As a result, the Office of Power's viewpoint dominated decision making. However, the Forestry Division's organizational situation was somewhat different from Health and Safety's and this helps to explain the difference in behavior.

A major buyer of strip-mined coal, TVA began giving serious attention to the damage caused by this method of coal production around 1960, when the agency's purchases were growing rapidly. Many inside and outside TVA felt that, as a resource development agency as well as a utility, it ought to do something about the consequences of surface mining. Concern among the general public was quite limited until the middle of the decade, but strip mining in general, and TVA's large-scale purchases of strip-mined coal, received increasing attention. Some critics of strip mining charged, in fact, that TVA's aggressive coal-purchasing efforts were a major force in creating a large strip-mining industry in the Southeast.[107]

From the first, the Office of Power opposed independent steps by TVA to require its suppliers to reclaim the land they mined. Clearly, the Office feared such action would put TVA at a cost disadvantage in relation to other utilities. For the most part, the Forestry Division shied away from advocating aggressive TVA action to control strip-mine damage. It concentrated its energies on conducting surveys of the problem, entering into discussions with state officials, and exploring the possibility of demonstration reclamation projects. It issued several reports on the subject of reclamation.[108]

In 1963 an interdivisional task force was established in which the Forestry Division was heavily represented. It tentatively advanced the argument that TVA had some responsibility for damage associated with strip mining in the Tennessee Valley and neighboring states from which TVA bought coal. It recommended that the agency insert reclamation requirements in its contracts with suppliers operating in states without strip-mine regulations. In its final report, however, the task force dropped this suggestion, although it retained the recommendation that suppliers in states with regulations should be required to comply with them. The head of the Forestry Division played down even this recommendation in a memo he wrote to accompany the report.[109]

Later that year, the TVA board issued a statement denying that TVA had a responsibility as a purchaser of coal for strip-mine damage. It pledged its support for state regulation of the strip-mine industry, which it called the best way to deal with the problem; but none of the states without a reclamation law made any progress toward adopting one, despite TVA's encouragement. The board then decided that the agency needed to take more direct steps. In 1965 it voted to include reclamation requirements in TVA's coal contracts, becoming the only major coal purchaser in the nation to do so.[110]

A Government Accounting Office investigation showed that TVA's initial requirements, adopted and administered with the involvement of the Forestry Division, were weak and poorly enforced. Until 1970 no TVA suppliers were shut down for noncompliance.[111] Several times revisions were made in the regulations. Director Frank Smith brought about some modifications of the requirements in 1968 and 1970.[112] A major strengthening of the program occurred in 1971 as the result of outside comments on an Environmental Impact Statement that TVA was compelled to prepare by an environmental suit. The Division of Forestry, however, did not take advantage of growing outside concern with strip mining to enlarge its sphere of influence within TVA.

Bruce Rogers has suggested that lack of aggressiveness on the part of the Division director, Kenneth Seigworth, may be part of the cause. Seigworth's own explanation suggests a more "systemic" reason: "I refrained from getting too far out front on the strip-mine issue because I did not wish to look like a conservation emotionalist to the TVA board—thereby jeopardizing other forestry, fisheries, and wildlife programs which I thought had much more positive and constructive benefits (both economic and environmental) to the region."[113] These other programs were, significantly, unrelated to the power program and were funded by appropriations, not revenues. Assured of a continuing program, Seigworth had little incentive to risk an unpleasant confrontation. The Division of Health and Safety, in contrast, had less choice in the matter.

In recent years, pressures on the Office of Power from inside and outside the agency have mounted, and its leadership has changed. It has responded by modifying both its strategy and its structure. Instead of "Spend as little as possible, especially on capital, in the short run," its decision rule on environmental matters has evolved into "If environmental expenditures today will help us to avoid troubles or still larger environmental expenditures tomorrow, go ahead and spend today."

The Office of Power did finally become committed to an extensive program of operational controls, as an alternative to the system-wide installation of scrubbers. Moreover, the Office agreed to invest more than $40 million in the development of a full-scale scrubber prototype at Widows Creek, probably envisioned as a gesture that would allow TVA to avoid or delay still greater expenditures.[114] Building a scrubber prototype also buttressed TVA's position that scrubbers were not yet available on a commercial basis. Additionally, Widows Creek is a site with special problems; a nearby mountain regularly receives high SO_2 levels, and TVA has settled damage complaints with neighboring farmers out of court, so that it did have to do something.[115] Recent amendments to the Clean Air Act have compelled TVA to go further with the installation of scrubbers, but this is something the Office of Power now seems prepared to do. According to one inside observer, once power system planners in the Office realized that legally TVA was going to have to comply with emission standards, they threw their support behind a settlement with the environmentalists.

Accompanying—and contributing to—the change in the Office of Power's attitudes is a certain amount of change in its internal structure and staff. Although Wessenauer formerly conducted a large amount of the Office's system-planning activities himself ("on the back of an envelope," someone said), this increasingly complex function is now carried out by a large and influential Division. And it is in this Division that the new, more future-oriented approach to environmental spending has come into play. Centralized and informal system-planning was once quite common in the utility industry. TVA's new organization in this regard reflects a structural adjustment to the increased com-

Figure 7. The $53 million limestone scrubbing facility under construction at Widows Creek. The open structure in front of the right-hand stack is the scrubber. Courtesy of the Tennessee Valley Authority.

plexity of planning tasks found in several other of our companies as well. Attention devoted to environmental matters in this Division became so great that the group often came into conflict with the Air Quality Branch over the division of environmental responsibilities. The Office's research staff has grown as well, particularly as a result of its involvement in the scrubber program. Thus, even the groups most resistant to environmental spending have begun, slowly, to modify their stance in response to changing external pressures and internal dynamics. The men now running the Office of Power also came to TVA long after the formative years of the Great Depression. Although they grew up in the organization when the low-cost power ideology was still strong, their emotional commitment to it may be less strong than that of their predecessors.

In summary, TVA illustrates the simultaneous and interactive impact of internal and external conditions in determining a utility's environmental performance. Relatively low incomes and less popular environmental concern than in other areas, combined with the fuel-price advantages of coal-fired plants, have provided the broad context for many years. Given what has until recently been a comparative isolation from both state and federal political pressures, these circumstances have provided TVA with substantial discretion in implementing environmental protection efforts. Internally, a strong strategic commitment to minimizing the costs of power—which is both rooted in the organization's history and reinforced by its internal structural arrangements—has served to determine how this discretion is utilized. Vertical promotion and limited internal mobility have produced strong group loyalties. In the context of a relatively weak top management, policy has often been formulated by negotiation among the heads of the various Divisions and Offices. Strong leadership, the apparent legitimacy of its arguments in light of the organization's history, and internal financial arrangements have all facilitated the ability of the Office of Power to minimize environmental expenditures—even when top management might have preferred a more aggressive approach.

TVA may now be on the verge of major changes. The president has apparently looked to the new chairman to restore TVA's "progressivism." (In fact, TVA has not really departed from its old "progressivism"; it seems that the definition of the word itself has changed.) The external world, which tolerated TVA's resistance to environmental regulation, is beginning to impose stronger constraints on the agency. Popular concern with the environment is growing in the Valley, and Congress has taken steps to see that TVA obeys state requirements. Yet, in an imperfectly coercive world, an organization in which socialization and self-selection produce the kind of loyalty and drive that TVA employees exhibit does not change easily.

5

The Pacific Gas and Electric Company

A sharp contrast with the Tennessee Valley Authority in many respects, the Pacific Gas and Electric Company (PG&E) serves most of the northern two-thirds of California. PG&E is one of the largest private utilities in the country, a status it has acquired and maintained in spite of the vigor and success of the public-power movement in California. It serves a population with a per capita income higher than the national average, which can afford to (and does) place a high value on wilderness preservation and environmental cleanliness. Its service area is one of extraordinary natural beauty, and the birthplace and national headquarters of the Sierra Club. (See Figure 8.)

Reflecting such circumstances, PG&E has acquired a national reputation as an industry leader in environmental consciousness. It has developed the diverse perspectives internally that allow it to propose innovative responses to external demands and the strong internal control system that makes effective implementation of innovation possible. Yet PG&E has also become involved in some of the most highly publicized and acrimonious battles with environmentalists of any of the companies we have studied. Ironically, some of the same features of the organization that account for its positive responsiveness on numerous occasions have contributed to these apparently inconsistent confrontations.

Background and Context

The Pacific Gas and Electric Company traces its corporate ancestry to a gas company that began operations in 1852 and an electric utility dating from 1879, making it one of the oldest utility organizations in the nation.[1] The current company was officially formed in October 1905 with the consolidation of the two largest existing gas and electric systems in the San Francisco area. But

Figure 8. Pacific Gas and Electric Company: service area, selected transmission lines, and generating stations. Based on annual reports of the Pacific Gas and Electric Company.

this amalgamation was only one act in a long drama of entrepreneurial adventure. In the booming environment of northern California at the end of the previous century, competing companies fought for service areas, the stronger organizations absorbing the weaker ones. The ultimate product of this process, PG&E continued its expansion until it established the limits of its present service area in 1941.

PG&E and its antecedent companies were based on hydroelectric power drawn from the foothills of the Sierras. The Folsom Water Power Company had first begun to generate power for Sacramento from its dam at Folsom in 1895. And even today, although water power alone is no longer sufficient to meet demand, as much as 60 percent of PG&E's power is derived from hydroelectric sources.[2] The technical experts upon whom the company has traditionally relied have therefore been civil engineers, who still dominate the engineering hierarchy.

Understandably, the leaders who guided the company as it absorbed 90 percent of the gas and electric companies in central and northern California were financiers and entrepreneurs. Of PG&E's first four presidents, two (John Britton, 1906-1907, and Wiggenton Creed, 1920-1927) were experienced utility lawyers, one (Frank Drum, 1907-1920) was a financier who had largely underwritten the 1905 merger, and one (August F. Hockenbeamer, 1927-1935) had been an investment broker before joining PG&E management. The fifth, James Black—who served successively as president (1935-1955), chairman of the board (1955-1963), chairman of the executive committee (July 1963-September 1963), and again chairman of the board from September 1963 until his death in 1965—was an engineer by training. Before coming to PG&E he had been the negotiator who had driven a hard bargain for the North American Company when the latter sold its California interests to PG&E in 1930.[3] From an early date (as is still true today) nonengineers have played a leading role in top management.

One early decision of PG&E's financial leaders deserves attention here because of its effect on the company's future. August Hockenbeamer, while treasurer of PG&E, came up with the idea of selling common stock to the utility's customers. This inaugurated the policy of "customer ownership" which was later adopted by utilities across the nation. Along with PG&E's practice of recruiting native Californians as executives, this policy would later be helpful to the company's ability to withstand the challenge of public ownership.[4]

The public-power movement posed problems for PG&E almost as soon as it began consolidated operations. In 1905 municipal power systems were already in existence in Palo Alto, Healdsburg, Ukiah, and Biggs, following the precedent set by Alameda in 1887. In 1913 the federal Raker Act authorized the city of San Francisco to undertake its own hydroelectric development of the Toulumne River in Yosemite National Park (the so-called Hetch Hetchy project), provided that the power was transmitted via publicly owned lines.[5] Proponents of public power also put a state constitutional amendment on the ballot three times in the 1920s which was designed to put the state of California itself directly into the water and power business. It failed to pass each time, however, partly as a result of opposition financed by PG&E, among others. Reflecting the same trend, in 1932 the voters of Sacramento authorized the establishment of a municipal electric system, although they did not approve the bonds to consummate the takeover until 1934.[6]

The biggest challenge to PG&E from the advocates of public power, however, was an outgrowth of the unsuccessful state constitutional amendments of the 1920s. This proposal had been based on an ambitious plan for hydroelectric generation developed by Colonel Robert B. Marshall of the United States Geological Survey. Despite the electoral failures, many features of Marshall's plan were incorporated into the State Water Plan of 1930. And in 1933 California voters finally passed a key piece of the plan—the Central Valley Project—along with $170 million in bonding authority. The onset of the Depression made the state reluctant to issue the bonds for the Central Valley Project. But by 1935 the Roosevelt administration was eager to promote hydroelectric projects. The Bureau of Reclamation, following the same plan, proceeded to construct a water distribution and power generating system along the Sacramento, American, and Trinity rivers, which was fully half the size of PG&E's capacity.[7]

This development was widely perceived, both in California and in Washington, D.C., as a possible step toward the establishment of a public power system in the state. After World War II the bureau pressed for congressional approval for the next steps: a backup steam plant to provide power during droughts, and transmission lines to distribute the power. Jim Black first tried to contain the threat by refusing to transmit "BuRec" power. But when it seemed likely that the public-power advocates would establish a competing system, he changed tactics. He offered to "firm up" the bureau's hydro power—that is, to guarantee its availability during times of low stream flow, and also to transmit, or "wheel," the bureau power over PG&E's lines to those municipalities that wanted to distribute it through their own local systems to individual customers. This in turn allowed Black to argue that the bureau had no need of public money to build steam power plants and transmission lines of its own. In 1955, after nearly twenty years of extensive lobbying—much of it by Black himself—Congress finally agreed, much to the disappointment of the public-power activists. The compromise has had costs for PG&E. By the 1960s eleven communities, representing about 5 percent of the total kilowatt-hours sold in PG&E's service area, had set up municipal systems to take advantage of the public power.[8]

This was not the end of attempts to create an independent public system. In the early 1960s several proposals were made for a publicly owned, long-distance, high-voltage transmission line to move electricity from the Bonneville Power Authority on the Washington-Oregon border down to California. This would make still more inexpensive wholesale public power available and (some hoped) might lead to the creation of still more municipal retail systems. Jim Black, in cooperation with several other private utilities, countered with an offer to build the lines in question with private utility company money and to guarantee wheeling and distribution of the power through the existing private grid. After extensive negotiations, PG&E built two 500-kilovolt lines extending from its Round Mountain and Indian Springs substations north of Redding, California, to its boundary with Southern California Edison's service area on the south. This made it possible for Bonneville power to reach municipalities in southern California as well as those within PG&E's service area. PG&E would have built even further north, had there not been congressional pressure for the federal government to build at least some of the lines in California.[9] Once again, Black's ingenuity had prevented the creation of an independent and competitive system, with its own transmission facilities, within PG&E's service area. (See Figure 8.)

Most recently, the municipal utilities within its service area (like those elsewhere) have taken the position that they wish to *own* part of any new generating facilities, and not simply buy power from PG&E. These eleven municipal systems, organized as the Northern California Power Association (NCPA), filed antitrust complaints and other litigation to further this aim. They claimed, among other things, that PG&E was seeking to create a monopoly and exclude them from the generating business. In response, PG&E offered NCPA members part of its own 25 percent share in the proposed (although since abandoned) Kern County nuclear plant, which was being undertaken by the Los Angeles Department of Water and Power.[10] Such a move would lower PG&E's long-run rate base, and hence its allowable profits. On the other hand, the municipal systems could have helped provide scarce, much-needed capital.

Local referenda on municipalization, which may be called by initiative petitions, continue to occur regularly within PG&E's service area. The company's opposing campaigns have usually met with success.[11] But the threat is always there. And in response to the demands of local activists, a San Francisco grand jury recently reopened investigations of PG&E's involvement with the Hetch Hetchy project and possible violations of the Raker Act.[12] In sum, although some PG&E managers argue that things have changed significantly since the 1930s and 1950s,[13] the possible growth of public power is still a major concern for PG&E. One manager after another told us that such matters were a central feature in corporate strategy: "We have to walk on eggs"; "We stand for election every year"; "The people keep us in office."[14]

As in any organization, these past experiences become the basis for current attitudes and perceptions, especially since most senior executives at PG&E have risen through the ranks. In the course of their long service, they have had direct personal experience with public-power battles and municipalization referenda. Robert Gerdes, long the dominant force in the company, was an attorney at PG&E when Sacramento municipalized its power system. He explains how the experience affected his views: "I formed the opinion early in my career that the most important thing was the best possible service at the lowest possible rates . . . Above all, we must want to protect our public image . . . This certainly has an equal place with, for example, profits. You do have to make profits to get money to build, but you'd rather maintain good standing. If the company doesn't keep that good standing, the public will take it over. If we can't do better, we shouldn't be in existence."[15] We would also hypothesize that his continuing involvement with the Central Valley Project helped solidify his long opposition to using large volumes of scarce inland water for power plant condenser cooling—a position that PG&E maintained until the difficulty of finding any acceptable combination of site and generating technology forced it to consider a wide variety of both conventional and exotic options.

PG&E also faces strong external pressures on environmental

questions. The Sierra Club was founded in California in the 1920s, and the company's service area has long been home to many environmental advocates and organizations. In the last fifteen years these groups have opposed PG&E projects more than once, often with the support and sympathy of the larger community. An area of great natural beauty, where access to the wilderness is less difficult than in many other parts of the nation, San Francisco and its environs have attracted and nurtured people sensitive to environmental values. Given the growth of population, motor vehicle travel, and population in the Bay area in recent years, one cannot help noticing the deterioration of air quality on days when the hills across San Francisco Bay, and the mountains behind them, disappear into the smoggy haze. At least one executive argued that the company's relatively good environmental record came in part from the personal sensitivity of its executives, who share the region's values.[16]

In addition to the wilderness values of its customers, PG&E also confronts intense local concern about the immediate aesthetic impact of its facilities. Much of its service area is composed of middle- and upper-middle-class suburban communities, like those on the Peninsula south of San Francisco. These towns are filled with comfortable homes on large and well-tended lots. The residents of such areas have the resources, the commitments, and the skills to take effective political action on local environmental and land-use questions. The Peninsula community of Woodside is a prime example. It fought an epic series of battles with the company over the routing of transmission lines and the undergrounding of distribution lines. In one case, the residents were so obstinate that PG&E (unwilling to put the transmission line to the newly constructed Stanford Linear Accelerator underground through Woodside unless the customer paid the extra costs) had to have the line built by the Atomic Energy Commission, relying on the federal government's powers of eminent domain and a special act of Congress.[17]

One of the more recent manifestations of environmental concern in California was the passage in 1972 of a referendum question called Proposition 20, which created a Coastal Zone Commission empowered to plan for and license all ocean-front land use and development. Along with other industrial interests, the utilities campaigned vigorously but unsuccessfully against the initiative. The Coastal Zone Commission now constitutes a major added constraint on constructing new generating capacity at coastal locations. On one occasion in 1974, under intense political pressure in the midst of the energy crisis, the commission did reverse an earlier decision in order to permit the addition of two units to Southern California Edison's nuclear generating facility at San Onofre. But most observers believe that new coastal sites are now foreclosed. Public unhappiness over proposed nuclear generating plants was, after all, a central concern of the campaign for the new law. (On the other hand, a very strict antinuclear initiative that would have imposed a moratorium on all such capacity failed on the 1976 ballot.)

The company also operates under the jurisdiction of a number of Air Pollution Control Districts, including the Bay Area APCD and the Monterey/Santa Cruz APCD, which are multicounty in scope. Under state law, the county board of supervisors, or some designated set of local officials in the multicounty agencies, serves as the board of directors of these Districts. The board has the power to promulgate regulations on air pollution emissions from stationary sources.[18] With local politicians on these boards, and occasionally politically ambitious young staff members, the APCDs have on occasion pressured the company to do as much or more than it felt was technically or economically possible. Taking on PG&E was often good press, given the pattern of local opinion.

PG&E must deal with what is perhaps the largest and most professional of all state public-utility commissions. Dating from a constitutional amendment promoted by progressive governor Hiram Johnson in 1911, the California Public Utilities Commission (originally the Railroad Commission) is composed of five members appointed by the governor. At the time of our study it was served by a staff of over 350 with an annual budget of over $10 million.[19] In contrast with their counterparts in Massachusetts, for example, most PUC staff are paid competitive salaries. Even among the utilities, they have a reputation for being competent and knowledgeable. The commission's willingness to take the initiative has been demonstrated in recent rate proceedings. Under prodding from the Environmental Defense Fund, which has an office in Palo Alto, the staff suggested that PG&E experiment with imposing peak-load pricing on large industrial customers. Recently the commission accepted the Environmental Defense Fund's suggestion that PG&E's allowed rate of return be adjusted to reward or punish it for its energy conservation efforts.[20]

In the last few years yet another state agency, the California Energy Resources Conservation and Development Commission, has come to play a significant role in constraining PG&E. This agency reviews and must approve the company's annual demand forecasts and supply plans. It, too, has a large staff of more than 300 professionals. It has already presented the California utilities with its own relatively elaborate econometric forecasting model and asked them to try to implement it in their respective areas. The commission must approve sites for new power plants and ensure that such projects meet the requirements of the California Environmental Quality Act of 1970.[21] Although its potential impact on the utility industries is great, the commission's functions are still evolving and changing. Procedural and jurisdictional questions with respect to the PUC have not yet been fully established.

The resources, aggressiveness, and competence of California state agencies are only partly due to the state's size and prosperity. Our own observations suggest that generally Californians take a greater interest in state and local politics than do residents of the Northeast, for example. They are further from Washington both geographically and psychologically, and local affairs seem relatively more important.

Not all the public pressures on PG&E, however, are on environmental or conservation issues. Public-power debates, for example, often focus on rates. PG&E must control costs in order to compete with nontaxpaying public systems. Like all private utilities, PG&E also faces important constraints from the capital market. It must maintain attractive earnings in order to raise equity and preserve its favorable bond rating (and hence its borrowing rates). Moreover, PG&E stock is widely distributed, quite literally, among the holdings of "widows and orphans" (one outcome, it seems, of August Hockenbeamer's drive for customer ownership). It must therefore maintain a credit rating attractive to the trust officers handling such investment accounts.[22]

This array of political, financial, and regulatory pressures has made capacity expansion for PG&E especially difficult in the last twenty years. With the development of the Central Valley Project, in addition to its existing resources, PG&E was able to depend on hydroelectric power until after World War II. It used steam generation only as needed, during peak-load periods or when water was low. But by the early 1950s it was clear that hydro had its limits—especially in the face of the growing demand that PG&E, like every other utility at the time, had tried to cultivate.[23] Consequently, PG&E began to build steam plants for regular use. The postwar industrial boom was hardly the doing of PG&E executives; but since the late 1930s and early 1940s, when it was clear that PG&E could no longer grow by expanding its service area, the company had campaigned vigorously to increase electricity demand.

The company's primary reliance on hydro power had left its mechanical engineering group relatively weak. An outsider, C. C. Whelchel, was brought in from Niagara Mohawk in the late 1940s as head of the mechanical engineering department to correct the situation. He took a leading role in planning PG&E's expansion of generating capacity.[24] In 1955 an executive reshuffling occurred, prompted by Jim Black's retirement as president and his appointment as chairman of the board. The new president was Norman Sutherland, sympathetic to Whelchel's views. In the same year, the company announced that henceforth it would place major reliance on nuclear power. Two years later, PG&E demonstrated the earnestness of its intentions by contributing $500,000 to an experimental nuclear power station at Vallecitos. And it then planned and built what was one of the first privately owned utility nuclear reactors in the country—the 63 MW plant at Humboldt Bay.[25]

Thus, long before most other utilities had seriously considered the nuclear option, PG&E had made a major commitment in this direction. Sutherland, however, realized that siting the new generating facilities was likely to be a major problem in the future. He charged two civil engineers with the task of locating future sites. After exploring approximately one hundred options over the course of five years, they narrowed the list down to twenty or thirty and let top management make the final choices. The resulting "Super System," designed to serve PG&E through 1980, was announced with some fanfare in February 1963.[26] This admirable attempt at long-range planning was not supported by as much staff work—particularly in the area of geological studies—as hindsight now suggests would have been desirable. In the final analysis, *none* of the Super System sites has ever been used.

Despite Sutherland's commitment, since Humboldt Bay the company has succeeded in building only one nuclear plant, at Diablo Canyon (not a Super System site), which is still surrounded by debate on geological questions and other licensing issues. Although one unit is complete and the other nearly so, as of this writing, in part due to the need to respond to questions raised by the Three Mile Island accident, the Nuclear Regulatory Commission has not yet granted it an operating license.[27] In part this reflects the physical difficulties of the situation. The coast of Northern California, unfortunately, is one of the most heavily faulted and earthquake-prone parts of the continental United States. In addition, much of the coast is composed of stark, lovely headlands and unspoiled, windswept beaches; it has great emotional appeal to many residents of the region. This has led to a combination of regulatory constraint and popular protest that has been very difficult to deal with.

Why then not locate nuclear capacity inland in geologically less hazardous areas? Unfortunately, doing so would involve using large amounts of water. Yet hundreds of millions of state and federal dollars have been spent to relieve an apparently critical water shortage in inland areas. Nuclear generating plant designs that require less water (by using dry cooling towers or the air-cooled version of the high-temperature gas reactor) are still experimental, risky, and very expensive.

Air quality considerations in PG&E's service area make fossil-fuel plants hardly more attractive. The San Francisco Bay area is a great natural bowl, with a narrow opening to the west through the Golden Gate. Thermal inversions, coupled with the prevailing westerly winds, often result in polluted air piling up inside the Bay. As a result of recent residential and industrial development along the southern and eastern shores, air quality has deteriorated noticeably. The combination of strong sunlight, hydrocarbons, and NO_x produces classic smog conditions.[28] Further north along the Sacramento Delta, industrial development has brought similar results. Some areas of the Delta risk violating state and federal ambient air quality standards. The air is cleaner in parts of the Central Valley, but even here local air pollution control authorities have shown themselves willing to develop and enforce stringent air pollution regulations.[29]

PG&E, in the past, was able to meet strict sulfur dioxide and particulate emission limitations by burning natural gas. Its larger fossil-fuel units, however, have at times created NO_x problems. Moreover, as natural gas supplies have tightened in recent years, the Federal Power Commission has designated power plants as low-priority users. This makes it unlikely that natural gas can be relied upon to such a degree in the future. Although very low-sulfur Indonesian oil is available, it is not as clean as natural gas and is increasingly expensive. The recent increase in the use of oil has raised ambient sulfur concentrations in some industrial areas, leading California air pollution regulators to require the use of oil with a sulfur content below .25 percent. Indeed, the Air Resources Board chairman recently suggested that unless ambient sulfur levels improve, the board may be forced to require a .1

percent ceiling on oil sulfur content.[30] This would imply that only the very lowest-sulfur oils in the world could be used, putting the company at the mercy of the international oil situation.

On the other hand, California air pollution regulations may effectively prohibit the use of coal in power plants, given available control technologies. Only very stringent control measures at the technological frontier might make such plants possible. Even with such controls, it is uncertain whether coal-fired plants would be acceptable. While other California utilities have constructed large-scale joint coal-burning projects out of state, which have been the focus of considerable environmental debate, PG&E has only recently decided to participate in two such proposed projects. Yet federal policies on nonsignificant degradation of air quality and recent California guidelines on out-of-state projects make this source, too, quite problematic.

In part because all options for new generating technology are so uncertain, PG&E has been the nation's leading company in developing geothermal energy — where steam produced naturally underground is tapped and used to drive the turbo generator. Having begun work on the first such unit at the Geysers site over twenty years ago, in 1958, PG&E now relies on geothermal power for 8 percent of its generating capacity (575 MW in five units). Another 660 MW of geothermal capacity is under construction.

In summary, PG&E is a company with a long tradition of entrepreneurial vigor and political self-consciousness. It seeks to maintain its acceptability with an often skeptical and politicized public, in a service area that contains more public-power activists and environmental enthusiasts than most others in the country. With an effective state Public Utilities Commission and myraid state and local environmental agencies with which to contend, PG&E has not had an easy time of it in recent years. Indeed, at the moment, it is not at all clear that there are *any* options for new capacity that simultaneously will satisfy technical, financial, and environmental requirements. What sorts of strategy and organizational structure have emerged in response to this pressure? What implications do they have for PG&E's corporate decision making?

Internal Organization

To satisfy external demands, PG&E's management faces two principal tasks. First, it must control costs in order to keep rates down while providing good service and environmental protection. Second, management must be able to identify changing public attitudes and then quickly choose and implement effective strategic responses. It is not surprising, then, that certain structural characteristics have emerged at PG&E that facilitate accomplishing these tasks. Most noticeably, a variety of nonengineering, outside-oriented groups — including a system of divisional managers who handle local problems on a decentralized basis — have considerable influence over corporate decisions.[31] In addition, a strong and deep control system, with a substantial number of general-management posts, allows top management to control the organization's behavior effectively. In many respects, then, PG&E is very different from TVA and has precisely the capacity to notice and respond to change that TVA has lacked. (See Figure 9.)

Like any system, the management structure at PG&E has some deficiencies that in a sense reflect its virtues. Strong controls, which facilitate implementation, can also discourage dissent. Tight budgets can limit not only costs but also advanced planning. And diverse perspectives can be difficult to integrate, especially when the technical and nontechnical sides of the company have differing views.

The most noteworthy among the nonengineering groups at PG&E, given its size and the scope of its activities, is the Law Department. At the time of our study, the Department (along with all other nontechnical functions) reported to the vice-chairman of the board and former general counsel Richard Peterson, and not to John Bonner, the president. The thirty-seven lawyers in the Department handled almost every legal matter affecting the company — including securities registration, contracts, environmental regulations, rates, pensions, and antitrust matters. Boston Edison, in contrast, had only seven full-time staff attorneys and made use of outsiders as necessary. All legal work at the Southern Company is done by outside firms retained for that purpose. TVA, too, now has a large legal department, but PG&E's lawyers are far more involved in company affairs of all sorts than their counterparts at TVA seem to be. The strength of PG&E's lawyers reflects the views of Robert Gerdes, who returned to the company as an assistant general counsel in 1944 on the condition that such a comprehensive legal organization be created.[32]

Gerdes' role in the company in turn reflects its historical need to defend itself against the threat of public power. As an attorney for the company in the early 1930s, he was deeply involved in PG&E's conflict with the advocates of municipal utility ownership

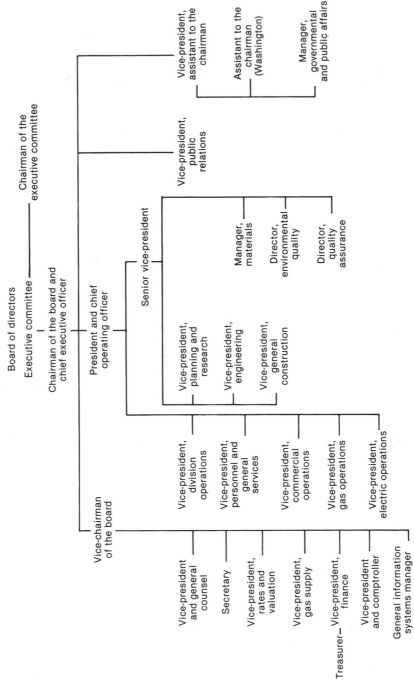

Figure 9. Pacific Gas and Electric Company: partial organization chart, fall 1972. Based on documents supplied by the Pacific Gas and Electric Company.

in Sacramento. He left the company in 1935 to go into private practice. But in 1944, in the midst of the congressional controversy over the Bureau of Reclamation's involvement with the Central Valley Project, PG&E president Jim Black asked Gerdes to return. Serving successively as general counsel, executive vice-president, president, chairman, and chairman of the executive committee for most of the last thirty years, Gerdes was, until his retirement in July 1977, in a position to oversee structural developments.[33]

Perhaps as a result of Gerdes' influence, the lawyers at PG&E are deeply involved in all phases of corporate decision making. At the time of our study, for example, the positions of treasurer, vice-president for gas supply, vice-president and assistant to the chairman, and manager of the Commercial Department were filled by lawyers who began their service in the Law Department — many of them hired by Gerdes himself.[34] As a result of the most recent reshuffling of top management in July 1979, lawyers occupied three of the top four positions in the company. Moreover, an engineer at PG&E (unlike, as we shall see, his counterpart at the Los Angles Department of Water and Power) would *not*, as a rule, go to talk to the Costal Zone Commission or local air quality regulators without the help or active participation of an appropriate member of the Law Department.[35]

What is the impact on PG&E of having such a strong legal group? The legal perspective emphasizes the legitimacy of conflicting perspectives, the political bargaining aspects of a situation, and the importance of complying with the law. Thus, lawyers tend at least to be aware of the need to consider how the other side might react. Legal education does not by itself necessarily create a tendency toward concilation. Lawyers surely have been known to exacerbate tensions by haggling over details or by opting in favor of litigation (as we shall see in the case of Boston Edison). The PG&E Law Department, however, appears to us to have taken its perspective from Robert Gerdes. He had a forceful personality, formal authority, strong views in favor of avoiding confrontation, and PG&E's strong control system at his disposal. He recruited many of the lawyers personally. It is not surprising that new lawyers joining the company were socialized to his view of "better a bad settlement than a good lawsuit," given the company's external situation. A few may have grumbled privately that he was too willing to compromise, but his views nevertheless prevailed.[36]

The lawyers at PG&E continue to function as a "group" even

when their formal functions transcend bureaucratic lines. Personal relationships, professional training, and shared experience within the company all contribute to this. Furthermore, the diagonal mobility of promising managers tends to weaken their attachment to any particular bureaucratic unit. In such circumstances, early associations and alliances tend to remain significant factors in a manager's motivation.

Another group within PG&E that is formally responsible for dealing with outsiders—and crucial to the company's success in dealing with environmentalists—is the Government and Public Affairs Department. At the time of our study, it reported directly to Fred Mielke, vice-president and assistant to the chairman. A key figure in this Department has been Kenneth Diercks, now retired. Diercks, a long-service employee, worked closely with Robert Gerdes over the years and had considerable influence with him. Diercks handled relations with local governments and activist groups, and had wide contacts with political and environmental leaders. It was through him, in fact, that Doris Leonard, a well-known conservationist now on the PG&E board, first came into contact with the company. Diercks worked his way up from the tough "south of Mission" part of San Francisco, ultimately to be chief of the department. He played a significant role in PG&E policy making whenever public protests seemed likely to cause difficulties.[37] As one senior manager put it, "Ken has the confidence of Mr. Gerdes and an extraordinary amount of influence on the thirty-second floor. Sometimes they have relied on him as if he were the only guy in the company with political knowledge . . . Still, he is very effective with opposition groups . . . and he knows an awful lot of people in the Democratic Party."[38]

Diercks, like the lawyers, advocated a flexible, negotiation-oriented approach for PG&E. His ability to obtain concessions from PG&E's adversaries depended on his ability to influence the company to be flexible. Only in that way could he convince outside groups that negotiation was more in their interest than confrontation. (As is often the case in an organization, strategic recommendations—consciously or not—turn out to be consistent with group interest, since either engineering or formal legal solutions would not require the same negotiating function.)

The Public Relations Office at PG&E is another outside-oriented group, headed by a vice-president who (unlike all other vice-presidents except for the assistant to the chairman) reported at the time of our study directly to the chairman of the board. This Office, however, tends to focus on such traditional public-relations tasks as advertising, education, and community service, leaving the more political aspects of public relations to other Offices in the company.

Another source of outside-oriented ideas in PG&E is the company's large divisional structure. PG&E's service area is divided into thirteen Divisions. Each of these is headed by a manager responsible for most of what happens in his region from day to day. The Division managers are senior figures in the company. Each supervises the physical provision of services. Each also stays in touch with local political developments, and responds to complaints from individuals, organizations, and local governments. The Division manager in turn has from two to four District managers reporting to him, in addition to assistants for marketing, gas operations and electrical operations.[39] As John Bonner, then president of the company explained, "To most of our customers, the Division manager *is* the company."[40] Although many managers are engineers by training, their experience and responsibilities in the Divisions tend to make them conscious of public-relations considerations. As one staff member explained, the "Division-level philosophy" at PG&E lays much emphasis on "being cool under fire, easy going, a nice guy . . . It's important to be able to meet people well." At the same time, the authority of Division managers in their own region is great. Even Government Affairs must secure permission from the divisional office before intervening within its boundaries. And senior executives will often clear even routine official visits to an area with the Division manager.[41]

The divisional structure, like that of the Legal Department, is a source of senior executives with orientation to more than technical concerns. A number of Division managers were seen as "rising stars" in the company at the time of our study. Several key vice-presidents, including those for personnel and general services, and for commercial operations, have served in that capacity. These jobs are considered good training, since they offer all-around management experience. The whole set of District and Division posts constitutes a distinct career system. Promising candidates move from smaller Districts to larger ones, from District to Division, and from smaller to more important Divisions.[42]

There are also units on the engineering side of the company with externally oriented responsibilities. An environmental group, for example, consisting of five professionals, reports to the senior vice-president for engineering and construction. The members of this group are technically well qualified and adept at public appearances. They act both as internal consultants and as witnesses in hearings or speakers at public meetings. Their roles are relatively unstructured, and they often develop their own assignments.[43]

Although we can only speculate, it appears to us that the small size of this staff is due in part to the fact that other units in PG&E were already conducting many of the functions the environmental unit might have performed when that Department was formally created. Furthermore, the Department's leadership has not aggressively fought for control over environmentally related activities. Thus, this group does not take the lead in preparing impact statements, nor does it oversee research and development activities (unlike its counterparts at Boston Edison or the Southern Company). Its influence is thus primarily informal, arising from the personal knowledge of and respect accorded to its members.

The engineering units responsible for general strategic planning at PG&E — which include transmission and generation planning, load forecasting, and the rapidly growing power plant siting group — report to the vice-president for planning and research.[44] The creation of this structure in 1971 raised some of the same problems internally that a similar move created in the Los Angeles Department of Water and Power. Much of PG&E's most challenging and attention-getting tasks were shifted to this new unit — which did not please people in other parts of the structure. The Land Department, for example, lost some functions to the growing siting group, which also coordinates work on environmental impact statements. And the mechanical engineers — whose main role had been the analysis of unit cost and of the relative efficiency of various options — wound up with still less to do relative to generation planning. Some of them were not pleased by this, given that the new structure was led by civil engineers.[45]

Yet civil engineers have always done much of the generation planning and site selection in the company. Siting used to be done by a few staff people on special assignment working directly with those at the highest levels of the company. Overall system planning was part of the Civil Engineering Department. Certainly, at least in the postwar years, the engineering leaders have been and still are mostly civil engineers. In 1975, for example, the president, the senior vice-president for engineering, the vice-president for planning and research, the vice-president for engineering, and the chiefs of the Siting and Land Departments were all civil engineers. Just as the lawyers dominate the nonengineering side of the company, the civils seem to dominate the engineering side. Several of the staff members we interviewed, civils and noncivils alike, attested to this. One said, "You've got to have a civil engineering degree from Berkeley . . . Civils run the company."[46]

As noted, the role of civil engineers appears to derive in part from PG&E's historical dependence on hydroelectric power. This same experience with hydroelectric generation in turn seems to have had other effects. For example, compared to TVA, PG&E engineers have followed a conservative policy on unit size. PG&E's opposition to the use of inland water for cooling purposes may also reflect this fact.

The top management of PG&E does seem to have effective control over this set of quasi-competitive groups—much more so than does TVA's general manager, for example. Responsibilities overlap, so that no one group has a monopoly of expertise on any given problem. The size, complexity, and fluidity of the company's top management structure are also crucial factors. When this study was conducted, no less than six people shared general management responsibilities at PG&E: Shermer Sibley, the chief executive officer and chairman of the board; John Bonner, president and chief operating officer; Richard Peterson, vice-chairman of the board; Robert Gerdes, chairman of the executive committee of the board; Fred Mielke, vice-president and assistant to the chairman; and Dean Worthington, senior vice-president for engineering and construction. In the intervening years there have been several other reorganizations, but the general structure of top management has remained similar. With so many general managers, there are more people to share the work, ask questions, and supervise than at TVA. Effective control of a company as large and complex as PG&E depends in part on having a group that is large enough to carry the substantial burdens involved.

The nature of PG&E's executive structure, however, has created some obstacles to effective strategic integration. To an outsider there appear to be two distinguishable lines of authority, one headed by lawyers and the other by engineers. When Gerdes succeeded Sutherland as chairman of the board in 1965 (and Sibley moved from vice-president and general manager to president), four senior vice-presidential positions were created—engineering, operations, law, and finance—in an effort to establish a more collegial managerial group than had been characteristic of the Black-Sutherland period. After successive reshuffling of top executive slots and titles, the younger two of the four initial incumbents, John Bonner and Richard Peterson, had by 1972 assumed the posts of president and vice-chairman of the board, respectively. They effectively divided engineering and nonengineering responsibilities between them. Only Sibley and Gerdes—as chairman of the board and chairman of the executive committee—really supervised the whole company. It was only at this most senior level that the two chains of command converged.

With the death of Shermer Sibley in 1976 and Robert Gerdes' retirement a year later, Peterson and Bonner moved into the two top positions. Reflecting the two executives' areas of expertise, senior engineering managers reported mainly to Bonner and nonengineers to Peterson. When Bonner and Peterson retired in 1979, the same dual reporting pattern continued, with engineers reporting to the new president, Barton Shackelford, an engineer, and nonengineers reporting to the new chairman, Fred Mielke, a lawyer.

The fact that the executive structure has changed several times illustrates a general flexibility which enhances top management's control. Senior managers have every reason to aspire to further advancement, since they can expect that new management posts will be created to fit available talent. In recent years, for example, several new vice-presidential jobs have been created. In each case, it seems probable that the slots were shaped both to meet corporate needs and to fit into the career paths and suit the skills of talented individuals.[47]

The most direct source of strong control for top managers at PG&E stems from their involvement both in substantive policy making and in personnel decisions. Senior executives have come up through the organization. They know many of their subordinates and their subordinates' job problems from personal experience. They believe that their own participation in personnel choices is justified, much more so than if they had come in from the outside. As John Bonner explained, "Down to the manager level [which includes some one hundred individuals] we all know each other pretty well . . . We've worked with each other over the years."[48]

In contrast, Boston Edison has often been led by "outsiders." Even now it has a president who joined the company in mid-career. Many of the top executives of the Southern Company, although long associated with the organization as members of closely related law firms, did not come up directly through the ranks. In the public companies, top managers have often had long service. Yet in TVA, personnel choices are heavily decentralized, and at the Los Angeles Department of Water and Power they are governed by civil service restrictions; in both these cases, top managers are not fully able to use their resulting knowledge in personnel matters.

The involvement of PG&E's top executives extends well beyond personnel matters. Particularly on the engineering side, senior management participates in many of the details of planning and decision making.[49] This brings them into regular contact with a wide variety of people throughout the company and reinforces their willingness to become involved in personnel matters quite far down into the organization. The lawyers operate in a less centralized manner, at least on routine matters. Perhaps they feel more need for fast responses and personal "feel" in negotiating situations, and perhaps this works toward decentralization. On critical decisions, however, top management becomes deeply involved. Indeed, it can take over detailed operational control.[50]

To an extent, this pattern (which dates from the days when Jim Black was president) appears to be a response to the pressures that PG&E confronts. The outside world often demands rapid, decisive action, in a context where wrong decisions could be very costly. This has led to a tradition — developed and reinforced by a series of strong executives — of having top management make key decisions. Richard Peterson stated the matter succinctly: "Outside forces demand personal and rapid responses . . . and such forces contrive to push decisions to the top."[51]

In such an environment, being noticed by top management can be of significant aid to advancement. Middle- and lower-level managers we interviewed agreed that "exposure" at meetings — and luck in drawing assignments that provide such exposure — are helpful to success at PG&E. Top managers have many demands on their time. Because they cannot know everyone equally well, decisions about promotion can be influenced by whom one happens to know. It is always tempting to pick a trusted individual with whom one has had a good working relationship in the past. This process in turn can reinforce long-standing group ties. The men who succeed under such a system tend to be personable, intelligent, hard-working, and able to handle themselves in public. In contrast, at the Los Angeles Department of Water and Power, an exam-based civil service system places much less premium on interpersonal skills.

The need for cost-consciousness at PG&E, strengthened by the ever-present threat of public takeover, enhances the tendency for effective top-management control. One employee, for example, described ex-president John Bonner as "a tight man with a dollar: if he gives you $1.00, he wants $1.27 back."[52] Capital-expenditure decisions and hiring are tightly controlled by the top. Even Division managers must submit annual capital budgets detailing proposed expenditures over a few thousand dollars. While Division managers are given considerable latitude for authorizing work required by new business, load growth, or storms, there is much tighter control over expenditures for offices, service centers, and equipment.[53]

The strong and deep control system has its costs as well as its benefits. It may be inevitable, in such circumstances, that middle managers will complain about their lack of authority. And some of those we interviewed at PG&E felt quite strongly on this point. One manager, for example, reported that when he was given his job his boss told him, "God dammit, you don't make any decision I don't know about."[54] Such a system can create bottlenecks and delays, so that the company is not always able to respond as rapidly as it might wish. "Things move very slowly at top levels of the company," one senior supervisor explained.[55] On the other hand, PG&E can move rapidly and flexibly when confronted with a crisis. However, the need to attend to such crises (always present to some degree) can lead to inattention to more slowly developing problems.

The assiduous efforts PG&E makes to control costs also can lead to personnel problems. Since the compensation of senior executives is public information, the company feels under pressure to keep such salaries down. Indeed, were it not for the fact that the Bay area offers relatively few engineering and management opportunities, PG&E might have more difficulty holding on to top technical and executive talent. As it is, several middle-level executives told us that some of their better people had left because of limited opportunities for salary increases, particularly compared to the high-technology growth industries of the Bay area. Restrictions on hiring designed to control costs also mean that good people tend to be overworked. Able younger employees can become so valuable to their short-handed Departments that they may not get the range of experience that is the best preparation for management responsibility. Several middle managers told us that they could not rotate technical people as much as they would like to because they had neither the time nor the money to train replacements.[56]

In such circumstances, long-range planning is relatively difficult. Instead, everyone becomes involved in trying to solve the current crisis. As one executive put it, "Everyone is so damn busy he doesn't have time to think about twenty years from now." Innovation in such circumstances is limited because no one has the time for it. An attempt to build a long-range corporate planning staff took several years because the proponents of the plan got caught up in a series of current crises.[57]

The power that top management at PG&E holds over careers and advancement within the company understandably puts those further down in the hierarchy in awe of the "thirty-second floor." This is illustrated by the fact that one executive thought it quite remarkable that another "stands up and talks to top management as if they don't scare him at all!" Subordinates at PG&E are eager for approval and anxious not to give offense. They will take pains to check things out with the boss, "just to make sure it wouldn't give him any problems." That, after all, is what a strong control system can be used to do — to ensure compliance. But such practices can also limit criticism and good ideas. Many professed to believe, for example, that one middle executive would have gotten much further if he had been less outspoken. Under such circumstances, top managers who are believed to be especially sensitive to criticism can make serious mistakes, because subordinates will be reluctant to disagree with them. No one, after all, wants to tell the chief the bad news, if the messenger is likely to become a marked man.

Ironically, when subordinates always "check with the boss" the question of who is responsible for what can become quite unclear. As one senior manager said, "When management doesn't delegate, how can anyone get pinned with the responsibility for a mistake? No one is ever responsible and no one ever gets blamed."[58]

One final element of PG&E's structure deserves mention, especially in contrast with TVA. This is the role of the board of directors. The board is composed, like most of its counterparts in private industry, primarily of local bankers and businessmen.[59] The board's executive committee was unusually active, at the time of our study meeting weekly for about an hour. Again, like most boards, the PG&E board depends on top management for information and analysis. Disagreement with top management is thus unusual. There have been occasions, however, when the board has delayed acting on certain management proposals. And having to prepare matters for submission to the board tends to force management to analyze its own proposals very carefully. The board is accorded substantial deference. One executive stated,

"When a board member coughs or sneezes, there is a great tendency to interpret that as a comment. If someone on the board asks a question, everyone drops everything to answer it."[60]

At the time of our study, chairman Shermer Sibley did not try to bring to the fore any internal disagreements about company policy. Discussions at the weekly meetings of senior managers were largely confined to reports on what was occurring *outside* the company.[61] This contrasts with the agendas of comparable gatherings at Boston Edison or the Southern Company. In the latter organizations such meetings were used to expose internal conflicts as a step toward developing a consensus on company policy. Several executives at PG&E complained that the weekly Monday meetings of the senior managers who constitute the president's advisory committee consumed scarce and valuable time and were of little value—"prayer meetings," someone called them.[62] (On the other hand, we must note that there were extensive formal and informal consultations, quite apart from these meetings, whenever major decisions were made at PG&E.)

The creation of the Planning and Research Department on the engineering side of the company seems to have been prompted in part by these problems of integration. The Department is supposed to provide an overall focus for technical planning activities. Indeed, a similar group at Ontario Hydro has had considerable success in this respect. But PG&E's Planning Department, unlike the Concept Group at Hydro, is not in a position to act as the *overall* integrating unit. It is merely one more participant in the internal decision process.

In order to provide greater integration, PG&E has tried other alternatives. For example, a complex interdepartmental task force was set up to try to pull together diverse perspectives in the case of one major generation project. The idea for such a task force grew out of the discovery that the plans, on the basis of which the project was well under way, might possibly lead to future violations of ambient air quality standards under certain circumstances. Some in the company argued that this discovery implied a need for a reorganization of planning activities to include more nonengineering input, in order to take such potential legal difficulties into account at an early stage. Rather than make a permanent change in the planning process, however, an interdepartmental task force was created to review the particular problem, with an engineer as chairman and a nonengineer as vice-chairman.[63]

Reactions to the task force experience were mixed. Some saw it as a creative departure. Others complained that the chairman did not have enough authority to secure the effective participation of the various Departments. Part of the reason for this may have been because top management did not fully delegate decision-making authority to the group, so that busy managers did not see it as a high-priority activity. Lacking clear signals from their superiors, the committee members may have been reluctant to take a strong position. Top management made the final decision, in any case.

The task force process, to an outsider, appears to reflect a certain change in the role of the engineers in PG&E in response to changing external circumstances. Historically, the civil engineers would have acted relatively independently to design and build new dams as a technical matter within their sphere of expertise — once the money had been raised, the market secured, and the threat of public power fended off. Now, however, engineering decisions are at the very core of the environmental controversies facing the company. As a result, lawyers, government-affairs types, and other nontechnical staff are more involved than ever in purely "technical" questions.[64]

Environmental Decisions

Environmental pressures have confronted PG&E in three principal areas: strong citizen pressure to underground transmission and distribution lines through residential areas; regulatory controls and broader public concern over air quality; and geological and aesthetic concerns about nuclear plant siting. In the first two problem areas, PG&E's lawyers and public-affairs specialists initiated policies that are very much "positively responsive." But in the area of nuclear plant siting, the company has been involved in some of the most bruising and costly environmental confrontations of any company in our study.

PG&E's approach to undergrounding transmission lines is a striking example of an imaginative response to increasing public concern. Although distribution facilities in various downtown areas were often routinely placed underground, PG&E, like most other utilities, had done relatively little undergrounding in suburban residential areas up through the post-World War II period. Beginning in the late 1950s, however, public pressure in this regard began to increase in the more affluent parts of the company's service area.[65] In 1958, for example, the city of Walnut Creek tried to force undergrounding by means of a local ordinance. However much the company wanted to avoid a confrontation, PG&E clearly could not afford such a precedent. It therefore decided to appeal the matter to the California Public Utilities Commission. The PUC agreed, in 1959, that it was perfectly reasonable for the utility to insist that anyone who wanted underground service had to pay the extra costs, in those cases where the company for its own reasons did not choose to provide it.

Nevertheless, public concern increased steadily. More and more communities tried various legal tactics to force the company to underground the lines within their borders. Richard Peterson, then general counsel, recognized that the company needed a way to avoid these disputes. He also was concerned that the tendency to respond to the most vociferous communities created an unfair cost burden on the rest of PG&E's customers. Peterson therefore proposed that the company annually devote a certain percentage of residential revenues from each political jurisdiction to undergrounding the lines in that jurisdiction. Specific projects would be chosen by the elected political bodies in each area. The plan was to get the PUC to adopt this formulation as a mandatory regulation. As recently retired assistant general counsel Bill Johns put it, "We decided to preempt these moves [to force undergrounding]. We cut them off at the pass."

PG&E's legal and community-relations expertise was crucial to the development of this plan. This was not simply a question of a utility, faced with inevitable regulations, working for a less stringent set of provisions. In this case what was impressive was the recognition that by taking the initiative to impose *added* constraints on itself, a company could disarm outside critics and thus be better off in the long run. In view of the diversity of outlooks within PG&E, however, obtaining internal agreement on the proposal was not easy. Top management ultimately overruled dissenters lower down in the hierarchy. "It was rammed down their throats," one executive explained. Still, vigorous disputes continued over such details as the percentage of revenues to devote to the program. The final figure of 2 percent was picked by top management; it was in the middle of a range of suggestions, and reflected the guiding principle that the cost of the project should not require future rate increases — assuming continued rates of productivity gain.

Developing the plan took about a year. In June 1965 the California Public Utilities Commission responded to PG&E's suggestion and opened proceedings on undergrounding. The company was able to convince San Diego Gas & Electric to go along. But

Southern California Edison remained opposed, partly on the grounds that local governments and utilities would not be able to work together. PG&E had a different view, as it said in print: "Edison's objections . . . are premised on an inaccurate and pessimistic characterization of cooperative ventures between utilities and local government . . . PG&E had found that it is possible to work with local government planning bodies . . . in an orderly and efficient manner."[66] And the company was able to convince a number of municipalities to support the proposal. Its success was in part a result of generosity. In addition to the 2 percent fund, the plan contained a proposal to lower the charges to homeowners who voluntarily paid for undergrounding on their own. It made them liable only for the difference between the cost of the underground line and *new* overhead service.[67] Previously they had had to pay for undergrounding minus only the (negligible) salvage value of existing lines.

In September 1967, the PUC accepted PG&E's plan with two changes. First, the commission chose to fix the percentage *ad hoc* each year, in order to avoid arguments between the company and some cities over how large the program should be. (In fact, however, the commission's figures have regularly been about 2 percent, as PG&E had proposed.) Second, the PUC decided to apportion the funds not according to revenues, as PG&E had suggested, but in proportion to *numbers of customers* in each area. This favored the relatively less affluent, lower-use communities.

The undergrounding program, which has since been refined and expanded, now serves the functions that Richard Peterson foresaw. Division marketing managers work year by year with local governments to develop projects. When necessary, they will intervene with the central office to help local people get what they want. There is relatively little controversy over undergrounding—in part because local citizens now have other worries. In 1973 the PUC and the California League of Cities did urge more vigorous prosecution of the program, however, since rising costs had begun to reduce the volume of work being accomplished. More recently, the rise in rates and revenues due to oil price increases has brought revenues so high that less than 2 percent of such funds are being spent.[68]

Many features of PG&E's strategy and structure are reflected in this story. Nonengineers took an initiative and removed a source of public complaints. A concern over costs led to the initial disputes and influenced the company's specific proposals. Top management played a key role in defining policy in the context of internal disagreement at lower levels. The company was willing and able to work with local governments and, if necessary, to disagree with other utilities. The Divisions played an important role in implementation and in fostering close community relations. Similar features of the organization and its attitudes are reflected in its policies on air pollution control.

Until the late 1960s PG&E had comparatively few air pollution problems. It burned natural gas only in a series of small units, many of which were not located in heavily urbanized areas.[69] The company thereby avoided the SO_2 and particulate problems that plagued the coal- and oil-burning utilities in the East. But, like the Los Angeles Department of Water and Power in the 1960s, PG&E began to encounter problems with regard to its emission of oxides of nitrogen, a major contributor to smog. In the early 1960s smog of the Los Angeles sort was not yet a serious problem in the Bay area. But during the winter of 1967-68, when the company fired up its two new 740 MW units at the Moss Landing station (thereby tripling the capacity of the plant to 2,000 MW), a detached brownish-yellow cloud about a half mile long would sometimes appear downwind of the plant.[70] Moss Landing station is on Monterey Bay, close to the city of Monterey and not too far north of the well-to-do resort community of Carmel. With aesthetics, property values, and the tourist business at stake, civic concern in a year of heightened environmental consciousness was considerable. The local newspaper and its publisher turned the matter of the yellow cloud into a cause. There were editorials, speeches, and public marches. (For a view of Moss Landing, see Figure 10.)

PG&E's divisional office serving the Monterey area was the first part of the company to call attention to the problem. However, it soon became a concern of top management. As Robert Gerdes later observed, "We were faced with a severe bonfire."[71] Unsure as to what exactly was causing the problem, the company commissioned a series of outside and inside studies. These revealed that the new boilers were discharging almost twice as much nitrogen oxide per unit of fuel burned as any other facility in the system. In part this was because they operated at such high temperatures (they were PG&E's first "supercritical" units). In view of their large absolute size, they produced a lot of NO_x—and this, in turn, caused the cloud. Because of the high stacks at the plant, ground-level concentrations were acceptable. The issue was one of aesthetics, not health. A new conference, called to announce the findings, failed to quiet local protests. Robert Gerdes then

Figure 10. The Moss Landing generating station near Monterey, California, whose initial nitrogen oxide discharges caused significant local concern. Courtesy of the Pacific Gas and Electric Company.

"pounded the table" and insisted on placing an advertisement in the local paper saying that the problem *would* be corrected. His unconditional commitment "froze the hearts" of some of the company's engineers, who were not at all sure that the emissions could be reduced at a reasonable cost.[72] But Gerdes prevailed, explaining that "the only way to put out the fire was to make it unqualified . . . We had to handle the matter, and we did."[73]

This episode illustrates how centralization and a strong control system can produce environmentally sensitive decisions when top management so chooses. Gerdes promised that PG&E would clean up an existing plant, even with major technical uncertainties and without any regulations compelling it to do so. The Los Angeles Department of Water and Power, on the other hand, persisted in trying to build a new plant that did not even comply with formally established NO_x limits. The explanation of this difference lies in a whole series of internal and external features of the two organizations.

As it turned out, the engineers developed some new methods that achieved major NO_x reductions and eliminated the offending cloud. Nevertheless, the Monterey/Santa Cruz Air Pollution Control District, in response to local political pressures, has imposed steadily more stringent emissions standards over the years. One member of this agency's board said some years ago that he was tired of setting standards PG&E could meet and wanted to enact just one they could *not* satisfy, for a change! In such circumstances, an effective response demands precisely the tight control, the political sophistication, and the sensitivity that PG&E's internal structure is able to produce.

PG&E's policy of avoiding direct confrontation has led to serious problems when the constraints imposed by public agencies conflict with one another. Company efforts to devise a cooling system for its fossil-fired generating unit, Pittsburg 7, provide a striking example. The 735 MW facility was planned initially as a standby, in the event that then-pending nuclear projects were delayed. When these projects did in fact get behind schedule, there was serious pressure to get the unit on line fast enough to avoid capacity problems.[74]

As work progressed, cooling water became a major problem. According to the provisions of the California Water Quality Act of 1970, the relevant state agency had to certify that the high-temperature outfall of the cooling system would not violate the state's new thermal effluent standards. To meet this requirement, PG&E replaced the originally designed cooling-water outlet with a more expensive diffuser outlet.[75] Since the intake and outflow structures were to be in a navigable waterway, a permit from the Army Corps of Engineers was also required (under the newly revived provisions of the federal Refuse Act of 1899). The Corps then consulted all other potentially interested agencies. The state Fish and Game Agency had no objection to the project. But its rival, the United States Fish and Wildlife Service, had recently pressed successfully for a major cooling tower installation on a Columbia River project. When approached by the Corps with PG&E's plan, the Fish and Wildlife Service opposed the permit. In an unusual extension of its operational sphere of influence to within California, the agency alleged that thermal effects of the discharge might injure the fish population in the river.

The Corps would not proceed further without the approval of the Fish and Wildlife Service. Bill Johns, an assistant general counsel, was handling the case. He thought that a public hearing and an our-experts-versus-your-experts confrontation might have been an appropriate tactic. But top management, eager to avoid delay and any bad publicity that might jeopardize the Diablo nuclear project, was not amenable. And Johns, seeing that, did not push hard. "Someone on the thirty-second floor killed the idea of a hearing," he said.

The first solution PG&E proposed to deal with the Fish and Wildlife Service's objections was the rather elaborate step of installing cooling towers. This would be expensive and would set a precedent that the company might prefer to avoid. But it seemed the only way. A multidisciplinary team from PG&E journeyed to the regional headquarters of the Fish and Wildlife Service in Portland, Oregon, to present the plan. The staff there was delighted. But the Bay Area Air Pollution Control District, at its executive director's initiative, now insisted that the APCD's rules on *particulate* emissions applied to the salt "drift" from cooling towers that occurred when the saline water vaporized during the cooling process. Unfortunately, tower manufacturers could not guarantee that available "drift eliminator" systems would perform well enough to meet the regulations. Again, some wanted to fight. But critical law and government affairs people, aware of the internal tensions in the APCD and of the political ambitions of some key participants, argued that such a response would be self-defeating.

The engineering group was thus forced to look for still other options. Some mechanical engineers began to consider a system of floating spray modules (essentially fountains) that were being

used for cooling at two small plants around the country. One of
the two manufacturers in the field (the smaller and newer concern) worked hard to sell PG&E on the idea. A long, U-shaped
cooling canal would be built, with modules installed along the
outflow side. The modules would probably lower the drift, and in
any event it would be easier to meet particulate rules using a large
number of individual cooling units because of the way the regulations were written.

It is not clear who was the principle advocate for the spray
module system, or who was responsible for approving it. It turned
out that mechanical and corrosion problems caused some modules to sink or capsize. And they did not provide sufficient cooling. In an attempt to increase its cooling capacity, the system was
steadily expanded until modules were installed on both sides of
the canal. But the 735 MW unit still could not be run above 500
MW on many days, because the system could not dissipate
enough heat. As a result, PG&E departed from its usual policy of
nonconfrontation and became involved in extended litigation
with the supplier over alleged failures to fulfill contractual obligations.

Now, some years later and after a change in personnel, the Bay
Area Air Pollution Control District has advanced a slightly less
restrictive interpretation of its own particulate rules. In addition,
cooling-tower designers will now guarantee better drift-control
performance. The company once again moved to install cooling
towers at the unit — writing off most of the $12 million investment
in the spray canal in the process.

The company was willing to spend substantial sums and to take
significant risks in order to avoid being the environmental "bad
guy" in confrontations with the public. Unfortunately, in this
case the outcome was not advantageous. In retrospect it seems
that the staff work was less than perfect, although it must be said
that the engineers were working under very restrictive time and
technical constraints. Even today it is not clear where final responsibility lay for choosing the spray module approach, because
the lack of formal mechanisms to integrate group perspectives at
middle levels tends to diffuse responsibility.

Both the undergrounding and the Pittsburg 7 experiences illustrate that a company with diverse internal perspectives and a
strong control system can move aggressively to deal with public-
relations and regulatory difficulties. In neither case would the
technical people have developed or implemented such options on
their own. Yet this same organization has also become involved in

a series of epic disputes over the siting of nuclear facilities — disputes that have been very costly to the company, apart from the tens of millions of dollars spent on sites later abandoned. The company's carefully nurtured public acceptance has been seriously jeopardized. These battles also appear to have contributed to the development of still more stringent regulatory controls, particularly those of the Coastal Zone Commission. Furthermore, the delay in nuclear capacity made it necessary to use additional and expensive fossil-fuel units, which led in turn to the difficulties at Pittsburg 7.[76] How, exactly, did such difficulties arise? Why was PG&E less successful here than in the cases we have just considered?

PG&E's commitment to nuclear power dates from president Norman Sutherland's announcement to that effect in 1955. This was in turn followed by the company's contribution to General Electric's Vallecitos plant, its construction of its own small nuclear plant at Humboldt Bay, and the development in 1963 of the "Super System" of proposed nuclear sites. One of these sites, and one on which substantial work had begun before the whole scheme was even announced, was at Bodega Head.[77] On a curving peninsula fifty miles up the coast from San Francisco, the site apparently had been of some interest to the company (for either fossil-fuel or nuclear purposes) since 1957.

Other parties were interested in the same site. In July of that year, for example, the state's Division of Parks and Beaches announced that its acquisition of the site for recreation purposes, planned since 1955, "had been forestalled by planned purchase of a major portion of the headland by a private utility company."[78] Since 1955, too, the University of California had been using the area for marine research and had begun planning for a permanent facility.[79] But despite the possible objections of such competitors, this was the site PG&E chose for its first large-scale nuclear plant. The selection was apparently made personally by Walter Dreyer, then vice-president for engineering, with Norman Sutherland's strong support and involvement.[80] "Mr. Sutherland wanted to bestow a power plant on Sonoma County," one executive recalled. And given the geography of the coastline, there were not many suitable coastal locations.

From the beginning, the company found that it had to be flexible in order to get local cooperation. Because of the potentially troublesome precedent involved, PG&E had hoped to avoid having to obtain county use permits. It argued that the state Public Utilities Commission had exclusive jurisdiction over such facilities, a view it had defended successfully in some earlier disagreements with the county. But as negotiations proceeded, the company had to agree to the permit procedure. From 1959 to 1961, with Kenneth Diercks (then with the Land Department) working full time with local officials, PG&E obtained several of the necessary permits, including one for a transmission line along a sandspit that was used as a park, and another for an access road over the inner edge of the harbor's tidal flats. The company also decided in October 1959 to move the site slightly seaward, away from one of the branches of the San Andreas Fault that ran through the neck of land connecting Bodega Head with the mainland.[81] All these factors would later provide a focus for public controversy.

Neither the competing land uses nor the potential geological instability of the area brought any substantial changes in the company's plans. In part this was because there initially was little organized opposition. In January 1962 an Army Corps of Engineers hearing on the access road over the tidelands produced some protests from local clamdiggers. But at the PUC hearings on the plant two months later, almost no opposition witnesses appeared.[82] Moreover, there were external pressures to push forward with the plant. Glen Seaborg, the new chairman of the Atomic Energy Commission (and former chancellor of the University of California) was running into heavy criticism from Congress for the slow pace at which nuclear energy was being used for peaceful purposes. Seaborg cited the Bodega Head project as evidence to the contrary.[83]

Thus, the company became committed to a project on a site that had been chosen by somewhat informal search processes and acquired before extensive geological investigation. Geological consultants ultimately declared the site acceptable. Their reactions were sufficiently mixed, however, that PG&E was reluctant to submit their reports as exhibits to the PUC (although it ultimately did so), and the company chose not to include some of the documents in its Preliminary Hazard Report to the AEC.[84]

Just after the close of the PUC hearings, the opposition began to organize. On March 14, 1962, the *San Francisco Chronicle* published an impassioned letter written by Karl Kortum, director of the city's Maritime Museum and a resident of Sonoma County. Kortum urged people to write to the PUC to demand a reopening of the hearings, advice that was heeded by over 2,500 people. New proceedings were held in May and June, at which many opposition witnesses appeared. Nevertheless, the PUC granted the permit in November, and in December PG&E applied to the AEC for a license.[85]

At about this time, the Northern California Association to Preserve Bodega Head and Harbor came into existence to take up the battle. It was headed by David Pesonen, a young Sierra Club member whose talents as an organizer came to be highly respected at PG&E. The association filed a series of suits. It demanded additional hearings from the PUC so that it could cross-examine the utility's geological consultants. And it commissioned counter-studies of its own.[86] In response, the secretary of the interior, Steward Udall (still smarting from conservationist attacks on proposals to build a dam on the Colorado River just below Grand Canyon), wrote to the AEC in May 1963 to express his concern. He announced that the United States Geological Survey was undertaking additional site studies.[87] By August the highly publicized furor had led Governor Edward Brown and the Democratic leadership of the state assembly also to write to the AEC, asking that the permit be denied. Through the fall of 1963, studies were made by the Geological Survey, the Stanford Research Institute, and the company's own consultants. Some additional evidence of a fault zone lying directly beneath the reactor was uncovered in these studies, and at least some of the company's consultants began to have second thoughts.[88]

In March 1964, in an attempt to save the project, PG&E altered the design of the plant. It proposed surrounding the containment vessel with compressible material, so that it would survive even the shocks of a fault slippage directly through the site. The AEC, in reviewing the proposal, was divided. The Advisory Committee on Reactor Safeguards announced in October that the plan was acceptable, but the staff of the Division of Reactor Licensing was unconvinced. The latter group, relying on Geological Survey estimates of possible earth movements, wanted a design to withstand two or three feet of rock slippage. Although PG&E said that its design could accommodate this much movement, the staff was of the opinion that PG&E could not prove that its design was adequate, and therefore refused to accept it. Governor Brown again urged abandonment of the plant. Finally, on October 31, 1964, PG&E's new president Robert Gerdes, announced the company's withdrawal. According to Gerdes' official figures, $4 million had been spent on excavation, grading, and road building.[89] Yet when all the costs of additional geological studies, reports, and time spent in negotiations are included, one can speculate that two to five times that amount may well have been invested in the project.

How could a company ordinarily so sophisticated about and responsive to public opinion become enmeshed in such a controversy? How did it come to propose building a large nuclear plant on the shores of a scenic harbor, a transmission line along a park sandspit, and an access road across the inner tidelands—and do this in proximity to the nation's most famous geological fault? Part of the answer is that PG&E was caught by changes in the outside world. When the project was proposed in 1957, words like "environmental" and "ecology" were not yet part of most people's vocabularies. Communities competed with one another to attract power plants, as valued additions to the tax base.[90] PG&E had recently built large fossil-fuel plants—which had more evident impact because of air pollution—at locations almost as scenic south of the city (at Moss Landing in 1950 and Morro Bay in 1951) without major public controversy. And the development of nuclear power to generate electricity seemed at that time to represent an extraordinarily promising technological solution to many of the region's resource problems.

If attitudes were changing, so were regulations affecting nuclear facilities. Bodega was one of the first plants considered by the Atomic Energy Commission, and standards—especially in regard to geology—changed rapidly during the course of the controversy.[91] The geology at Humboldt Bay, where PG&E already had a nuclear plant, also raises some problems, although there are different kinds of difficulties in each case.[92]

In buying first and studying geology later, the company was simply carrying over procedures it had used for fossil-fuel plants, for which geology was not seen as so critical a matter. Furthermore, geology was *not* the initial point seized on by the project's opponents, who first raised land-use and procedural issues, made accusations of secret deals, and used radioactivity as a scare tactic. It was only as the argument developed that geology became a major concern.[93]

But why did the company persist when circumstances changed? Why didn't the lawyers or public-relations people alert top management to the problems? Part of the explanation lies in the attitudes of top management itself, which are especially important, in view of the company's strong control system. One senior executive, for example, suggested that "Norman Sutherland became personally committed to building the plant at Bodega. Perhaps that is why things went on for so long." This view is implicitly confirmed by another executive, who observed that when Gerdes succeeded Sutherland, it was much easier for him to withdraw from the project because he was not so strongly attached to it. (We do not know to what extent Sutherland's commitment discouraged dissenting advice even from being offered, rather than just being rejected when it was advanced.) Moreover, although Gerdes was already quite influential in the company, the influence of the lawyers as a group did not yet have the same institutional basis it was later to acquire. Fewer lawyers held key middle-management positions, and there was not yet a distinct top manager to whom the nontechnical Departments reported. Whatever the reasons, PG&E's inflexibility in this case contrasts noticeably with its behavior in the other incidents we have recounted.

The technical people in the company were not happy with Gerdes' withdrawal.[94] But paralleling the strategy he followed in other instances, Gerdes saw nonconfrontation as the best way to advance the corporation's long-term interests. As executive vice-president he had kept in close touch with Kenneth Diercks and others dealing with local politicians and interest groups. Now Diercks was shifted to the Tax Office and then into a new Department reporting directly to Gerdes. When the next controversy over siting arose, Gerdes was apparently determined to be in control and in touch with politically important outsiders from the very beginning.[95]

In its next attempt to build a nuclear plant, PG&E worked hard to avoid a confrontation with conservationist critics. As a result, it ended up with a site that was, at least for a while, acceptable to such people because it was chosen with their participation. But if the company was attempting to co-opt its opponents, as it had done in its earlier undergrounding policies, its efforts in this instance were not successfully institutionalized, although its approach to the matter was extremely sophisticated.

After Bodega, PG&E tried to acquire a site on one of the few major sand dunes on the California coast — the rolling Nipomo Dunes south of San Luis Obispo, at the southern end of PG&E's service area. This area was widely used for recreation in spite of the proximity of a Union Oil refinery. Here, too, as at Bodega Head, the state had long-term plans for park development. But like Bodega, Nipomo Dunes was among the locations included in PG&E's "Super System." In October 1963 the company bought 1,100 acres from the Union Oil Company. Shermer Sibley, then vice-president and general manager, asked Kenneth Diercks (fresh from his experiences at Sonoma) to take a trip down to the site to sound out the local opposition.[96]

Diercks' reports were not encouraging. County officials were eager for the added tax revenues. But local members of the Sierra Club, as well as its national office, and various other conservation organizations were prepared to oppose nuclear development at the site. Despite the objections of some company engineers, Gerdes gave Diercks and a colleague in Government Affairs authority to negotiate with conservationist interests. As one lawyer explained, "After Bodega, the company was not eager for another head-to-head confrontation." Said one engineer, "Mr. Gerdes wanted a site where there would be no protests."

The initial plan called for a plant 500 feet from the ocean. Environmental groups proposed that it be set back 4,000 feet. The company countered with 1,700 feet, arguing that it would be too expensive to pump the cooling water in and out from 4,000 feet. But conservationists would not accept the compromise. Subsequent discussions focused on other alternatives. First on the list was a site north of Nipomo, at Wild Cherry Canyon. But the large landholder who owned the property wanted it for a home. He suggested instead another part of his holdings, Diablo Canyon, just a bit farther up the coast.[97]

Within the company, opinion as to how best to proceed was divided. Some of the engineers argued that Nipomo was the superior site. They pointed out that certain elements of the Sierra Club had been strenuously opposed to the compromise and would certainly continue to protest, in any event. But as one senior engineer put it, "The political/legal people torpedoed the site over Engineering's strong opposition. Diercks told Gerdes that Nipomo would be another Bodega . . . Gerdes was still bleeding from Bodega and said that if it was trouble, he wanted no part of it."[98]

In September 1966 a group of PG&E people invited some environmental activists to take a jeep ride to the Diablo Canyon site. The next day, the Sierra Club board voted nine to one to approve the project, provided that the Nipomo land be turned over to the state for park use. For a while, then, it seemed as if the company's efforts had been worthwhile. But the Sierra Club was split over the issue. David Brower, then executive director, resigned in March 1969 when the membership twice upheld the board's decision not to oppose the plan. He formed a new organization, the Friends of the Earth. The board, too, had second thoughts on the

matter. In September 1968 a letter was sent to PG&E president
Shermer Sibley, in which the board "regretfully acknowledged
. . . a mistake of principle and policy" in its acceptance of the
previous compromise. But the Sierra Club stood by its agreement
and did not actively oppose the project.[99]

Here again, as in the NO_x controversy at Moss Landing or in
the development or an undergrounding policy, we see a highly
centralized decision-making process at work. Top management
was deeply involved in the details and used its authority to impose
a decisive course of action on the organization in spite of substantial internal disagreement. Again, the views of diverse groups,
including nonengineers, were crucial to the choice of a flexible
approach. The Diablo Canyon plant cost more to build than was
anticipated, and still lacks a Nuclear Regulatory Commission
operating license.[100] Nevertheless, PG&E clearly learned some
important lessons during the Bodega controversy, which it put to
good use in the case of Diablo. (For a view of the plant, see Figure 11.)

What, then, are we to make of the company's third nuclear
siting controversy? In 1966 — not two years after the withdrawal
from Bodega Head and before Diablo was even settled — the company revealed plans for a nuclear plant at Point Arena, in Mendocino County, about fifty miles north of the Bodega site.[101] At
first, the machinery built up during the previous battles went
smoothly into operation. In 1968 the State Resources Agency, in
an informal agreement with PG&E, accepted the site and pledged
not to oppose its development. By January 1971 the company had
acquired 586 acres of land; the Mendocino County Board of Supervisors had issued a use permit; and the Point Arena city council had passed a resolution in support of PG&E's plans. In March
1971 the company let contracts to General Electric for the reactors, and in August submitted formal applications to the PUC
and the AEC. Less than eighteen months later, however, in January 1973, the company halted further work on the site and officially withdrew its applications — once again after a considerable
investment.[102]

In the interim, some young geologists studying the site for the
Geological Survey (acting as the AEC's consultant) discovered
what they believed to be evidence of a fault right through or close
by the proposed location. (The San Andreas fault zone is not very
far offshore at this point.) In the process of reviewing the company's geological analysis, they noted some gaps and insisted that
the company's geological consultants submit additional seismo-

Figure 11. The Diablo Canyon nuclear generating station, located on a site chosen in cooperation with local environmental organizations. Courtesy of the Pacific Gas and Electric Company.

logical studies which had either not been performed or were not initially reported. The AEC became quite skeptical of the site. In September 1972, at a joint meeting of the Geological Survey, the AEC, and PG&E, the company's consultants disputed the Survey's interpretations and evidence. Despite its skepticism, the AEC agreed with the Survey that the company should be allowed to try to establish the site's acceptability. Soon after the meeting, PG&E proposed and then began extensive new investigations to resolve the disputed geological issues.[103]

Once again, the project began to unravel. In November 1972 California voters passed Proposition 20, establishing a Coastal Zone Commission with the power to regulate all coastal land use. Meanwhile the Sierra Club's opposition to the site was growing. The local chapter had apparently been persuaded by PG&E representatives to cooperate. But the national office was not amenable to compromise, after the internal turmoil that the Diablo controversy had created. The company's earlier informal understanding with the State Resources Agency—labeled by environmentalists as the "secret agreement of 1968"—came under particularly heavy attack and was ultimately invalidated by the courts.[104] In August 1972 the United States Department of Justice, responding to complaints filed by the municipal systems in PG&E's service area, suggested that the Point Arena plant would violate antitrust laws unless the local distribution systems were allowed to own part of it.[105]

The handwriting was clearly on the wall—especially since the passage of Proposition 20 promised to create a whole new set of unpredictable regulatory hurdles. There is also evidence that PG&E's geological work was not turning out as the company had hoped. Engineering people talked of "floating" the plant to ensure its integrity, even in the case of massive horizontal or vertical ground slippages. But finally, seven years after work on the site had begun, Robert Gerdes again decided in favor of withdrawal.

In retrospect, several people in the company claim always to have had doubts about Point Arena. One anonymous middle-level manager, for example, said, "You might have envisaged what would happen when the civil engineers bull-headedly picked Mendocino, especially if you didn't fight." Some of those closely involved at early stages in the project now say that they proposed locating the plant inland (at least inside the coast highway), but that cost considerations kept this view from getting much attention. Others now claim that the site always had certain disadvantages because it would have required expensive, and perhaps controversial, transmission lines over the coastal mountain range. Even Gerdes acknowledged that the parallels to Bodega were not unforeseen.[106]

But what were the company's alternatives? Only two sites were left from the "Super System" (at Collinsville and South Moss Landing), and these raised serious geological questions, even on brief examination. The whole coastal area of northern California is heavily faulted. The company either had to take the risk or go inland and use expensive and scarce water for cooling. By training and experience, neither Gerdes nor the civil engineers in the company could accept the wastefulness inherent in the latter approach at the time. (Yet their inability to get coastal options approved has led them to explore inland sites in their most recent proposals.) At the same time, too, the Diablo project was moving forward. And a site north of the city seemed best suited to the company's transmission network.

With such reasoning, top managers at PG&E saw little choice. The decision was made at the highest levels of the company with only a limited amount of staff work, by today's standards. In this instance, then, the failure was not one of public relations; it was, rather, a failure to evaluate technical data properly. According to some outside observers, the company's geological consultants deserve some of the blame in this connection. Although PG&E's management does not share this view, these outsiders argue that the widely respected academics who were retained seemed more committed to rationalizing away apparent objections than to genuinely assessing the merits of the case. To whatever extent this view is valid, it would seem to reflect the fact that when top management is so committed to a project, no one, inside *or* out, is eager to be the messenger who carries the bad news.

The Pacific Gas and Electric Company is an example of a utility that has tailored its structure and behavior to meet the considerable demands of its service area. In a region that has a strong history of public ownership and where environmental consciousness and political sophistication are high, such adaptation is vital to survival, even more so to success. PG&E learned this lesson early in its history. The entrepreneurs who ran the company during its years of expansion recognized that public relations and legal expertise were often as important as engineering skill in delivering good service to PG&E customers and in fending off challenges from the public sector. Such functions have now become firmly institutionalized in the divisional offices, the Government and Public Affairs Department, and in the Legal Department.

PG&E has not responded equally effectively to all the environmental pressures it has faced in recent years. To a large extent, this is because so much depends on top management. Certainly, senior executives have the power to force action, even when staff members disagree. They must, however, also depend on that staff for critical information, and this may not be forthcoming. Outside-oriented groups have been incorporated into PG&E's organization structure in a way that gives them considerable access and influence. But this does not mean they will determine the outcome of every decision.

PG&E's tradition of strong and aggressive leadership, firmly established during Jim Black's thirty years of service with the company, has been another crucial element of its success. Personalities, of course, like Jim Black's or Robert Gerdes', are inseparable from this tradition. But the strength of top management does not depend only on charismatic personalities. The leadership's firm control over corporate policy and its implementation is maintained by means of a flexible executive structure, which can expand and adapt both to suit the skills of talented individuals rising through the ranks and to handle the increasingly complex job of managing a utility company. A deep control system and a certain amount of interdivisional mobility give some effective training to rising young executives, although a gap between technical and nontechnical functions does exist.

This structure has placed an even greater burden on the two or three most senior executives. Yet as we saw in the case of the generation planning task force, efforts to create multidisciplinary groups at lower levels have run into difficulties. Since top executives still made the decisions, the task force was not able to resolve major policy conflicts.

PG&E now faces an even more complex array of externally imposed difficulties — compounded by drought, fuel shortages, and new regulatory constraints — than it did when we began our study over six years ago. The new generation of managers is still struggling to find ways to integrate diverse perspectives without, at the same time, losing their strong control over corporate policy — that is, they are still struggling with the problem of how to construct an appropriately responsive organization.

6

Ontario Hydro

Not all public companies are as insulated from external pressure as the Tennessee Valley Authority; Ontario Hydro is much more sensitive to governmental concerns. Established in 1906 by the legislature of Ontario Province, Canada, the Hydro-Electric Power Commission of Ontario, as it was originally named, is one of the oldest and largest publicly owned utilities in North America. Today it supplies 95 percent of the province's electricity. Primarily a wholesaler, Hydro sells most of its power to 353 municipal utilities, as well as directly serving a small number of large industrial users.[1]

Operating in Canada's richest and most environmentally conscious province, Hydro has faced considerable pressure to control its pollution. In addition to popular preferences, Hydro is also more closely supervised and controlled by its parent government than either TVA or the Los Angeles municipal system. But despite its sensitivity to environmental concerns its behavior has not always pleased the public; it has pushed ahead with an ambitious program of capacity expansion that has raised rates and strained the capital resources of the province. The confrontation over this program reflects a strong strategic commitment rooted in the organization's past history and perpetuated by its internal structure. It shows that an organization's behavior is not merely the product of the opportunities that the larger world offers. In the long run, however, this external context is steadily forcing changes not only in Hydro's behavior, but also in its internal organization.

Background and Context

Ontario Hydro's early history is similar in some respects to that of the Los Angeles Department of Water and Power. Both came

162

into being early in the century, principally at the initiative of businessmen who were seeking cheaper and more reliable sources of energy. Both were active participants in several decades of intense political turmoil. Both helped organize and sustain what were essentially political machines, which campaigned actively for measures that supported the utilities' survival and growth, in the face of prolonged private-utility opposition. Finally, both utilities withdrew from or were forced out of politics at the time that each came to be accepted as the primary source of electricity in its region.[2]

At the time public power became an issue in Ontario, the province depended principally on American coal for its energy. In 1901 groups of Ontario businessmen began meeting to discuss the alternative of setting up a public agency to exploit Niagara Falls and other sources of hydroelectricity in the province. The ruling Liberal government resisted their plans. In 1904, however, the Liberals were replaced by the Progressive Conservatives, who were more sympathetic to public power. Adam Beck, a prominent and ardent supporter of public power, was a member of the new cabinet. In 1906 Beck, who was to serve as Hydro's chairman for its first eighteen years, introduced the legislation that created the organization. This legislation, called the Power Commission Act, established a provincial agency authorized to sell wholesale power "at cost" to any municipalities that contracted with it.

On New Year's Day, 1907, after some hectic local campaigns, nineteen municipalities voted to become Hydro customers. Hydro continued to battle for over a decade before it became established as the chief supplier of electricity in the province. Beck, a proud and willful man, played a leading role, writing numerous pamphlets and traveling throughout Ontario seeking new municipal customers. He was supported by the Ontario Municipal Electric Association (OMEA), an association of Ontario's municipal customers, which helped him create a political organization. Indicating the importance of this "machine," a government inquiry commented in the 1920s: "No head of any department of the government doing the things which he did [spending Hydro funds for political purposes, approving expenditures without consulting fellow commissioners, etc.] would have kept this position. [He stayed in office because he] created a political force which governments as a rule are unwilling to antagonize."[3]

The Liberals' return to power in the 1930s had a disciplining effect. Hydro had used every possible means to help defeat them during the campaign, going so far as to issue pamphlets charging

that the Liberals were tools of the private utilities and hiring de-
tectives to seek proof of this dubious allegation. Retaliation was
thus inevitable. The new government instituted an investigation
of Hydro and removed its ruling commissioners and many top
staff members. No major change in policy was made, but apparently a lesson was learned: even after the Conservatives returned
to power in the mid-1940s, Hydro never resumed the political
activism of its earliest years. Another reason for its withdrawal
from the political sphere was the fact that, having established
itself as the principal supplier of power in its area, the company
no longer had fundamental battles to fight. For a map of the
company's service area, see Figure 12.

This situation persisted for several decades. With abundant
hydroelectric sites and a favorable tax and interest-rate situation,
Hydro's rates have been below those of neighboring private utilities.[4] There was little for Ontario's citizens to complain about,
and Hydro was largely free of close government supervision. This,
however, did not last. In the late 1960s concern with Hydro's
environmental impact grew and in the early 1970s the company's
rates began to climb. Popular protest put the government in the
position where it had reason to start controlling Hydro more
actively.

Of the three public companies in our study, Hydro today appears to be the most closely supervised by its parent government.
The government's legal controls over, and close ties with, the
organization reflect the role Hydro plays in the life of the province. TVA serves only a small portion of its parent government's
jurisdiction and is but one small agency among many in the federal bureaucracy. And although the Los Angeles municipal system is important to its government, many of those affected by its
activities live outside the city boundaries. Hydro, in contrast, is
one of the largest agencies of the Ontario government and its
operating territory matches the Ontario government's jurisdiction. Hydro's policies are therefore highly visible to all the Ontario electorate, and any individuals or groups unhappy with the
company have an obvious set of political institutions to appeal to.
Furthermore, unlike the nonparty, district-based Los Angeles
City Council elections, in which local constituency service can be
an issue, Ontario's parliamentary form puts a premium on issues.
To phrase the matter another way, citizen action in relation to
Hydro is likely to be effective given the government's interest in
avoiding citizen displeasure, and such action is likely to be easy to
mobilize given the evident benefits that citizens can receive from
altering Hydro's behavior.

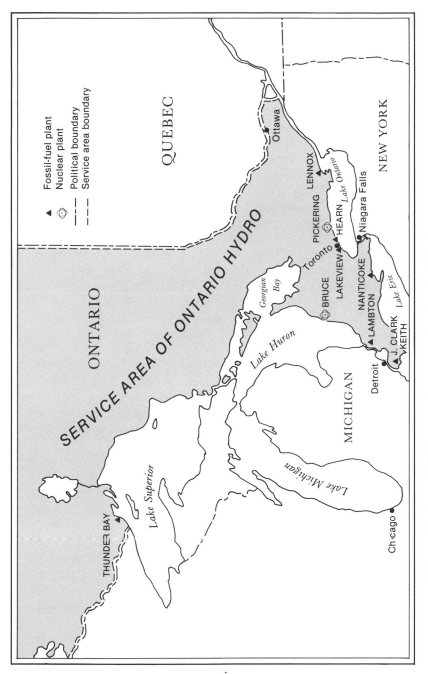

Figure 12. Ontario Hydro: service area and major fossil-fuel and nuclear generating stations. Based on annual reports of Ontario Hydro.

The nature of party politics in Ontario tends to reinforce the government's concern. The Progressive Conservative party has been Ontario's governing party for most of the century, having remained continuously in power since 1943. At the time of our study, the Conservatives (as they are generally known) were ruling as a minority government (although they still held more seats than either of their rivals, the Liberals or the New Democrats), and hence they were especially insecure. But even when they have had a solid majority, the Conservatives have sought to minimize sources of potential voter dissatisfaction; they have generally tried appeasing and co-opting their critics (particularly those on the left). Indeed, making an issue of some Hydro contracts in the 1930s helped the Liberals oust the Conservatives from power, which illustrates the government's vulnerability on matters relating to Hydro.[5]

Although it has not always employed them, the government has had reason to develop and retain a wide array of formal and informal powers by which it can constrain Hydro's behavior. It appoints the Hydro board of directors (until recently, known as "commissioners"), and must approve every major construction project and bond issue.[6] TVA, in comparison, has been empowered since 1959 to issue bonds independently for its power program and has never had to obtain approval from Congress for the expenditure of power revenues. The Los Angeles Department of Water and Power is somewhat more constrained, but still has more formal freedom than Hydro; since the late 1940s it has been empowered to issue bonds, although it does require the city council's approval for major contracts.

Until the mid-1970s, when Hydro's policies began attracting substantial criticism in the province, the Ontario government rarely exercised its approval and appointive powers to change Hydro policy. It preferred to exert influence informally, through frequent consultations with Hydro officials at the top and middle levels. With Hydro's headquarters only a few hundred yards from the legislature, this contact was easy to maintain. As the pressures on Hydro have mounted and formal controls have been increasingly used, this informal contact has apparently increased as well. Hydro's chairman often discusses major policy announcements with the premier of the province or a member of his cabinet; these announcements are sometimes made by the government itself in the legislature. Hydro engineers are now in frequent contact with staff counterparts in the government to discuss pending Hydro or government decisions.[7] The existence of formal powers that could be used by the government must inevitably affect the ways in which these informal discussions proceed.

In this regard, Hydro's relationship to its parent government parallels that of public corporations in other countries (for example, the United Kingdom and Australia) where formal directive measures are legally possible but seldom taken, while informal consultation is frequent and generally decisive. Such relationships allow political figures to avoid responsibility for the actions of public corporations, and allow the corporations to preserve their apparent autonomy while still achieving the ends the government seeks.[8]

When Hydro's policies have led to political controversy, the government has generally tried to defuse criticism by appointing a Royal Commission or a special task force to inquire into the matter. This has occurred throughout Hydro's history, and led to a number of wide-ranging inquiries in the 1970s. In 1972, for instance, the government used this approach to resolve an important environmental controversy concerning a major high-voltage transmission line that Hydro proposed to build. The commission's inquiry led to new efforts by Hydro and the government to consult the public on new Hydro facilities as a matter of course.[9] Another royal commission, the Porter Commission, is presently reviewing a wide array of electricity-related issues. Its mandate includes the safety of nuclear power, alternative energy sources, energy conservation, and the process by which Hydro decides how much to expand its facilities.[10]

The use of royal commissions reflects some distinguishing features of Canadian political culture, which is unlike that of the United States and which forms an important part of the context in which Hydro operates. In Canada there seems to be a widespread belief in the possibility of using a methodical, technical, and "reasonable" approach to solving social problems — a belief that perhaps stems from British traditions. In the United States a dispute over utility planning would be very difficult to settle via a single, agreed-upon technical body; each side would insist on "its own" experts, studies, and judgments. Moreover, there would be less optimism about the possibility of defining new methods that the utility could use in the future, to avoid recurrences of the same kind of problems. In Canada, however, attention to method is an important aspect of political style.

In the last several years, with growing public concern over Hydro's environmental and financial policies, the government has begun to move beyond informal contacts and independent reviews and to exercise its formal approval powers. Hydro must now go through extensive review procedures to obtain approval for new facilities. In 1976 the government, because of its concern about the combined borrowing requirements of the government and the utility, formally requested that Hydro limit the borrowing for 1976-78 to $1.5 billion per annum. In response, Hydro cut $5.2 billion from its capital program for the next ten years, necessitating large curtailments in its planned expansion program.[11]

This formal request represented a more open intervention in Hydro affairs than was typical in the past. It occurred, in part, because the government's objectives came into conflict with the previously developed strategy of the organization. In such a situation the usual informal controls were no longer sufficient. Yet such a confrontation is embarrassing to the government, and its powers, although significant, are still limited. For these reasons, even when major political concerns are at stake, outside pressures are both imperfect and applied only after a delay — leaving Hydro significant discretion.

To limit its need to impose such external restraints, the government has intervened directly to alter Hydro's internal organizational structure. It created Task Force Hydro, a government-appointed group with representatives from Hydro, business, and the government, to study the organization. On this group's recommendation, Hydro was transformed from a provincial commission into a public corporation. At the same time, the position of minister of energy was created in the provincial government. Whereas Hydro previously had reported directly to the premier, considerable communication between Hydro and the legislature now occurs through the minister of energy. These changes were designed in order to "emphasize that Government involvement with Hydro is on a policy level and in order to define a clear channel for policy direction from Government to Hydro."[12] The contrast between the old and the new organizational structures is shown in Figures 13 and 14.

Internally, Hydro's top management was strengthened significantly. The explicit aim was to increase its ability to formulate overall policies consistent with government objectives. Its six-member board was reconstituted as a thirteen-member board of directors, in part to make room for a substantial increase in business and government experience in this group. Soon after, R. B. Taylor, a former steel company executive, was made chairman; a member of Task Force Hydro, Taylor had received extensive informal training for the job. He replaced retiring chairman

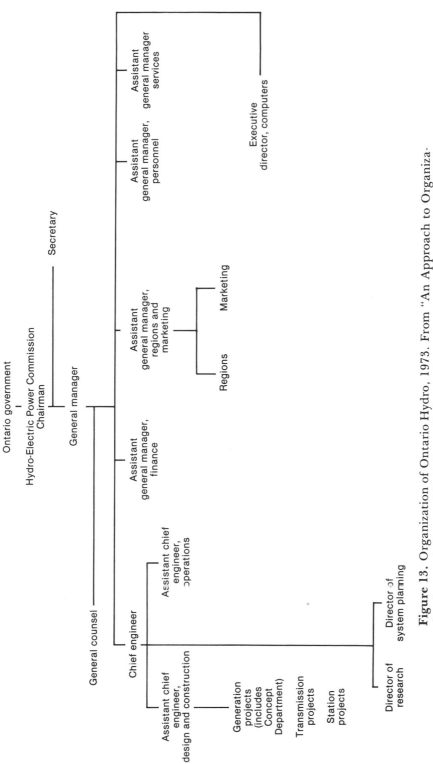

Figure 13. Organization of Ontario Hydro, 1973. From "An Approach to Organization," second report of Task Force Hydro, 1972, p. 4.

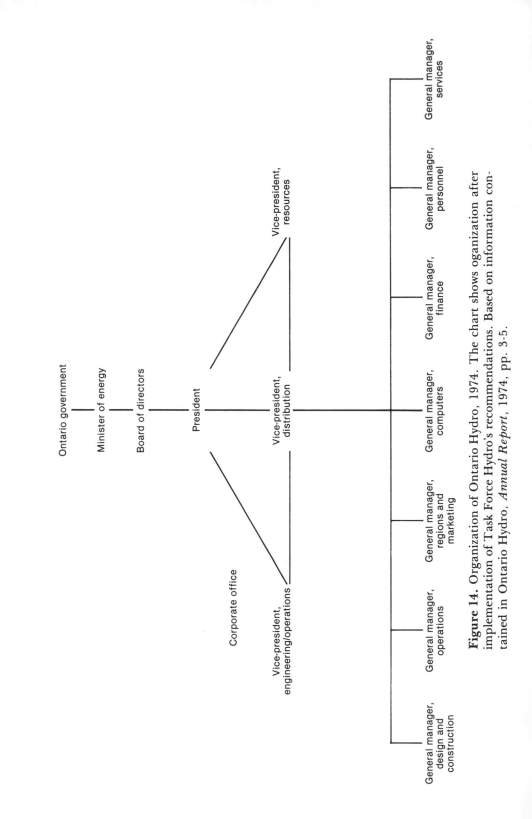

Figure 14. Organization of Ontario Hydro, 1974. The chart shows oganization after implementation of Task Force Hydro's recommendations. Based on information contained in Ontario Hydro, *Annual Report*, 1974, pp. 3-5.

George Gathercole, whose departure was politically opportune and was reportedly encouraged by the provincial government. Gathercole had been one of the principal figures in a scandal — sometimes called the "Hydrogate affair" — involving the award of a major contract for Hydro's new headquarters to a friend of Ontario's premier. A select committee of the legislature cleared the premier of wrongdoing, but criticized Hydro for not encouraging more competition and Gathercole for supplying misleading information to the legislature. Although the government did not remove Gathercole at the time of the scandal, his retirement hastened the disappearance of this controversy and facilitated the process of change within Hydro.[13] (See Figure 15.)

The most significant organizational change was the establishment of a Corporate Office at what had been the general manager's level. Several new vice-president positions were established to increase management support for the agency's chief administrative officer. Douglas Gordon, Hydro's former general manager and a member of Task Force Hydro, became head of this office as Hydro's president.[14]

The Task Force's study reflected both the Canadian attention to method and the Ontario government's strong interest in minimizing embarrassing conflicts with Hydro. Neither TVA nor the Los Angeles Department of Water and Power has experienced a similar intervention into its internal structure.

Even before these changes were made, however, Hydro was responding positively to many of the pressures it faced. Having been relatively free of outside constraints for a number of years prior to the late 1960s, Hydro may sometimes have seemed insensitive to external opinion. As a report from Task Force Hydro put it, "The briefs submitted to Task Force Hydro confirm that certain citizens and corporations perceive Hydro as being remote, impersonal, monolithic, and indifferent."[15] Yet even though Hydro was not perfectly receptive to public or government wishes, it did in a number of cases seek to respond to external expectations before they became official constraints. This receptivity was particularly marked in the environmental area.

Since the mid-1960s environmental concern has been high in Ontario. Perhaps sensitized by the growing pollution problems in the United States, Ontario was the first province to establish a water quality commission, and later, a ministry of environment.[16] In 1967 a candidate running mainly on an antipollution platform was elected to the board of aldermen in Toronto, Ontario's capital and largest city. In 1968 the province established numerical

Figure 15. The new and modern Ontario Hydro headquarters office building in downtown Toronto, the construction of which led to the "Hydrogate" controversy. Courtesy of Ontario Hydro.

ambient air quality standards—four years before such standards were universally established in the United States.

Hydro's air pollution control choices began to provoke organized citizen opposition around 1969. One of the most persistent citizen groups, Pollution Probe (based at the University of Toronto), sponsored a "citizen inquiry" at Toronto City Hall. The inquiry was sparked by Hydro's decision to build a tall stack at its coal-burning Hearn plant on the Toronto waterfront, rather than to limit sulfur dioxide emissions. Hydro subsequently converted the plant to burn natural gas as well as coal, in part because of this environmental pressure and in part to provide greater flexibility in the plant's fuel supply. (At that time the availability of American coal was in doubt, and Canadian natural gas had become available at a good price.) In more recent years, Pollution Probe has attacked Hydro's policy of exporting power to the United States (significant exports are often possible because of Hydro's extensive capacity reserves), charging that this effectively amounts to a policy of "importing" pollution.[17] A new group, Energy Probe, has since broken off from Pollution Probe and has intervened often against Hydro in rate proceedings. For a view of Hearn, see Figure 16.

In 1972 Hydro encountered its first strong opposition to a planned transmission line when it announced its intention to build a major line between its Nanticoke and Pickering plants. The plans were cleared with the affected town governments, but were objected to by local citizens and provincial conservation groups. A group known as the Coalition of Concerned Citizens, along with the Sierra Club and the Conservation Council of Ontario, petitioned the premier to review the route of the proposed line. The government appointed a one-man royal commission to inquire into Hydro's plans and its efforts to consult public opinion. After lengthy public hearings and public-participation procedures, the commission advised locating the line further south than Hydro had planned, along a proposed highway route.[18] As a result of this controversy, Hydro itself began to use extensive public-participation procedures in the planning of all new major facilities.

Hydro's responsiveness to these environmental pressures seems consistent with its close connections with the Ontario government. At the same time, Hydro has made other strategic commitments that were not so clearly the result of external imperatives.

Particularly notable is Hydro's commitment to system reliability and energy independence, which has clear historical roots.

Figure 16. The Hearn generating station, which is located relatively close to down-town Toronto. Courtesy of Ontario Hydro.

Hydro was founded to harness the province's hydroelectric potential and reduce its dependence on American coal. It relied almost solely on the province's hydroelectric resources (supplemented by hydroelectric power from Quebec) throughout the first half of the century. By the early 1950s, however, sufficient new hydro was unavailable and the company began to turn to American coal to fuel its new steam electric plants; less than a decade later this had become the chief form of new capacity, despite the hydroelectric development of the St. Lawrence River. Beginning in the early 1950s, Hydro sought to offset this trend by working, along with a federally chartered public corporation, to develop nuclear power of a sort that would satisfy the independence objective. They developed a distinct Canadian nuclear technology: using heavy water as a moderator, the reactor runs on unenriched uranium mined in Canada, eliminating the need to send the fuel to the United States for enrichment.[19]

Hydro has made a major — and at times controversial — commitment to this technology. The program is known as CANDU (officially, the name signifies Canadian-Deuterium-Uranium, but the allusion to Canadian competence is obvious). In 1965, with a 200 MW prototype CANDU plant still under construction, Hydro and the Canadian government decided to go ahead with plans to build a full-scale nuclear plant at Pickering, Ontario, using the CANDU technology. In 1968, with the 200 MW prototype operating only sporadically and the Pickering plant incomplete, Hydro committed itself to still another large CANDU plant — the Bruce station. Given the lack of successful experience with CANDU up to that point, the Bruce decision generated considerable skepticism and suggestions by some that Hydro should employ American technology. Hydro's experience with its Pickering plant has somewhat assuaged these doubts, since it has had one of the best operating records of any nuclear plant in existence.[20]

The early commitment to CANDU was very risky. Doing so required both optimism about the technology and a willingness to risk the costs and difficulties that a poor result would impose on Hydro and the provincial and national governments. This willingness reflects the views of key managers in Hydro and their commitment to its historical mission of Canadian self-sufficiency.

In the latter half of the 1960s Hydro's concern with energy independence was reinforced when the organization suffered a shortage of generating capacity. Hydro had underestimated the growth in demand that occurred during this period. Icy water conditions had impeded the operation of its hydroelectric plants, and it had failed to get new units on line according to schedule. It had also had trouble with the new generating units for its coal-burning Lakeview plant; some of these had breakdown rates nearly three times greater than the average for comparable units in the United States. Because of this unfortunate mix of circumstances, Hydro was forced to rely heavily on neighboring utilities in Canada and the United States for added power. But because these utilities were able to make up only part of Hydro's capacity deficit, the company occasionally had to cut back delivery to large industrial users who were on explicitly "interruptible" contracts—contracts that offered a lower price for electricity but allowed for occasional interruptions in service. There were no brownouts or blackouts for regular customers.[21] Yet this situation evidently gave Hydro's engineers a sense that their ability to supply power was highly fragile, and reminded some of power shortages after World War II that had led to blackouts in the province.

This *near* failure of the Hydro system had a marked effect on the utility's thinking. More conservative planning criteria were introduced, apparently including a rule that allowance would not be made for potential power loans from American utilities in an emergency. These new criteria, along with the advent of larger units on the system, meant expanding reserve margins to nearly 30 percent—that is, Hydro decided to have on hand almost 30 percent more capacity than was needed to meet peak demand, to protect against unexpected breakdowns. The CANDU program, too, called for higher reserve margins, to guard against uncertainties in the performance of this new technology. Added reserves, however, meant added expenditures.[22] In addition, Hydro greatly increased its attention to plant reliability; it developed sophisticated procedures for ensuring that reliability, as well as capital cost, was given due emphasis when new plants were designed.

This concern with system performance led, interestingly enough, to greater attention to environmental problems. Environmental complaints could delay the expansion of the system, as happened with the Nanticoke to Pickering transmission line. Moreover, as Hydro began the 1970s, it was not yet under substantial pressure to prevent rate increases. This affected its attitude toward environmental expenditures and toward spending to enhance system reliability. Even though Hydro's rates had begun to rise, they were still very low compared to the rates charged by many of Hydro's neighbors. In 1970, for example, Ontario consumers paid an average of $8.72 for 750 kilowatt-hours of electricity, while users in New York paid an average of $17.36, and consumers in Michigan paid $12.32.[23] Presumably because of its low rates, Hydro faced no official review or regulation of its rates until the mid-1970s.

Public power has not generated nearly as much antagonism in Canada as it has in the United States. Reflecting this openness, since Hydro's founding several other provinces have established provincially owned utilities. Hydro encountered some harsh opposition from private utilities in Ontario when it was first established, but the public-power issue was more or less completely settled in Ontario by the mid-1920s. For this reason, too, Hydro has not faced the same historical pressures as, say, TVA, to minimize rates in order to justify its existence.

With fuel and other costs going up, Hydro's rates began to rise just at the time the commitment to CANDU was made. These rising rates and the prospect of heavy borrowing generated concern over the company's financal impact on the province. From a long-run viewpoint, Hydro's strategy made sense, at the time, in terms of costs and energy security. Hydro estimated that a CANDU plant could generate electricity at about half the cost per kilowatt-hour of a coal-fired plant. The problem, however, was that the initial capital costs of CANDU plants were more than two and a half times greater, per megawatt of installed capacity, than the costs of fossil-fuel plants.[24] With Hydro's expansion program leaning heavily on nuclear plants, then, the strain on the province's capital resources was tremendous. Yet because Hydro could, in theory, issue reasonably low-rate bonds guaranteed by the government, these capital costs appeared acceptable in terms of narrow financial calculations.

All the public saw, however, was the increase in rates. For the first time, the Ontario Energy Board was called upon to review — although not to regulate — the wholesale rates Hydro charged. This group held extensive hearings on Hydro's entire approach to expansion planning, even before the establishment of the Porter Commission. In 1974 the Ontario Energy Board strongly suggested that Hydro reduce its planned reserve margin by 5 percent. Hydro refused. Subsequently, the government limited how much the utility could borrow. Essentially, the government declared that an annual growth rate of 7 percent in generating capacity was unrealistic. If increases in the price of electricity could not reduce the growth in demand to 6 percent a year, new ways would have to be found to encourage the conservation of electricity.[25]

To the disappointment of Hydro's critics, the Energy Board did not take a strong stance with regard to the company's rates. One year it even recommended that Hydro *add* to an already large proposed rate increase. The government reacted by appointing a legislative committee to oversee the rate question, a move that resulted in some reduction of the increase. As one government observer commented, "They [the government] didn't want to go down to defeat on support for the Energy Board."[26]

Rates, then, have ultimately become a significant issue in the province, and Hydro's failure to respond more positively eventually resulted in a tightening of formal mechanisms in this area. Even after pressures began to increase, however, Hydro was emphasizing performance concerns other than cost minimization. To a much greater extent than TVA, Hydro has an image of itself as a public company concerned with providing service as well as maintaining low costs. TVA saw low rates as a way to promote the well-being of the Tennessee Valley residents; Hydro's chosen mission is noticeably broader. As senior Hydro engineer, Bill Morison, described it: "We fell we should be better than most. I think this is the feeling pretty much throughout the organization. That's the way we should do the job, as opposed to saving the last buck. We're not a profit-making organization. We're here to serve the people of Ontario. And that gives us a chance to assess: What do the *people* want? And to use the resources of our company, which are tremendous, to serve those ends."[27] In fact, Hydro did not — and could not — give the people everything they wanted, since various objectives conflicted and priorities had to be set. Insofar as people wanted lower rates, Hydro was less responsive. Still, a desire to perform well, a responsiveness to outside concerns, and a willingness to forego short-term cost minimization were all characteristic of Hydro's behavior in the 1960s. All were encouraged by the company's external context, as well as by the structure of the Hydro organization itself.

Internal Organization

The outlook and organization of Hydro's engineering groups have been the key to Hydro's response to environmental pressures. In the face of growing ecological concern in Ontario, the engineers adopted a strategy of staying "one step ahead" of environmental regulations. Their efforts were facilitated by a well-integrated organizational structure developed in the latter part of the 1960s.

To some extent, the engineers' strategy may have been a description of what they felt they *should* do, as opposed to what they actually did do. For instance, we were told in some cases that steps were taken to protect the environment before government directives required action, when in fact the government directives came first. In many cases, however, Hydro has demonstrated significant responsiveness to environmental pressures. Interestingly, these policies developed without the guidance of a strong top management and initially without much input from outside-oriented staff groups—two factors that seemed especially important at Pacific Gas and Electric.

Hydro's "one step ahead" approach to environmental policies was closely related to its efforts to improve system reliability. In the late 1960s the company's engineers tried hard to ensure the smooth expansion and operation of the power system. This heightened their sensitivity to environmental issues as a potential obstacle to that expansion. Moreover, the aspects of Hydro's structure that facilitated attention to environmental matters were developed in large part to facilitate Hydro's expansion efforts.

As Hydro's top engineer for the past two decades, Harold A. Smith was central to the evolution of its strategy and structure. Smith enjoyed a formidable reputation for technical brilliance as a result of his key role in developing the CANDU nuclear technology. In the mid-1950s, in the face of skepticism from some scientists, an engineering team headed by Smith made a number of important breakthroughs that defined the nature of the CANDU technology. In 1957 Smith was placed in charge of Hydro's engineering activities.[28]

Quiet but self-assured, Smith has been willing to choose bold courses of action while clearly recognizing the risks involved; alternatives that are apparently safer, he feels, would only cripple Hydro in the long run. Committed to reducing the province's dependence on the United States for energy supplies, he has pushed for the development and use of CANDU despite considerable financial and technical uncertainties. "It should have been obvious that this was the only way to go. Without CANDU, we would be relying on the United States and other countries for 80 percent of our primary resources by 1980," he said. Smith's concern with internal organizational arrangements—and his willingness to make changes in these arrangements—also reflect his unusual combination of long-range thinking, caution, and decisiveness.

Smith is a staunch yet philosophical patriot. Speaking about problems with one of the early CANDU plants, he said, "The problems [at the Douglas Point pilot plant] were blown up all out of proportion by nitwits. This [lack of national self-confidence] is a very Canadian characteristic. You've got to look inward and see what you've got around the place."

Smith's views have clearly affected the pace and nature of Hydro's expansion program, but he has played a less active role in shaping the organization's environmental policies. While not an advocate of greater environmental spending, he has shown enough flexibility in this area to encourage his subordinates to do what they thought best. They, in turn, have tended to make responsive choices.

In emphasizing Smith's role, we are not suggesting that he has acted in defiance of higher authorities, or without their approval. The CANDU program, for instance, has depended critically on the support of successive general managers and chairmen at Hydro. Without Smith's commitment to the program, however, one wonders how quickly it would have gone forward. Smith's influence was increased by a number of organizational features.

Historically, many members of Hydro's top policy-making body, the Hydro Commission, had little administrative experience, although some members, such as J. S. Duncan and R. L. Hearn, were able administrators.[29] Moreover, before the Task Force Hydro reforms, the general manager was not in a position to exert extensive direction over the utility, given the large sweep of his responsibilities and his lack of a personal staff.

Officially, the heads of the various functional branches within the agency constituted the general manager's staff, and were in fact known as assistant general managers. Yet they were heavily involved in the work of their own branches and could not really serve as independent advisers to top management. As Douglas Gordon, formerly Hydro's general manager and now its president, commented: "In the general manager's setup, the assistant general managers, who were engaged full time in directing their own functionally and operationally oriented branches, found it difficult to allocate time to strategic planning. There was a tendency for the committee to act in a compartmentalized manner. The degree of analysis of each other's operations was minimal, and it was recognized that greater emphasis on strategic planning and corporate planning was required."[30]

As at TVA, weak general management and a divisional-based advancement pattern favored the emergence of strong leaders one level down. On occasion, the Hydro Commission overruled or superseded Engineering Branch recommendations, but this did not occur very often. For this reason, Smith was relatively free to make decisions designed to emphasize energy independence and system-reliability considerations. Ultimately, the expansion program he favored encountered constraints on capital, but this reversal seems to underline the extent to which Smith's outlook influenced Hydro policy. If there had been more nonengineering input into capacity planning, Hydro might have taken earlier account of capital constraints. On the other hand, Hydro was aware of the potential cost advantages of nuclear generation, assuming that financing were available.

On technical matters, top management's ability to evaluate engineering recommendations has been limited by the increasing concentration of engineering functions under the chief engineer's authority. Even when the general manager had some engineering training, as Doug Gordon did, Smith's acknowledged technical expertise put his critics at a disadvantage.

At the beginning of the 1960s some technical functions still remained outside Engineering. The managers in charge of these functions, however, reported to nontechnical bosses who could not provide strong leadership or control. Mainly at the general manager's initiative, these functions were moved into the Engineering Branch during the 1960s: research in 1961, system operations in 1965, and power plant operations in 1970.[31] Thus, Hydro lacked the competing centers of technical expertise that, partly for reasons of historical accident, existed in TVA.

Nonengineering personnel have had little input into Hydro's engineering decisions. In TVA the Division of Law or the Division of Environmental Planning has sometimes been able to confront the Office of Power and bring about changes in its decisions, but Hydro has had no similar mechanism for questioning decisions or actions of the Engineering Branch. There has been no independent environmental organization, and independent nontechnical staff have been few. TVA, for example, now has forty-eight lawyers, including about five lawyers who specialize in environmental matters. In contrast, at the time of our field work, Hydro had a total staff of five who had virtually no input into environmental decision making.[32] Public relations personnel have come to play an important role in some of Hydro's planning activities, but they have never functioned as a separate power center the way the lawyers or government- and community-affairs specialists have in PG&E.

How then did Hydro's environmental responsiveness come about? As head of the Engineering Branch, Smith took a great interest in organizational matters. Throughout the second half of the 1960s, he and some of his lieutenants restructured the Branch in a way that reduced the conflicts and misunderstandings often found among different technical groups—TVA's situation being a striking example. A key participant in the reorganization of engineering was P. G. (Pat) Campbell, whom Smith appointed as assistant chief engineer in charge of Design and Construction in 1965. (Campbell is now general manager for Design and Construction under Task Force Hydro's plan to delegate operational responsibility to divisional general managers, freeing the newly created vice-presidents—one of whom is Harold Smith—for long-range planning.) Putting Campbell, former head of construction, in charge of both activities was a big step toward greater integration. According to Smith, the designers formerly treated the construction engineers as a contractor, rather than as a partner.[33]

It is difficult in retrospect to know exactly why Smith and Campbell began to reorganize engineering at the particular time they did. Smith explains Campbell's appointment, which set the process in motion, as a result of his belief in the need for cooperation among functional groups, and also as a result of a historical accident—the death of the head of Design, which made Campbell's dual post easier to create. Smith expressed his management philosophy concerning the need for cooperation: "It used to be that, in many respects, one Division acted as if the other Division belonged to another company. We only make one product, round-the-clock, and it has to be high reliability. We can't have any of this five-quarterback stuff. It has to be a team."[34] Moreover, the same year Campbell was appointed, System Operations was moved into Smith's Branch, at the general manager's behest. So Smith needed more supervisory help in the design and construction part of his organization. Once a manager of both design and construction had been appointed, other changes to integrate engineering functions could take place.

Yet this is not the whole story. Soon after the restructuring began, Hydro encountered capacity shortages that were exacerbated by delays in constructing new plants. This was a serious difficulty when viewed against Hydro's concern with energy self-sufficiency. While the initial changes in Engineering may not have resulted from these shortages, the shortages clearly had an impact on later organizational developments. The gradual concentration of all technical functions in one Branch also reflects the absence of any other strong and independent focus for such activities within Hydro. In TVA, for example, the Office of

Power wanted to control environmental engineering, but there was a separate and competitive center of expertise that fought to maintain a distinct role for itself. Thus, Hydro's structural evolution — as is generally the case — has not been shaped only by present needs and by the character and beliefs of key individuals; the previous history of the organization, as embodied in the organizational structure, also played a significant role.

At TVA there was a tendency to promote engineers up through the functional Division in which they began their career. Smith, in contrast, encouraged diagonal mobility in the Engineering Branch as a way of breaking down parochial loyalties and viewpoints.[35] Beginning in 1966, he and Campbell began a series of structural changes that greatly increased integration among the various functional groups within Hydro's Engineering Branch.

One of their first changes was to reorganize design and construction from engineering disciplinary lines (civil, mechanical, and so forth) into new groups based on types of facilities. Groups were created for generating plants, substations, and transmission lines. In order to improve coordination between design and construction, they were responsible for both tasks.[36] Promoted to head the new Generation Projects Division was H. A. Jackson, a career construction man. His assistant was Bill Morison, the chief designer for the Pickering plant.

The next steps came in 1969. A new advance-planning group, the Generation Concept Department, was established within Generation Projects to collect and synthesize all possible inputs at the earliest stages of planning for new plants. Among other things, this group was instructed to ensure that Hydro was able to build plants that would operate reliably and with adequate protection for the environment. To keep projects on schedule, subsequent design and construction activities were put on a "project management" basis: a special team was established to handle the design and construction of each new major line or plant.[37]

The "project" approach was designed to increase attention to plant reliability and operability. Project teams included not only design and construction engineers, but also representatives of plant operations. Since the CANDU nuclear program had started, Harold Smith had taken steps to see that the men who would operate the new nuclear plants were involved in the process of their design. This approach was now extended to all thermal plants.[38]

Thermal operations activities were also reorganized, further increasing the operators' ability to influence design decisions.

Until 1970 the plant operators had been part of the Regions and Marketing Branch.[39] Each plant had reported to the manager of the region in which it was located, and as a result operations had lacked strong representation in the head office. In 1970 operations was made part of Engineering. A central office organization for thermal operations was established. Fossil-fuel operations had never had more than half a dozen engineers in the head office under the old organizational scheme. The new office, consisting of nine sections, now has about forty members attending to a wide variety of operational concerns. Contrast these efforts to improve the operators' position with the difficulty TVA's operators had in getting to "sit at the table" when decisions were made.

The new operations group was headed by Lorne McConnell, former head of nuclear operations. Like most nuclear men, he was committed to methodical approaches to monitoring and solving operating problems. This view in turn necessitated the kind of extensive central-services organization for fossil-fuel plants that was set up soon after the Thermal Generation Division was established.

Even before most of these structural changes occurred, Hydro's strategy had changed to give noticeably more emphasis to plant reliability. Hydro's reliability problems at its Lakeview station, built in the mid-1960s, had spurred a large-scale effort. "We've taken more steps to improve reliability than any other utility on the continent or in the United Kingdom," Arthur Hill, a long-time Hydro design engineer, commented in 1973.[40] Among the steps taken was a decision not to go above the 500 MW scale on new fossil-fired units. (In general, most new fossil-fuel units built by large North American utilities in recent years have been 700-1000 MW.) A decision was also made to avoid prototype units wherever possible, since prototypes, like those at Lakeview, almost always proved less reliable. The only exceptions to this policy were in cases where Canadian-manufactured units were purchased for nationalistic reasons. A deliberate policy was adopted of designing new plants for ease of operations and maintenance. Hydro also began training engineers in mathematical techniques for estimating the impact of various design options on plant reliability.

This emphasis on reliability and maintainability added to the capital cost of new units. But Hydro's designers justified their approach with a mathematical analysis showing that reducing outages — planned and unplanned — could save money in the long run by reducing the amount of reserve the system needed to assure adequate availability of power.[41]

This represented a major change in strategy. During the first ten or fifteen years of Hydro's use of thermal generation, the reliability of its plants was quite poor compared to those of the North American utility industry as a whole. The first four units at the Hearn plant had forced-outage rates averaging 7.6 percent for the years 1965-71, compared to an American utility average of 3.88 percent for similar units. And while Lakeview units 3-8 had forced-outage rates in the high teens, similar American units averaged about 6 percent.[42]

These reliability problems seem to have stemmed from just those features of Hydro's internal organization that recent reforms have altered. One long-time operating man described the problems that arose from having plants under the supervision of the regional managers—whose main job was marketing: "We could have had a major fossil generating unit out of service for several months, because of a lack of expensive spares. A request would go up and it could sit at the regional office for months before being processed. We had great difficulty in getting the regional managers to recognize the needs and importance of spares in fossil plants."[43] Although the operators had a small central office, their role in the design process was limited. "We would write directly to the head of the design section," the same operator recalled. "We would leave it to them to incorporate whatever they recognized as important." Until the mid-1960s, many of the operators' requests were rejected.[44]

Hydro's reliability problems were also exacerbated by inadequacies in its engineering organization. The utility's first two fossil-fuel plants were designed and built by outside consultants. It was not until 1957 that Hydro even had its own thermal design group; in that year fifteen to twenty engineers were brought in from outside to supplement a group of about thirty existing employees who had worked previously on hydroelectric plants. The group's newness and lack of experience hampered its ability to make judgments about equipment quality. "On reliability, you had to accept the manufacturers' statements," commented Arthur Hill, one early member of this group. "We didn't have any background in judgment. We didn't have a background in maintenance costs."[45]

The overall structure of Hydro's generating system had an impact on the value of and emphasis placed on reliability. Initially, fossil-fuel plants were not a large part of the system and were used mainly during peak-load periods; it was not critical that they be consistently available. "In the early years," said one thermal operations manager, "we could take a fossil unit out of service over a weekend for maintenance, and as long as it was back in by Monday, it was no problem. Now that we are required to run them far more regularly, reliability has become extremely important."[46]

The Generation Concept Department was charged with helping Hydro stay "one step ahead" of obstacles to smooth system performance. Given Smith's interest in system expansion, and the strong control system, members of the group were motivated to avoid possible difficulties even if doing so cost money. Given the low costs and rates Hydro had enjoyed, this seemed to some an acceptable trade-off in light of economic-development objectives. Moreover, having been given the responsibility for synthesizing a single strategy, the Concept Department was faced with the need to build a consensus in order to prevent others from complaining about its performance — again, even if this meant spending a little more on this or that ancillary objective. In TVA, in contrast, instead of the pivotal group accommodating the others, the Office of Power used its control over decision making to pressure other groups to accommodate themselves to its commitment to cost minimization.

In 1975 and 1976 the internal structure was changed again. Responsibility for coordinating advance planning in Hydro was divided among several groups, to facilitate handling the enormous work load created by the building program. These groups retain the tendency toward integrating perspectives characteristic of the Concept Department.

The Route and Site Selection Division identifies possible locations for new generation and transmission facilities, coordinates public participation in such decisions, and obtains government approval for the sites selected. Directed by Arthur Hill, the Division includes groups formerly in public relations and property as well as staff from other engineering divisions. Outside-oriented groups have become involved in Hydro's planning, but characteristically they have been brought within the engineers' domain.

Responsibility for designing new generating plants rests with the Generation Planning and Development Department. Part of the former Concept Department, it is backed up by two other groups that were also formerly in Concepts. One is responsible for energy and environment matters, and the other for nuclear studies and development.[47]

In this structure, there is really no independent group analogous to the Division of Health and Safety in TVA. There is no one who has the role of internal "policeman." Precisely because he dislikes this kind of competitive "five-quarterback" situation, Harold Smith has opposed the establishment of a separate environmental affairs staff in Hydro, preferring to locate responsibility for environmental decision making in the line groups responsible for planning in general. The new energy and environment group is less of a departure from this approach than it might appear, since it is drawn from the old Concept Department and is responsible to Bill Morison, as the old Concept Department was. This new group, too, continues to work closely with the generation planners, perpetuating the integrated approach to decision making.[48]

There may be losses as well as gains from this approach. Competition can encourage groups to develop new policy initiatives or promote particular viewpoints as a way of increasing their role in decision making. This dynamic is lost when organizational rivalry is carefully suppressed. In TVA, top management has deliberately used intergroup rivalry to establish a system of checks and balances; its early and extensive air quality monitoring program was largely a result of this process. In Hydro, where no strong environmental group has existed outside the line organization, a potential source of internal criticism and advice on environmental practices was eliminated. As a result, where Hydro is not strongly pressed from the outside on environmental problems the organization has done less than one might expect. Its cooperativeness in areas that have attracted outside attention is not matched by initiative in other spheres because there is no internal competition to generate such initiatives. This is most evident in the areas of air pollution monitoring and scrubber research and development.

Hydro does have a large and established Research Division which has undertaken some environmentally related work. But until the very end of the 1960s the organizational and financial basis for this effort was very limited. Air pollution monitoring was conducted by a section of the Chemistry Department within the Research Division. Initially, the group had too little money to buy any automatic monitors and, later, not enough to buy as many as it needed to do complete analyses at specific plants. The managers in charge of this research expected little sympathy for a request for more funds, and did not ask for them.[49]

The Research Division's lack of aggressiveness in this area follows in part from its role and circumstances. The group traditionally functioned as a service organization, performing tasks and developing expertise in areas where other parts of the organization requested assistance. Its members have had little incentive or opportunity to venture into a more aggressive and policy-oriented role, and their organizational situation has further discouraged such efforts. Throughout the 1950s, when Hydro first started building coal-fired generating plants, the Research Department was not part of Engineering. Rather, it reported to Hydro's assistant general manager for services, a nontechnical man who could not give the Research Division strong leadership. In 1961 Research was incorporated into Engineering, but Smith, although encouraging more research and development activity, wanted to avoid intergroup competition.[50]

The Public Relations Division is the one nontechnical staff group that has come to have considerable influence in Hydro's environmental affairs. This is especially so in connection with Hydro's public-information and participation procedures for siting new generating and transmission facilities. In part, the background of Jim Durand, the group's head from 1970 to 1975, helps to explain its success. A former engineer (in Distribution), Durand wanted his Division to handle more than routine activities, and he had enough experience in engineering to "open many doors" in Hydro, in the words of a subordinate.[51] The Division approached its job in a manner consistent with Smith's view of how a staff should operate. This undoubtedly facilitated its participation in the decision-making process. Public Relations looked for opportunities to be of help to the engineers, and *offered* its services to them. Since managing public participation activities called for skills that engineers do not always possess, this tactic led to a significant role for the group in such processes and in decision making generally. Ultimately, as in Pacific Gas and Electric, these outside-oriented personnel have come to play a large part in facilitating Hydro's responses to outside concerns.

The way in which Smith has used his authority over the Engineering Branch has been crucial to its environmental performance. As chief engineer, Smith employed personnel policies that gave him strong control over Hydro's engineers. He encouraged, and involved himself in, the movement of subordinates among Divisions. Subordinates thus did not have to depend on their immediate supervisor for advancement; they could (even had to) look to top management for rewards and promotion. And once a diagonal move occurred, the person promoted was likely to feel loyalty to the higher-up who put him into that position.

In addition, Smith was able to rely on the personal loyalty and shared perspectives of trusted lieutenants. Engineers who had been involved with Smith in the development of CANDU held key positions in the organization, Bill Morison and Lorne McConnell being two principal examples. Smith also placed considerable responsibility in the hands of Pat Campbell, for many years the assistant chief engineer for design and construction, a man obviously supportive of Smith's administrative approach.

Central to the engineers' environmental responsiveness is Smith's tolerance, indeed enthusiasm, for the expression of opinions different from his own. Smith has demonstrated that a top manager with strong controls *and* strong opinions can avoid the "LBJ effect": a powerful chief executive does not have to discourage all useful criticism of his own preferred policies. The failure of an organization to discipline its chief's enthusiasms can have serious consequences, as illustrated by PG&E's nuclear siting efforts. Having a manager with tight control over the organization is not enough to ensure its survival in the face of extreme external pressure. A manager with such controls can be too aggressive. Decisions that are ultimately disastrous are not opposed by those lower down who often know better.

For example, Smith would seem to have inculcated in his subordinates a strong sense of the importance of improving system reliability. Yet he has given his organization considerably leeway in defining the best tactics for achieving this objective. In particular, in the environmental area, the organization evolved a policy of making environmental expenditures that reduce obstacles to smooth system expansion. Thus, when a Committee on Amenities recommended that Hydro buy more attractive transmission towers (which would increase the cost of a new transmission line by over 50 percent), Smith initially argued against the plan. Eventually he went along, though he personally thought that it was not worth the cost to society. "Just because the Amenities Committee was reporting to me," he said, "I wouldn't lock their recommendation in the drawer. We're a team. I don't know how you can keep a team spirit if you play God and block someone out. We're talking about a range of judgments here. If you're running a team operation, you've got to let the team guys speak."[52] This management perspective has clearly influenced Hydro's reaction to environmental pressures. Subordinates feel it is their own responsibility to take a broad look at problems. As a result, even when Smith personally doubts the good sense of vocal public protests, those in Engineering feel free to take the public's sensitivities into account.

Whether a strong manager does or does not impose his own views on subordinates does not tell us whether or not the company policy will be environmentally sensitive. Smith had only to allow his organization to respond to obtain good environmental performance in some areas. In contrast, PG&E chairman Robert Gerdes got action by *insisting* that his engineers find some solution to the sky discoloration problem at Moss Landing.

On other occasions, PG&E and Hydro have both behaved in ways that outsiders perceived as undesirable, when their top managers' personal commitments guided company policy. Several times, mainly on the basis of his personal judgment, Smith has recommended large investments. By doing so, he has led the organization into a political thicket that his subordinates might have avoided, if only out of timidity. Smith had a strong personal belief in the necessity and workability of CANDU. He also favored large capacity reserves to guarantee energy independence. These views help explain why the organization has proposed such large investments in these areas. There was no outside pressure to do this; indeed, Hydro made these investments in the face of public skepticism.

This is not to say that Smith or any other Hydro manager created a policy direction that the Hydro Commission did not back. The commission stood behind the principle of energy independence in general and the development of CANDU technology in particular. In committing itself to both the Pickering and Bruce plants, however, the Hydro Commission relied heavily on Smith's expert judgment that the plants would perform as projected. Smith stresses that his superiors did not depend on his judgment of the plants from an overall economic and strategic point of view.[53] But his views were clear and strong: Smith believed CANDU would work, indeed that it had to work.

Hydro's commitment to large reserve margins also reflects Smith's influence. He not only encouraged his subordinates to work toward larger reserves but, at one point in the 1960s, personally made the decision to add two 500 MW units to the expansion program. This choice, Smith admits, was not based on any detailed numerical analysis, but rather on overall, informal balancing of risks and benefits. "To overcome the shortfall, at my insistence, we committed two more 500 MW units—without a detailed economic analysis. One unit was to cover for Pickering. This seemed prudent to me as a matter of insurance. I would not have taken the action if the system planners had been adamant against it. But they weren't. They concurred with my judgment."[54] On the basis of Smith's recommendation, the commission decided to approve the two additional units.

The changes in Hydro's organization brought about at the recommendation of Task Force Hydro potentially could reduce Smith's influence. Top management's control of the engineering groups has been relatively weak and unorganized. As publicly owned utilities mature, they are often viewed as carrying out non-controversial, technical functions, and this perhaps reduces lay involvement in engineering decisions. The problem, then, as Task Force Hydro recognized, is to find a way to take into account nontechnical values and considerations: "The choice of a nuclear reactor system, for example, has an important bearing on system security and the cost of power well beyond the comprehension of most laymen. Such comprehension is, however, vital, if the political decision maker in government and at the top levels of the Hydro organization is to arrive at decisions which will result in effective, consistent policy direction for Hydro."[55]

Task Force Hydro's recommendations are a definite step in a new direction. As we noted previously, the company's six-member board was expanded, in part to permit the inclusion of more experienced, expert, and diversified membership. A new corporate office, composed of a series of functional vice-presidents, was established to support the agency's chief administrative officer. The day-to-day supervision of operations was placed in the hands of Divisional managers, in order to free the vice-presidents for long-range planning.

In the short run, it is not clear to what extent the changes have affected the manner in which Hydro policy is formulated. As vice-president for engineering and operations, Harold Smith retains a major role in the new structure. In the long run, however, the creation of a corporate office and greater professionalism of the new board should increase top management's ability to evaluate independently the recommendations of the engineering staff. In fact, the new Hydro board has cooperated with the government's induced cutback in the expansion program that was so dear to Smith.[56] This may not reflect any change in internal (as opposed to external) power. In the long run, however, the new management structure seems likely to reduce the influence of the engineers.

Environmental Decisions

Hydro's circumstances and structure have led it to anticipate and respond to environmental demands before they develop into major conflicts. This strategy has not been followed in all cases, nor has Hydro successfully anticipated all external pressures. Nevertheless, Hydro has demonstrated a readiness to spend today to meet future requirements, to go beyond official regulations, and to seek out and try to provide what the public wants.

Consider, for example, the decision to spend $7 million for precipitators at the oil-fired Lennox generating station. The ash content of oil is only about 1 percent of the ash content of coal, and only a few utilities have installed particulate control equipment on oil-fired units. Concerned, however, about the appearance of the plant's smoke plume, Hydro's engineers recommended such measures at Lennox.

This decision reflects many of the factors that have affected Hydro's behavior. In part, it was a response to the high level of environmental concern in Ontario. In the 1960s Hydro had been publicly criticized for the air pollution caused by coal-fired plants, particularly the two located in Toronto. The engineers did not expect that particulates from the Lennox plant would actually constitute a health hazard. But they were concerned about the *appearance* of environmental negligence that a visible smoke plume might create.[57]

Wes James, the Hydro engineer who recommended installing the precipitators at Lennox, said that he was concerned that the plume might exceed opacity standards even though only a small amount of ash would be emitted. When asked why Hydro did not apply for a variance to cover this contingency, he responded, "We would not design a plant on the basis of a variance if we thought that the expenditure of a reasonable amount of additional capital would correct the problem. If we did so, and concerns were expressed about the opacity of the stack plume after the units commenced operation, the Ministry of Environment would be very sensitive to them. The result could be a considerable expenditure in both time and money to correct the situation, and, in the meantime, we would have to continue with a plume that was of concern to our neighbors."[58]

Ministry officials had explicitly told Hydro that precipitators would not be necessary at Lennox. The decision to install them came as quite a surprise.[59] Hydro was reacting very strongly indeed to the risk of possible political problems and showing less concern about the rate implications of the pollution controls.

Several features of Hydro's internal structure contributed to this response. Lennox was the first plant that the newly created Concept Department had planned. Its members, including Wes James, were no doubt eager to have the project proceed without major objections or difficulties. Furthermore, the members of the Concept Department took their job especially seriously because of the incentives they faced; strong control from the top, loyalty to their superiors, and the prospect of diagonal mobility made them eager to do what was expected of them. They had been given considerable discretion in the environmental area, which they felt a responsibility to use in Hydro's best interests, all things considered. Thus, James gave consideration to the way in which complaints about Lennox would affect the Ministry of Environment and the way in which this, in turn, would affect Hydro.

Such concern about overall priorities is the job of a senior manager. It is unusual to find that the incentive and control system has effectively posed the same strategic problem to an engineer seven steps down in the organization. At Hydro the process of delegation—without decentralization—to this group of "integrators" had precisely this result, and the company showed noticeable flexibility on environmental issues. The engineers who made the decision had reasons to avoid taking the narrow view that "this is how we have always done things down here in mechanical engineering." Their leader, Harold Smith, whom they wanted to please, would have disapproved of such a narrow view—and would have been unlikely to reward them for taking it.

Even before the engineering reorganization of 1965, Hydro had installed better particulate controls than some of the other companies in our study—although this comparison is not straightforward. Starting with its first coal-fired plants, built in the early 1950s, Hydro installed electrostatic precipitators to control its particulate emissions. By the late 1950s it was installing precipitators that were 98 percent efficient. In the early 1960s the Hydro Commission initiated the regular use of precipitators that were 99.5 percent efficient.[60] TVA, in contrast, put mechanical collectors on new plants throughout the 1950s, but many of these plants were in rural, nonindustrial areas with clean air. Boston Edison installed precipitators with design efficiencies of only 95 percent at urban plants as late as 1961. Boston Edison aside, however, Hydro's record in this regard was not very different from that of a number of other major American utilities such as Commonwealth Edison in Chicago, Detroit Edison, and Consolidated Edison in New York, which operated coal-burning plants in northern urban areas.[61] Thus, it was only in the early 1970s that the relative lack of cost constraints on Hydro, combined with the changes in Hydro's structure, produced some decisions that were unusual in their environmental sensitivity.

Hydro has responded with similar sensitivity to external pressures to increase the public's role in the selection of routes and sites for new transmission lines and generating stations. In a sense, it had little choice, given government pressure to change its procedures. But rather than waiting for the government to spell out requirements, Hydro plunged into the process of developing new planning methods. Both technical and nontechnical groups participated in this endeavor. The engineers, concerned with system reliability, have been especially strong proponents of responsiveness rather than confrontation.

Following its normal practice, Hydro had selected the initial route for a major transmission line between its Nanticoke and Pickering stations on the basis of internal evaluations and discussion with local officials, provincial agencies, and citizen groups. In the absence of strong opposition Hydro would normally have simply proceeded, with ready government approval. In late 1971, however, a coalition of local landowners and conservation groups began to oppose the line. In June 1972, in response to their petition, the premier of the province appointed Omond Solandt, past chairman of the Science Council of Canada, as a one-man royal commission to conduct a review of the project. That fall, Solandt held hearings on the proposed route. He then issued an interim report asking for permission to hire a consultant to undertake a whole new route-selection process, involving extensive public participation. The government granted his request, and between February and July 1973 Solandt's consultant, Bruce Howlett, conducted three sets of public meetings to sketch out possible routes for the line and to obtain public comments on them. In September 1973 Howlett recommended a new route that would follow a proposed new parkway for much of its distance. After further hearings, in April 1974 Solandt himself recommended this route.[62]

At the time of Solandt's appointment, Hydro had already chosen routes for two other transmission lines — from Lennox to Oshawa and from Bradley to Georgetown — and had already received government approval for the latter. Following Solandt's appointment, the government withdrew its approval for the Bradley-Georgetown line and Hydro withdrew its Lennox-Oshawa proposal.[63] Both recognized that in view of changed public expectations the old methods for selecting transmission routes were no longer adequate. So while Solandt was restudying the Nanticoke-Pickering line, Hydro began to conduct new studies to select routes for the other two lines.

The question was how best to involve the public in the process. Solandt's 1972 hearings and interim report and Howlett's on-going work would help. But Hydro—and the consultant it employed to assist with its new Lennox-Oshawa study—still had to exercise some creativity. A special steering committee of Division directors, some from Engineering and some from other Branches, came up with a plan, which was sent to a larger coordinating Committee on Amenities, chaired by Pat Campbell, and then on to Harold Smith. The steering committee proposed the creation of multidisciplinary teams to coordinate the planning process for these two lines, and a third line for Nanticoke to London, Ontario. Each team would include not only regular transmission-line planners but also ecologists and experts from the Public Relations and Property Divisions.[64] This, in fact, is how Hydro proceeded. The establishment of these teams evidently reflected the engineers' sense of what was needed to assure an adequate response to public pressure. They may also show the results of the efforts of public relations director Jim Durand, a former distribution engineer himself, to increase his Division's involvement in engineering affairs.

Using an approach similar to the one used by Howlett, the teams' work included several phases. Each team collected extensive data on the region and a wide variety of opinions from municipal authorities, provincial agencies, and the public, using public meetings and in some cases opinion surveys. On the basis of this information, the team selected a number of alternative, minimum-impact "corridors" for the proposed line. At subsequent public meetings and meetings with special-interest groups, these corridors were presented for public discussion and comment. Specific alternative routes were plotted, and, in some cases, more public meetings were held.[65] What is significant here is the strategic flexibility Hydro displayed in developing new procedures and accommodating new pressures. Perhaps its political circumstances would have ultimately made some degree of responsiveness necessary. But instead of resisting until coerced, the organization instituted a very large change in its standard operating procedures. Doing so may have been in its interests, but different organizations in the same circumstances might well have chosen differently.

Although Solandt had been appointed to review only the Nanticoke-Pickering line, the government extended his authority to include the Lennox-Oshawa line. Hence, when Hydro had developed its proposal in April 1974, it was submitted to Solandt. A year later he issued his report, making some changes in the route but generally approving Hydro's plans. Because the Bradley-Georgetown line intersected Nanticoke-Pickering, his review of the latter helped to define the former. In May 1975 the government asked its new Environmental Hearing Board—established to carry out Solandt-type reviews on a regular basis—to review a piece of the Bradley-Georgetown line. In December 1975 the board recommended that Hydro change the route of this segment also.[66]

Hydro began to involve the public in the process of planning new generating stations, although the government never specifically instructed it to do so. Again, such a strategy facilitated Hydro's expansion program and protected it—and the government—against charges of unresponsiveness. Hydro moved more slowly in this area than it did on transmission lines, however. In 1974 public-information meetings were held on units being added at the Thunder Bay and Pickering sites. Here, the choice of site was not an open question, and the meetings were conducted largely to get information to the public. But in 1973 Hydro did make a siting choice for a new plant on the basis of public comment—even changing its intended design of the plant to conform to the site the public preferred. In 1975 Hydro began a public-participation process, similar to the ones used in the selection of transmission-line routes, to choose the site for yet another new generating station; this process combined the choice of transmission routes with the selection of generating sites. In March 1976 two citizen committees were formed to participate in this work. Within a year they had developed transmission-band alternatives and had gone on to consider sites compatible with these zones.[67]

The multidisciplinary approach to siting now has a permanent organizational basis. Since 1975 the job of finding acceptable locations for new generating plants and transmission lines has been the function of a new Route and Site Selection Division. Clearly, there are important structural similarities between this Division and the old Concept Department, which handled some of the early public-information efforts related to new generation sites. However, nonengineering functions and engineering functions are integrated directly into a single organization—thus taking the philosophy of previous developments another step forward.

Members of the new Division have taken steps to bring representatives of various interest groups into the planning process on an ongoing basis. In this way Hydro will have more continuous feedback, and the groups will be able to confront problems posed by their competing needs and desires. Hydro will be in a better position to maintain some control of the process, even though under the provisions of the new Environmental Assessment Act the provincial minister of the environment may submit Hydro's route and site proposals to the Environmental Hearing Board for further review.

The Route and Site Selection Division has initiated a two-stage process to develop siting plans with the participation of citizens' committees. In the first stage, the focus of study is a large region encompassing thousands of square miles, and the citizens' committees involved include representatives from a variety of regional organizations. As alternatives become more specific, locally based organizations become involved in the assessment of particular routes and sites.[68]

Meanwhile, the Royal Commission on Electric Power Planning chaired by Arthur Porter has been conducting a large study, involving extensive public hearings, of the way in which Hydro's need for new facilities should be determined. As time goes on, Hydro's public-participation procedures — and the issues exposed to public comment — are becoming more extensive, reflecting the high level of both public and government concern with Hydro's choices in this area.

Hydro has been less aggressive in ameliorating environmental damage where its impact is less visible and less likely to produce disruptive public protest. Sulfur dioxide emission control is a case in point. While utilities in the United States are generally required to limit SO_2 emissions, Ontario's regulations only limit ambient sulfur dioxide concentrations at the point at which emissions "impinge" on the ground or on some object outside the plant. There are specific emissions regulations pertaining to Hydro's two Toronto plants, but Ontario's regulations in general allow Hydro to employ a tall-stack strategy and to rely on atmospheric dilution to keep ground-level concentrations below set standards.

TVA, facing different regulations, decided to build a prototype SO_2 scrubber big enough to serve a 500 MW unit at the Widows Creek plant. Boston Edison, in 1970, began to operate an experimental magnesium oxide prototype scrubber, having worked for some years on the concept jointly with a chemical company. Southern has done considerable work on methods of removing sulfur from coal before it is burned, and has also built three 20 MW prototype scrubbers for purposes of selecting one technology for further development. Hydro, in comparison, built only a 1.5 MW prototype scrubber system and canceled plans to build a 100 MW prototype when it did not receive the subsidies it had requested from the provincial and federal governments.[69]

Hydro has taken some actions on sulfur. It switched from coal to sulfur-free natural gas at its Hearn plant in 1970, following the Pollution Probe hearings on Hydro's plans to abate pollution there through the use of a tall stack. Hydro engineers, however, note that the switch — to Canadian gas from Alberta — was made largely to reduce dependence on the American coal market, in which labor and transport problems raised the possibility of sudden shortages that Canadians could not control.[70]

The organization has tried to be forward-looking on the problem. Several years after it was founded, the Concept Department initiated a joint effort with the Air Management Branch of the Ontario Ministry of the Environment to develop some guidelines on the total concentration of SO_2 that would be acceptable in the vicinity of future generating sites. The result was a range of permissible SO_2 levels, varying according to the degree of other development in the vicinity of a proposed plant. This analysis appears to have played a part in the decision not to locate additional units at the Lennox site — the least-cost option; a new location, Wesleyville, was chosen in order to spread out the SO_2 emissions.[71] But these steps seem only to emphasize the fact that there has been little attention paid to sulfur emissions control technology.

Hydro's policies in this regard partly reflect the lack of any internal group in a strong position to expand research and development work in this area. The Research Division has been making some efforts in the area of air pollution research for about twenty years — longer than most other utilities in our study. But given the work's limited funding (until quite recently), the effort has been low-key. In 1956 Doug Harrison, a Hydro research engineer, and a few others began looking into the air pollution situation at the Hearn plant in downtown Toronto, in anticipation of a major expansion in generating capacity. Harrison's group was until 1969 a section in the Research Division's Chemistry Department. This status, far down in the organization, both reflected and reinforced a pattern of low budgets, low visibility, and low priority. While TVA was using automatic monitors and doing helicopter surveys to chart the course of plumes from its steam plants, Hydro's group relied on lead peroxide candles for SO_2 monitoring

—fairly crude equipment that yielded only monthly averages. To track short-term variations continuous automatic monitors, costing three thousand dollars each, would have been necessary. Harrison felt that his group could not afford a significant number of them.[72]

By the mid-1960s Hydro had installed some automatic monitors. In retrospect, Harrison felt that the group would have needed quite a few more to do an adequate job. "We have lost a good deal of confidence in the meaning of our [earlier] results," he commented. "It seems that with half a dozen monitors [the most that Hydro had at any one plant], the chance of a plume impinging on a monitor at any one time is exceedingly small." He pointed out, however, that by positioning the monitors in locations where maximum concentration could be expected and taking readings over a period of time, his group was in a position over time to measure the severity of the plant's impact on its surroundings.[73] Given the climate at the time, inside and outside the organization, neither Harrison nor C. H. Clark, the head of the Chemistry Department, felt that their superiors would want to give air pollution research a much larger budget. "These things level off at various plateaus," Clark said. "The plateaus are higher over time, but you can't start from nothing and pole-vault right up to the top."[74]

The Research Division's unwillingness to play the environmental advocate is shown in other ways. In response to complaints from Toronto officials and newspapers, Don Gillies, a meteorologist associated with the System Operations Division, urged the occasional use of low-sulfur coal at Hydro's Hearn plant in 1967. The Research Division had concluded that this measure was not needed, stating on the basis of surveys it had conducted with lead peroxide candles that it had found no evidence that the plant was having a serious impact on SO_2 levels in the city. This may have been true for monthly and yearly averages, but not for specific events. Gillies tried the simple expedient of watching the Hearn plant for his office window, noting when its smoke plume was blowing in the direction of a continuous automatic SO_2 monitor operated by the province's Ministry of Health. He would later check the monitor readings, which increased substantially when Hearn's plume blew in the monitor's direction. By this somewhat unorthodox method, Gillies provided evidence of the need for tighter controls. As a result, Hydro's fuel purchasing group began buying low-sulfur coal to be stockpiled at Hearn for use under adverse weather conditions.[75]

The Research Division had neither the incentive nor the experience to act more aggressively. It already had a fairly large and stable sphere of activity, and there was no precedent in Hydro for it to take an initiative independent of a request from Engineering. The Division, which now comprises over four hundred people, traditionally has been a service and resource group for the rest of the organization. Over the years it has developed expertise concerning various technologies and materials, and has given advice on such matters to others in the organization. Much of its work is done on request, or in anticipation of future requests.[76]

The contrast with comparable groups in our other companies is instructive. TVA's Division of Health and Safety did not have the same broad laboratory and testing functions; it concentrated on monitoring the health effects of the power program, particularly outbreaks of malaria due to dam construction and reservoir management. TVA's switch to steam plants in a sense forced Health and Safety to find new areas of expertise or risk a decline in its organizational position. In focusing on its traditional activities, Hydro's Research Department acted more like the Division of Forestry, Fisheries, and Wildlife in TVA, which tried to avoid taking a strong regulatory role in relation to TVA's purchases of strip-mined coal.

Another contrast is offered by the small environmental group in PG&E that has remained in a relatively minor advisory and consulting role, while law, public relations, and public affairs fill many of its potential functions. Hydro's research directors (like the head of PG&E's environmental group) have not been especially aggressive. Alternatively, Southern's Research and Environment Division, a new group headed by an outside expert, has vigorously tried to expand its budget and activities; but although an aggressive individual at Hydro might have done more, aggressiveness was neither necessary for the group's continued functioning nor a natural outgrowth of previous strategies.

Consider the role of Don Gillies. In a staff position in an odd corner of the organization, he has several times taken the initiative within Hydro on air pollution matters. Yet Gillies, unlike the people in Research, was accustomed to offering advice to the power systems operators. Moreover, he was something of a lone operator in his Division, and so had fewer reasons to take a conservative view than the manager of a large, functioning Division.

In 1969, when public outcries about Hydro's air pollution were reaching a peak, Harrison's group was reorganized as a special environmental task force. With more personnel and funding,

Harrison was able to buy considerably more equipment — twenty automatic monitors for the Nanticoke station, among other things. With external concern growing, Hydro's top management felt the need for a bigger research program in the environmental area.

In this atmosphere, Harrison felt hopeful enough to broaden his activities to include scrubber development work, believing that public concern with SO_2 required some effort by Hydro in this area. Considerable enthusiasm for this work eventually developed among Hydro's engineers; some suggested building a 30 MW prototype. At Harold Smith's suggestion, plans went forward for building a 100 MW facility. Harrison had built two small prototypes, one on a .25 MW scale, and the other on a 1.5 MW scale. Hydro's plan was to pay 50 percent of the cost of the 100 MW prototype and obtain the other half of the funds from the provincial and federal governments. Government support for the project was not forthcoming, however, and the project was terminated.[77] This illustrates how internal initiatives do not always change an organization's behavior, especially when external pressures are not great enough to bring top management fully behind the efforts.

Similarly, lack of public concern about heat discharges into the Great Lakes helps to explain why Hydro has followed a practice of using once-through cooling at all its plants. Certainly, the low temperatures and large volumes of the lakes make thermal emission control less important in Ontario than in some other regions, but even so, Hydro has been relatively unaggressive in this area. In fact, the Ministry of Environment reports that "on many occasions the temperature restrictions of 20° F and 15° F [on temperature rise on Lakes Ontario and Erie, respectively] at Ontario Hydro power plants are being exceeded. This occurred on 110 days during 1973 at Pickering Generating Station."[78]

In Ontario Hydro external pressures, organizational strategy and structure, and important elements of individual personality have interacted to account for environmental decisions. Public concern and the potential influence of the government over Hydro gave the organization much reason for seeking to accommodate public protests. This tactic was reinforced by the organization's own strategic emphasis on both generation and transmission reliability, which could be compromised by protest-induced delays in project completion. Where public pressures have demanded a response contrary to the organization's basic strategy, Hydro's response has been noticeably less cooperative. In particular, the organization had planned to develop a nuclear system based on the CANDU technology, with high generating reserves to guarantee reliability in the face of technical uncertainty. This strategy required enormous capital expenditures and had serious rate implications. When public concern about rates and about Hydro's role in Ontario's economy became widespread, the system definitely was *not* "one step ahead" in responding to them. The government had to exercise its latent power and impose investment and rate restrictions to bring about a change in Hydro's system development plans.

These events also illustrate our general observation that managers, when they have at their disposal a strong and deep control system, can shape an organization's behavior if they so choose. Smith was willing to be persuaded to spend more on the environment than he otherwise might have, partly because such decisions did not go to the heart of his strategic commitments. Generation planning was another matter, however. Here his views clearly dominated, even when he had to directly overrule subordinates' work.

Hydro's various decisions demonstrate clearly the dynamic interaction between internal and external influences on an organization's behavior—especially when external constraints, and hence the organization's opportunities, are in a period of flux. Hydro's (and Smith's) strategy of national self-sufficiency was well adapted to an older set of circumstances, but less well adjusted to more recent pressures. At the same time, nothing in the external situation demanded either the commitment that Hydro made to CANDU or its sustained effort to build up reserves.

In retrospect, successful organizations are those whose internal structures lead them to strategies that are adapted to their external circumstances. An imperfectly coercive environment will tolerate more than one strategic choice. Hydro has been positively responsive in some areas and less so in others. The historical development of the company has produced a structure giving power to individuals whose strategic commitments have led to these results. At the same time, the overall structure has shown fluidity in fostering appropriate lower-level integration and strategic planning. Delegating so much responsibility to a staff group can be risky—unless one exercises the sort of leadership that Smith does. It remains to be seen whether Hydro's new structure will enable top management to transmit government concerns more effectively into operational strategic priorities.

7

The Southern Company

The Southern Company, a multistate, multicompany system, provides electricity to the area immediately to the south of TVA, including most of Georgia and Alabama and parts of Mississippi and Florida. Expanding environmental requirements have posed new challenges for Southern, as they have for other companies. Yet given its situation, it has had less to fear from public-relations difficulties on environmental issues than Pacific Gas and Electric or Hydro; Southern's customers are less concerned with environmental matters, and institutionally have fewer ways to exert control. A well-managed organization in such a situation could plausibly choose the strategy that Southern has generally followed: communicating its views on regulatory requirements to state agencies who are likely to be sympathetic, given the general climate of opinion; and, to avoid legal complications and delay, making sure through advance planning that it is able to comply with whatever regulations do emerge.

Implementing such an approach is not easy. To accomplish the first task a company needs effective political and bureaucratic contacts with regulators. To accomplish the second, it needs technical and organizational creativity and forward-looking management. Yet Southern has achieved both goals through a complex organizational structure that is capable of both initiative and stubbornness in varying circumstances. A leader in utility efforts to amend federal environmental legislation, it has also been able to find the supplies of low-sulfur coal for its plants that TVA long claimed were unavailable. But although Southern's structure has enabled it to comply with external demands, the company has not developed an overall strategy of positive responsiveness.

In most cases, the company responds only as much as it has to, given the pressures it faces. It does make exceptions to this rule, and may approve added expenditures when it perceives that there will be long-run benefits. But the company's general stance illustrates that there is no necessary one-to-one link between an organization's structural capacity for responsiveness and the strategy it actually chooses with regard to environmental regulations.

In view of the fact that the system comprises four separate operating companies (one in each state), a jointly owned service company, and a parent company, we might expect maintaining policy coherence to be a problem. But a well-designed internal structure has helped minimize coordination difficulties. A large and collegial top-management group has enabled Southern to respond effectively to most outside demands. A distinct exception is Southern's limited capacity to deal with organized citizen groups; having faced much less pressure from such groups than companies like Pacific Gas and Electric, it has not developed the same kind of sophisticated strategies and structural units.

Background and Context

The four operating companies within the Southern Company System are the Alabama Power Company and the Georgia Power Company (which serve most of their respective states), the Mississippi Power Company in southeast Mississippi, and Gulf Power Company in northwest Florida. Southern's operating subsidiaries are responsible for their own plant construction, operation, distribution, and marketing, but their electrical systems are interconnected and jointly operated. On a minute-to-minute basis, power is dispatched from whichever plant can produce it most economically. The operating companies also decide together where to add new capacity.[1] Figure 17 shows the service areas of the four operating companies.

Joint dispatching has several advantages. It reduces operating expenses by allowing the most efficient capacity in the region to be used at any one time. It also permits capital savings: by creating a larger system and allowing for risk-sharing, it reduces the absolute amount of reserve capacity that any one company must maintain in order to achieve any given target level of service reliability; and by increasing the size of new plants that can be built at any one time, it enables the companies to enjoy economies of scale in design and construction.

Although the Southern Company as presently constituted has been in existence only since 1947, its subsidiaries have been part of a unified system since the mid-1920s.[2] Initially they functioned

Figure 17. The Southern Company System: service area and major coal and nuclear generating stations. Based on information supplied by the Southern Company.

within a holding company known as the Southeastern Power and Light Company, subsequently becoming part of the larger Commonwealth and Southern holding company empire. Although the system's name and membership have changed several times over the years, the relationship among the four system companies has remained much the same.

The system really began in 1912. In that year James Mitchell, an adventurer and utility engineer who had previously worked in Brazil, England, and Japan, came to Alabama. With the assistance of a local attorney named Thomas Martin he formed the Alabama Traction Company to consolidate a number of small utility holdings and hydroelectric franchises in the state into a single system. They named the combined system the Alabama Power Company.

From the beginning, Mitchell envisioned an electric system extending throughout several Southern states. Evidently he was motivated in part by the fact that Alabama's hydroelectric potential greatly exceeded the likely demands within the state. In 1919 he had Eugene Yates, Alabama Power Company's first chief engineer (later president of the Southern Company), begin planning for such an interconnected system. In 1920 and 1922 Alabama's first out-of-state interconnections were established, with two companies in Georgia.

James Mitchell died in 1920, leaving Thomas Martin, who succeeded him as president of the Alabama Power Company, to bring his dreams of a multistate electric system into being. Martin served as president until 1949 and as chairman and general counsel until his death in 1964. In 1924 he established the Southeastern Power and Light Company to replace the Alabama Traction Company. Southeastern then advanced capital to the Georgia, Mississippi, and Gulf power companies so that they could consolidate independent utility properties in their states, in much the same way as Alabama Traction had brought together independent utilities in Alabama. These new companies relied on Southeastern's capital and on administrators provided by Alabama Power Company.

Georgia had only limited hydroelectric capacity of its own, and Mississippi and Florida had none at all. The companies in these three states, therefore, obtained a substantial amount of their electricity from Alabama Power, via specially built transmission lines. Financially and physically, Southern's four subsidiaries were operating as a single system as early as the mid-1920s. Although these companies continue to operate as a unified system, today 84 percent of the system's electricity is derived from coal and only 7 percent is generated at hydroelectric plants.[3]

In the late 1920s, in the midst of explosive nationwide growth in electric utility holding companies, Southeastern was absorbed into a larger conglomerate. The new Commonwealth and Southern Company, the product of this merger, included utilities in Michigan, Indiana, Illinois, Ohio, and Tennessee, as well as the five Southeastern companies. Physically, however, the Southeastern system remained separate; most of the northern companies were geographically isolated and were not interconnected electrically, either to each other or to the companies in the South.

Under the new structure, staff functions such as purchasing and engineering were performed for the company's operating subsidiaries by a service organization with headquarters in New York. But most of the staff members doing engineering work for the southern subsidiaries worked in a regional office in Birmingham, Alabama. Many of these people were drawn from the old Southeastern system and functioned with substantial independence from the New York headquarters. To a considerable extent, then, the southern utilities continued to operate as a separate system throughout their association with Commonwealth and Southern.[4]

Under the leadership of Wendell Willkie, then president of Commonwealth and Southern, the organization stood together against the challenge posed by the Tennessee Valley Authority. Following its creation in 1933, TVA began to encroach on the service areas of several Commonwealth and Southern subsidiaries. Unable to compete with TVA's low rates, the Alabama, Mississippi, and Tennessee power companies sold some of their transmission and distribution lines to TVA in 1934. Competition from TVA continued, however. In response, Commonwealth and Southern, along with several other utilities, filed a suit challenging the constitutionality of TVA's power program. Willkie conducted a nationwide speaking campaign against TVA's encroachments—a campaign that vaulted him into the 1940 presidential race against Franklin Roosevelt. After the utilities' suit failed, Commonwealth and Southern ultimately sold its entire Tennessee system, as well as parts of its Alabama and Mississippi properties, to TVA. In exchange, it obtained an informal promise from TVA not to expand further (an understanding that did not receive the force of law until the TVA Revenue Bond Act was passed in 1959).[5]

Undoubtedly influenced by the TVA threat, the southern utility companies made several rate reductions during this period. The rate reductions also reflected the decreasing incremental costs of producing electricity, as larger and more efficient units were installed. Both Thomas Martin and Wendell Willkie appreciated the benefits, in the form of greater electricity use, that would result from lower rates. At the time Southeastern was formed, the South had little industry. The system's growth was clearly dependent on the economic expansion of the region. As Martin put it, the "manufacture . . . of customers" had to be an important function of the companies—paralleling the "manufacture of power"—if they were to find markets for their electricity.[6]

The utilities furthered this aim in a number of ways. Industrial-development departments were established in all Southeastern operating companies in the 1920s. These departments served as unofficial departments of commerce in their respective states: they collected data on industrial opportunities, located potential sites for new plants, advertised in the North, and lobbied during World War II for placing war industries in the region. The system companies also became active supporters of local and state chambers of commerce. In 1941 Thomas Martin himself played an important role in the establishment of the Southern Research Institute, an organization designed to conduct scientific research and enhance the South's attractiveness as a setting for modern, technologically sophisticated industries.[7] This attention to the prosperity of the region paid off in terms of expanding demand for electricity, establishing a rapport with leading political figures in state government, and improving the public image of the companies.

TVA was not the only federal challenge that Commonwealth and Southern faced during the 1930s. In 1935, concerned that control over utilities was passing into the hands of a "power trust," Congress passed the Public Utilities Holding Company Act. Commonwealth and Southern was apparently innocent of the worst abuses uncovered during an eight-year investigation of the utilities that preceded passage of this law. Its financial foundations were relatively sound, and it had refrained from various practices used by other holding companies to drain extra profits from their subsidiaries. But because its holdings were not physically unified, Commonwealth and Southern was condemned to dissolution by Section 11 of the Holding Company Act—called the "death sentence" clause by Wendell Willkie and widely known by that name.[8]

Court proceedings, and possibly the reluctance of the Securities and Exchange Commission to force major changes in the utility industry during World War II, delayed the dissolution until the late 1940s. The system was not entirely disbanded, however. Because the Alabama, Georgia, Mississippi, and Florida companies were physically unified, they were allowed to remain under a holding company umbrella. In 1947 the Southern Company was established to assume ownership of their common stock. In 1949 Southern Services (renamed Southern Company Services in 1976) was established as the Southern system's central service organization. It inherited much of the staff of Commonwealth and Southern's service company office in Birmingham.[9] Thus, the Southeastern system, which had been absorbed into Commonwealth and Southern, reemerged relatively intact.

Economically, the Southern Company's service area has grown rapidly since the company was established, and consequently, Southern has been one of the fastest-growing utilities in the country. Even with its rapid economic growth, however, the South has continued to lag behind the rest of the nation in average per capita income.[10] Concern with continued industrial development has made environmental protection a lower priority in Southern's territory than in some other parts of the nation. It is probably a reflection of the region's pro-business sentiments that as late as 1971 industrial representatives sat on environmental agency boards in Alabama, and continue to do so in Mississippi. John Farley, now at Southern Company Services and for many years the environmental manager at Alabama Power Company, was one of the industry representatives to the Alabama Air Pollution Control Commission.[11] From Southern's viewpoint, having industrial representation on environmental boards is a good way to ensure objective consideration of the facts, as industry experts perceive them, but in areas where there is more hostility to business the emphasis has been on creating a greater distance between the regulators and the businesses they regulate.

Part of the success that Southern has had in dealing with state agencies lies in its ability to identify each operating company with the state in which it functions. The task of dealing with state agencies falls to the operating companies, an arrangement that facilitates communication and accommodation between agency officials and the power companies. Southern's various subsidiaries are seen in each state as insiders, not outsiders. Given the companies' role in state economic development, the overall balance of public opinion and political pressures has been favorable instead of hostile. It is a very different kind of context in which to operate than the one that confronts PG&E or even Boston Edison. Future increases in income and industrialization may lead to more environmental pressure. In the past, however, environmental agencies in Southern's service area have been willing to listen to company arguments.

The agencies have generally shared Southern's view of what constitutes a reasonably cost-effective approach to environmental control — if not immediately, then after Southern has had a chance to make its case to them. In Georgia, Mississippi, and (after some dispute) Alabama, state regulations were established permitting the system to burn relatively high-sulfur coal at most existing plants and to use tall stacks to disperse its emissions. There are, of course, details on which the Southern Company still differs with the regulators. But company spokesmen indicate that there has been a gradual process of adjustment and reconciliation, which has resulted in final standards that are closer to company preferences than some of those instituted originally. These results indicate both the relatively relaxed regulatory situation Southern has faced and the effectiveness of its own efforts to communicate its viewpoints to the regulatory authorities.

The company's experience in Georgia is a good example. Consistent with Southern's own viewpoint, Georgia's Department of Natural Resources made the judgment that techniques for controlling SO_2 emissions were not available and decided that the electric generating stations within the state — most of which belong to Georgia Power — should not be required to use them. The department established regulations permitting the utility to increase the sulfur content of its coal (up to a maximum of 3 percent) as the height of its stacks was increased.[12]

The Natural Resources Defense Council (NRDC), a national environmental group, challenged Georgia's regulations in federal court, partly on the grounds that the Clean Air Act called for limiting emissions to protect the air, not diluting them through tall stacks. The courts agreed, and ordered the Environmental Protection Agency to review the adequacy of Georgia's emission rules. In doing so, however, the EPA decided to give credit for stacks up to a certain height that had been built since the standards were first adopted. As a result, emission limits were made more restrictive at only two Georgia Power plants.[13]

The history of Alabama's SO_2 standards for existing plants is somewhat different. Initially, much to Alabama Power Company's dismay, the Alabama Air Pollution Control Commission established standards requiring the use of coal with sulfur content of less than 1 percent. The commission itself lacked adequate technical expertise and so was forced to rely on advice it received from an outside consultant selected by EPA. Under severe time constraints, the consultant, TRW, developed its report for Alabama using the relatively crude "worst-example region" and "linear rollback" methods that the EPA recommended. The inevitable effect of this approach was to encourage the adoption of very stringent standards. Used together, the techniques involve determining by what percentage ambient *concentrations* in the most polluted region of the state exceed federal standards and curtailing *emissions* everywhere by that same percentage. The result, when applied to Alabama, satisfied the EPA but almost no one else.[14] Representatives from Alabama Power Company met with the commission and argued that they could not meet the standards as written because scrubbers were commercially unavailable. By building higher smokestacks, however, they could meet ambient standards at their plants while burning higher-sulfur coal.

In 1973 Alabama's Air Pollution Control Commission modified its SO_2 standards so that, in many cases, Alabama Power Company could burn coal with a sulfur content of close to 2.5 percent. The new standards that the commission adopted appeared implicitly to permit the use of tall stacks as a method of SO_2 control, although the Clean Air Act does not sanction such an approach. The commission's executive director has stated that tall stacks are not an integral part of the plan. Figures provided by him, however, indicate that, without the new tall stacks which Alabama Power has built, the company would be violating ambient standards around some of its plants.[15]

The lack of ongoing environmental activity in Alabama played an important role in the relaxation of the standards. In 1971 demonstrating environmentalists had prompted the state legislature to abolish the existing air pollution agency, which had included representatives from pollution sources, and replace it with a stronger commission. However, in 1973, when the commission was considering the relaxation of its original SO_2 regulations, the hearings were attended by only one environmentalist, who weakly opposed the changes.[16] There was thus little support and little reason for maintaining especially stringent regulations. The commission has taken a much stronger stand against TVA, in part because of TVA's "stonewalling" approach to the SO_2 regulations. The commission has tenaciously pursued TVA in the courts, and has obtained a settlement agreement with TVA that would include the installation of at least one scrubber, at Widows Creek 7.

In Florida, the political climate initially was very different. There was continuing interest in air pollution control regulations among such groups as the Florida Lung Association and the Easter Seal Association—groups with a large proportion of older members. This made it much more difficult for the Gulf Power Company, Southern's Florida subsidiary, to get its point of view across to the air pollution control agency. The Florida "clean air" advocates were drawn particularly from downstate areas, where older and retired people (many from the North), whose susceptibility to air pollution is especially high, constitute a large proportion of the population.

The environmentalists' level of interest and activity was very high. The state's pollution control board held a series of hearings in various cities in late 1971 in preparation for setting air quality standards. Representatives from a coalition known as the Florida Council for Clean Air traveled around the state in order to present their viewpoint at all the hearings. This group remained involved right up through the enforcement process. When Gulf Power applied for a variance from the SO_2 emissions standards, representatives of the council appeared as intervenors at the hearings and participated in the negotiations held between the state and the power company. The administration responded to this political climate. The state's young "reform" governor, Reuben Askew, made it clear to the Air Pollution Control Board that he would support its position on strict standards. "He more or less gave us the go-ahead. He didn't tell us what to do but said, 'Don't worry about anyone backdooring you. Do what is right,'" said David Levin, former chairman of the control board.[17]

Eventually, the political climate changed in Florida, and the regulations were relaxed. Under the state's original regulations, Gulf Power had been in the position of having to burn low-sulfur coal by July 1975 or move into an agreed-upon schedule for installing scrubbers on its plants. But in May 1975 the pollution control board virtually suspended its SO_2 emission standards for two and a half years, pending the outcome of a $2 million study conducted by a group representing a diversity of perspectives but financed by the state's utilities. During the course of the study, the state's standards for coal-burning plants were relaxed on an interim basis from 1.5 lbs of sulfur per million Btu to 6.17 lbs. This new standard eventually became permanent. In the spring of 1978 the study group reported that the interim standards were adequate for protecting the public health and should be continued. The pollution control board accepted this recommendation.

In the first part of the 1970s, the staff of the Florida pollution control board had favored strict standards requiring the best available technology, particularly because of the highly susceptible population of old people in the state. But by 1975 various pressures had built up that made it virtually impossible for the agency to maintain its stance, despite some continuing environmentalist support for the original standards. Most important was the energy crisis, which in 1973 led the EPA to begin advocating less stringent measures where ambient standards could be met with existing fuel use patterns. In particular, the agency urged that emission standards, where these required a switch to lower-sulfur fuel, should be relaxed. This meant relaxing many of the strict standards developed using the EPA's 1971 methods. In 1974, at congressional request, the EPA reviewed the state plans and specifically pointed out where they could be modified.

Within the state of Florida, there were broad political changes as well. The Florida utilities—which initially had not worked together against the SO_2 standards—eventually united in a campaign for their modification. While some observers feel there was no real diminution of popular support for environmental controls, others agree that environmentalist fervor had quieted considerably by 1975—or at any rate was not articulated as effectively. Certainly the climate of state government had changed. In 1975 the legislature enacted a bill to abolish the state's emission standards. The governor vetoed the bill, but the pollution control board clearly sensed the change in the political climate; it modified its standards on its own initiative.[18]

The Florida story suggests that Southern's good relations with its regulators in Georgia, Alabama, and Mississippi depended on the political circumstances in those states as well as on Southern's political approach. Particularly in situations where proenvironmental groups are persistent and well organized, Southern's government-relations strategy may not be adequate. In situations where direct contact with state regulatory agencies was effective, however, the company was well equipped to develop good relationships and arrive at understandings that were "reasonable" from its viewpoint.

Although Southern has frequently ended up with environmental regulations it could "live with," this has not meant that the system has enjoyed an existence free of constraints. For Southern's subsidiaries, much more than for TVA, there are potentially damaging legal consequences for direct disobedience of pollution control rules. For example, when Georgia Power failed to do required in-stack emission testing, it was charged with a violation and ultimately agreed to pay fifteen thousand dollars to Georgia state authorities in place of fines. (TVA, in contrast, was immune from state enforcement authority.) State regulatory authorities suggested that the problem developed because Georgia Power wanted to do the testing with its own personnel and could not develop the capability rapidly enough. Ultimately, to expedite the required work, it agreed to hire an outside firm to do the needed tests.[19] In addition, for all of Southern's operating companies there is always the possibility that poor public relations will lead to repercussions with regard to its publicly regulated rates.

Where regulators have required Southern to limit its emissions, it has taken steps to do so. It has, for example, acquired significant amounts of low-sulfur coal, whereas TVA for a long time would not or could not do so. Part of the explanation is that Southern is planning to continue building fossil-fired plants. In view of the fact that the region is growing so quickly, and the fact that the company has no government guarantees for its bonds, it cannot afford the capital costs of TVA's strategy of relying solely on nuclear plants for baseload generation. Thus, it will have to continue to get permits from state agencies and meet tough new source performance standards at fossil-fuel plants. In other areas as well, Southern has acted more readily than TVA to comply with regulations. Its precipitator upgrading has gone more quickly than TVA's, although its program, too, has lagged somewhat. Southern has also been much readier to install cooling towers than TVA, at least at new plants. At many existing plants, however, Southern's political acumen and prevailing regional attitudes have allowed it to reach a fairly comfortable accommodation with state agencies on costly water pollution controls.

Southern's ability to live comfortably with its regulatory situation depends, in part, on its fuel situation. Traditionally, its system has used coal with a much lower average sulfur content than that used by TVA—1.5 percent compared to TVA's 3.5 percent.[20] Certainly, as long as state standards allow coal with up to 3 percent sulfur content, Southern can comply relatively easily.

In nonenvironmental areas, too, regulatory authorities have been less sympathetic to Southern's viewpoint where there has been strong public opposition to the company. The system's experiences during the 1970s with state rate commissions were quite stormy; the publicly elected rate commissions in Southern's territory — particularly the Georgia Public Service Commission — refused a considerable proportion of the rate increases it requested. Southern's subsidiaries insisted that they needed these increases to keep up with rising costs and to help finance the rapid growth of the system.[21] The fact that state rate commissioners are elected rather than appointed in Southern's territory does not automatically lead them to take a stance hostile to the utilities. Conventional belief holds that companies like Georgia Power Company and Alabama Power Company have traditionally had good success in having "their" candidates elected. However, with rates rising, the rate-setting process has become politicized, and the commissions have been under increasing pressure to hold the line against the companies.[22]

In Georgia, rate-increase hearings have been well attended and have received considerable newspaper and television coverage. The unions have sometimes campaigned hard (and successfully) against proposed increases, although, in the last few years, the unions have been supporting the company's rate-increase requests — perhaps because of slowdowns in new plant construction. An Atlanta-based public-interest group known as the Georgia Power Project has intervened frequently in Georgia Power rate proceedings. In Alabama, too, the rate process has been highly politicized. Governor George Wallace twice brought suit, attempting to overturn rate-commission rulings granting increases to Alabama Power. In 1977 the Alabama legislature met in special session to consider a variety of bills submitted by the governor to impose new financial controls on the state's utilities. The only outcome of this session, however, was an independent audit of Alabama Power Company which resulted in a tremendous vindication for the company: the auditor, Price Waterhouse and Company, concluded that Alabama Power was well managed and had been compelled to raise its rates because of economic factors beyond its control.[23]

Despite the rate pressures the system companies have been under, the organization has felt less vulnerable to general political repercussions than, say, Pacific Gas and Electric. While PG&E typically accepts rate decisions once they have been made, Southern's subsidiaries have often taken their states' public-service commissions to court seeking higher rates. Both Georgia Power and Alabama Power have gone public with their complaints, both having delayed construction of new nuclear plants on the avowed grounds of inadequate revenue (slower demand growth also, no doubt, played a role).

From Southern's perspective, the fiscal problems it faces have been significant. Georgia Power Company has made arrangements to sell substantial shares in several new plants to Rural Electrification Administration cooperatives and municipally owned utilities, in large part to raise capital. This strategy—like the one PG&E has followed—is a major reversal for Southern. Throughout the 1960s Southern lobbied hard and brought several court suits to prevent cooperatives in its territory from obtaining federal money to build their own generating plants.[24] While this new tack seems to be to its current advantage, the ability of the company to change a long and deeply held strategic commitment reveals its general managerial sophistication.

Internal Organization

Southern may be lucky to face less severe pressures than some other companies in our study, but it has not relied on luck to deal with its problems. Southern's managers—going back to James Mitchell and Tom Martin—have been enterprising problem solvers, and the system's structure is well designed to cope with the pressures it confronts. Even in a situation in which centrifugal forces would appear likely to dominate, Southern's organizational design provides a surprising amount of policy coherence. It creates appropriate central coordination while assuring recognition of the particular problems and opportunities of each subsidiary.

These potentially conflicting purposes are achieved by having many decisions decentralized to the operating companies while administration of the system is in the hands of a collegial group consisting of the president of the parent company and the chief executives of the subsidiaries. These executives are all members of the board of directors of the Southern Company and of Southern Company Services, the in-house engineering and service company. They also constitute the executive committee of the parent company, and they meet together regularly to discuss system problems.[25] Figure 18 shows the organizational relationship of these executives.

A shared responsibility for system decisions helps develop a common perspective on system problems among this group. This counterbalances—but does not eliminate—the tendency for individuals' viewpoints to be influenced by the particular activities for

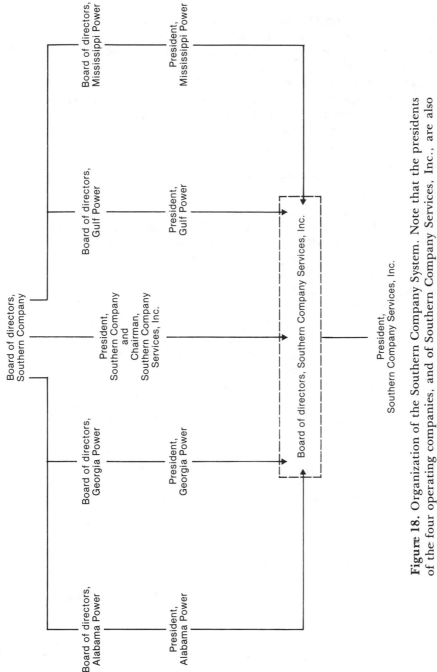

Figure 18. Organization of the Southern Company System. Note that the presidents of the four operating companies, and of Southern Company Services, Inc., are also members of the Southern Company's board of directors. Based on information supplied by the Southern Company.

which they are responsible. The structure produces compromise in company policy and at the same time ensures that the concerns of the subsidiaries receive top-management attention. The executive group is also a useful forum for discussing the system's problems, encouraging objective examination from a number of different perspectives. This facilitates the strategic flexibility that is one of Southern's virtues from a management viewpoint.

Many of Southern's executives have moved into top management by similar routes, though in different subsidiaries of the system. This makes it easier for them to understand and cooperate with one another. Frequently they began as members of one of the outside law firms serving the operating subsidiaries, moving, while still young, into a relatively senior position at one or another of the system's companies. Alvin Vogtle, Southern Company president; Harllee Branch, his predecessor; Joe Farley, Alabama Power Company president; and Edwin Hatch, recently retired chairman of Georgia Power Company, all moved up in this way. As Alvin Vogtle commented, "I and the operating company presidents — we've grown up together."[26]

The prominent role played by lawyers in Southern's top management is in part a matter of tradition. Tom Martin, cofounder of Alabama Power Company and of the whole system, was a lawyer. In addition, the company's active involvement in legislative and regulatory matters exposes promising young lawyers to a wide range of company affairs — and to the system's top management. This facilitates their movement into positions of general responsibility.[27]

Several system executives are engineers who came up through the technical ranks of the subsidiaries. One is an engineer who was brought into the system at a fairly high level. A surprising number are both lawyers and engineers. Joe Farley, a lawyer, has an undergraduate engineering degree, and Bob Scherer, president of Georgia Power Company, is an engineer who got a law degree along the way.[28] Given the broad background of this group, it is able both to supervise technical activities and remain alert to the political consequences of the company's actions.

Southern's collegial management thus provides a unifying force within the system. Yet, from the start, considerable emphasis has been placed on the autonomy of the operating companies. In certain spheres, they function with considerable independence. Southern personnel stress the advantages of having the operating companies handle state government affairs — a policy that apparently goes back to the system's earliest days. State-by-state responsibility for these matters enables each company to develop the contacts and knowledge of local circumstances that are essential in the delicate business of influencing government policy without having such efforts backfire.

The organization of Southern's legal activities complements this strategy. Unlike PG&E and TVA, each of the system's subsidiaries has employed an outside law firm rather than build up a staff of lawyers in-house. As Alabama counsel Eason Balch commented, the companies have benefited from the experience and contacts their law firms have developed in doing work for other clients. The system provides the company with advocates having wide and deep community ties. Although it may be difficult for such lawyers to be as closely involved in day-to-day decisions as those at PG&E, Balch himself says that he doesn't think this is a problem.[29]

Clearly, these arrangements have advantages in responding to the rate and tax issues that come up before state agencies and legislatures. The president of a local company who goes before the rate commission to argue the necessity of an increase is himself a local man, and the lawyer with him is likely to be a prominent local figure. If an apparent outsider were involved, the politics and psychology of the situation would be less favorable to the utility. "The intervenors still refer to the 'hounds of Wall Street' in opposing company rate requests," Alvin Vogtle commented.[30]

Perhaps for this reason, the Southern Company has maintained a low profile in its service area until quite recently. Even within the system, operating subsidiary employees do not strongly identify themselves as part of the Southern system (and in some cases may even be unclear about the nature of the link). They see themselves as working instead, say, for the Alabama Power Company.

This policy has changed somewhat in the last few years. The system's chief executives apparently have felt that the parent corporation needed greater visibility, in part to help attract the increasing amounts of required capital. The system companies are now using a common corporate symbol, and Southern Services was renamed Southern Company Services in order to highlight its role in the Southern Company system.[31]

In dealing with new environmental regulations, however, state-level management of state regulatory affairs will no doubt continue. As John Farley put it, "It's sort of a First Commandment here. If there is a question of going to a state agency, Southern Company Services would not go to the state agency concerned as the representative of the operating company . . . [As a member of the Alabama air pollution control agency], I could see that it never went too well when some hotshot from out of state would run in with his briefcase. We had never seen him before. He might really know his stuff, but it left a bad flavor when he would run off and get back on a plane home."[32] In contrast, the operating company engineers responsible for environmental affairs have been around long enough to develop ongoing relationships with state agency personnel. They know whom to approach and when and how, and what the likely reaction will be. In turn, they provide someone for these personnel to complain to if they are unhappy with the company. Such contacts facilitate cooperative interaction between the company and state agencies (although they do not exempt the companies from established regulatory requirements).

Despite this practice and Southern's traditionally low profile, many technical functions within Southern have historically been centralized in order to save money. This practice has made the system's service organization an important source of policy coherence, complementing the impact of top management. In particular, capacity expansion planning (like system operations) is usually done jointly. The system has its origin, after all, in the attempt to make efficient regional use of surplus Alabama hydropower. The service company (like its predecessor organizations) plays a central role in all this by analyzing the economic desirability of various options (although some intersubsidiary bargaining also can influence the outcome). Once a broad plan is agreed to, Southern Company Services designs the new power plants and — in the case of the two smaller companies in Mississippi and Florida — transmission lines as well.[33]

Rapid system growth, the use of more complex technologies, and the need to meet environmental regulations have led to a steady increase in the size and influence of the service company over the last decade. New functions have been established at Southern Company Services — computer services, fuel purchasing, research, nuclear plant licensing, and preparation of environmental impact statements. Some of these were formerly handled by the operating companies, but as the activities reached a certain critical size or level of sophistication, centralization and joint financing became more attractive. Reflecting and encouraging Services' expansion, a new management team was brought in from the outside in the late 1960s to supervise this growth.

The conventional view within the system is that Southern Company Services does not — or is not supposed to — play a strong leadership role. It functions, instead, as an in-house engineering and special service firm, performing work for the operating-company clients at cost. The service company has probably always done more than passively provide consulting services project-by-project, however. Since it is a central locus of technical expertise in the system with ongoing responsibility for the system's engineering and other service needs, it inevitably has had a strong influence over the technical choices of the system.

The increasing complexity of the problems facing the Southern system has allowed the service company's staff to assert more than ever its crucial role as the system's "experts." In playing this role, they have had reason to explore and urge the adoption of innovative methods and practices capable of solving those problems. It is their initiative that has enabled Southern to satisfy a number of difficult demands that have been placed upon it.

Two new groups at Southern Company Services stand out in this respect. One is the fuel-purchasing group. Until the mid-1960s, coal purchasing was carried out on a decentralized basis by the operating companies. In 1965, to take advantage of potential economies of scale, a new group was established at Southern Services to carry out this function.[34] Given the resistance of the operating company staffs to such centralization, this group had every incentive to work hard and be successful, thereby justifying the assignment of this task to a central group of experts.

Even more important has been the Research Department. Established in 1969, the Department was headed by William B. Harrison, formerly dean of the Research Division of Virginia Polytechnic Institute, who came to the service company as a vice-president. (Now in charge of computer services as well, he has become a senior vice-president. Research is headed by a new vice-president, who reports to Harrison.) The Research Department's members have extensive backgrounds, by utility standards. Besides Harrison, several members of its original staff had doctoral degrees. The group is effective at obtaining outside financial support and has the motivation to undertake technically sophisticated projects. Through its work on solvent refining — a process used to remove sulfur from coal before it is burned — the group has propelled the Southern Company into the role of a technological leader in the utility industry.[35] Figure 19 shows the prototype solvent-refining installation that the group initiated.

The service company's growing influence has created some tension with the operating companies. Intergroup rivalries are less

Figure 19. The Southern Company's solvent-refined coal pilot plant near Wilsonville, Alabama, completed in 1973. Courtesy of the Southern Company, Inc.

intense in the Southern system than in TVA, but the question of exactly who should do what work is not always clear. This leads to tensions and disputes that top management must resolve. Southern Company Services has never tried to control operating companies the way TVA's Office of Power has tried to manipulate other TVA Divisions, and the operating companies often accept the service company's expertise. At other times they have become jealous of their own engineering functions, particularly when the role of Southern Company Services first began to grow; they protested that the service company was trying to impose a uniform, system-wide perspective on them.[36] Such tensions were only natural in this kind of transition. They have apparently diminished in the last couple of years, as the operating companies have come to accept the need for more centralization within the system and have gained respect for Southern Company Services' ability to provide solutions to the system's problems—and as the service company has, at the same time, taken steps to make sure the operating companies' viewpoints continue to be recognized.

The ability of operating companies to compete with central services is limited. Their own engineering staffs are generally small. They do mainly small-scale design work (on substations and distribution lines, for example) and coordinate the planning and design of major facilities with the service organization. Yet, at least during the early 1970s when Southern Company Services was growing rapidly, the career patterns of operating-company personnel fostered a certain amount of bureaucratic possessiveness on their part. Intercompany mobility among middle-level engineering personnel was fairly limited, although less limited than in TVA. Low diagonal mobility tends to reinforce group perspectives, so it should not be surprising that men of the middle ranks of the subsidiaries seemed more dedicated to their companies' interests than their more mobile superiors. An engineer working for Alabama Power (or Southern Company Services, for that matter) was likely to spend his entire career in that company, and was thus likely to take a special interest in the question of what responsibilities his group would have. The answer would affect the kind of work he did, the likelihood that his group would grow, his own promotion prospects, and the status of his group within the system. The operating-company employees who move to the service company when their specialties are centralized may not have these feelings to the same extent. But they stand to lose far less than those left behind in the operating companies.

There have also been questions of whose opinion would prevail with regard to design problems. Organizational rivalry, as well as differences in experience and perspective, have created occasional friction in this area. Rapid system growth implies the need to build many generating plants at once. In response, Southern Company Services has sought to use standardized designs to limit the level of engineering effort. This was a departure from the previous practice of designing each plant to a specific company's requirements. William Reed, president of Southern Company Services and an architect of the policy, explained, "There was more making-to-order in the old days — tailoring plants to the needs of the individual companies. When you were only building one unit a year, you could do this, but there's so much to do now. We can't continue this policy. You can't keep reinventing the wheel. It just doesn't make sense."[37] However sensible, this new policy caused apprehension and resentment within the operating companies. Operating-company engineers seemed hard-pressed to come up with concrete cases where standardization has led to problems.[38] However, the symbolic importance of having each plant designed to their specifications seems to have mattered to the operating companies.

The appointment of three outsiders from General Electric as top managers of Southern Company Services is a third area in which tension developed between the service organization and the operating companies. Apparently concerned about the service company's ability to cope with rapidly growing demands, Alvin Vogtle brought a new top management into the service organization soon after he became head of the Southern system. These managers were hired explicitly to fill gaps created by a series of retirements in the late 1960s. The team was headed by Clyde Lilly, Jr., president of the service company, and included William Reed and William Lalor as vice-presidents. Vogtle also brought in William Harrison as a vice-president charged with organizing a new research department. In passing over some obvious internal candidates, Vogtle risked morale problems and increased tension with the operating companies. But he did get a tough, loyal management team as a result.

When he first came to the system, Clyde Lilly was made head of Gulf Power Company. But, Vogtle said, "We used Clyde at Gulf with the expectation that he would come in at Services." The complaint had been lodged often that no one at Services had *operating* experience. "Giving Lilly the job [at Gulf] meant that he was free of that taint."[39] Lilly's term at Gulf also reduced the distrust that might attach to him if he had had *no* experience in the system before coming to Services.

By appointing his own people, Vogtle would seem to have gained greater control over the service company. The new executives had more personal ties to him and fewer to their subordinates than they would have if they had "risen from the ranks." By appointing men with strong leadership ability, he also increased his control over the entire system. The new team was able to exploit opportunities for centralization, thereby shifting activities into a context in which Vogtle's ability to influence them was greater. It is quite understandable, therefore, that some in the operating companies were unhappy with this pattern, at least at first.

Southern Company Services' top management underwent considerable change in the spring of 1977, however, following a plane crash that killed Lilly and Lalor. William Reed was moved up to become the service company's president, but two operating company vice-presidents, Doug McCrary from Alabama Power and E. L. Addison from Gulf Power, were moved to the service company to serve as senior vice-presidents. William Harrison was promoted and became the company's third senior vice-president. Since then, Addison has rejoined Gulf Power as its president, but a number of other operating-company men have joined Southern Company Services as vice-presidents. Meanwhile, additional functional staff from the operating companies have been brought over to Southern Company Services to work in newly centralized departments. The strong presence of operating-company executives and staff at Southern Company Services has apparently improved the relationship with the operating companies. At the same time, the trend toward centralization of responsibility in Southern Company Services has not been substantially reversed: the movement of operating-company personnel to the service company has probably legitimized the service company's expanded role. Southern Company Services' strong influence in the system seems clearly established.

This is especially true in view of the fact that the system's top executives — unlike some men in the ranks — evidently accepted the growing centralization of influence in the service company. As members of Services' board of directors, they have not feared losing control to Southern Company Services. They have been able to identify much more easily with the service company than could their subordinates.

Yet there have been pressures on Southern Company Services not to take too much independent initiative. For example, the rapid growth in expenditures by the service company's Research and Environment Department generated internal controversy.

Initially there was pressure on the Department to justify its spending carefully, and the Department's first head, William Harrison, developed a new and fairly rigorous budget justification procedure.[40]

Conversely, the operating-company presidents have also checked tendencies within their own organizations to take over functions from Southern Company Services. Vogtle commented, "We've done some reorganization to assure that there's no duplication. Since Services is staffed with experts, that's where the emphasis [in design] is going to be."[41]

Joseph Farley, Alabama Power Company president, expressed a similar view:

> It's inevitable that when you have a service organization, and have a lot of full-time staff people doing engineering yourself, it's difficult not to have sparks at the point where you cut off between the operating company and Southern [Company] Services. It's never going to be a smooth break. In fact, there are sparks within the operating company, too. For instance, the question comes up: "Who's going to drill borings at a new plant site—engineering or construction?" Between the operating company and Southern Services, you have to be careful not to overlap. There's nothing new about this problem, though as we get bigger the problem may get bigger. We have to make constant efforts to avoid overlap. We [the executives] all agree that we can't afford to duplicate. Starting from that premise, we try to resolve conflicts at the lower levels when they come up to us. There's a common premise that Southern Services is an effective at-cost organization. I'm a director of it. We've got to make it work and work right.[42]

As this suggests, the existence of sparks at the cutoff point is not necessarily unhealthy. The competition has kept Southern Company Services responsive to the needs of the operating companies and of the system as a whole. It has reinforced whatever control Southern's executives exert directly over Service's staff. Without such a check, Service's staff might not work as hard or be as careful in their recommendations.

Moreover, without such competition and the incentives and checks it produces, some innovations would almost certainly not have taken place. For instance, largely at the urging of Alabama's design liaison group, the Southern system is now employing "hotside" precipitators at a number of locations. Such units are designed to remove particulates from stack gas even when low-sulfur coal is burned — coal that inhibits the efficiency of normal units. At first, Southern Company Services' engineers questioned the value of hotsides, given their greater cost, but after a series of meetings and discussions with representatives of Alabama Power, they agreed that hotsides might be useful.[43]

Given their different responsibilities and perspectives, the operating companies and Southern Company Services have had some of their sharpest disagreements over the issue of how much to spend on plant reliability. The operating companies run the plants, and plant operators are an important part of their organizations. It is understandable, therefore, that they would be more concerned than Southern Services with reliability, even if this entailed increasing the capital cost of a plant. Such views are typical of plant operators in all the companies we studied.

A notable example of this difference of opinion involved the choice between two types of coal-fired boilers. Several years ago, in keeping with industry trends, Southern Company Services began advocating the use of pressurized boilers, in which the coal is burned in a firebox with air at above atmospheric pressure to enhance combusion. It also recommended supercritical temperature and pressure conditions for the steam produced at such new coal-fired units. The argument was that these boilers promised considerable savings in capital and fuel costs, and on the basis of this analysis the operating companies agreed. Once the boilers were in operation, however, the operating companies encountered considerable difficulty. The pressurized firing was particularly troublesome. The boilers were difficult to seal perfectly, because of their large size and their expansion and contraction as they heated and cooled. Since there was positive pressure inside, they emitted large quantities of ash and coal dust whenever a leak occurred; this caused problems with all the other equipment in the plant — fans, motors, pumps, and so on. Supercritical steam conditions also caused difficulties, especially in maintaining proper control when starting up or turning off such units.

Eventually, Alabama Power began to advocate a return to balanced-draft boilers, in which there was no internal pressure to cause the leaks that occurred with the pressurized boilers. The operating company also wanted lower steam pressure, making possible a drum-type boiler that would be easier to control. Unable to resolve this disagreement at lower levels, it was brought to the top level of the system. Ultimately, some of the other operating companies adopted Alabama Power's viewpoint. A decision was made to return to the use of balanced-draft, lower-pressure boilers. Plans to use pressurized, supercritical boilers at Alabama's newest plant, the Miller Electric Generating Plant, were dropped in favor of using smaller, balanced-draft, drum-type boilers.

Such controversies occur less often now. Perhaps because of the stronger presence of operating-company men in the service company, reliability considerations are given more attention. The pressurized versus balanced-draft issue clearly demonstrates, however, how organizational forces can become involved in supposedly technical decisions.

During this controversy, economic analyses comparing the two alternatives were done and redone. A review was necessary because, according to Roy Krotzer, manager of engineering services for Alabama Power Company, "many factors relative to plant operation were not included in the [initial] evaluation that should have been." At Greene County, where pressurized boilers were first installed in Alabama, "there were equipment failures in components that never had failures, because of the leaks of the combustion products."[44]

The number pushing was never completely decisive. The calculations were not easy, since they involved computing the costs of readjusting system-reserve margins to take account of changed unit reliability. "More data proved that balanced-draft was better," Bill Reed, head of Southern Company Services, stated.[45] His own design staff, however, did not come to the same conclusion. According to a Southern Company Services' engineer involved in the design choice, "We were not able to come up with anything large enough to change our [initial] economic assessment. Since that time, we have made a turnaround. There is now a consensus in the operating companies that balanced-draft is preferable, for reliability, cleanliness, etc., but balanced-draft installations are still not justifiable solely for economic reasons."[46] Whether the influence of the operating companies led the organization to higher costs in the interests of making the operators' job less difficult is very hard to decide. What are the gains in morale and other areas, and what are they worth? The decision to discontinue the use of pressurized boilers and supercritical steam conditions is one that many other utilities have reached. Still, the impact of the operating companies on engineering choices is evident from the chronology.

This controversy demonstrates that the operating-company staffs can serve as a check on the discretion of Southern Services, when the operating-company presidents are willing to back them up. Despite the fact that they tend to be sympathetic to Southern Company Services, supporting their own staffs' viewpoints on occasion clearly fosters loyalty from their own companies and provides added discipline. Although they do not intervene frequently, their influence can be decisive. One consequence is that the plant operators' viewpoint gets considerably more of a hearing in the Southern organization than, say, in TVA. Thus, for example, when the operators wanted to install more expensive, but fireproof, synthetic "fill" in a cooling tower—as opposed to wood, which was cheaper—they won here also.[47]

The system's executives seem to have strong controls within their own organizations. They involve themselves actively in the promotion process and have developed a pattern of substantial diagonal mobility. For example, engineering vice-presidents in the subsidiary companies do not typically move vertically directly into such jobs (unlike in TVA). Alan Barton, executive vice-president at Alabama Power, was an engineer in operations and served as vice-president for transmission and distribution (where he also managed labor relations for the company) before assuming his present position. Some senior vice-president positions are filled from outside the company. Reed and Lalor entered Southern Company Services as vice-presidents from General Electric. Two of their successors as senior vice-presidents at Southern Company Services came from Georgia Power and Gulf Power, and Georgia Power's executive president for engineering and operations came from Alabama Power, where he was in charge of operations.

These kinds of promotion patterns give managers considerable incentive to please their superiors; movement up the line on a seniority basis is by no means assured. Upper-level middle managers have some reason to be grateful to their superiors for their present position, and feel loyalty to them as a result. Moreover, they are given a relatively broad perspective on the company and its problems, lessening any tendency toward a narrow definition of group or corporate interests. Hence, middle managers are willing to ensure that top management has the opportunity to intervene as it likes in important aspects of a decision. For instance, Alabama Power's president, Joe Farley, mentioned that he expected to be consulted about establishing new precipitator efficiencies when some recent upgrading was underway.[48]

Summing up, several features of the organization's structure help ensure a coherent and on occasion innovative policy, even in the face of the centrifugal tendencies of the multicompany aspects of the system. These features include the operating companies' skill in dealing with state agencies; Southern Services' interest in being more than a passive contractor; the collegial top management system; the broad background of chief executives; the competitiveness of the operating companies' staffs; and a strong control system. As we will see in the next section, these structural characteristics have clearly aided the Southern Company in responding to the new sorts of consequences it has faced as a function of its environmental decisions.

Environmental Decisions

Serving a region in which environmental protection has not been as high a priority as in some others, Southern has not been under extreme pressure to limit its environmental impact. Given Southern's need for capital and the uncooperativeness of state utility commissions, the company has always been fairly intent on minimizing costs. In some cases, it has installed less than the best pollution controls available, but in line with its readiness to respond flexibly to specific situations its executives have been willing to spend more in particularly sensitive situations. In the face of stringent requirements, the company has shown itself capable of developing creative solutions.

The SO_2 requirements imposed in the 1970s illustrate both the virtues and the limits of the organization's structure and strategy. Southern worked hard to persuade state agencies to apply "reasonable" standards for existing coal-fired plants—standards that could be met without either the use of scrubbers or system-wide use of very low-sulfur fuel. The low level of air pollution and of environmental concern in the region clearly made it easier to convince the regulators, but Southern's decentralized strategy and structure for handling state governmental relations also contributed to its success.

The company's efforts, however, have not gone equally smoothly. The difficulties that Gulf Power had in persuading the Florida Department of Pollution Control to modify its stringent SO_2 regulations illustrate the limits of Southern's skills. The company is much better able to handle regulatory situations where public-interest groups are less involved on a continuous basis. Where such groups lead and articulate public opposition to the company's position, maintaining close contact with state and local agencies is less effective.

The company's lack of experience and expertise in dealing with such groups is reflected in and reinforced by its organizational structure. There seem to be no parallels to PG&E's Public and Government Affairs Department or Ontario Hydro's Route and Site Selection Division, both of which spend a considerable amount of their time making contact with and coming to understand concerned citizen groups that might object to planned company projects.

While the company faced what it considered to be reasonable standards for existing plants, it still confronted the problem of what to do about the stringent federal "new source" standards which apply to any fossil-fuel generating plants whose construction began after August 17, 1971. An all-nuclear strategy like TVA's would be risky and taxing for Southern, in view of the company's high growth rate, the high capital costs of nuclear generating plants, the large engineering input required, and the problems encountered so far in bringing nuclear plants on line.[49] As a result, Southern has already built one coal-fired plant in Mississippi which is subject to these standards. It is building another in Alabama, and it has several more planned.

Parallel to its efforts on the state level, the company's primary response to federal regulations has been to seek a change in the standards. In an effort led by William Lalor until his death, the system joined other utilities to campaign in Washington for a change in the Clean Air Act. The utilities supported the goal of protecting ambient air quality, but opposed the use of emission requirements. They asked that Congress waive these and permit utilities to disperse their SO_2 emissions through tall stacks. Ironically, because TVA was seeking approval for use of the latter control method at its existing plants, Southern and TVA were on the same side of this controversy. The utilities' campaign proved less successful than Southern's efforts to communicate its viewpoint to state-level regulators, however. Congress has consistently reaffirmed its commitment to the emissions control approach.[50]

Unable to change the law, Southern has sought to comply with it; TVA, in contrast, continued to delay until David Freeman replaced Aubrey Wagner as chairman. In part, this can be explained by the fact that Southern, unlike TVA, cannot claim immunity from state regulation. Perhaps because it must cope with such demands, Southern's internal structure is capable of generating flexible responses to external requirements. Southern Company Services has had both the opportunity and the incentive to take technical initiatives. Hence, the company has often simultaneously pursued several possible solutions to its problems to ensure that it has some feasible response.

To an outsider, corporate strategy for meeting both the "new source" and the Florida SO_2 standards appears to have been this: rather than install scrubbers, use low-sulfur coal for the short run while pursuing other options that might prove viable in a few years' time. This strategy provided considerable flexibility, since it permitted the company to meet current standards without installing permanent controls—which will not be needed if the Clean Air Act is modified. Even if the law is not changed and Southern decides to pursue other alternatives, these are likely to be less expensive, more reliable, and better understood in the future. In particular, Southern is becoming more and more enthusiastic about a method it is helping to develop to remove the impurities from coal before it is burned, through a process called "solvent refining." This may turn out to be a better method of SO_2 control than the use of stack gas scrubbers.

The low-sulfur fuel strategy has not been totally successful as a means of avoiding long-term commitments. In some cases, Southern has had to enter into long-term contracts to obtain sufficient supplies of low-sulfur coal. But such commitments are certainly less binding than an investment in stack gas cleaning equipment. Furthermore, as long as existing mines (or new mines financed by others) supply the coal, the approach does not require any capital investment on the company's part. This is a major benefit to Southern, in view of its recent difficulties in raising enough money to finance its capacity expansion program. Indeed, because of its capital problems, the company recently divested itself of mining properties it had owned for some time.[51]

Finding supplies of low-sulfur coal was not a simple matter. TVA had concluded that only minute supplies of such coal were available in the Southeast, and had argued that western low-sulfur coal—besides being expensive to transport—was not satisfactory for use at its plants, given its low heat value and high ash content. Yet, Southern Services' fuel department, with no greater organizational resources or experience than TVA's Fuel Procurement Branch, was quite successful in finding supplies of low-sulfur coal. (Southern also contracted for some low-sulfur oil, but after the Arab embargo the company shied away from further dependence on this fuel.)[52]

For the recently built Miller plant in Alabama, the company contracted to buy the total capacity of several new, deep mines in that state. The coal is of metallurgical quality and was originally intended for export. When members of Southern Services' fuel department learned of its existence, they approached the mines' owners and, after some extended discussions, persuaded the owners to sell the coal to the Alabama Power Company. Meanwhile, to meet the Florida standards and supply a proposed new Georgia plant, the company's Fuel Department was exploring the possibility of buying low-sulfur coal in the West, despite the transportation problems this would involve. (Now the plan is to burn the coal at the new Daniel plant in Mississippi.) Mined in a different area than the western coal TVA purchased, this coal has a higher heat content that makes it more acceptable in plants designed to burn eastern coal. At the same time Southern was approached with offers of low-sulfur coal from mines in South Africa and Australia. The Fuel Department knew little about purchasing foreign coal, but sent representatives to investigate; it subsequently negotiated contracts to buy coal from both countries.[53]

Besides the external pressures that made it necessary to find some way to meet the SO_2 standards, a number of internal factors help account for the Fuel Department's aggressive efforts. In addition to the group's interest in proving its worth, it reported at the time directly to Bill Lalor. Lalor had been brought in from General Electric to help the service company cope with the increasingly complex problems facing the system. Accordingly, he had considerable incentive to show that he—or his subordinates—were capable of finding a way to meet the SO_2 standards, while he simultaneously pursued his campaign in Washington to get the standards changed. Lalor had a strong interest in the success of the Fuel Department's efforts to make the low-sulfur coal strategy work.

However enterprising, the company's coal purchasing activities have led to adverse public-relations consequences of the sort Southern is not well equipped to handle. This development was ironic, since once the South African purchase was made, Lalor had seen the importation of low-sulfur coal from distant foreign mines as something that could make the Clean Air Act's requirements look patently unreasonable.[54] But the purchases from South Africa generated strong protests from the United Mine Workers—nationally and locally—and from other groups, obscuring any other lesson that might have been drawn from the imports.

The company had anticipated union reactions against the imports on the grounds that they took jobs away from American miners. But to Southern's surprise, the miners and other groups raised a larger moral issue, attacking the imports on the grounds that they supported apartheid. Southern personnel found themselves denying that they were encouraging slave labor practices.

The United Mine Workers of America countered with vivid accounts of poor conditions and harsh discipline in the South African mines.[55]

To demonstrate their concern, five hundred union members picketed the 1974 Southern shareholders' meeting. One member, who got inside as a guest of some shareholders, confronted company officials and stockholders over the coal purchases. Later, the attorney general of Alabama joined the UMWA in a motion to the United States Customs Commission. They sought to block the imports under an old customs regulation that prohibits the importation of goods produced by slave or indentured labor under penal sanctions, unless such goods are unavailable in the United States. (The coal was entering the country in Mobile, Alabama, although destined for use in Florida by Gulf Power Company.) Meanwhile, a coalition of church groups holding Southern Company stock sponsored a proxy resolution challenging the imports.[56]

These challenges to Southern's purchases did not succeed directly. The Customs Commission rejected the UMWA motion, accepting Southern's contention that sufficient low-sulfur coal was not available in the United States. Only a small percentage of shareholders supported the proxy resolution. But in August 1975, Southern announced that it would not extend its contract for South African coal past 1976.[57] Florida's decision to delay by two years the imposition of strict SO_2 emissions standards made such a change less troublesome than it otherwise might have been. But the controversy over conditions in South Africa may have played a role as well.

Why did Southern buy South African coal, and why did it fail to anticipate the consequences? The UMWA contended that at higher prices and for long-term commitments, mines would have been opened to exploit some of the large reserves of low-sulfur coal in the Southeast.[58] During the customs case, the union produced a list of local coal companies that it claimed would sell low-sulfur coal to Southern under these circumstances.[59] In fact, the company did make some long-term contracts for Southeastern low-sulfur coal, but it is unclear why it did not make more.

Certainly, Southern may have wished to avoid making added long-term commitments. It also could have wanted to conserve capital: the South Africans did not need any financing from Southern, and Southern's chief purchaser said that his group had had little success in locating "viable" domestic suppliers of low-sulfur coal without supplying part of the capital. Price, too, would seem to have been a factor. The local coal for the Miller plant was purchased at what turned out to be bargain prices. And because of its low mine-head price, even after being shipped nine thousand miles South African coal was priced attractively, in view of rising American coal prices.[60]

On the other hand, the failure to foresee and respond effectively to adverse public-relations consequences has structural explanations. The coal purchasing group was part of Southern Company Services, which is much less experienced in dealing directly with the public than are the operating companies. Only after the controversy over the South African coal began was a full-time public-relations office established at the service company's engineering headquarters in Birmingham—a development that also reflects the growing role of Southern Company Services within the system.[61]

To end this discussion, in 1976, Gulf Power entered into a further ten-year contract for 7.7 million tons of South African coal —about 20 percent of its requirements—at a price considerably below locally available sources. Thus, the public-relations costs, even when recognized, did not ultimately play a decisive role in determining the system's policies on South African coal. On the other hand, the company made efforts in 1976 to persuade local groups that circumstances in South Africa were changing.[62]

While the fuel department was devising a short-term strategy for meeting the "new source" standards, Southern Company Services' Research Department embarked on an energetic investigation of stack gas scrubber technologies and solvent coal refining. Setting out to build one small scrubber prototype at Gulf Power's Scholz Plant in Florida, it ended up constructing three separate 20 MW prototypes there in order to compare the systems to each other and to other existing scrubber designs. Rather than repeat prototype work that was already under way, the group decided to make a virtue of Southern's lateness in entering the scrubber research field and chose to explore some relatively untested "second-generation" approaches to flue gas desulfurization. Formulating the program in this way gave an incentive to the manufacturers of these new technologies to provide money and personnel for the research effort, which is why the multiunit effort could proceed within a budget initially developed for a single-prototype experiment. Out of the initial work with the three prototypes has come EPA funding for a full-scale demonstration of one of these technologies at another utility site, and continuing research at Plant Scholz on other scrubber approaches that the manufacturers wish to test.[63] Figure 20 shows the three scrubber systems at the Scholz plant.

Figure 20. Three experimental flue-gas desulfurization systems (Japanese, West German, and American) as they appeared in 1976 at Gulf Power's Scholz generating station in northwest Florida. Courtesy of the Southern Company, Inc.

Supplementing the research group's investigations of scrubber technology, William Harrison looked into work on solvent coal refining that the United States Office of Coal Research had sponsored during the 1960s. He began exploring with the office the possibility of a joint undertaking to test this control approach.

Attracted by Southern's interest, a chemical firm named Catalytic became interested in participating as well. After Southern Company Services and Catalytic had partially completed planning for a fifty ton per day project, however, Congress decided to build the project entirely with federal funds in Tacoma, Washington. Rather than dropping their work, Southern and Catalytic proceeded with their own six ton per day prototype, which the companies felt could make a significant contribution to the development of this technology. Catalytic personnel designed, built, and operated the facility.

Initially, two-thirds of the funding for the project came from the Edison Electric Institute. Later, a new industry organization, the Electric Power Research Institute, took over as the source of this funding. Today funding also comes from the United States

Department of Energy. The results of this research have been very promising. In 1977 the company described a test burn of solvent-refined coal as "an unqualified success," and now says it believes that commercial quantities can be produced at costs that will make solvent-refined coal competitive with scrubbers. On March 1, 1978, the company called attention to its work in a half-page advertisement in the *Wall Street Journal*.[64]

Southern's serious exploration of these control technologies would seem to be in conflict with the company's avowed desire to use tall stacks rather than SO_2 emission controls. Yet the system's top management evidently supports these research activities, despite its interest in persuading Congress to modify the stringent new source standards contained in the Clean Air Act. How, then, did Southern's research fit into the company's overall strategy?

Southern's research program appears to be part of a plan designed to meet a number of different contingencies. Southern is *not* committed to using the control methods it is developing; if the emission standards are modified so that scrubbers or similar controls are not needed, it is unlikely that such controls will be installed.

In Florida, Southern's scrubber research at Plant Scholz was an integral part of Gulf Power Company's strategy for responding to state air quality regulations, which originally required the company to meet very restrictive emission standards by July 1975. Each of the three scrubber systems tested at Plant Scholz was designed so that it could be expanded to larger capacity at relatively little additional cost, and each system was managed as it if were to become a routine part of the power plant operation. The company also used the argument that it needed more time to conduct its scrubber testing, to help convince the state to extend the 1975 deadline by several years. Meanwhile, Gulf launched a search for low-sulfur coal and continued its efforts, along with other Florida electric utilities, to work with the state in order to maintain the desired ambient air quality. Ultimately, after a $2 million study lasting two years, the state substantially altered its original emission standards, so that scrubbers were not required after all.

Yet Southern — in line with its policy to be prepared for a variety of eventualities — sought to have a thorough understanding of the different control methods it might use if it had to resort to emission controls. John Craig, former senior research engineer at Southern Company Services and now director of environmental affairs for El Paso Natural Gas, stated, "The Southern Company is interested in having alternative strategies available in case the Clean Air Act is not amended."[65] Clearly, the research group's activities helped prepare the company for this contingency.

The particular makeup of Southern's research group also helps explain the innovative nature of the company's work. Southern's researchers are not typical of electrical utility technical personnel. Four of the original group had doctoral degrees and most had done engineering or scientific work in a nonutility setting, such as a university or a large research institution. The fact that El Paso Natural Gas recruited one of the group's members to be its director of environmental affairs underlines the quality and range of the unit. This unit evidently had the motivation and ability to undertake technically sophisticated projects that were of interest outside as well as inside the Southern System. Moreover, these researchers knew from past experience how to obtain the funds to mount such an ambitious program. "We developed partial outside funding for many of our projects," said John Craig. "Because of our academic backgrounds, we're used to raising outside funds to support our work. We were brought up in a frugal atmosphere and we know how to attract money for research."[66] Without this ability, the group might not have been able to do nearly as much, given its relatively limited budget.

Because of their unusual talents and backgrounds, Southern's researchers were able to see opportunities and take initiatives that others might well have missed. Perhaps this is what top management intended, when it created the unit. Yet because the members' own thinking played such a key role in determining what work it did, the consequences of creating such a group were not entirely foreseeable by top management.

Having such a sophisticated research unit at Southern was a departure from traditional utility practice; utilities have generally relied on their equipment suppliers to carry out research and development work. Given the group's novelty for Southern and the company's complicated organizational structure, the new unit did not immediately fit into a niche in the Southern system. It took some time for managerial procedures and expectations surrounding the research group to evolve. Some of the more conventional people in company management, particularly in the operating companies, expressed doubts about the scope of the group's work. The detailed budget justification procedure that Harrison created for his research department appears to have quieted these doubts considerably, and facilitated the adjustment of these managers to the presence of the group.

At the same time, the research group itself had to learn what type of work top management would support. On at least one occasion, the system's executives rejected an ambitious proposal by the research unit which would have required a large investment by the company. Thus, the process of adjustment was not one-sided. After a period of transition, the research group's place in the organization became better defined.

Although Southern Company Services' current structure has influenced its response to SO_2 emissions standards, the company's ability to take some initiative in particularly sensitive situations predates recent organizational developments. In the area of particulate controls Southern has, on occasion, gone further than the law requires. Where there has been no reason to be positively responsive, it has been quite restrained in its expenditures.

The particulate control equipment originally installed on many of Southern's plants would be inadequate by today's standards. Some plants were initially equipped only with mechanical collectors. And precipitators—as in many other utilities where they were installed before the late 1960s—were generally not very efficient or reliable. One Southern Company plant, Alabama's Gorgas plant which began service in 1929, operated with no particulate controls whatsoever until 1975 when it was shut down.

Interestingly enough, three Southern plants built during the 1930s and 1940s were equipped with precipitators. Their particular locations led the company to take these measures, although there was no legal need to do so. In 1936 precipitators were installed at Plant Atkinson, near Atlanta, as a result of complaints by the owner of a nearby tree nursery. In 1948 precipitators were installed at Plant Mitchell because of its proximity to Radium Springs, Georgia, a local health resort. And in 1949, when Plant Gadsden was built within sight of the city hall of Gadsden, Alabama, it too was equipped with precipitators. Because of the visibility of the facility, the precipitators at Gadsden were upgraded in 1970-1971, before the new state implementation plan was instituted.[67]

Although Southern relied primarily on mechanical collectors throughout the 1950s, a general switch to precipitators at new plants began in 1959. This was initiated by the steam projects planning unit of the service company. Sherwood Lawrence, who now oversees the steam projects group, explains that the switch was made in part because the mechanical collectors then in use were continually breaking down. But, he said, there was also a "growing concern" with air pollution, which was reflected in newspaper and trade journal accounts. "There was a feeling that we should put in a design that would work and avoid the issue in the future," Lawrence said.[68] To put this initiative in perspective, however, it should be noted that many utilities (including several in our study) had already been using precipitators as a matter of course for a number of years.

The paradoxical nature of Southern's decision making is revealed by the fact that once the company converted to precipitators it did not choose to aim for high performance. Its first units were consciously designed so that they did not provide highly effective particulate removal under the most difficult conditions — that is, with the dirtiest coal or with the boilers operated over design limits. The designers did not feel that the added cost of building in margins to assure the extra efficiency was justified. The operating companies were not happy with the frequency of breakdowns and pushed for more reliability. But it was only in the late 1960s and early 1970s, when the Southern states began adopting air pollution regulations, that precipitator specifications were tightened.[69]

Even though efforts have been made to improve reliability, no one in the company seems to have advocated efficiencies higher than those required by law. Unlike TVA and Hydro, Southern has not adopted a policy of installing 99 or 99.5 percent efficient precipitators. It plans only to comply with state regulations, with some design margins built in to ensure that this level is actually met. On the other hand, Southern will come closer than TVA to meeting state deadlines; the company was two years late in retrofitting precipitators on some old plants, but TVA was up to three years late in a number of cases.

Overall, the history of Southern's particulate controls shows that the organization has sought to balance the costs and benefits of varying decisions. Its strategy reflects the company's concern with holding down costs, the fact that the managers are politically minded, and a collegial top management structure that facilitates constructive interchange and pragmatic rethinking. The history shows how Southern Company Services has effectively carried out this strategy, in part because doing so was consistent with the goals of some of its key members. Yet this strategy has been functional only because modest environmental pressures make modest, slow, and considered responses acceptable. One cannot determine what its value would be in a context like PG&E's.

Other environmental choices have been dealt with in similar

fashion. For instance, Southern's early plants were built with very low stacks. But in the mid-1960s, before the Research Department was established, Services' steam projects group had noted national trends in this area and had begun building taller stacks. It also began cooperating with the operating companies on a program to monitor the impact of stacks on plume dispersion (drawing heavily on TVA's work).[70] Similarly, Southern and its subsidiaries have campaigned against federal requirements that it retrofit cooling towers on its older plants. Yet the steam projects group has included cooling towers or ponds or other forms of closed-cycle cooling in the design of all new plants built since the early 1970s. In part, this was in order to overcome water availability problems, but no doubt a sense of national trends in this area influenced the decision.[71] Doing so allowed Southern to avoid the costly retrofitting TVA has had to undertake at the Browns Ferry nuclear station. In the nuclear power area, Southern Company Services' Nuclear Licensing Department has kept track of requirements that the Atomic Energy Commission (now supplanted by the Nuclear Regulatory Commission) could be expected to impose on nuclear plants already built or under construction. It has successfully argued, sometimes over operating-company protests, for the addition of new control systems in Southern's nuclear plants in anticipation of what *might* be required.[72]

As a last example, Southern Company Services' Fuel Department has pushed for greater reclamation efforts on the part of Southern's strip-mine coal suppliers, who supply about 45 percent of Southern's coal. This is in contrast to TVA's Fuel Procurement Branch, which sided with TVA's Office of Power in opposing proposals to impose reclamation requirements on suppliers. Explaining why he saw the need for Southern to take some action in this area, Jim Ludwig said, "There's an element that would like to ban strip mining outright. That's because of exposure to some very bad situations where the land really has been raped. We've got to have coal production, but we can't afford to have [negligence] which would cause this very large segment to be banned. Some suppliers have created a problem for all of us by doing just a token effort or nothing at all. We feel we ought to do more."[73]

In summary, Southern has been under considerably less pressure to demonstrate environmental concern than utilities in some other regions. It has been able to follow a policy of minimizing pollution control expenditures in many cases, but has also demonstrated flexibility in dealing with environmental matters. It has taken some significant initiatives—from solvent refining to purchase of overseas coal. In many cases, Southern has invested only what it had to in controls, and has worked for the relaxation of such controls where this seems feasible and economically valuable. But where curbing certain impacts has seemed necessary, or where the savings achievable by installing only limited controls did not seem worth the problems that would result, it has acted more vigorously to protect the environment.

As we have seen, the organization's battles with TVA and the operating companies' attention to local political trends have enhanced the organization's sensitivity to external pressures, as has the presence of so many lawyers in its top management. The decentralized structure facilitates Southern's ability to relate successfully to state agencies. At the same time, technical creativity has been assured by Southern Company Services' organizational circumstances. As system-wide consultants, staff members have the incentive, the opportunity, and the background to take a longer view. Tension between services and the operating companies has some costs, but there are also evident benefits.

A collegial top management has been combined with significant diagonal mobility, especially at the upper levels. Outsiders have been brought in where this has seemed appropriate, but insiders too reach many top jobs. This has produced a team with a broad identification with the organization, and a corporate structure that facilitates strategic reexamination. With relatively deep and strong controls at their disposal, management is in a position to implement its decisions effectively, even where this means structural change to respond to new circumstances.

As pressures from citizen groups increase, Southern may face added challenges to its current mode of operation, since it has not been extremely effective in dealing with such groups. However, it has many structural features that should facilitate further adaptation.

8

The Los Angeles Department of Water and Power

The Los Angeles Department of Water and Power (LADWP) is the largest municipal electric utility in the nation. Built with a combination of technological virtuosity, local boosterism, and machine politics, for the first four decades of this century it waged a long and difficult campaign against neighboring private companies before becoming secure in its service area. During this battle the DWP functioned as a central force in local politics, but reforms in the 1940s reduced its political involvement just as its territorial fight was ending.

For a time after World War II, the DWP had a fairly trouble-free existence. With low rates and adequate service, it functioned for the most part as an uncontroversial, technocratic organization. In the last fifteen years, however, with increased environmental concerns and rising energy prices, it has become enmeshed in a series of difficult situations. Los Angeles was one of the first areas in the country to become seriously concerned with air pollution. In the process, the DWP could not help being an object of growing regulatory efforts. Its internal structure, based on a strict promotion-through-examination type of civil service system, limited the ability of top management to hire, fire, promote, and demote. Having adapted to a less taxing situation, the utility at first did not have the managerial or technical resources to respond to these new pressures in a coherent, effective manner. Instead, its behavior varied a good deal from issue to issue, depending on which groups happened to be responsible and on their particular orientation. While the city government had more levers to control the DWP than the federal government had to guide TVA, the city's impact was attenuated by the DWP's internal administrative weaknesses. In some cases, changes in its behavior came about only as the result of assiduous use of external regulatory mechanisms.

More recently, particularly with the arrival of a new general manager from outside the organization, the DWP has undergone significant evolution. Concern on the part of the city council and the mayor has been translated into a more active Board of Water and Power Commissioners. Simultaneously, the new top management has undertaken several organizational innovations designed explicitly to enhance the utility's ability to notice and respond to outside pressures. The nature of these developments and the contrast with earlier structure and behavior are suggestive. They tell us something about the general problems of designing organizations with the capacity and inclination to respond positively to changes in the larger world.

Background and Context

The municipal generation of electricity began in Los Angeles as a by-product of the city's efforts to secure an adequate water supply, which explains the current organizational connection between water and power services.[1] The Los Angeles Department of Water and Power owes its existence to the fact that under Spanish law, the residents of the village founded on the banks of the Los Angeles River in 1781 held a common right to the use of the river's water. When California joined the United States in 1848, these communal rights were interpreted as belonging to the municipal government. Early experiments with private operation of the city's water supply produced unsatisfactory results, however, so in 1902 the city purchased the existing private works and established a public board of water commissioners to operate them.

The new municipal management soon found that the Los Angeles River was unable to supply the water needs of a rapidly growing population. A prominent local engineer, Frederick B. Eaton, convinced the superintendent of the waterworks, William Mulholland, that the only solution was a 250-mile gravity aqueduct from water-rich Owens Valley, high on the eastern slopes of the Sierra Nevadas. Together they promoted the ambitious project, and in 1905 and 1907 Los Angeles voters approved the bonds to pay for it.[2]

It was apparent that the falling water along the aqueduct could be used for power generation. A consulting engineer, Ezra F. Scattergood, had been building small hydroelectric stations to power the construction effort. In 1909 the city council asked him to investigate the possibilities of expanded power production and then formed a Bureau of Aqueduct Power with Scattergood in command. He would continue to head the municipal electric system until his forced retirement in 1941. In 1914 the Power and Water Bureaus were consolidated in a single Public Service Department, which in 1925 was renamed the Department of Water and Power. Only after 1941 (except briefly in the early 1930s) were the two bureaus administered by a single head; until that time, separate chief engineers reported directly to what came to be known as the Board of Water and Power Commissioners.

Many Los Angeles industrialists, anticipating the commercial development that low-cost reliable electric power would make possible, supported the growth of the Power Bureau. But the private utility companies opposed the municipal system. To either build its own facilities or buy out the private firms, the Bureau needed money. The only way to get it at the time was to convince two-thirds of the city's voters to approve a bond referendum. Whenever this was tried, the private utilities mounted well-financed and carefully organized campaigns in opposition. These were intermittently successful, especially when the press and the chamber of commerce sided with the private companies, as they occasionally did.

From 1910 until 1937, when the city came to own most of the distribution facilities within its borders, a seesaw battle was fought both in election campaigns and in the courts. Scattergood, like Adam Beck at Ontario Hydro, developed a political machine of his own to battle for the cause of public power. It was made up of people from the DWP and other municipal employees, and was run out of the utility's headquarters, through the business agent's office. System employees, for example, were given election day off but were well organized for poll watching, turning out the vote, and so forth.

The expansion of the municipal power system was a major focus of Los Angeles politics for about twenty-five years. But in 1936 a 287-kilovolt transmission line to Boulder (now Hoover) Dam was completed. This line, at the time the longest and highest-voltage transmission line in the world, freed the city system from dependence on Southern California Edison for its power supplies. The following year, the last of the private distribution systems in the city were purchased. Public power, it seemed, had prevailed.

The DWP's expansion was not without costs. The people of Owens Valley were unhappy with the terms they were offered for their land and water rights. In 1922 they organized an irrigation

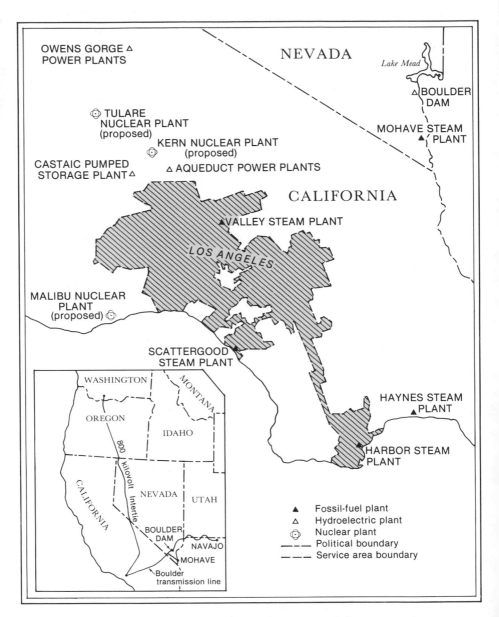

Figure 21. Los Angeles Department of Water and Power: service area, principal transmission lines, and generating stations. Based on annual reports of the Los Angeles Department of Water and Power.

district so they could sell together and get a better price. Frustrated by the failure of this project and lacking any political control over the utility, some resorted to dynamiting the aqueduct, sniping, and so on. Armed guards were posted and at one point the governor called out the National Guard. In 1933, after years of controversy, headlines, and a special investigation, DWP offered more generous compensation terms and the matter was gradually settled. But in the minds of residents outside Los Angeles, it left a legacy of skepticism about the DWP's intentions that has continued to affect the utility to the present day.[3]

Meanwhile, the political climate was changing. To the early progressives, municipal ownership promised to remove the private power companies as a potential source of local political corruption; there would be one less greedy interest to sway public officials. In Los Angeles it had not worked out that way. The DWP itself became an "interest" and some of its political friends were charged with involvement in corrupt practices. But as the city grew and became more cosmopolitan with increasing immigration, the old system could not survive. In 1940 a former judge, Fletcher Bowron, succeeded in winning the mayoralty on an anticorruption reform platform.[4] Overriding Scattergood's suggestions, he appointed a new majority to the Board of Water and Power Commissioners who were sympathetic to his aims; he used that majority to take control of the organization.

Scattergood was subsequently removed as chief electrical engineer and made a consultant for a time. A new single head of both systems (a water engineer) was appointed. In 1944 he was succeeded in that post by a former dean of engineering at Stanford — an able, technically oriented man with no history of involvement in the city's power politics.[5]

Over the next few years most of Scattergood's men resigned or retired, including the business agent, whose office had been the focus of the Bureau's political activity. The staff and budget of that office were immediately cut in half. Efficiency surveys and an elaborate job classification effort provided the basis for a strict civil service system. This made it difficult or impossible for anyone to use the utility for patronage purposes.

Perhaps even more important, the city charter was amended in 1947 to allow the DWP to issue revenue bonds without voter approval. This made its political machinery unnecessary. As with Hydro and TVA, steps were taken to insulate the organization from politics at just about the time that the most pressing political question it raised — namely, the scope of its activities — was settled.

In a sense these reforms accomplished their purpose. The DWP lost most of its outside-oriented groups and became almost exclusively a technical organization. Reflecting the change from the Scattergood era, recently retired general manager Robert V. Phillips said, "My motto and that of every general manager is 'Keep politics out of the Department.' "[6] But by implementing these changes, internal conditions were created that made it much more difficult for the DWP to grapple with the energy and environmental controversies that waited in its future.

In the meantime, however, its problem in the post-World War II period was to supply power to a growing community, and to supply it cheaply so as to attract additional development to the region (an objective the DWP shared at the time with TVA and Ontario Hydro). A growth-oriented municipal administration tended to appoint to the Board of Commissioners local businessmen who accepted the organization's objective. It was also necessary to keep the city council happy and to minimize citizen complaints. During this period, the utility's management was basically intent on operating and expanding the system in a relatively crisis-free atmosphere. With favorable tax and borrowing advantages, and with a series of new and efficient plants being added to the system, it was able to keep rates below those of its neighbor, Southern California Edison.[7]

A review of the authority relationships governing the utility is useful for an understanding of its operations. By city charter, the public's interest in the DWP is represented by the Board of Water and Power Commissioners. The five unsalaried commissioners are appointed to staggered five-year terms by the mayor, although by tradition the board resigns *in toto* when a new mayor is elected. DWP business is reviewed and decisions are made at weekly board meetings, following an agenda prepared by the board office from material submitted by the general manager and the chiefs of each system. Most agenda items are handled by one of the board's six standing committees before being heard by the board.[8]

The role of the board has changed greatly in the last decade or so. Previously, despite its substantial formal power over DWP affairs, the board rarely interfered with the policies adopted by the utility's management; it was a part-time group and lacked technical expertise. Members had clerical assistance but relied on the general manager's office for additional staff support, thus having to work with limited resources in carrying out its oversight responsibilities. As politically sensitive environmental issues have arisen, however, commissioners have begun digging into DWP issues much more deeply, balancing technical factors against broader social and economic concerns. Recent commissioners have taken an active interest in matters such as nuclear power, conservation, and rate restructuring.

Whatever their initial viewpoint, however, commissioners generally become sympathetic to the DWP's problems. As an observer within the utility put it, "Once commissioners assume office, they become responsible for directing a public utility. In the process, they learn to view projects from *both* the utility's and the public's perspective."[9]

The city council too has clearly defined, if limited, authority over the DWP. This elected body must approve all changes in the rate structure and must approve any DWP contracts of more than three years' duration. It has no budget control over the utility, however. And although the council and the mayor may disapprove a bond issue within fifteen days of its announcement, the DWP is no longer required to secure council or voter approval in advance.[10]

Until about ten years ago, the DWP had few dealings — and hence few clashes — with the city council. To be sure, council members were sensitive to their constituents' concerns with regard to distributing stations and transmission lines, and the utility responded to this concern. But for the most part, the DWP felt little need to "play ball" with the city council. Robert Phillips said, "We had the reputation of being independent — more than independent: we were accused of being arrogant."[11] The utility could afford this reputation, however, only as long as it was in the position of not needing the council's approval. During and after World War II this was the case, since the DWP's revenues from increased power consumption were more than enough to offset inflation and to finance capital expenditures. With declining fuel costs and steady industry-wide technical change, it had no need of rate increases. Moreover, the DWP undertook its own construction projects, so it did not need to ask the council to approve long-term contracts.[12]

On a less global level, however, individual council members can be quite concerned with DWP actions. With no strong local party organizations, council members are dependent for reelection on their personal appeal and whatever supporting organizations they can create. Hence, protest groups with a specific neighborhood base can be an effective political force. This helps to explain the interest the council has taken for many years in the beautification of substations and use of transmission rights-of-way for park purposes. The DWP, in response, has made a conscious commitment in this area, striving to make its facilities as aesthetically pleasing as possible.[13]

The mayor's formal authority over the Department of Water and Power derives from the fact that he appoints the Board of Commissioners and the fact that as the city's chief executive, he holds veto power over the city council. However, after the reforms of the 1940s, mayors troubled themselves relatively little with DWP affairs. Only two men, Norris Poulson and Sam Yorty, held the post from 1952 until 1973. Politically they were conservative advocates of regional development. They found the utility's "low-cost power-good service" objective and its interest in a smoothly operating, steadily expanding system perfectly congenial.[14] From their point of view, the DWP was doing a good job and no intervention was called for.

Thus, although the utility was subject to significant line authority — certainly more than TVA, although less than Hydro — this was not much used to influence its behavior. Outside regulatory authorities have produced the greatest changes in DWP activities, especially in the environmental area. Unlike TVA, the DWP could not claim exemption from the jurisdiction of such agencies. Foremost among these has been a county agency, the Los Angeles Air Pollution Control District.

The APCD was created in 1947 by state legislation, after the city's wartime industrial growth had caused its first smog crises in 1943. The city's largest paper, the *Los Angeles Times*, began a major public campaign that helped get the agency created. Rule making and appeals authority for the APCD was vested in the County Board of Supervisors, whose five members were elected by districts.[15] This placed air pollution control authority on a governmental level different from that of the DWP.

In light of current understanding of the chemistry of smog, it seems fairly certain that the smog incidents of the 1940s were brought on not by industrial expansion, but by the increased use of automobiles which expansion brought with it. At the time, however, this was not understood. The Air Pollution Control District began by focusing on SO_2, whose harmful effects were known but which in fact we now know had little to do with smog. Then it moved to hydrocarbons (which were more relevant), looking to obvious, large industrial sources such as steel mills and oil refineries. Citizen pressure led to tough regulatory measures despite vigorous protests from those regulated. Several times the APCD's chief administrator was fired because of worsening air quality. After several bad incidents in 1954 and 1955, for example, a county supervisor lost an election over the smog issue, and another agency reorganization followed. A 24-hour enforcement squad—complete with patrol cars and two-way radios, and headed by a former state trooper—was established.

After 1954 the APCD turned its attention to power plants, beginning with Southern California Edison because until 1957 government organizations were exempt from its jurisdiction. The pattern of relations between the APCD and power companies was thus established not by the DWP, but by Southern California Edison.[16] Edison was denied construction and operating permits in 1956, primarily on the basis of SO_2 emissions and the plume opacity that resulted when its units burned residual fuel oil instead of natural gas. To some extent, this was only a gesture, since closing the plants would have left the area short of power. But the gesture did not go unnoticed. Edison responded by announcing a $1.7 million research program into the use of precipitators, bag houses, and other flue-gas cleaning devices. It also appealed the denials to the independent three-member Air Pollution Hearing Board, which granted the company the first of a series of one-year operating variances as well as construction permits for the new units. The DWP came under APCD supervision the following year, when the agency convinced the state legislature to expand its authority. The same pattern of rejections and variances was characteristic of the DWP's early plant applications as well.[17]

Air quality worsened steadily, however, and the regulations were tightened. In 1958 the APCD began to require large sources (that is, power plants) to burn low-polluting natural gas whenever it was available. They also had to use fuel with less than 1 percent sulfur during the summer months or in smog emergencies (in practice, this meant using natural gas). By 1968, when the oil import quota program was abolished, a year-round limit of .5 percent sulfur had been imposed, which implied burning natural gas, or very low-sulfur oil that could now be imported from Indonesia.[18] (In comparison, fuel sulfur-content regulations did not begin in Boston until 1970, twelve years after they were first instituted in Los Angeles.) In 1968 the DWP began to confront strict rules on emissions of NO_x, which utilities outside California are generally still not required to control. Thus, the special air pollution problems of southern California have repeatedly created for the DWP difficulties that other companies in our study have largely escaped.

For about ten years the Air Pollution Control District's relations with the DWP were quite amicable. To some extent, the utility benefited from Southern California Edison's research into emissions controls.[19] The APCD could justify its willingness to cooperate with the utilities on the grounds that progress was being made, or at least attempted. The APCD attempted to set standards that were technologically feasible and it worked closely with industry to this end. The result was that the DWP was usually able to meet fuel requirements and emissions standards, and each party considered the other to be quite cooperative.[20]

During the 1950s and early 1960s, then, the political and regulatory atmosphere in which the DWP built new generating capacity was relatively relaxed, despite the growth of fossil-fuel generation within the Los Angeles basin. In the 1920s and 1930s the utility had acquired most of the power it needed by adding hydroelectric plants along the route of its aqueduct and by buying generating units and distribution systems from local competitors.[21] It had also lobbied successfully for the Boulder Dam project. When these sources proved inadequate to meet the demand created by the industrial boom of World War II, the Department of Water and Power began to construct a series of fossil-fuel steam generating plants in the Los Angeles basin, the first of which (the 65 MW Harbor Generating Station 1) began operation in 1943. After 1947, when the DWP no longer needed voter approval to issue revenue bonds, funds for construction became more readily available and the projects continued. In all, between 1943 and the early 1960s seventeen units at four different sites within the basin were constructed, with a total generating capacity of 3000 MW.[22]

By the early 1960s the problems of capacity expansion had become more complicated. In the fall of 1964 the APCD urged that no new fossil-fuel power plants be built in the Los Angeles basin because of continuing air pollution problems there. In late 1966 the Air Pollution Control officer reported to the supervisors that such a strategy would work, since the last units of the Haynes plant within the basin were just coming on line. At about the same time, Floyd Goss, who had recently become DWP's chief electrical engineer, assured the supervisors that the utility had no plans to add any fossil-fuel generating capacity in the Los Angeles basin.[23] This turned out to be impossible, at least from the DWP's point of view. As a result, the utility tried to build a new plant in the city and hence to take on a regulatory body whose chairman, county supervisor Dorn, had unseated an incumbent over the smog issue. One observer commented that "Dorn was making a big political thing" over the DWP's plans, forcing the utility to deal with the kind of context that companies like TVA and Southern seldom had to confront. It did not do so with great success.

Partly in response to these local environmental and political pressures, the DWP began to place renewed emphasis on the strategy of importing power over long distances from large federal projects or mixed (public and private) projects of which it was only a part owner. Greater flexibility on environmental matters was only one of several benefits to this approach. Such a scheme offered a relatively small utility the opportunity to obtain power at low cost from efficient-size (that is, large) generating plants. It also enabled the DWP to diversify its generation among sources and so improve system reliability. If it had been forced to "go it alone," large, low-cost generation projects would simply have been beyond its fiscal capacity. In addition, such projects could have made the system dependent on only a few power sources, and a failure in any one of these would have been most serious.

Since the construction of the original aqueduct and Boulder Dam, the DWP has relied on power sources outside Los Angeles. In 1970 the utility completed an 850-mile, 800-kilovolt direct current line to the Bonneville Power Authority. It was, and still is, the longest and highest-voltage transmission line in the country (see Figure 21).[24]

Drawing on power sources outside the Los Angeles basin does not free the DWP from environmental constraints, but it does provide some alternatives to the stringent regulations and intense environmental concerns within Los Angeles itself. Yet these alternatives, too, have often aroused intense debate.

In 1943, for example, the DWP began lobbying for a major federal hydroelectric development at Bridge Canyon on the Colorado River. In the mid-1960s, the United States Bureau of Reclamation began to pursue the idea in earnest in order to provide power and revenue for the Central Arizona Project. But the scheme evoked vigorous objections from environmentalists across the country, since it would have backed up water into Grand Canyon National Park. The secretary of the interior, Stewart Udall, ultimately abandoned the project in the face of congressional opposition. A proposal for a pumped-storage project on

Kanab Creek (a tributary of the Colorado River in the same region) was likewise withdrawn.[25]

This strategy of diversification by importing power from distant, low-cost joint projects was somewhat more successful when, in the late 1960s, the DWP joined with several other utilities and federal agencies in the construction of two large coal-fired plants in the southwestern desert: the Navajo plant in Arizona, and the Mohave plant in Nevada. With considerable coal close at hand, the desert locations offered the prospect of low-cost power with environmental regulations less stringent than those in the heavily polluted Los Angeles basin. (These same attractions had already led some of these utilities—although not the DWP—to build an earlier plant in New Mexico, near "Four Corners," where New Mexico, Arizona, Utah, and Colorado meet.) A number of other plants have been planned or constructed in the same general area.

As it turned out, however, various local agencies have imposed on Mohave and Navajo environmental constraints that were more stringent than the utilities had anticipated. Several other projects in the region (not involving the DWP) have been delayed or canceled in response to local or federal regulatory requirements.[26] Nevertheless, given apparent economic advantages and the utility's limited options in the face of the APCD's position, the DWP continues to pursue this strategy where it seems feasible, as its proposed participation in the Intermountain Power Project attests. Whatever restrictions do govern such sites and facilities, the rules the utilities must comply with are usually more lenient than those that would govern a fossil-fuel plant in the Los Angeles basin. Coal-burning plants, even with high-efficiency precipitators, would simply not be possible in the city's own service area.

The DWP's other alternative has been nuclear power, where it faces the same difficulties as PG&E: both coastal and inland sites confront distinct and significant objections. There are no easy answers to a utility's (and the public's) need for additional electric generation sources.

As pollution control has become a growing problem, the utility has had to develop new relationships with the city council. Rising fuel costs, environmental expenses, and energy conservation have brought the need for larger and more frequent rate increases. However necessary, they are never popular, and the DWP's financial pleas are not always enough to override the council's political concerns. Contracts with coparticipants in joint construction projects (such as the Mohave and Navajo plants) need council approval—which is another avenue for environmental or other pressures to reach the DWP. It seems to DWP's decision makers that the utility can hardly make a move without securing the council's approval. The adjustment has been an awkward one.[27] In 1974, for example, the DWP waited a year for a requested rate increase, because the mayor and the city council (half of whose members were standing for reelection at the time) found it politically inopportune.[28]

Water and Power officials believe that most council members recognize the need for rate increases as costs go up, even if the council cannot fully evaluate the specific technical and economic analyses that underlie such requests. At the same time, council members have constituents to worry about. And the council's control over rates gives it an important, and sometimes effective, political handle on the utility. For several years, for example, at the council's request, the City Administrative Office had a team of auditors working full time at the DWP. The utility has had little choice but to cooperate, and now reports that the auditors have made "constructive contributions."[29] Similarly, the council's refusal to consider any more rate increases without an examination of the rate structure led the mayor to appoint a blue-ribbon committee. The committee's recomendations were adopted, resulting in lower rates for small residential and small commercial users while raising rates for larger industrial and large residential users, presumably removing some of the political opprobrium from granting rate increases.[30]

Decisions concerning out-of-state generating plants have received some city council attention, too. An example is the 1972 controversy over the jointly owned Navajo coal-fired plant in Nevada. In May of that year, after six months' discussion, council member Tom Bradley, who was chairman of the Water and Power Committee, convinced the council to reject certain new contracts for the plant unless a number of conditions were met. These were designed to protect the environment and the interests of the residents in the area of the plant. The proposed changes (such as a cleaner stack emissions, coal-mine reclamation, and compensation to Indians and shepherds) would have provided only ideological, not material, gains to residents of the city. But environmental organizations appeared to be a major political force. Tom Bradley, a black ex-policeman, was preparing to run for mayor against incumbent Sam Yorty and would need votes from white, middle-class, and environmentally conscious areas.

The instructions to the DWP to reopen negotiations with other participants led nowhere; the utility reported that it had been bluntly rebuffed. Ultimately, the council reconsidered and approved the contracts, whereupon Bradley, by now the mayor, vetoed them. There the matter rests, with the project going forward on the basis of a number of earlier agreements.[31] (The last of these contracts was finally approved, with minor revisions by the city, in 1978.)

What is striking about this narrative is the limited power the council has to impose its will on the DWP—unlike that which the Ontario government, for example, has with respect to Ontario Hydro. The council could provoke a major confrontation by threatening to reject rate increases, or could try to get the mayor to change the board or the top management. But either course has high costs relative to the potential gains. It would probably take a major issue before a strong and persistent majority of the council would undertake such a battle. Thus, even when the city council took the unusual step of intervening in one of the DWP's out-of-state activities, it was not in a position to enforce its will, especially since Navajo was a joint project with other utilities.

This incident also illustrates an important general point. Utilities, like other organizations, never have absolute independence from the sovereign political authority. Structural and procedural arrangements make effective intervention more or less costly to would-be intervenors, and hence more or less likely to occur. In the long run, the city charter could be changed to make control by the council easier—if this seemed important enough. (Such change did seem important to the Ontario government recently.) But, in the short run, institutions influence outcomes.

Tom Bradley's victory in the 1973 mayoral election brought unprecedented pressures from the mayor's office on the DWP. Bradley had an interest in, some knowledge of, and a major political stake in the DWP's activities. Like Fletcher Bowron, he began by appointing new commissioners to the Water and Power Board. Commissioners now pay close attention to the environmental impact reports which (in compliance with the California Environmental Quality Act of 1970) must accompany proposed DWP projects. Although the board has not turned down a project outright, members have at times requested additional information before giving their approval.[32] The financial constraints of recent years have also increased the commissioners' interest in budgetary matters. Shortly after he assumed office, Bradley appointed a blue-ribbon committee to identify potential commissioners who have some interest in and qualifications for the appointment.[33] The excitement of the earliest months has died down somewhat, as people have become acquainted with one another, but the current board clearly has the potential for constraining the DWP in ways that its predecessors did not.

On the other hand, the DWP staff is not without its resources when it comes to convincing the board. The mayor—eager to expand his general supervisory powers and to diminish the utility's isolation—has been trying to get civil service classifications and salary levels in the utility amalgamated with the rest of the municipal system. Yet his new appointees to the Board of Water and Power disagreed on this issue, accepting the view of the DWP management that it was preferable to allow separate salary determination. The mayor's proposal to establish a "common unit" for describing jobs and setting salaries throughout the city administration would, in the DWP's view, have limited the ability of the utility to manage its own personnel affairs. The mayor persisted, however, and in May 1977 the voters approved a charter amendment that gave the mayor the power to set salaries, subject to council approval.[34]

The mayor has used the device of the blue-ribbon committee on other occasions, as a means to compensate for his administration's lack of technical expertise. It is also a subtle way to introduce different political values into what appears to be a technical problem. When the Arab oil boycott temporarily brought the DWP to within ninety days of exhausting its fuel supply, the utility recommended to the city council a stringent energy conservation program, which included rolling blackouts and a fifty-hour business week. Neither the city nor the public was in a position to argue with the utility over the need for strict conservation efforts, but elements of the DWP program (especially the fifty-hour business week and the layoffs it would entail) were vehemently criticized. The mayor responded by appointing a blue-ribbon committee to come up with a "better" program, several features of which were finally adopted by the city council. Many observers saw in these events a deliberate and well-publicized attempt by the mayor and city council to extend their influence over the Department of Water and Power.[35]

When Robert Phillips retired as general manager in 1975, the Board of Commissioners chose to seek candidates from outside (as well as inside) the DWP and, instead of conducting the search itself, to entrust it to the city's personnel department. Louis H. Winnard—the first outsider to serve as general manager in the more than thirty years since Samuel B. Morris had come from

Stanford in 1944—was ultimately recruited from the Jacksonville Power Authority. While it is clear that the board was ultimately the decision maker on these matters, there is some disagreement as to the role played by the mayor in the selection process. At least one source who was close to these events at the time is convinced that Tom Bradley was critically influential in the decision both to extend the search outside the DWP and to have it conducted by the city personnel office. The Department of Water and Power, on the other hand, maintains that the decisions at every point were those of the commissioners, who wanted to find the best person for the job in as efficient a manner as possible. Regardless of these disagreements, it is understandable, in view of the mayor's relations with the DWP, that Bradley might have preferred a candidate without strong internal loyalties.[36]

In the last decade not only have line authority relationships within the city government been strengthened, but the regulatory constraints that the DWP faces have been greatly expanded. In 1976 the county-level APCD was abolished in favor of a regional South Coast Air Quality Management District.[37] The state Air Resources Board is taking more seriously its responsibilities to review local plans before submitting them, on the state's behalf, as implementation plans under the Clean Air Act Amendments of 1970. With Governor Jerry Brown's appointment of Tom Quinn as Air Resources Board chairman, the board began to exercise its expanding powers—instituting, for example, stiff source-review guidelines for the South Coast Air Basin (October 1976) and requiring the use of .25 percent sulfur oil (February 1977).[38]

In 1972 California voters created, through initiative and referendum ballot, the Coastal Zone Commission—a direct expression of environmentalists' antagonism to the use of any California coastline for industrial purposes.[39] The commission's approval is needed for any coastal project and, as with PG&E, it has been one key element in the DWP's decision to seek inland locations for nuclear development.

The California Environmental Quality Act further requires that the DWP assess the environmental impact of any project it proposes to undertake—a process that entails notification of and consultation with state or local agencies and offices, and with interested persons and organizations. In 1976 the state attorney general, Evelle Younger, interpreted the act to mean that projects *outside* California in which state and local agencies participate (including the DWP) would also be subject to its provisions. In contrast to recent court decisions on the National Environmental Policy Act, Younger stated that environmental impact reports must precede major commitments on any project. DWP officials are quite vocal in their disagreement with these opinions, and, along with other California utilities, have recently achieved legislative relief.[40]

The newest environmental regulatory agency confronting the DWP is the Energy Resources Conservation and Development Commission, established in 1974. This commission's jurisdiction includes approvals for all thermal power plants larger than 50 MW, as well as review and approval of periodic electrical demand forecasts. The commission has greatly complicated the DWP's problems because of its generally antinuclear and antigrowth position; it acts with the air pollution control agencies to block almost any capacity expansion proposal. In recent years three nuclear plants, two within California and one in Arizona, in which the DWP would have participated (Kern County, Sundesert, and Palo Verde's units 4 and 5) were repeatedly delayed and ultimately killed, partly as a result of the commission's efforts.

In summary, the Department of Water and Power has gone through a cycle in terms of its exposure to outside pressure. Despite its highly political early history, the utility became insulated from politics during the industrial expansion of the war and postwar years. With its service area established and its need to obtain bond approval eliminated, the political occasions that had provoked its previous involvement had vanished. But in the 1960s circumstances once again brought the DWP and its activities into the public spotlight and altered its relations with political and regulating institutions. Unfortunately, it was not always well equipped internally to deal with these new pressures.

Internal Organization

The internal machinery that evolved after the utility's reorganization in the 1940s combined a civil service system with a lack of functional or professional groups oriented to the outside world. To a large extent, these features were the product, whether deliberate or incidental, of efforts to depoliticize the DWP's functions. They were also a key element in the utility's environmental troubles. As a result, the DWP has begun to evolve a more sophisticated ability to notice and respond to outside pressure.

It is important that an organization have a top management group with general oversight powers and without day-to-day operating responsibilities. At the DWP there is more of such a structure—at least potentially—than, say, at TVA or under the old Hydro system. The general manager, appointed by the Board of Water and Power Commissioners to oversee the Water and Power systems, has the help of several top-level assistants. The Office of Finance and Accounting and the Office of Management Services report directly to him, as do several small staff groups such as Public Affairs. Within the Power System (the focus of this study) general oversight responsibilities are shared by a chief electrical engineer and two assistants (reduced to one in late 1979), to whom the Division heads within the Power System report.[41]

Diluting the advantages of this structure is the civil service system, which limits top managers' ability to hire, fire, promote, and demote, thus minimizing the incentives they can offer subordinates for good-performance. The DWP's present top management is aware that it is possible to exercise leadership and control within the constraints posed by such a personnel system, and that employee professionalism compensates for top management's limited ability to offer rewards and punishments. Yet the structure of the personnel system has in the past handicapped top management in creating and implementing responses to external demands.

Six top managerial positions are exempt from civil service, and the general manager has two "wild cards," or unassigned exempt slots, with which to maneuver.[42] Otherwise, all appointments and promotions are based on performance on written and oral competitive examinations. Managers are required to pick one of the top three scorers on any exam. In recent years, there has been considerable pressure from the mayor's office to pick the number-one person "or explain why," in order to eliminate any suspicion of unjust discrimination.

Upper-ranking positions in the Power System are filled by promotion from within the DWP, since higher-level examinations are restricted to those who have passed all lower-level exams. (The only exceptions are so-called "open" lists, or else newly created slots such as those that occurred in the nuclear area.) Bonus points are awarded for seniority, on the basis of one quarter of a point for each year of service up to twenty years. Since only a few points typically separate the top scorers, seniority is often the deciding factor. Pay, too, is determined according to job classification and length of tenure (although the charter provides that DWP salaries be "competitive" with private industry), and there is no allowance for merit raises.[43] Thus, managers at all levels

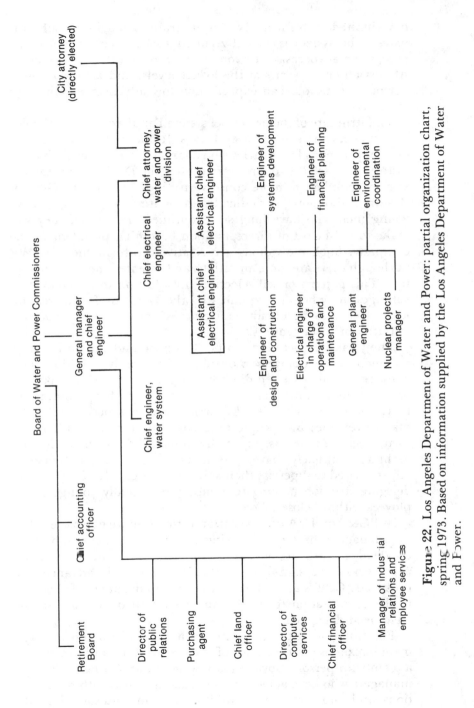

Figure 22. Los Angeles Department of Water and Power: partial organization chart, spring 1973. Based on information supplied by the Los Angeles Department of Water and Power.

have limited tools for motivating desirable behavior in subordinates. The system is virtually closed to experienced outsiders, except for an occasional promotion from another city agency. Almost all entry occurs at the lowest levels, and a bright young person starting out can expect only slow advancement through the ranks.

The structure of the personnel system has affected the behavior of managers and staff in several ways. It does not attract the sort of entrepreneurial visionaries who characterized the utility's early history. The security of civil service and the DWP's high starting salaries look best to more conservative individuals. At PG&E or Boston Edison one periodically encounters bright, aggressive young men who have long since outlined the speech they will make to the board of directors upon becoming president of the company. Such individuals are relatively rare in the LADWP (although there are some ambitious and talented men on the way up). This pattern of self-selection (in addition to economic advantages) may help to explain why the DWP prefers to rely on joint projects to meet load requirements, rather than aggressively initiating its own projects.

The weak link between job performance and promotion does not encourage employees to overextend themselves. Middle-level managers we interviewed did not complain of having to take two or three hours' work home every evening, in sharp contrast to their counterparts at PG&E. Crisis situations occasionally demand overtime, but people take compensatory time off in return.[44] Such managers, especially older ones for whom further mobility is unlikely, have little incentive to make the personal effort needed to supervise their subordinates closely. They tend to delegate decision making to junior (and usually younger) employees without close follow-up.[45]

In PG&E or TVA centralization is much more extensive. Middle managers insist on reviewing subordinates' actions because they will, in turn, be held responsible for them by senior managers who have significant influence over their advancement prospects. Others at the DWP have taken advantage of the slack in the organization to involve themselves in detail that should have been delegated.

The situation at the DWP makes it difficult for top management to exercise certain kinds of leadership. It is hard to assemble a team with personal loyalty (as Vogtle did at Southern). Middle managers who have achieved their current status with no obligations, and who have limited ambitions, could (and sometimes do) feel little impetus to please their superiors.

Although recent managers have explored alternative ways to influence and motivate subordinates, the workings of the civil service system and the patterns of decision making of the DWP hampered policy formulation and implementation in the changing climate of the late 1960s and early 1970s. Top management found, on occasion, that its options had been foreclosed by prior lower-level decisions. This was an integral feature of the difficulties surrounding the construction of the Scattergood Steam Plant 3. On the other hand, the weak hierarchical control system has allowed a certain amount of creativity among lower-level engineers — and this has, at times, led to some sensitive environmental decisions.[46] The civil service system, by limiting the power of "patrons" to reward their "clients," has also restrained the formation of the bureaucratic and personal political alliances that have characterized some of the other companies we have studied.[47] It also appears to have made advancement easier for those who lack the social skills or the ethnic background that are prerequisites for success in some corporate environments.

One countervailing mechanism in the DWP that helps overcome these difficulties is the lack of emphasis on going through channels. The chief electrical engineer will sometimes deal directly with those down the line who are handling an important problem.[48] Young, technically accomplished employees doing the work on a key problem will thus find themselves dealing directly with top management, even in the absence of a formal structure to facilitate such interaction.

Also, in spite of the apparent rigidity of the civil service system, there are ways of working around and through the regulations. The board that conducts the oral examinations that are the basis for the very top jobs may know which people are next in line for promotion, and may be favorably disposed toward them. The chief electrical engineer can shape their perspectives and reactions by telling them what he is looking for.[49] Some of the more aggressive managers in the history of the DWP developed a certain amount of skill in using the system this way. Within limits, therefore, promising individuals may be identified and moved up, even though such activity must be carried out within the civil service framework.

The current chief electrical engineer, James L. Mulloy, seems to have advanced in this fashion. Within the space of five years he rose through the ranks as section head, assistant division head, division head, assistant chief electrical engineer, and finally chief electrical engineer. When Floyd Goss retired on September 1, 1972, Mulloy was a division head. He was made chief ten months later.[50] This rapid rise was made possible by the fact that Mulloy achieved the civil service rank of principal electrical engineer by passing the appropriate examination. Subsequent promotions to assistant division head and division head did not require a new civil service classification. Promotion to assistant chief electrical engineer did require passing the appropriate exam. The chief electrical engineer position is civil service exempt.

Traditionally, the general manager — until recently appointed alternately from the Water and the Power systems — assumed very little administrative responsibility over the system with which he was less familiar. But in the early 1970s, with the DWP coming under closer scrutiny from outside, the utility's top management began to develop tighter control. When Robert Phillips became general manager in 1972, the electrical engineers in the Power System encountered a "waterman" who was determined to make his presence felt. Phillips tightened reporting procedures — especially on budgetary and fiscal matters — and became much more active than his predecessors had been in the budget process. With the aid of one of his assistants, he began to pay closer attention to appointments and promotions. When Phillips retired in 1974, his successor, Louis Winnard, carried the trend even further.[51]

Winnard, an electrical engineer by training, had managed in succession three smaller publicly owned electric utilities before coming to the DWP in February 1976. Under his administration, a number of steps have been taken that have strengthened the general manager's ability to supervise and motivate the organization. Winnard has reorganized and combined functions such as financial planning, rate setting, maintenance, and supplies — functions that formerly had been duplicated to some extent within each system. Perhaps more significantly, he has emphasized the need to develop management skills throughout the structure and to groom future managers in a much less haphazard way than has been done in the past: "I have told all my key managers they must groom their replacements." To this end, Winnard's office has employed management consultants to devise training programs that will provide upper-level managers and lower-level supervisors with broader experience.[52]

The Financial Office's newly inaugurated "responsibility budgeting" program allows field managers to devise their own budgets and makes them accountable for controlling their own costs. It is also designed to broaden the horizons of lower-level managers. Many line managers know very little about the budgetary process, despite years with the utility, according to one of the architects of the new program.

At the same time, the new budgeting system extends the arm of the financial control system directly from the general manager's office down to the lowest levels of the hierarchy. And by working through a Power System Budget Committee composed of representatives from each Division, the Financial Office has bypassed the formal Power System hierarchy.[53] In the absence of mechanisms for strong internal controls, Winnard has also attempted to use external pressure as a tool to motivate appropriate behavior. Project managers and field supervisors have been "strongly advised" to be prepared to testify publicly on any environmental matters relating to their work.[54] Like Phillips, Winnard has made sure that his office retains the power to decide whether to fill any new or existing positions at the engineer level or above.[55]

Although aware of the constraints of the civil service system, Winnard argues that it does not necessarily pose any greater obstacle to advancement than do bureaucratic entrenchment or union regulations elsewhere. One cannot simply thrust change on an organization, he argues, but must work with the system one inherits.[56] Significantly, however, several key members of his team are relative newcomers to the DWP—nonengineers who entered the utility from the outside through the civil service open lists, rather than by working their way up through the ranks. The heads of both the reorganized Financial Office and the new Management Services Office joined the DWP from the outside—which is possible in these nonengineering areas. Neither, however, was brought in specifically by Winnard. The reorganizations themselves seemed timely when several old-timers retired or became ill.[57]

It is also worth noting that the principal changes instituted by Winnard's administration have been focused *outside* the Power System per se. Financial Planning and Rate Setting, for example, were combined with a similar Water System function and centralized in the Finance and Accounting System, reporting directly to the general manager.[58]

Other characteristics of the organizational structure have had an impact on its policy. Within the Power System there is no place in the managerial hierarchy for nonengineers. All management positions are subsumed in the broader category of "engineer" and require a person to move up the whole engineering ladder. Moreover, the Power System is run largely by *electrical* engineers, who occupy the top two positions.[59] In the past, nonelectricals who have made it into upper management circles seem to be exceptions—a pattern that apparently has caused some resentment among nonelectrical engineers. We suggest that this situation reflects and reinforces the DWP's capacity expansion strategy of participation in a portfolio of large, jointly owned, efficient-scale generation facilities which have often been located at long distances from its service area.[60]

The Power System did not have a centralized planning organization until fairly recently. Load forecasting and transmission planning were part of Electrical Operations, and the specification of generating plants was undertaken by Mechanical Design. The critical intermediate step of forecasting and then deciding what capacity should be added was done largely by the chief electrical engineer.[61] Since it took only two or three years to build a new unit on its own, such *ad hoc* judgments seemed quite adequate. On the other hand, when it came to large, remote, jointly owned capacity, much of what occurred was both unpredictable and outside the utility's control.

By the mid-1960s, the world in which the DWP operated had grown increasingly complex. To function effectively amid the political pressures, government regulations, and complicated joint projects, top management in the Power System needed a well-developed set of alternatives with carefully developed contingency plans.[62] Recognizing this fact, chief electrical engineer Floyd Goss created a new Division in the Power System early in 1967: "I established the System Development Division. I needed more direct control over planning, because of the increasingly critical nature of it. It was taking more of my time, and there were dispersed planning groups in different Divisions, duplicate efforts, with little communication. As the decisions became more complex, you couldn't just leave them to a guy in Mechanical Design, for example."[63] Goss thus recognized the need to create an internal mechanism for devising a coherent and responsive policy. Personnel from Design and Construction, Operating and Maintenance, and the Executive Office were combined into the new Division, and it was hoped that its functions would gradually expand.[64]

Although the civil service system within the DWP was flexible enough to allow for such a reorganization, budgetary stringency and the opposition of some senior managers in the Power System prevented the concept from being fully implemented. Part of the problem was that Planning wanted to write specifications that were too detailed for the liking of Design and Construction, where personnel were accustomed and committed to working without close supervision and constraints. Since senior managers and staff engineers are tenured civil servants, there was very little

Goss could do to replace uncooperative subordinates with individuals more sympathetic to his strategic and structural objectives.

In areas other than system planning, the Power System has lacked groups whose functional responsibilities might provide a focus for policy initiative or evaluation. No one in the system, for example, is charged with research and development. Like system planning before 1967, such activities are scattered among various Sections in various Divisions and conducted on an *ad hoc* basis. In TVA and the Southern Company, research and environmental groups have been advocates of new technologies and approaches because they stand to gain in size and influence when such policies are adopted. Lacking such centers of initiative, the DWP has had to rely primarily on external sources for research in generation, distribution, and transmission problems. For instance, the DWP contributes (along with most other major utilities) to the research activities of the Electric Power Research Institute. On the other hand, some fruitful research on vibration suppression and insulation characteristics has been conducted in-house.[65]

Also, until 1973 no one had responsibility for following environmental issues. A former engineer in the Nuclear Project Office was appointed engineer of environmental coordination in that year, reporting (like Division heads) to the chief electrical engineer. But this was long after the DWP's first major entanglements over such matters. The responsibility for responding to environmental regulations is still widely scattered among fairly low-level staff members in various Sections of the Design and Construction Division. Air pollution is handled by a group in Mechanical Design. Water pollution is the responsibility of a group in Civil Engineering. Noise is a concern of Electrical Engineering. The engineer of environmental coordination, with the assistance of one supporting staff member, keeps abreast of appropriate state and federal regulations, supervises the preparation of environmental impact reports (but does not himself prepare them), and handles formal relations with some regulatory agencies.[66] The communication problems implicit in this fragmentation and decentralization of responsibilities would be even more serious were it not for the informality of internal working arrangements. Still, no one except top management is in a position to make a comprehensive assessment of the system's options from an environmental viewpoint.

Most of the groups or individuals who are outside-oriented are located *outside* the Power System. This limits the set of perspectives represented in decision making and deprives Power System executives of routine access to these perspectives and opinions. Furthermore, the DWP's history of insulation from politics has left such groups small and relatively weak.

The Public Relations Office, for example, whose director reports directly to the general manager, is fairly small. Until 1972 its activities were devoted largely to advertising and drafting press releases; its staff members had little routine input into engineering decision making. In 1971, for example, when the DWP announced plans for a proposed nuclear plant in Tulare County in the Central Valley, residents and local officials were angry that they had not been contacted about the project in advance; they had first heard about it from the Los Angeles newspapers. The Public Relations Department itself did not learn of the plan, or the decision to announce it, until the head of the Division read the board agenda the day it happened.[67] This is in contrast with the current role of Public Relations in Boston Edison, where the vice-president for public relations is a major figure in the company. The director and his staff at DWP are now extensively involved, in advance, in all such decisions.

As a publicly owned utility, the DWP was hard pressed to justify the Public Relations Office's advertising campaigns. Goss, growing more sensitive to such criticism, apparently urged the Public Relations people to drop the promotional advertising campaign — which they did.[68] However, they resisted the pressure to drop *all* advertising because of the need, in management's view, to have access to the public for a controlled message on sensitive issues. In June 1972, under pressure from the mayor, all advertising was dropped. Since then, essential institutional announcements are advertised only with specific board approval.

The Public Relations Office has changed noticeably, although it is still limited in size and power. Under the influence of a new director (another outsider who joined the utility from the Memphis municipal system in 1969), the Office has made a determined effort to become involved, and to involve the public, at earlier stages of decision making.[69] In keeping with its new image, the Office was changed from "Public Relations" to "Public Affairs" in December 1973, although the name change was apparently not accompanied by a structural reorganization.[70]

The DWP's Government Liaison Office (also located outside the Power System, under the general manager) is even smaller than its Public Affairs Office. One man, a legislative representative, handles relations with the city council assisted by one staff person and a secretary. The general manager alone has formal responsibility for dealings with the mayor's office.[71] In none of the environmental decisions we focused on, however, did the legislative representative play a role. The increase since the late 1960s in the frequency and intensity of the DWP's contact with the city council has not changed the Liaison Office significantly. More attention is being paid, however, to the *kind* of person who fills the position, as is evident in the current legislative representative, a civil engineer from the Water System.

Top managers at the DWP have taken more personal notice of the council in recent years. Phillips recognized that it was not enough to leave matters to the legislative representative; he gained a reputation for maintaining more frequent personal contact with the council than his predecessors and for keeping council members informed of DWP activities.[72] Winnard and Mulloy, although they rely on the legislative representative, also report having frequent contact with the city council.[73]

The DWP ostensibly has no special representative handling its interests in Sacramento. Since it is a city agency, it cannot appeal independently (that is, without council approval) to the state legislature. Until three years ago, the utility used the city's legislative advocate only occasionally. At that time, specific state environmental regulations led it to join with the city's two other proprietary units (the Airport and Harbor Departments) in sponsoring their own "lobbyist." The DWP's man is paid by these Departments, but is legally registered as the city's advocate.[74] He has actively sought legislative relief from provisions of the California Environmental Quality Act that affect the DWP's out-of-state projects, and that require it to submit environmental impact reports early in the planning process.[75] The DWP feels that the advocate plays an important role — one that the city's other representatives in Sacramento do not play. One state legislator from Los Angeles — a man who had lived in the city his whole life — did not know, until the DWP advocate told him, that the utility was *not* a private company.[76]

The DWP's status as a city agency also limits (and confuses) the role of lawyers in the organization. Only in Ontario Hydro, with its major differences in cultural style and political structure, do lawyers play such a small role. Like the legislative advocate, the attorneys assigned to the DWP are employed by the city attorney's office and not by the utility. They report organizationally to the city attorney's office, and for purposes of DWP business they report to the general manager. They are a small, overworked group with much responsibility for routine matters such as purchase contracts. Since DWP plays virtually no role in their own career advancement, their response to the utility's management is based on their sense of professionalism rather than simple incentives. Although they guide the Power System's engineers in regulatory matters, the Water and Power attorneys have not taken an active part in policy making. Nor, in contrast to the lawyers at PG&E, do they take much initiative in following regulatory situations and anticipating problems. They are not viewed, internally, as a central part of the management structure.[77]

Among the groups that do help the DWP maintain some outward-oriented perspective — potentially, indeed, the most influential such group — is the Board of Water and Power Commissioners. The board's scrutiny over budgetary matters has, for example, forced the DWP to try to explain and justify its projects and expenses.[78] The attention it now pays to the utility's environmental impact reports also makes it less likely that DWP projects will evoke public outcry.[79] Although in the past the board has had limited policy involvement, it has recently been involved with policy in many areas such as conservation, nuclear power, and rate setting. However, the board's ability to scrutinize details closely is hampered by members' time constraints and lack of technical expertise.[80]

In summary, the ability of the Los Angeles Department of Water and Power to respond to changing external pressures has been undermined by two principal features of its internal organization — a weak control system and the limited role of outside-oriented groups. These features stand out in sharper contrast when we compare the DWP with other utilities in this study. Recent administrations, however, have sought remedies for these weaknesses, with varying degrees of success.

Environmental Decisions

Over the last three decades, the LADWP has seen great changes in external pressures and has exhibited clear internal evolution in response. Its environmental decisions — previously *ad hoc* and uncoordinated — have become noticeably more effective and positively responsive. In the early postwar years, the substantial decentralization and delegation fostered by the weak control system led to widely varying choices, depending on the preferences and perspectives of the group making the decision. This resulted in public satisfaction with well-designed substations in some cases, and public protest over insensitively routed transmission lines in others. But as pressures increased, especially with regard to generating plants, the approach led to difficulties varying from project terminations to cost overruns. Although recent internal changes have improved the DWP's ability to deal with these problems, external constraints continue to become more severe. Today, it is not clear that the utility—or indeed anyone—will be able to find acceptable methods for capacity expansion.

Illustrative of earlier practice was the DWP's long-standing concern for aesthetically pleasing facilities. Chief electrical engineer James Mulloy declared, "While the DWP Power System has always been concerned with environmental matters, prior to the early 1970s aesthetics were the prime environmental concern."[81] The strategy goes far back into the DWP's past. Floyd Goss, who worked directly for Ezra Scattergood as a young engineer, noted: "Ezra Scattergood used to lecture us that 'Los Angeles is, most of all, a place to live.' Our philosophy has been that we should put in the best-looking things available. We want to be the best-looking in the neighborhood."[82] For the most part, the utility has succeeded in this effort. It has responded quickly and effectively to complaints about noise, for example, and has won several architectural awards for the design and landscaping of its substations. In cooperation with the Department of Parks, DWP rights-of-way have been turned into recreation sites—as city parks and play areas, or as fishing and picnic areas outside town. Several substations have been built entirely underground.[83] Compared with PG&E or Boston Edison, which also have large urban service areas, the DWP's record in this regard has been quite good.

In part, this is a response to external constraints. The municipal Planning Board and the Art Commission must approve new installations. In practice, the Planning Commission often will not issue a permit until local groups have been appeased. It now requires walls twenty feet high around substations so that the equipment is not visible from outside. The Power System's architects make formal and informal presentations and try to work out compromises. One substation in an attractive residential area off Mulholland Drive consumed five years of negotiations. The DWP does not always have to satisfy local groups, however. When local demands are "excessive" and the utility is at least partially responsive, it can obtain approval over local opposition.[84]

In this particular sphere of decision making, decentralization leads to sensitivity. The lack of groups with expertise in relating to the outside world is not serious here, because the architects take care of such matters reasonably well on their own. Their professional perspective is such that the demands of the "client" are respected—at least within limits. Their professional pride helps produce good design, interesting wall treatments, and effective landscaping. One recently built substation in a well-to-do suburban area was put underground beneath the parking lot and first tee of a municipal golf course—an expensive solution in an area where land is not in short supply.

The DWP's decision making on aesthetic questions also reflects the concerns of the city council. (The utility now routinely notifies council members of projects proposed for their districts.) An example is DWP's decision to install the first 230-kilovolt underground transmission line west of the Mississippi River. This particular line, six to eight miles long, went through a relatively well-to-do residential area. In 1961 and 1962 the council member for the district helped organize citizen pressure in favor of undergrounding—even running for reelection on the issue. Undergrounding at that time was approximately ten times more expensive than overhead construction for such a facility. But after many meetings between the council member and his staff and DWP's management, the line went underground. Floyd Goss remembers a number of other occasions on which such discussions with a council member or others led to changes in a proposed line or substation—when this didn't cost "too much."[85]

Transmission-line engineers traditionally have been oriented toward straight-line, low-cost routes, and the DWP's engineers were quite aggressive in carrying out this approach in the old days. One staff member recalled: "Probably our initial problem of this kind was with the Boulder lines in the early 1930s. The southern portion was very controversial and the objectors were getting an injunction, so we worked all night and weekends to finish the lines. The people were very dissatisfied and have never forgotten."[86]

The DWP now shows more concern for public opinion. When controversy arose over routing some replacement lines from Boulder, changes were made in response to public protests. The objectors wanted the utility to avoid what was later designated the Piro Canyon primitive area, and to upgrade existing rights-of-way. The DWP did computer studies indicating that putting this much power along one right-of-way implied unacceptable risks in the event of an accident. The utility did, however, relocate portions of the line as objectors had requested.[87]

This change in behavior reflects the strategy of, and stronger control of, the new top management. Local people strongly pressed for a public hearing on the project under the provisions of the California Environmental Quality Act. The hearing was held, but not before top management overrode middle-management objections. The DWP also had to decide whether to spend an extra $6 million on aesthetically pleasing tubular-type transmission towers (instead of old-fashioned lattice towers) on a proposed upgrading of a transmission line in the same area. That decision went to chief electrical engineer James Mulloy, who chose the more expensive tubular towers.[88]

Unless major controversies develop, however, decisions are often made quite far down in the organization. For example, on yet another line, several protesters at a public hearing argued for rerouting. To the technical people, some of the critics made arguments that seemed unreasonable and self-serving. But others had what appeared to be a legitimate complaint, pointing out that a section of the proposed route required houses to be removed when the line could easily be put through nearby vacant land instead. Out of a combination of reasonableness and political calculation, such a change was subsequently made. This was a noncity area, but the county supervisor for the district was concerned about the problem. The decision came at a fairly low level in the structure, where the engineers were young and did not remember the "old days."[89]

Before recent developments, however, the decentralized structure of the Department of Water and Power had not allowed it to respond nearly so effectively to complicated environmental pressures. Nowhere is this more apparent than in the story of the DWP decision to add a third fossil-fuel unit to its Scattergood Steam Plant—a decision that has involved it in a running battle with the Los Angeles Air Pollution Control District since 1968 and, more recently, with state and federal regulators.

The controversy surrounding Scattergood 3 has focused on NO_x emissions—a pollutant for which most eastern utilities face no emissions standards, but which is a key element in Los Angeles smog. This smog is made up of so-called "photochemical oxidants" produced from the chemical interaction of nitrogen oxides and carbon monoxide with ozone, which is abundant on sunny days.[90] In 1949 Arie J. Haagen-Smit, professor of biochemistry at the California Institute of Technology, first discovered the nature and causes of photochemical smog and the effects of NO_x. Although his work initially was controversial, by the early 1950s the APCD staff had become concerned about NO_x emissions. As a result of their prompting, Southern California Edison in 1956 began a series of experiments to see how boiler modifications might limit NO_x emissions. Nevertheless, the problem grew steadily worse. In 1959 the state established its first motor vehicle emissions standards. But in 1960 and 1961 "first alert" levels of NO_x were exceeded several times at at least one downtown monitoring station. Pressure on the APCD mounted, and in the winter of 1961-62 it worked with two small, newly licenced generating plants to limit NO_x emissions—a step that Haagen-Smit, then a consultant for the APCD, urged for all power plants.[91]

In the meantime, the Department of Water and Power, under the leadership of chief electrical engineer Floyd Goss, was seeking with little success to expand its generating capacity. Time and time again Goss and his predecessors encountered unanticipated obstacles. The federal government had backed out of the Bridge Canyon project, which the DWP had been urging for over a decade. The utility's first attempts to build nuclear plants along the coast were turned down by the Atomic Energy Commission on seismological grounds, and inland projects were restricted by a critical shortage of cooling water. Goss had announced in 1967 that the DWP would build no new fossil-fuel plants in the Los Angeles basin, but under the circumstances he didn't see any alternatives. The DWP needed new capacity. The Scattergood Steam Plant, close to the city center and to the airport, seemed a logical place to expand, especially since its water-intake pipes had been designed to handle additional units which had been planned but never built.[92]

In January 1968 Floyd Goss and an engineer in Mechanical Design who was responsible for air quality reviewed the DWP's plans with APCD officer Louis Fuller and his staff.[93] At this meeting, and in an exchange of letters later that month, Fuller stated that he personally would have to oppose the plan. According to later public and private testimony, however, Goss and his staff received the distinct impression from Fuller that a permit would be granted. Acting on this assumption, the DWP formally applied for a construction permit in February 1968. In March the DWP air quality engineer spoke with an APCD staff member, who told him that the permit would probably be denied. The engineer assumed that the DWP could simply apply for a variance, as it had done many times in the past.[94] A week later, Fuller wrote for additional information on the proposed unit and urged the DWP to consider a coal-fired plant *outside* the Los Angeles basin as an alternative.

In subsequent exchanges, the DWP made attempts to counter APCD objections by arguing that the new unit would have the effect of lowering total NO_x emissions in the basin, because it would allow older and less efficient units to be retired. In July 1968 the APCD published a draft regulation limiting NO_x emissions from stationary sources — a regulation that would have been impossible for the proposed Scattergood unit to meet. Yet in July and August, the utility ordered the boiler and turbine generator anyway, and sent the APCD additional data on boiler design in October. Construction on the unit was begun without a permit. For a year the APCD continued to press the DWP to substantiate its claims that the unit would lower total NO_x emissions, but the utility did not supply corroborating evidence. Floyd Goss later explained that precise data were not available because the prediction was based on uncertain future contingencies. There the matter stood. The APCD neither granted nor denied a permit, and the DWP continued construction.

In the fall of 1969 — a year and a half after negotiations had begun — the APCD began to act more decisively. On September 30 Fuller informed DWP general manager Edward Kanouse that he would take legal action to halt the Scattergood construction.[95] In December the Air Pollution Control District formally adopted Rule 67, severely restricting NO_x emissions from all new stationary sources. The next day, on the basis of this new rule, the DWP's application for a construction permit for Scattergood 3 was turned down. Work at the site stopped immediately, but top managers at the DWP were not content to let the matter rest.[96] The Scattergood unit had been designed to meet all *existing* APCD regulations, they argued; clearly, Rule 67 had been written specifically to stop its construction.[97] Infuriated, the utility took the APCD to court. After lengthy and widely publicized proceedings, the APCD's action was upheld.

It was apparent that further appeals would only add delay and expense without guaranteeing victory. DWP managers decided to try to bring the unit into compliance. Rule 67 put a simple numerical limit on the pounds of NO_x that could be emitted from any facility. This required a very low *rate* of emissions from a unit the size of Scattergood 3. A consultant from KVB Associates, B. P. Breen (who had handled most of the NO_x research work at Southern California Edison) approached the DWP with an offer of assistance. Breen suggested that combustion modifications might solve the problem, and after two years of work he and the DWP's air quality engineer worked out a plan. Even with the suggested combusion changes, the boiler could only meet the limits by burning natural gas and by being run at 315 MW (instead of the 465 MW for which it was designed), but Scattergood 3 was finally in compliance. In February 1972—four years after the initial application—the APCD issued a permit for the construction of the unit, restricting it to natural gas and to the lower operating rate.[98]

Given the history of the Scattergood affair, however, APCD staff were concerned that granting the permit would be construed as "going soft" on NO_x emissions or on utilities. Working closely with Southern California Edison and the DWP, the APCD developed and adopted Rule 68, which restricted NO_x emissions on old sources as well. The adoption of this rule was timed deliberately to coincide with the issuance of the Scattergood permit.[99]

It was a mixed victory for the DWP. A substantial portion of the boiler and generator capacity remained unused. Interest charges had been heavy, construction costs had risen during the two-year delay, and "bad press" for the DWP had resulted. Furthermore, by the time Scattergood 3 was ready to go on line, the DWP (along with the other electrical utilities in California) no longer had the abundant supplies of natural gas it had counted on. For the first several years of its operation, the unit was used only sporadically, when gas was available.

Ironically, the most recent events in the Scattergood story reflect the latest change in environmental pressures: emphasis on energy conservation has superseded air quality concerns, even in Los Angeles. A DWP proposal to burn low-sulfur oil at Scattergood—instead of scarce natural gas—has had some appeal in this context. (So, apparently, has the argument that Scattergood would lower total NO_x emissions when run at full capacity.) During the most recent reorganization of the ACPD, air pollution control officers decided that Scattergood 3 should be considered an existing unit, thus falling under the more liberal NO_x standards of Rule 68. In these circumstances, the DWP does not even need a variance to burn low-sulfur oil, although the project must still meet state and federal new-source standards for nonattainment areas. During the public hearings on the change required by the California Environmental Quality Act, the only objections were raised by nearly El Segundo residents, who were concerned about the noise made by trucks unloading oil. A representative of Friends of the Earth even praised the plan and suggested that such projects should be considered as alternatives to nuclear development.[100]

To what extent did the DWP's internal organization contribute to the entanglement with the APCD over the construction of Scattergood 3? Given a different structure, how might the utility have acted differently, and to what effect? Perhaps the most obvious feature of the Scattergood story is the recurring evidence of the DWP's weak planning capabilities. This was a key element in the decision to add a unit at Scattergood in the first place. As its proposals fell through one by one, the DWP did not have a well-developed set of contingency plans. Goss recognized this problem and established System Planning, but in the meantime he saw no alternative but to expand Scattergood.

The DWP's estimates of future capacity needs, upon which it justified the Scattergood decision, were also questionable. The court suggested that the DWP's own advertising played a significant role in the increased demand. More telling, Scattergood was *not* ready on time — yet no catastrophe occurred, in spite of the fact that the DWP had freely predicted disasters during the negotiations with the APCD and at the trial.[101] The credit for bringing the unit into compliance with Rule 67 must be given to Breen, an outside consultant; the DWP had no centralized research and development group to undertake such a task.

The utility showed a persistent inability to understand and deal with the APCD. DWP managers simply did not anticipate the APCD's objections to a unit which, they emphasized, had been designed to meet all existing standards. A group or office within the DWP charged with handling regulatory matters would have been better able to appreciate the pressures on the board of supervisors and on the APCD staff. But except for Floyd Goss (an engineer by training, with many other responsibilities), there was no one to do such an analysis. It was beyond the scope of the Public Relations Office or the legislative representative, and the position of environmental coordinator had not yet been created. Several people familiar with the APCD commented that the control officer, who had a law enforcement background, may have been unsure of himself on technical matters. They contend that he postponed or avoided hard decisions, which may account for some of the long delays in the APCD's actions.[102] But a well-informed utility would have been aware of this fact and would have tried to respond accordingly.

The lack of public relations acumen hindered those who conducted the negotiations with the APCD. The principal negotiators from the DWP acknowledge that communications were poor.[103] APCD engineers complained that the DWP was not conscientious in preparing its application and in justifying its arguments, that the utility complied with procedures only in a *pro forma* manner and with a "holier than thou" attitude.[104] In spite of the fact that the DWP would not (or could not) substantiate its claims that the Scattergood unit would lower total NO_x emissions, for example, DWP managers saw no reason why their estimates should not be accepted at face value.[105] They apparently felt confident that the utility's need, as always, would prevail.

There was enough circumstantial evidence to convince the trial judge that the DWP was trying to present a *fait accompli*. The APCD's procedural rules included a provision that a thirty-day silence on a pending application could be assumed to be a denial, thus allowing the applicant to seek a variance from the independent Hearing Board. This was designed to prevent the sort of interminable delays the DWP later complained about. The DWP did not take this option. It sought to keep its application alive at least until May 1968 by asking the APCD to state formally that the application was still open. The judge later speculated that the utility had chosen not to move for a variance hearing at an early date because it had hoped that denial would be more difficult once construction was well under way.[106]

What would have happened at PG&E in such a situation? First, the adverse public-relations consequences would have been taken more seriously. Ironically, the management of PG&E feels much more exposed to political pressures than do the managers of publicly owned LADWP. At PG&E, too, specialists familiar with the regulatory agency and its key personnel would have been active in the entire process. With PG&E's strong control system and vigorous intergroup competition, nine months would never have passed (as happened between November 1968 and September 1969) with only one contact with the regulatory authority.[107] Nor would the lawyers at PG&E have been eager to litigate the matter.

The LADWP's attempts to construct a nuclear generating facility reflect not only these internal structural difficulties, but also the multiplicity of physical and social constraints that PG&E has faced. The California coast offers ocean water for cooling, but is geologically unstable. Fresh water for cooling at geologically acceptable inland sites, on the other hand, is costly and scarce. The DWP has tried, so far unsuccessfully, to find a way around these barriers.

Since Samuel Morris was chief engineer in the early 1950s, the DWP has talked of using nuclear power.[108] In the early 1960s a management committee within the utility, assisted by geological consultants, chose Corral Canyon in Malibu as the most likely site within a reasonable distance to be licensed.[109] It was north of the city, but not too far away, and in an area not yet heavily developed. Almost immediately, the project provoked fierce opposition from a large real-estate development corporation which feared that its extensive holdings in the area would be adversely affected. Preliminary research by the United States Geological Survey, on behalf of the Atomic Energy Commission, indicated that the site was satisfactory. But at public hearings on the project, the real-estate interests produced their own Cal Tech experts who argued convincingly that the Corral Canyon was seismologically unacceptable. The Atomic Energy Commission then asked the DWP to redesign the plant. But the commission, the Geological Survey, and the DWP had a hard time agreeing on the amount of earth slippage to allow for. After many meetings and some attempts to redesign the unit, there was still no clear prospect for a resolution. Floyd Goss then ordered the project cancelled — in part because the original design was becoming technically obsolete.[110]

All California utilities were having similar problems with nuclear siting. The Geological Survey suggested that the lower San Joaquin Valley, among other regions, might be seismologically more acceptable. Acting on this advice, the DWP began to explore a site in Tulare County, but local residents were vigorously opposed. The DWP had not anticipated this reaction, and had done little or nothing to forestall it. Part of the protest focused on concern that mist from the plant's cooling towers would damage crops and contribute to winter fog conditions. Furthermore, since the DWP was a public agency, it would pay no local taxes. Tulare County citizens were hard pressed to see what benefits they would derive from the project, in return for the use of their land and water. Some of the more vocal protesters drew parallels between this new DWP project and the "rape of Owens Valley" in the 1920s. The DWP management had little choice but to withdraw.[111]

The DWP's more recent plans for a plant in Kern County (also in San Joaquin) demonstrated increased sophistication and better management. But not all the gains are the result of the DWP's efforts. After hearing of the utility's plans, the Kern County planning director took an early initiative. He discussed the matter with local community and political leaders and was appointed to act as liaison with the Department of Water and Power. At his suggestion, the project was restructured to include about 45 per-

Figure 23. The Los Angeles Aqueduct and power line from Owens Valley. Courtesy of the Los Angeles Department of Water and Power.

cent private ownership, making the proposal more attractive from a local tax viewpoint. Before any public announcement was made, he organized a series of individual meetings between local leaders and DWP representatives, including members of the Public Affairs staff. These sessions not only helped gain local community acceptance, but also informed the DWP about local concerns and political complexities.[112]

In planning the Kern County plant, the general strategy was to spend a little extra money in order to lower the probability of protests, lawsuits, and delays. The DWP considered expensive options to ensure that the plant's cooling facilities would not exacerbate the occasional dense, low-lying fog. The former manager of the project explained that he thought the DWP should not contribute to this condition for even a few days a year, and felt it was worthwhile to spend a substantial amount of money to avoid this. The utility also worked on ways to use agricultural waste water for cooling and employed a biological consultant to help relocate rare animals (kit foxes and kangaroo rats, for example) inhabiting the area.[113]

This more sensitive and aggressive posture illustrates the new directions of top management, but it also reflects the somewhat anomalous position of the nuclear power projects group. The group has had less trouble with the civil service system since some of its positions were newly defined and since it has been allowed outside recruitment. Furthermore, the group's existence obviously has depended on the continuation of the nuclear program; it is thus in the members' interests to do everything possible to facilitate the project. The decentralized management structure at the DWP has allowed the nuclear office leeway to pursue independent, aggressive action toward that end. And since it has been able to add staff while other groups have been subject to hiring limits, the nuclear office has had less difficulty expanding as the situation has demanded.[114]

Despite these efforts, the Kern County project was eventually dropped. A March 1978 referendum in the county produced a two-to-one vote against the plant. Though the vote was nonbinding, the county supervisors said they would abide by it. Newspaper accounts attributed the result to antinuclear feeling and concern over the plant's water use, intensified by the recent drought.[115] The DWP's proposal to use agricultural waste water for cooling was not an absolute promise. With Owens Valley as a precedent and the support of the governor, a statewide lobbying group (headed by David Pesonen, who spearheaded opposition to

PG&E's Bodega and Mendocino plants) was able to overwhelm a DWP organization that had lost its capacity to fight such battles more than thirty years before. Ultimately, the opposition of the California Energy Commission helped put an end to the project.

The history of the DWP's involvement in jointly owned projects reflects the same combination of internal decentralization and external limits that is evident in its own construction decisions. The incentives to participate in large, joint projects were economic and environmental. Air pollution control regulations in the Los Angeles basin made it increasingly difficult to construct fossil-fuel units within the DWP's own service area. In addition, as a relatively small system, the DWP could hope to lower its costs without risking unreliable dependence on a few units, by participating as a minority owner in a number of large, efficient, jointly owned generation projects.

Such a strategy, however, ran the risk of abandoning substantial engineering control to another system, if the DWP was not itself the lead company. In other organizations with larger and more influential mechanical engineering groups, such an approach would have met strong resistance — especially in organizations where promotion opportunities depended on a group's size and where size, in turn, was related to work load. The DWP, in contrast, had an examination-based personnel system and was led by electrical engineers. This made it much easier to accept a generation expansion strategy based on distant joint projects. Given its internal incentive structure, the DWP was not well equipped to ensure that its staff made the assiduous, even extraordinary efforts required to monitor and influence a project run by another company.

An example is the Mohave project, a large coal-fired plant (consisting of two 770 MW units) built in the desert Southwest. This was the first such venture in which the DWP participated. Some of the utility's engineers opposed the venture because of the lack of autonomy it involved. Nevertheless, in 1968 a formal agreement gave the DWP 20 percent ownership in the project, the Nevada Power Company 14 percent, and a public power district in Arizona (the Salt River Project) 10 percent. Southern California Edison retained 56 percent and the lead role in engineering.[116] The plant was plagued by engineering difficulties and environmental controversies, but with Southern California Edison in the lead the DWP felt little reason or ability to become involved in the technical problems.[117] And since residents of the area had no direct access to the DWP through the electoral process, the utility could stand back and allow Edison to negotiate with local environmental agencies (whose rules the project did have to meet), without worrying about political consequences to itself.

In the even larger Navajo project (three 770 MW units), the lead company is the relatively small Salt River Project with a 22 percent share. The DWP has 21 percent, the Federal Bureau of Reclamation has 24 percent and three private utilities own the remaining 33 percent. With an improved joint management structure, in part a response to earlier problems, the project has proceeded more smoothly than Mohave. Even though it is not the lead company, DWP engineers have been able to contribute to critical design decisions through a series of intercompany committees that deal with important phases of the project.

Some of this involvement has reflected traditional DWP decentralization. For example, middle- and lower-level staff members made environmentally sensitive decisions affecting the project. The head of the DWP's System Planning Division, who was also the utility's representative to the Colorado Technical Committee, persuaded the other participants in the Navajo project to install a closed-cycle cooling system that would reduce salinity downstream—despite the fact that the project's water-use permit would have allowed some of the cooling water to be returned to the river.[118]

On the other hand, when the DWP's top management became involved in project decision making, it did not always have environmental sensitivity as a top priority. DWP managers argued that they could not commit the Navajo project to strict environmental controls, despite the considerable pressure of public opinion in Los Angeles. A major disagreement with the city council and with council member Tom Bradley ensued over contracts for the project. The *Los Angeles Times* editorialized that it was incumbent upon the city to use whatever influence it could to improve the quality of the environment.[119] But general manager Robert Phillips contended that the DWP was only one minor participant, hardly in a position to dictate terms to the state of Arizona or to the federal government.[120] The DWP has been able to proceed under the old contracts. Current political and regulatory constraints will make future participation in joint projects more difficult. But with no hydro or nuclear alternatives, it is not clear what the DWP will be able to do to meet future demand. The organization will surely need whatever added toughness and effectiveness recent changes have produced—and then some.

The history of the Los Angeles Department of Water and Power shows once again that public ownership does not guarantee environmental sensitivity. After a period of early turmoil the DWP was assiduously depoliticized, but the resulting internal incentives and practices fostered decentralization and a lack of outside-oriented groups. When environmental pressures increased, the organization's responses were inconsistent and not always well organized. Results depended heavily on the particular groups responsible. Given the DWP's environmental and economic circumstances, participation in large joint projects and importation of long-distance power often seemed appropriate. The political and regulatory context and the professional orientation of the utility's management also fit well with this approach. Yet as regulatory barriers to new generating capacity multiplied, it became more and more difficult for the utility (and all electric utilities) to pursue any of its options successfully.

Since the organization was so insulated from the line authority of the mayor and city council, many of the changes in its behavior resulted from the pressure of regulatory standards — of the sort that TVA, for example, has not had to face. Within the DWP's strict civil service system, the ability to reward and punish has been so limited that even managers who have wanted to respond to outside forces have not been able to do this effectively. But the world has been changing. A new mayor, city council, board of commissioners, and general manager have all put greater pressure on the DWP than was the case two decades ago. DWP managers have made attempts to change, although the utility's rigidity has made this difficult. Floyd Goss sought to make long-range planning more coherent and to coordinate diverse activities by creating the System Development Division. But this was not done soon enough to save him from the Scattergood 3 imbroglio. Nor did this unit develop as much as he hoped, because of internal implementation difficulties. James Mulloy later established within the Power System the position of environmental coordinator, whose office tries to keep abreast of environmental developments. He also established the Governmental Affairs Office and instituted the use of briefing documents to coordinate and manage the preparation of environmental impact reports. But the work of responding to environmental regulations is still widely dispersed throughout the ranks of the Power System.

If changes are slow, they are nevertheless visible. Environmental and public-relations personnel are now involved more integrally and at much earlier stages in the planning process. The most important impetus for change seems to have come from the general manager's office. Robert Phillips and, to an even greater extent, Louis Winnard have become actively involved in the affairs of the Power System. Both have attempted to train and develop future managers within the confines of the civil service system. Both have tightened and centralized financial reporting procedures.

Winnard recognizes the obstacles posed by an established civil service bureaucracy. He has relied on relative newcomers to the DWP and on changes outside the Power System to achieve increased control and to introduce new people and perspectives. His emphasis on financial and public accountability seems to be an attempt to overcome other weaknesses of the internal control system. These changes will have to proceed rapidly and deeply to enable the DWP to cope with a steadily less congenial external situation.

9

Boston Edison

Boston Edison is the smallest utility in our study in terms of service area, population served, and generating capacity. Confined to an aging yet diverse metropolitan area, it deals with everything from large concentrations of liberal academics to stable, working-class ethnic communities. Its customers are neither as affluent nor as environmentally conscious as those in PG&E's territory, nor as concerned with economic development as those in Tennessee and Alabama.

Edison, like our other companies, confronted the rising tide of environmental concern of the late 1960s and early 1970s. The impact of that concern on the company was conditioned by the lack of technical sophistication in the state government. The new pressures, however, were strong enough to force changes in Edison's management and organization, which were necessary in order for the utility to prosper in a steadily less accommodating world. Stronger control systems, new managers, an increase in diagonal mobility, and a new pattern of reporting have all developed in the last few years. Ironically, these same internal changes — which increased environmental responsiveness — have also led Edison to respond to more recent pressures for cost control. Thus, the company has opposed some environmental expenditures that it believes would not provide sufficient benefits to justify their costs. Edison's history illustrates that a responsive organization will not necessarily advance a particular objective once the consequences for doing so are no longer advantageous.

Background and Context

Founded in 1895, Boston Edison was based on one of the earliest central-station generating systems developed by Thomas Edison after his successful experiments at Pearl Street in New York. The five other companies in our study all began as hydroelectric facilities. Edison from the beginning relied on relatively small fossil-fuel generating units located in the heart of its urban service area.[1] Figure 24 shows the scope of this service area.

New England did not offer the same hydroelectric potential as the Sierra Nevadas, Niagara Falls, or the Tennessee Valley. The water power that did exist had been developed intensively for manufacturing purposes — principally for textile mills — since the 1830s. Many sites in eastern New England that might have been attractive for hydroelectric development had long since become the nuclei of major urban centers. The construction of new hydroelectric dams would often have meant flooding the downtown area of an old mill town. At the turn of the century the remaining sites were far from Boston, either in Maine (where the state legislature had prohibited power exports) or along the Connecticut River in Vermont and New Hampshire.[2]

Edison consolidated its service area in metropolitan Boston during the early years of the twentieth century. It took no further steps toward regional integration and expansion, due partly to the fact that Massachusetts legislation made the merger of power companies difficult. Not being a hydroelectric system, the company did not have large blocks of surplus power to sell or the need to recover the high fixed costs of dams or transmission lines. Edison thus had less incentive to expand its service area than, for example, PG&E or Alabama Power.

The company's early history was shaped by its leadership. Charles Edgar, whom Thomas Edison dispatched as supervisor of the first generating station in 1895, served as general manager from 1900 to 1932. Unlike Martin of Alabama Power or Hockenbeamer and Black of PG&E, Edgar's interests were technical rather than entrepreneurial. During his long tenure Boston Edison established a notable record of engineering innovation with regard to boiler temperatures and pressures, and underground construction of transmission lines. Edgar's particular engineering perspective (he had grown up with fossil-fuel systems) may also have contributed to the company's failure to pursue hydroelectric sources. Even in political battles over public versus private power development of the Connecticut River, Boston Edison played a minor role. Several smaller companies in western Massachusetts were the focus of the controversy.[3]

Edison's slow growth reflects the slower-than-average growth in the demand for electricity in its service area. Boston has high labor costs, high local taxes, few natural resources, and a geo-

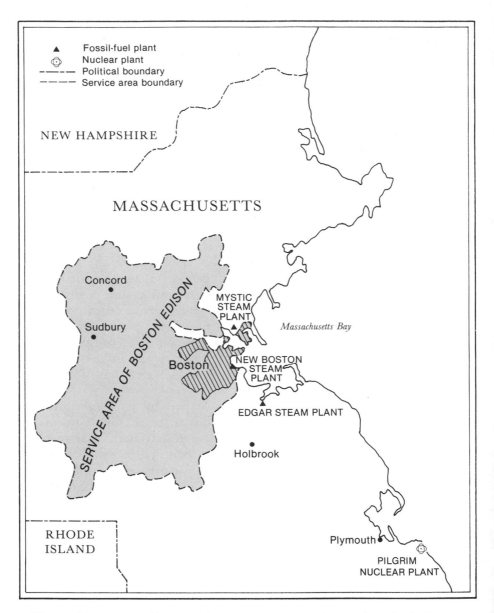

Figure 24. Boston Edison: service area and generating stations (including bulk purchasers). The shaded area represents the city of Boston. Based on information supplied by Boston Edison.

graphic location somewhat remote from the country's growing markets. This makes the area less attractive to heavy industries, which are the greatest users of electricity. The resulting slow growth in demand is self-perpetuating, since it leads to relatively greater use of older and smaller units. The high operating costs of these units (combined with high property taxes and high fuel costs) lead to utility rates that are among the highest in the country. These rates discourage large industrial power users from locating in the Boston area — which in turn means more slow growth, older plants, and higher costs.[4] Not surprisingly, the region's economic growth in the post-World War II years has focused in areas such as optics and electronics, which use the scientific skills provided by the region's academic centers. The products of these industries have a high value/weight ratio that offsets transport cost disadvantages. But the industries demand relatively little electricity.

Boston Edison for a long time was not a company to attract the best and most aggressive young engineers or managers. New generating projects occurred infrequently. The company did not maintain a large in-house design and construction unit, relying on outside architect-engineers for such projects. Why, then, should ambitious young engineers work for Edison, especially when they could easily find work in the new high-technology businesses that grew up in the postwar years? The company's uncomplicated financial affairs did not demand a large staff or offer promising career opportunities. Much of Edison's daily activities were routine and could be handled by plant operators, transmission and distribution repair personnel, clerks, and so on. This situation in turn led to a shortage of internal candidates for top-management positions. From Edgar's retirement in the early 1930s until Charles Avila's ascension to the presidency in 1960, the company was run by a succession of outsiders.[5] This pattern had a significant impact on company performance.

The political and cultural environment of the Boston area has been important in shaping the company's growth and development. Like any other long-standing Boston institution, the company has reflected the rivalry between old Protestant Yankees and immigrant (mainly Irish) Catholics — a rivalry that has been a central feature of Boston life for at least a century. These larger social tensions were reflected in the patterns of promotion and control within the company. The structure of local politics has also been important. Since World War II, Massachusetts has had a large state legislature — over four hundred members, each of whom serves a very small constituency. Working part time at low pay, state legislators typically have been minor local political figures whose futures depended on being able to get out the vote on primary day. In such circumstances, patronage is essential to survival, especially in traditionally one-party areas. This pattern prevailed in urban, ethnic Democratic areas in the eastern part of the state and among rural Republican Yankees in the west.

As a result, the various committees of the state legislature have maintained extraordinarily detailed budgetary supervision over the state administrative apparatus. Individual positions have been specified in separate budget lines. It is not unknown for specific people to be given lifetime job tenure by special legislative acts. Nor has it been unusual for committee heads to insist on favors in hiring as the price for cooperation in securing an agency's appropriations. Furthermore, state legislators' ends are best served by creating more low-skill, low-pay slots instead of fewer higher-paying positions with more demanding technical qualifications.[6]

These practices influence the state's ability to regulate utility rates and environmental performance. Prior to a recent reorganization, the Massachusetts Department of Public Utilities, for example, had 150 employees but only two professionals to deal with electric utility matters. The professional positions are so low-paying that one slot was recently vacant for over two years. The more senior position was filled by an accountant of long service whom the commissioners considered invaluable and whose salary was between sixteen thousand and eighteen thousand dollars per year. When rate cases arise, the Department of Public Utilities must call on lawyers from the attorney general's office to prepare an answer to the applicants, and perhaps an opinion as well. Until 1977 only one of the seven commissioners in the DPU worked full time. Most were obvious political appointees with little expertise and few incentives to work hard or to take controversial positions. The personal secretaries of at least two governors (not to mention various town solicitors, state representatives, and a Democratic national committee member) have been appointed to the DPU in recent years. A number of these faithful party servants remained in the part-time posts only until full-time patronage slots on the superior court or as administrative law judges became available.[7]

Under two recent governors, appointments to the Department of Public Utilities have evidently improved. One recent board chairman—an ambitious and effective young man, with more imagination than many of his predecessors—helped resolve a transmission-line dispute in which Edison was involved. Under the governorship of Michael Dukakis, an effort was made to attract more capable commission members by raising commission salaries and making the positions into full-time jobs. For most of its lifetime, however, Edison's rates have been regulated by a commission that was considerably influenced by the patronage emphasis of Massachusetts state government.

Such an agency is not likely to be very effective in ensuring that the savings resulting from improved technology or lower fuel prices are passed on to consumers in the form of lower rates. After a much-publicized rate reduction in 1929 (initiated by an angry group of Edison customers and Boston mayor Michael Curley), the DPU took no action for thirty years. Two rate increases were granted Boston Edison in the 1950s with little controversy, followed by two reductions (of 2.5-3 percent) in the 1960s without public hearings. Such lax regulation gave the utility the freedom to engage in inefficient practices without facing penalties. Contributing to this tendency was the fact that no public power system, like TVA, or the Central Valley Project in California, challenged Edison for its customers.[8] Until very recently there was no movement toward municipalization, as there has been in California. Since 1926 Massachusetts law has placed significant obstacles in the path of any towns seeking to take over local electricity distribution.[9] In sum, Boston Edison has until recently faced few external consequences for its high costs.

Environmental regulatory agencies in the state were not much more vigorous. In the late 1960s, when air pollution began to be taken seriously, the Department of Public Health operated only one monitoring station in the metropolitan Boston area. Qualitatively and quantitatively, the staff and inspection resources available to the DPH were extremely limited. Throughout the 1960s Edison was frequently cited for air pollution violations on the basis of visual inspection of its smoke plumes. Instead of undertaking formal enforcement actions, however, the DPH followed a "consultative" approach. This placed fewer demands on its limited resources and technical capacity, but it did not put much pressure on the company. Under state law the attorney general had to bring successful court action before any penalties could be assessed. Edison faced only one enforcement action in the period we studied (directed at the Edgar plant in 1968), an action that was dropped when the company agreed to certain cleanup measures.[10] Given the political system in which they functioned, environmental regulators in Massachusetts did not face personal costs by failing to act vigorously. This is in strong contrast to Los Angeles, where, perhaps because air quality problems were much more serious, people lost their jobs or lost elections as a result of smog-control issues.

The state's most recent regulatory initiatives have encountered similar difficulties. The Energy Facilities Siting Council, created in the early 1970s, is supposed to review and approve capacity expansion forecasts and generating plant sites for all gas and electric utilities. It operated for the first year of its life with a professional staff of two: a young lawyer and a nontechnically trained administrator with a degree in public administration. (It has since added additional staff members.) The Energy Commission in California, with comparable kinds of responsibilities, has a professional staff of about 250.

The weakness of the regulatory system reflects the fact that there is less environmental concern in Boston than in California. The reasons for this difference are physical and socioeconomic. Air pollution is less severe and less apparent in Boston than in parts of California; there is little heavy industry, and prevailing westerlies tend to push air pollution out to sea. The city is not bounded by high inland mountain barriers, as in Los Angeles or the San Francisco Bay area, which can trap polluted air. Combined with less sunshine, the meteorology means that California-type photochemical smog is much less prevalent. Also, the gentler topography of the Boston area offers no visual reference point comparable to the San Gabriel Mountains in Los Angeles or the East Berkeley Hills in San Francisco by which poor visibility can be instantly detected.

The citizens of eastern Massachusetts do not have the environmental enthusiasm of residents in California. Fewer wilderness areas remain to serve as a rallying point for conservationist efforts, or to attract environmentalists to live in the region. In Boston, a large proportion of families arrived from southern and eastern Europe one or two generations ago to work in the factories. Their lower-middle and working-class descendants are less willing to pay for environmental protection than are the more affluent citizens of northern California.

These cultural and political forces are in constant evolution, which has had its effect on the state's politics and on its regulatory bodies. By the mid-1960s the growth of technology-oriented industries and of the area's universities had begun to produce a reformist political constituency. The long-standing cultural and ethnic basis of party affiliation also began to break down under pressure of suburbanization, rising education levels, and so on. The Democrats elected the patrician Yankee Endicott Peabody as governor in 1962, while the Republicans elected the Italian Catholic John Volpe (whose two terms straddled Peabody's). A major impetus for reform in the state government came from Volpe's Yankee Republican successor, Francis Sargent. Sargent's commitment to environmental protection became evident in his 1970 gubernatorial campaign against Boston mayor Kevin White, and his victory was in part a reflection of the growth in public environmental concern.

The same constituency that supported stronger air pollution control regulations has also challenged Boston Edison's nuclear program. The Union of Concerned Scientists, a group including people from Harvard and the Massachusetts Institute of Technology, and one of the most technically sophisticated antinuclear groups in the country, has raised repeated objections before the Nuclear Regulatory Commission concerning Edison's Pilgrim power plant in historic Plymouth, about fifty miles from downtown Boston.

Edison is probably correct in maintaining that a large proportion of its customers do not share the views of this opposition group. Particularly when Pilgrim first went into service, many were sympathetic to Edison's arguments that nuclear power meant less use of high-cost oil, and hence lower rates. Though they did not obtain power from the Pilgrim plant, residents of Plymouth also generally supported the plant because of the property-tax benefit.

Although the Union of Concerned Scientists lacked public support for their initial challenges to Edison, it and other groups have been able to involve the company in prolonged regulatory hearings on technical issues. And quite apart from the challenges of environmental organizations, the growing complexity of the regulatory process meant that, by late 1979, Edison still had not obtained a construction permit for a second unit at Pilgrim — a unit it had once planned to bring on line in 1979. In the meantime, public skepticism about nuclear power had grown, if only because of the growing costs of building nuclear plants. While the Nuclear Regulatory Commission was studying Edison's financial capability to build the unit, the state Department of Public Utilities began questioning the need for the plant and examining Edison's plans for financing. Public concern with air pollution became less pronounced during this period of scrutiny. The energy crisis, inflation, and high regional unemployment focused public attention once again on high utility rates.

High electric rates are only one of many factors that contribute to the region's economic problems, and probably not the decisive factor in most cases. The utilities, however, have emphasized it when making proposals to the legislature. For example, their arguments convinced the legislature in 1975 to relax certain pollution regulations, including the sulfur standards that Governor Sargent had insisted upon. A bill was submitted by a legislator who was worried about the plastics industry in his district, but it is well known in the legislature that it was written by the chief lobbyist for the state's utility association — and ushered by him to an easy voice-vote victory.[11]

In summary, the external context in which the Boston Edison Company has operated has not been as coercive as those in other cases in this study. This has influenced both the style and the direction of the company's development. Nevertheless, Edison has faced environmental pressures in the last decade that are similar in kind, if not in degree, to those confronting the other companies we have studied. The utility has also encountered broader pressures brought on by changing economic, cultural, and political patterns. It has responded to these changes in ways that seem likely to influence its behavior, and the evolution of its structure, for some time to come.

Internal Organization

Boston Edison's organizational structure has undergone a striking transformation in recent years — a change that has been affected by the changing cultural and political climate of the Boston area. In the 1950s and early 1960s, Edison's internal structure reflected the relaxed regulatory climate, the unexciting nature of the business, the leadership of outsiders with little technical knowledge, and the ethnic rivalries of the area as a whole. The result was a fragmented and decentralized organization containing diverse groups that tended to go their own separate ways. In the last fifteen years, as the larger world has become less accommodating, new leaders have developed a structure that has increased top management's control and lessened the isolation and mutual suspicion of various internal groups. The result has been improved efficiency and greater strategic flexibility. See Figure 25 for a view of Edison's organizational structure during the mid-1970s.

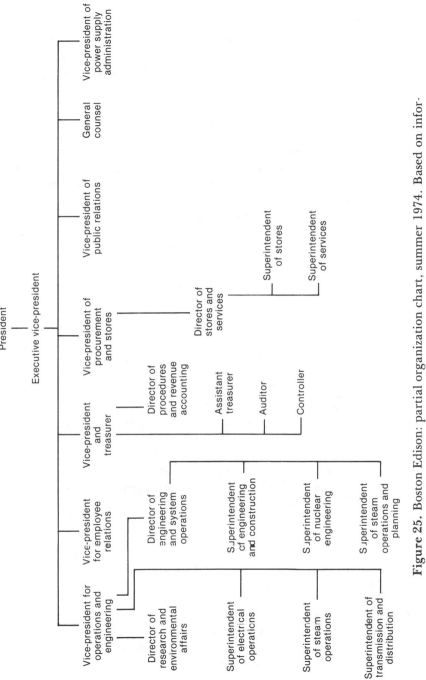

Figure 25. Boston Edison: partial organization chart, summer 1974. Based on information supplied by Boston Edison.

Top management's limited control in the early period stemmed from a number of structural characteristics. There were few incentives that managers could offer to Division chiefs. Throughout most of the 1960s, the senior technical manager in each group held the rank of vice-president and reported directly to the president. The only promotion the president could offer a group leader was the presidency itself. This opportunity was available infrequently, and presidents tended to be recruited from the outside, anyway. Why, then, would the vice-president for operations, for example, carry out the dictates of his superior enthusiastically if these conflicted with his own unit's short-run interests? Edison's structure was similar to TVA's. In contrast was the situation at PG&E, where several senior or group vice-presidents each supervised several areas of company activity and participated in overall strategy development. At Boston Edison, chief executives recruited from outside also had no fund of shared experience or mutual loyalty to draw upon as a means of controlling the organization's activities.

Top management's control over subordinates was further limited by a lack of technical expertise. From 1932 to 1960, the company was led by two lawyers and an accountant.[12] Unlike the lawyers at Southern, these people had little technical background; they were unable to make independent assessments of the decisions and operations of the various technical units. They did not have the same capacity to identify errors or evaluate performance, which is essential for imposing discipline. Lack of expertise and concern with engineering matters also made it harder for top management to play a role in promotion decisions at lower levels in the organization, further weakening the top's control.

The old organization of the company gave each functional group a relative monopoly in its particular area of expertise. In TVA, the Division of Environmental Health and the Office of Power both claimed authority over certain pollution matters. At PG&E, the lawyers and Public Affairs disputed Engineering's monopoly of system-planning decisions. In contrast, there was little competition for jurisdiction at Edison. Top management had fewer alternatives available and was less able to control any one part of the company. One employee of long service explained, "The chief of operations told the president, in effect, 'You just let me run the plant and leave me alone.' "

Weak control by top management does not mean that the control system as a whole was weak. The head of each Division within the company apparently had substantial authority and could dispose of senior-level positions. The Engineering Department included a superintendent, two deputy superintendents, a number of lower-level managers, and a cadre of senior technical specialists. Decentralized control over personnel decisions to leaders of each functional area produced strong group loyalties and a sense of group identification.

The resulting control system could be arbitrary. Many complained that seniority, friendship, religion, or even membership in a particular club could influence promotion decisions. For a time members of the Masons (predominantly a non-Catholic group) played an important role in the company. Over time, other ethnic and religious groups came to play a major role — reflecting the changes in Boston's population and society. Such patterns had an obvious effect on incentives. One observer commented, "When I first came to work here, you would see guys promoted who you knew hadn't done a useful day's work in ten years, and had gotten it on friendship."[13]

Within this overall structure, the engineering group was small and weak — a fact that reflected the company's slow physical growth. Most detailed design work was done by outside architectural/engineering consulting firms. Even some engineering functions (like transmission planning and design) were not in Engineering at all, but were under the Transmission and Distribution department. Plant operators, on the other hand, were well organized. Since all the company's plants were in the Boston area, they were able to form a cohesive group and to influence the main office's decisions in a way that the more geographically dispersed operators at Hydro or TVA could not. Most of the operators were not trained engineers; they were people who had risen from the ranks who were used to relying more on experience than analysis. In the 1950s some strong personalities emerged as heads of operations — notably Henry Kurth and Henry Wellington (known to some as "Henry VIII" and "Duke" Wellington, respectively). Their experience and influence helped produce conservative, reliability-oriented power plant design.

The operators had an impact on plant design in part because consulting architectural/engineering firms tend to "give the client what he wants." Unlike an internal engineering group such as Southern Company Services, an outsider will seldom take a strong stand on a design issue. Design choices are often a judgmental matter, which analysis can only imperfectly resolve. A consulting engineer who does what the client wants is given credit if it turns out right. If it comes out wrong, the client shares the blame. Consultants who go against the client's views bear the full burden of any failure and the risk of resentment if they succeed. Thus, when Edison's operators pushed for investment designed to enhance reliability and ease of operation, there was no one willing and able to oppose them.

Edison's plant operators, for all their influence, did not have any overarching professional or group "mission" that provided strategic coherence for corporate policy. This contrasts with the commitment to low costs of the Office of Power at TVA and the Engineering Branch's push for energy independence at Hydro. Under the old organizational structure, as with the LADWP during the same period, decisions were not necessarily either consistent or effectively implemented. This did not produce adverse results in part because the outside world was sufficiently compliant to allow such behavior.

When Charles Avila became president in 1960, Edison for the first time since 1932 had a chief executive with the technical expertise to intervene in the decision making on new plant design. The organization was in the process of constructing Mystic station units 4, 5, and 6 at the time Avila took over the job. Concerned over the costs, he had some backup equipment removed from the design (the unfilled concrete pads are still visible in the station). He became even more involved in the next facility, the New-Boston plant, changing both the architect/engineer and the construction firm that had long done Edison's work. Avila wanted better service from suppliers and better cost control. Boston Edison also exercised much tighter control over design changes and equipment purchases on the new units. The result was a station that, in dollars per kilowatt, cost only a little more than *half* its predecessors.[14]

Avila's strong action symbolized the beginning of Edison's evolution. Even without making changes in Edison's structure and control and incentive system, Avila was able to make a concrete change in Edison's policies. During the next fifteen years, he and his successor, Tom Galligan, restructured the organization so as to increase top management's ability to develop and implement effective policies. Group solidarity and mutual hostility declined — a change that is partly a generational matter. Many of the current leaders in the company disliked the old ways they encountered as younger people and worked to change them when they succeeded to senior positions. In this sense, Edison has mirrored the social and political evolution of the Boston area.

Several management actions contributed to these developments. Top management began to take a direct interest in personnel matters and greatly increased the depth of its control. In the mid-1970s, company president Thomas Galligan reviewed all personnel decisions down to the level of Division head — that is, appointments to the top one hundred positions in the company. Frank Staszesky, then executive vice-president, looked even further down. Responsibility for making appointments below the level of Division head has since been delegated to the company's ten vice-presidents; Galligan and Staszesky, however, now chairman and president respectively, continue to review appointments down to the level of Division head.[15] There has also been a significant amount of diagonal mobility among promising younger managers. One executive went from head of Generating Plant Design to manager of Nuclear Operations; later he took over the Transmission and Distribution Department. Another went from System Planning and System Operations to Public Relations, then to vice-president for environment, research, and planning. These changes reflect a fluidity in organizational structure. Various functions and groups have been shifted among executives in order to use their skills most effectively, and to coordinate interdependent activities.

Such changes have had a number of mutually reinforcing results. The new managers, chosen on the basis of merit, have a certain loyalty to the top management who advanced them. Since they are seldom long-standing members of the groups they now manage, it is easier for them to be merit-oriented in their own use of the personnel system (especially since this is what top management wants). The example of their own advancement provides performance incentives to others down in the ranks. Chosen for their ability and performance, their success says that by working hard it is possible to achieve similar gains.

Edison today resembles PG&E, with its strong and deep control system. Doing a good job in a way that attracts top management's attention can bring rapid advancement. For example, Steve Sweeney, now a senior vice-president in engineering, gained much credit in the eyes of top management when as assistant head of Electric Operations he adroitly handled public questions during the great Northeast blackout of 1965. Similarly, when the town of Brookline, Massachusetts, was considering taking over some of Edison's system, Bruce Damrell prepared a staff report that was well received. Work like this helped him later when the time came to select a new superintendent of engineering.[16] Even Charles Avila's rapid rise seems to have been facilitated by his effective management of a key underground transmission project, when he was a young supervisor.

This characteristic of the personnel system nevertheless seems arbitrary to those subject to it. When asked how one gets ahead, middle-level people (as at PG&E) will often say it is a result of "luck" or "being in the right place at the right time," as well as "doing a good job." Middle managers recognize that it is of career value to their subordinates to attend meetings where they can gain exposure to top management.

Other structural changes have enhanced the control of top management. Compared to the old days, there are many more general management positions above the departmental level. The structure at this level is quite flexible. Group leaders are likely to perceive the possibility of further advancement, and thus aspire to it. Not only are there jobs to move into—beyond running engineering or operations—but it is clear that new positions can and will be created to suit especially talented individuals.

The number of senior positions within specialist organizations has been simultaneously decreased. The two slots for assistant superintendents of engineering, for example, have been abolished. Since this reduces the rewards available for group leaders to dispense, a person's career advancement is more dependent on top management's assessment and the possibilities of diagonal mobility. Control from the top is thereby enhanced.

Recent top managers at Edison have been able to maintain better control over technical matters, even when they lacked a technical background. Tom Dignan, a lawyer who came to the presidency from the outside in the late 1950s, began deliberately to share overall supervisory responsibility with rising young engineer Charles Avila.[17] Dignan apparently chose Avila as his successor, and picked the latter's second-in-command. As president, Avila continued his scrutiny over technical matters; nontechnical managerial responsibilities he delegated to the "number two" whom Dignan had chosen, Tom Galligan. Galligan himself was being groomed for the presidency in a much more conscious way than managers had ever been. When he assumed that office, he carried the trend toward collegial management even further than his predecessors. Galligan and executive vice-president Frank Staszesky have operated together as the "president's office," such that each speaks with full authority.[18] They continue to share responsibility, now that Galligan has become chairman of the board and Staszesky has moved up to president.

Combining expertise among top managers is not a novel practice in utilities. PG&E, for example, has a dual leadership of lawyers and engineers. Genuine sharing of responsibility is not easy to achieve, however. The individuals involved must identify primarily with the company, rather than with their particular spheres of authority. The apparent differences in corporate strategy between the lawyers and engineers at PG&E have at times put a strain on the system, of a sort that does not seem to have developed at Edison.

To help reinforce the company-wide perspective, Galligan gathers all senior executives to weekly meetings at which major policy matters are discussed. It is understood that such meetings serve an advisory function; the group is not a committee and no votes are taken.[19] The practice helps to broaden the perspectives of key managers, to improve communication, and to develop common perspectives. In this respect, the top management at Boston Edison seems better integrated than TVA's, for example.

Galligan and Staszesky have not only exerted extensive control over personnel choices, but have exercised close supervision over budgeting as well. Financial controls have been very strict at times. During an extremely cash-tight situation in the early 1970s, they imposed strong restrictions on travel and hiring. Substantial responsibility for spending has since been returned to the vice-presidents, who must operate within a specified budget that is reviewed annually by top management.[20]

At the time of our interviews, some middle managers were irked by existing restraints, which made it hard for them to attract or promote good people. It could take time to get approval for a new slot, and meanwhile the person they wanted to hire may have gone elsewhere. Energy and environmental problems have made utilities more interesting places to work than was the case in the past, but until recently Edison had difficulty attracting bright young people. One executive explained, "Years ago it was even harder to get good people to go into utilities. You could get a lot of C-pluses, but not many B-pluses."[21]

The new structure at Boston Edison has changed the relative influence of various groups in the strategic bargaining process. Most notably, the changing status of the operators is reflected in new reporting procedures. Until Charles Avila's presidency, the operators reported directly to the president. Avila placed engineering and operations under one vice-president. Subsequently, another level of management was added between operators and the company president.[22] The Public Relations group, in contrast, has been given more access to policy-making levels. Jim Lydon, once a vice-president for public relations, is now senior vice-president for corporate communications. This makes him a major figure in the company and gives his area wide-ranging representation in decision making.[23] In addition, a new Public Affairs Department has been established out of, but distinct from, Public Relations — a recognition of the political and promotional aspects of public relations.

The rise of public relations reflects Galligan's own beliefs and experience. He came in mid-career from the company's auditors to head the Stores and Services unit. He then served as vice-president for public relations before becoming president.[24] This example of a chief executive expanding the role of his former area of responsibility is similar to that of Robert Gerdes' expansion of the legal department at PG&E. The phenomenon is understandable. Members of such a group are likely to share the top manager's strategies and priorities, which leads him to believe he can rely on them. It also makes sense from the company's perspective that those qualities that make a manager desirable should lead to added work and influence for similar individuals. Compatibility and Galligan's personal respect for its members' talent has increased the influence of the public-relations group. So has the fact that, unlike PG&E, there was no one else to play the outside-oriented role. There was no strong structure of regional managers. Neither the lawyers nor those in Environmental Affairs had the resources to compete with Public Relations. The work of this group is easiest for Galligan to supervise, given his background, and requires the least amount of control.

The lawyers at Edison hold a position that is somewhere between that of their colleagues at the Southern Company and those at PG&E. As in Southern, some of the company's legal work is referred to outside firms, especially when litigation is involved. Edison, however, also has an in-house legal staff of five. Although much smaller than PG&E's, the staff has a similar degree of flexibility within individual areas of competence. A lawyer involved in a crisis situation will talk to top management almost daily, when critical immediate choices must be made. Yet given the small size of the group and the lack of "alumni" in top management, the lawyers at Edison assume a much lower profile in the policy-making process than those at PG&E. "I don't consider it my role to make policy decisions for others in the company," said one of them. "Rather, I provide advice on the legal aspects of proposed actions or inactions in an attempt to help company management reach legally sound decisions."[25] In part, this may be a reaction to the hostile attitude toward lawyers that developed during an early transmission-line controversy.

The environmental affairs group also remains small. When established in the early 1970s, it included two engineers, a lawyer (who has specialized as an environmental spokesperson for the company), and a former power plant operator who had responsibility for managing oil-spill problems. The lawyer, Frank Lee, now heads the unit.

The group's main role has been as a focus for particular staff functions, such as oil-spill reporting and regulatory relations. It is not a large operational unit like Health and Safety at TVA, nor has it developed into an aggressive policy advocate in corporate decision making. Even in areas where it does play a role, such as the preparation of environmental impact statements, its tasks are limited. Preparing such statements for new nuclear generating capacity is largely the responsibility of a unit in nuclear engineering, leaving the Environmental Department with a coordination and editorial role. Not surprisingly, there have been communication problems with the environmental people in nuclear engineering in the course of preparing documents for the proposed Pilgrim 2 unit.[26]

The division of environmental functions reflects the dual nature of the engineering organization in Edison. There are separate groups for nuclear and fossil-fuel plant engineering. When Edison began to build Pilgrim 1, its first nuclear unit, it wanted to bring in experienced nuclear engineers and allow them to address their assignment without being subject to existing procedural constraints. The concern was that existing organizational procedures and patterns might not be compatible with implementation of the complicated new nuclear technology — technology that was governed by a major body of federal design requirements. The separation of nuclear and nonnuclear engineering continued when the nuclear project group became a regular Department.[27]

There were strong arguments for setting up a new nuclear group rather than fitting new people into the existing engineering organization. Integrating a stream of new people into the existing structure would have been difficult. There were large differences in background, style, and perspective between the old and new personnel. The nuclear people tended to be younger, to have more years of formal professional training, and to be self-consiously committed to the "scientific" approach. Combining nuclear engineering with fossil-fuel plant design could have raised innumerable problems about who was competent to supervise whom, and so on.

The difficulty of such an approach was that the nuclear engineering organization — or "nuclear company," as some called it at the time — was not well integrated into the rest of the corporate structure. Nuclear engineering was an obvious and sometimes resented exception to the strict hiring freeze of the early 1970s. For a number of years, the nuclear group even had its own location across the street from headquarters. To complicate matters further, although the Pilgrim plant was designed by a distinct engineering group, it was initially operated as a regular generating plant within the existing Operations Department. The nuclear operations group thus had communication problems with both Nuclear Engineering and Fossil Operations.

In response to these problems, the nuclear group was reorganized in August 1975. Both Engineering and Operations now report to the former head of Nuclear Engineering, who became a vice-president. This change was made deliberately to improve communication and to strengthen operating practices at the Pilgrim plant.[28] It has apparently contributed to a closer mesh between the nuclear group and the rest of the company. Nuclear Engineering was moved into headquarters, and J. Edward Howard, the head of the group, has assumed a greater role in company management.

Boston Edison has undergone a transformation under recent presidents, shifting from a collection of loosely controlled baronies to a more centrally directed organization. Central development of promising young managers, structural changes, and budgeting controls have all been used to increase top management's influence. How and why did this structural evolution take place?

When an organization is functionally adapted to a noncoercive environment, as was Edison, managers throughout the structure have little reason to exert or demand high levels of effort. In the words of March and Simon, "organizational slack" develops. People use resources to acquire psychological and material gains. The resulting patterns of behavior become deeply entrenched and difficult to change — even when they become less functional — in part because they depend on so many unexpressed (even unrealized) assumptions and biases. Someone has to exert significant effort to overcome the resulting inertia and hostility if change is to occur.

In Edison, a change in top management was critical to its structural evolution. Previous managers perhaps saw that the new situation was making new demands on the company. They were able to choose successors who could do what they themselves could not. Charles Avila and Tom Galligan were directly chosen by Tom Dignan, the president before Avila and the man who really began the transformation of the company's management. Avila recalls that Dignan once called them in and said, "Charles, I want you for first man, and Tom, I want you for second man."[29] Avila was Dignan's personal protégé. Galligan, an accountant by training who had been working for Edison's auditor, was brought into the company by Albert McMenimen, vice-president for finance and one of the major barons under the old system. McMenimen in effect was Galligan's sponsor, and helped move him around to give him varied experience, first as head of stores and services and later as head of public relations. The selection of these men to lead the company had to be approved by the board of directors. But, as boards often do, it accepted management's suggestions.

First Dignan and then Avila and Galligan moved aggressively to develop new managers and a new structure. Avila said that because he came up through the ranks he had a clearer idea than his predecessors of the company's faults and how to fix them. An outsider with a managerial as opposed to a technical background, Galligan had no commitment to the old ways and has been able to build on Avila's groundwork. It may be that the increasing pressures on the company have left him little choice. In any event, Galligan, like Avila, employed a team approach, relying heavily on Frank Staszesky in technical areas.

The demands of modern utility management have required the development of a cadre of middle-level managers, thus creating a larger pool from which to draw top management talent. The current team has advanced a number of promising younger people, who will become future senior managers. Indeed, the Jacksonville Electric Authority (the second largest municipal utility in the United States, after the Los Angeles Department of Water and Power) drew on this pool when it hired William Irving, head of Edison's Environmental Department, as its new managing director in 1976. Bringing in outsiders to fill the company's top position thus may be less common in the future than it was in the past.

Edison's experience in recent years illustrates the interaction among strategy, structure, and changing external constraints and pressures. The rise and fall of various groups and perspectives depended on their changing relevance to the organization's evolving problems. It depended also on the personalities and backgrounds of key people and on the history of the company. Nothing in Edison's external environment, for example, coerced the company to place the emphasis it formerly did on improving generating plant operation characteristics. What is more interesting is how and why the company has chosen to spend money on environmental amenities.

Environmental Decisions

Boston Edison's environmental decisions illustrate the importance of a strong control system and a flexible strategy if an organization is to respond successfully to rapidly changing external pressures. During the 1960s Edison did not have such characteristics and suffered unpleasant consequences. More recent decisions show that once an organization develops the capacity to formulate and implement coherent and positively responsive policies, it will not necessarily be "proenvironmental." Top management might conclude that other policies offer greater advantages, especially in light of changing public priorities and perceptions.

Like other coal-burning utilities, such as Consolidated Edison in New York and Commonwealth Edison in Chicago, Boston Edison had installed electrostatic precipitators on its plants beginning in the late 1930s. The earliest precipitators were not especially effective. Those installed in the 1940s were better, with a collection efficiency of 90 to 95 percent. While these precipitators could meet specifications under test conditions, their performance tended to deteriorate noticeably when generators were run above their "nameplate" levels.[30] It was well known that turbines could produce above their rated capacity and so Edison, like other utilities, often operated boilers and generators above their official design level. In a lax regulatory situation, the resulting problems in controlling fly ash were not a major issue. "The precipitators turned the plume from black to gray," said one engineer. Evidently, given the prevailing official climate, this was good enough.

Edison's design practices with regard to its precipitators did not reflect a general policy of underdesigning to save money; operators insisted on conservative designs in other aspects of the generating plants. On the other hand, during this period most utilities devoted little attention to the fine points of precipitator design. Around 1960, when many coal-burning urban utilities were deliberately increasing the collection efficiencies of their precipitators to 98 or 99 percent, changes in the costs of oil and coal led Edison to switch to oil exclusively.[31] Oil produces such a low level of particulate emissions that there was no longer any strong need for Edison to use particulate controls. Even without precipitators, fly-ash emissions were equivalent to those from a coal-burning plant using 99 percent efficient precipitators. And, at the time, the technology for using precipitators on oil-fired units was not well developed. Although a few units built in the early 1960s were designed to have precipitators, these controls were either not completed or were never turned on.[32]

The switch to oil did not eliminate the problem of sulfur emissions. TVA and Hydro had been monitoring SO_2 levels and developing expertise with fuel switching since the late 1950s. Edison did not begin to worry about the sulfur problem until 1966. A serious atmospheric inversion during the Thanksgiving holiday of that year resulted in poor air quality, as well as some public concern and discussion of the possible health effects of air pollution. This led the state to begin considering emergency measures and regulations that would require Edison to switch to a more expensive, lower-sulfur fuel. Edison began to investigate the impact of its operations on ambient SO_2 levels and to explore measures to deal with the problem.

The company began installing monitoring equipment around the city to check SO_2 levels. Frank Gottlich, a member of the engineering staff who later became head of Edison's Environmental Affairs Department, was responsible for this program. Edison installed four monitors at different locations around the city where it owned property.[33] (Note that TVA, with mainly rural plants, had been doing extensive monitoring since the 1950s and by this time had many monitors in service. TVA, in fact, believed that ten to twenty instruments were needed to track emissions from a single plant.)

Edison began experimental fuel switching at one of its plants to investigate the impact on ambient sulfur levels and to show it could switch fuel on short notice. These experiments were carried out at the Mystic plant in Everett, just north of downtown Boston. Low-sulfur oil was burned when wind direction and plume appearance were a special problem. These efforts were promoted in part by a *Boston Globe* photograph of a particularly dark plume, described as "whiskey brown" in color.

Low-sulfur oil was initially used only in some units so that plumes from various stacks could be compared. When the experiments indicated that there was some benefit from the program, a permanent system was developed. It was, however, put into effect only a few times in the succeeding year.[34]

Edison during this time was also getting complaints about fall-

out from its New-Boston plant in South Boston and from Edgar
Station in Weymouth, a suburb south of the city. Even though
average particulate emissions from these plants were low, the
accumulated ash stuck to the sides of the smokestacks and from
time to time was ejected in the form of messy "acid smut," which
neighbors claimed was damaging automobile finishes and laun-
dry hanging in nearby backyards.

Repeated complaints about the Edgar station eventually resulted in a suit by the attorney general in 1968—the first major
environmental enforcement action Edison had faced, despite
having been cited previously by the Department of Public Health
for sixty-nine violations.[35] The suit helped provoke more serious
efforts to solve air pollution problems. As part of the settlement,
the company agreed to invest half a million dollars at Edgar to
alleviate the problems. New, more efficient oil burners were installed. In addition, experiments were conducted with an old
precipitator at one of the Mystic station units while the unit was
burning oil, to see if precipitators might help alleviate the problem. The experiment was not encouraging. Given the low level of
ash and the small size of the particles, the unit had a collection
efficiency of only about 38 percent, and on one occasion there
was a small fire in the accumulated ash. The ash was so fine that
it tended to blow out of the stack in clumps, worsening the problem. Based on this experiment, Edison felt justified in its original
decision not to use precipitators when burning oil.[36] (Today,
while most utilities do not use precipitators on their old oil-fired
units, new design developments now make such controls possible.
Ontario Hydro, for example, installed them on a recent oil-fired
plant, and Boston Edison has installed them at its newest oil-fired
unit, Mystic 7.)

At the New-Boston plant, operators tried various alternatives.
They experimented with different additives in the boilers to
change the way the ash was formed. They also tried to heat the
air going into the boiler in order to increase the temperature of
the exit gases and retard the formation of acid smut. According
to a key participant, it was not clear whether any of these approaches was particularly effective. Regulatory changes forced
the company to switch to low-sulfur oil in the midst of these experiments, and this eliminated most of the problem.[37]

In the course of these efforts, and while discussions of the need
for sulfur-control regulations continued in the state, Edison's
mechanical engineers began exploring ways to develop a scrubber
to deal with the SO_2 problem. In the 1930s the company had used

one of the nation's first stack gas scrubber systems to control particulate emissions from its old L-Street Station. Several engineers approached the manufacturer of this system to discuss the feasibility of developing a scrubber to control SO_2 emissions. The idea was to develop a system that would produce usable sulfur byproduct for recovery and resale to a nearby chemical company, thereby paying some of the cost. In the summer of 1970, when sulfur regulations were becoming a reality, Edison announced its intention to construct a test and demonstration unit at the Mystic plant.[38]

Although top management followed the work that was proceeding in different areas of the company, these efforts took place in a relatively decentralized and uncoordinated fashion. No one unit was responsible for considering all the company's air quality problems and for instituting an integrated research effort. Various subgroups pursued their own ideas. The operators at Mystic tried fuel switching—a technique that was not tried at Edgar (although atmospheric conditions made it potentially applicable), where new burners were used instead. At New-Boston, operators experimented with more powerful air heaters. The scrubber project was pushed hard by a few key people in Mechanical Engineering. There does not seem to have been systematic planning or careful allocation of scarce engineering resources nor was there much communication among the groups.

Decentralized efforts can result in positive responses to environmental concerns. At the Los Angeles Department of Water and Power, architects went to some length to improve substation design in response to public concern. At Boston Edison, however, decentralized efforts were less successful. When hearings were held in 1969 and 1970 to consider new air pollution standards, Edison confronted not only environmentalists and student activists, but also working people from South Boston and Weymouth. Housewives came to hearings at the State House and displayed bedsheets with holes from the acid smut fallout. The resulting political climate was not favorable to the company.

By 1969 Boston Edison's own polls showed a dramatic rise in public concern about air pollution. In September David Standley, then executive director of the Boston Air Pollution Control Commission, a city agency, proposed a 1 percent sulfur content limit on fuel burned in the city. Later in the fall, under the Clear Air Act of 1967, the state's Public Health Council held hearings on ambient air quality standards that had been recommended by an *ad hoc* advisory committee. The standards were opposed by a variety of environmentalists, including the Union of Concerned Scientists. After the Public Health Council nevertheless adopted the recommendations, environmental critics put pressure on liberal governor Francis Sargent to reject them. Sargent twice sent the standards back to the Public Health Council for tightening — an effort that led to only minor readjustment.[39]

The next step under the Clean Air Act was to prepare a plan to meet the ambient standards. In the spring of 1970, the Department of Public Health proposed to do this by issuing permits to new sources on the basis of reviews of engineering drawings of planned facilities, without establishing numerical emissions criteria. This approach drew unfavorable comment from both industry and environmentalists. The former said it gave the agency too much arbitrary power; the latter believed that such discretion would lead to lax requirements in the face of industry protests. The Department of Public Health then proposed a sulfur content limit of 1 percent for fuel burned in the metropolitan Boston area, following the lead of the Boston Air Pollution Control Commission. When the final regulations were issued, however, the regulations called for an initial limit of 1 percent which would then drop to .5 percent after one year. Although the sequence of events within the Department of Public Health is not clear, many believe that the move to a more restrictive standard resulted from Governor Sargent's intervention. He was then running against Kevin White for governor, and both men saw a need to take strong positions on environmental protection.[40]

Edison responded in several ways. It announced its experimental scrubber prototype at Mystic and it applied for a variance from the sulfur regulations, proposing that it be allowed to burn higher-sulfur oil except when adverse atmospheric conditions required cleaner fuel. As part of its variance request, Edison offered three alternative fuel-switching plans, which would cost between $75,000 and $7.5 million. In contrast, the company estimated, burning low-sulfur oil on a continuous basis would add $22 million to its costs. Edison submitted an analysis prepared by the engineering firm of Stone and Webster on the basis of Edison's monitoring data. The study concluded that Edison was responsible for only 15 percent of the ground-level SO_2 in the city, averaged over the course of a year.[41]

In requesting the variance, Edison's managers felt that they were acting responsibly. The public interest, they felt, meant avoiding unnecessary environmental expenditures. If fuel switching would protect air quality at lower cost, then the company felt it was appropriate to argue for this approach.[42] However, the public at this point wanted strong action on air pollution control. Any attempt at modification of the rules was greeted with hostility and suspicion. The Public Health Council, sensing the public and political mood, dismissed Edison's plans without even hearing any opposition testimony. The world was changing more rapidly than the company realized. Years later, Edison executives still expressed surprise and dismay at the depth of skepticism and the strength of the feelings they encountered.

In July 1974 Edison applied again for a variance in order to pursue fuel switching, and was again turned down. By this time, the company had begun to show greater sensitivity to public concerns, particularly with regard to transmission-line routing, and was better equipped to respond to public concerns in general. Many managerial changes had occurred, including the establishment of an Environmental Affairs Department. Why then did Edison seek a replay of its early difficulties and apply a second time? By 1974, company opinion surveys showed, there had been a noticeable shift in public sentiment from environmental to economic concerns. Still convinced that selective burning was a more economical way to protect the environment, top management wanted to reopen the issue, despite staff reluctance. They wanted to communicate to their customers that they were in earnest in their desire to control costs. External pressures had grown more complex and ambiguous, and the company found that it could choose which groups to appease and which pressures to respond to. The second variance request reflected this strategy. It was born of knowledge and calculation, not naiveté or isolation.

Although the application for a variance was denied, the company's assessment of the situation proved accurate. Shortly thereafter, the state legislature passed a law requiring the state Department of Public Health to relax emission standards as much as possible, without violating federal secondary air quality standards, as a way of providing financial relief to consumers. This legislation was widely attributed to the utility industry's lobbyist. The sulfur content minimum for Boston was raised from .5 percent to 1 percent, and outside Boston the allowable level went from 1 percent to 2.2 percent. (In contrast, the allowable level in California has been .25 percent.)

Edison's strategy for dealing with air pollution has thus become steadily more sophisticated. The company appears to have initially misjudged the political climate, and to have assumed that a good working relationship with the small and cooperative staff at the DPH would be sufficient to accomplish its purposes. In this respect, the story resembles the problems of the Southern Company. Yet Edison quickly began to deal with the political dimensions of its problem. On the state legislative level, it helped launch an effective lobbying effort that led to legislative relaxation of the standard. At the same time, it has worked hard to keep the stacks of its Boston plants as clear as possible to minimize opposition to the changes. This is not idle concern, since the shift back to higher-sulfur oil has reintroduced some of the plume-opacity and fallout problems of several years ago. (Indeed, the Salem Harbor station of New England Electric was forced by the state to abandon a similar plan after heavy fallout in the plant area.) Tom Galligan—who can easily see most of the stacks from the company offices—has insisted that his staff deal with these visual problems. He drastically overhauled the leadership of steam plant operations when the existing, long-time managers could not seem to do the job.[43]

Another result of the change in the law is that Edison decided to discontinue the scrubber program. Some utilities have lobbied for changes in sulfur regulations on the grounds that a workable scrubber technology was not available, but the Edison engineers who worked on the test model believed that they could build a successful full-scale version. Because of the new sulfur limits, the program is no longer economically defensible, however. In comparison to the fuel the scrubber would allow the company to use, the fuel Edison now has to burn without the scrubber is not sufficiently more expensive so as to make the cost of the scrubber justifiable. Tom Galligan long took a personal interest in the scrubber project, but he was not willing to proceed unless the dollar gains were clear.[44]

Edison's problems with transmission-line routing reveal much the same change in the substance and coherence of corporate decision making. Here, too, there has been an evolution from defensiveness to flexibility, but in this case the outcome has been less equivocal from an environmental viewpoint.

The first of Edison's major transmission-line battles began in 1960 over a 115-kilovolt line through Sudbury, a town with a history of opposition to Edison projects.[45] The proposed route ran along a marshland near the Sudbury River, just touching the towns of Wayland and Concord. Some Sudbury residents wanted the part of the line that went through the town put underground. Since undergrounding costs ten or twelve times as much as a conventional line, the company was understandably reluctant to go

along with the request, especially since such a move would encourage other communities to make similar demands. Once some
local people started to object, the situation rapidly polarized.
Undergrounding became a major issue in Sudbury. Within Boston Edison, the general counsel decreed that the problem was a
legal one, and he therefore took control of the negotiations. The
town selectmen and Edison's attorneys soon became too antago-
nistic to compromise. Several Edison executives, in retrospect,
blame the combativeness of the lawyers. Edison's top public-
relations official, James Lydon, explained, "I think . . . that some
poor judgments, some mistakes were made. People got to feel
very strongly, and things got quite polarized. And then once it
got into court, the lawyers wouldn't let you do anything. I think
that we might have been able to work something out, but we were
told that we couldn't get involved."[46] Another manager re-
marked, "The lawyers really bothered us here . . . I sense that, if
the lawyers had just gone home, we could have made a compromise." To build the line, Edison had to obtain a number of permits from the state Department of Public Utilities. Despite strong
local opposition from Sudbury, Concord, and Wayland, the DPU
granted the permits, but at each point its decisions were appealed
to the courts by the towns. Edison repeatedly won these appeals,
but the court challenges extended the application process over a
number of years.

Because of its concern that local governments might choose to
take over the job of providing electric service, we can speculate
that Pacific Gas & Electric would have been noticeably more hesi-
tant to engage in such a confrontation. Perhaps because municipal takeovers are much harder to arrange in Massachusetts and
occur much less frequently, Edison could afford to be less fearful.
It was willing to "go to the mat" on these questions, and did so
again and again.

Ultimately, the towns found a way to block Edison outside the
DPU permit-granting process. Sudbury scored one victory when
it secured a commitment from the secretary of the interior, Stewart Udall, not to allow the line to proceed through a federal wildlife refuge so long as there were local objections. Edison altered
the route to circumvent the refuge. The towns then discovered a
new power, refusing to issue street-crossing permits for the lines
in question. Edison took the towns to court, and lost. A superior
court judge ruled that aesthetic concerns were a legitimate basis
for the exercise of town authority. In 1970 the line was built
underground. It was a costly defeat in view of legal fees, construc-

tion delays, poor public relations, and the time of key executives. Inflexibility does not appear to have been advantageous in this case.

Before the first battle was fully resolved, Edison proposed another line—a 230-kilovolt line from Medway to Waltham via a number of communities, including Sudbury. Although some towns approved, others took the matter to court. Edison began construction on the segments where it had approval, but the sight of the towers provoked more opposition. This time, however, as the battle began to escalate, a compromise was arranged. The architect of this agreement was Bill Cowen, then chairman of the Department of Public Utilities, later Governor Sargent's secretary for administration, and still later an unsuccessful candidate for state attorney general. Cowen represented a sharp departure from previous DPU leadership. He was a liberal with political ambitions, not the normal semiretired party stalwart seeking a modest sinecure. After several public meetings, a small working group hammered out a compromise that left the line aboveground but made the company responsible for improved tower design and landscaping.[47]

The time, money, and public-relations costs of these experiences led to a noticeably different approach to more recent transmission-line problems. An example that Edison executives point to with some pride is the major new transmission line from Plymouth to Holbrook, which helps carry the output of the Pilgrim nuclear reactor to Edison's grid. Edison's representatives, from Public Relations and Engineering, began discussions with local authorities two years in advance of the line's construction. The Transmission and Distribution Department, working with Public Relations, retained an outside consultant to help develop a more attractive design for the transmission towers.[48] The same strategy is shown in two other recent decisions. On one particular underground transmission project, Edison agreed to some changes that made the transmission route longer and costlier and that put the line partly under a parkway route. The company also agreed to pay to restore the parkland. These steps increased local support for the project and pleased a local politician who had previously wanted to improve the park. In another recent case, a tree-clearing crew for a new overhead line (along an existing right of way) found itself in the backyards of some houses that had been built years ago on Edison's easement. Instead of insisting on its legal "rights" in the matter, the company chose to limit its clearing operations and to pay for planting shrubs to screen the view.

In spite of the money involved and the precedents set, these matters were handled, for the most part, by the manager of Transmission and Distribution, in conjunction with district public-relations people and field supervisors.[49]

Several features of this new strategy deserve mention. Public Relations is prominent but not dominant. The approach is genuinely multidisciplinary, involving the close cooperation of functional units such as Law, Public Relations, and Engineering. On the Plymouth-Holbrook line, for example, the public-relations people favored the more aesthetically pleasing single pole lines, but they acquiesced to the engineer's view that more massive, A-shaped towers were less costly to construct and maintain and (being shorter) less visible than the single poles. (See Figure 26.)

The current strategy is subtle. The approach is not simply "Spend more on aesthetics and environment," as the efforts to relax air pollution limits indicate. Although Galligan would not accept the formulation, other Edison executives agree with our characterization of the current strategy as "Do what you have to do to avoid, or at least minimize, local objections." On one right-of-way that was recently upgraded, for example, Public Relations persuaded engineering to rework the older transmission-line towers and not to replace them with single-pole units. Reversing its position on the Plymouth-Holbrook line, Public Relations noted that new towers would be higher and in different locations, and that this disruption would disturb local residents more than a failure to put in more attractive structures.[50]

Top management has communicated this new strategy down through the ranks. It is understood now that company policy is to combine reasonable conciliation with the effective use of public consultation and enough advance notice to avoid the sort of polarization that occurred at Sudbury. Top management still makes the final decisions—for example, on tower design and route changes for the Plymouth-Holbrook line. The engineers running the project, however, are expected and allowed to develop and refine options and make decisions on their own.

These episodes clearly illustrate a dilemma that all managers face in implementing a complex strategy. In an organization of any size, one or two people at the top cannot review every decision in detail; some decentralization is unavoidable. "I didn't bother them with every little detail," said one manager. "I make decisions myself. That's what I am paid for. I only send it up if it involves a serious precedent, or lots of money, or for their information if they should get asked about it." At the same time, when

Figure 26. One of the unusual towers designed for the Plymouth-Holbrook line, as it appeared while under construction. Courtesy of Boston Edison.

tradeoffs among competing objectives are involved, how can top management ensure that middle management will strike the appropriate balance? The opposite traps of eliminating initiative and independence and of losing control of corporate policy must both be avoided. In these instances, at least, Edison appears to have found some viable middle ground.

At PG&E, in contrast, middle managers less often make, and take responsibility for, a decision on their own. This may reflect historical differences: there has been long experience with autonomous and powerful group leaders at Edison and an equally long tradition of strong top management at PG&E. PG&E also has more overlapping and competitive groups. Other people are always ready to call attention to, and harp on, any apparent failures. There is also less strategic consensus; hence, subordinates at PG&E may find it harder to know what policy to follow, and whom to try and please. PG&E also appears to have more promising management candidates. The limited number of good people at Boston Edison means that able staff members can look forward to promotion with more confidence, even if they make some mistakes. Finally, PG&E confronts a much more demanding external situation. The adverse consequences of a mistake could be noticeably more severe for PG&E than for Edison.

Edison's recent siting decisions reflect a similar strategy of minimizing community protest. Note that this does not necessarily mean minimizing environmental impact. The utility chose, for example, to locate its newest large fossil-fuel unit at its Mystic plant, just north of downtown Boston. The urban location makes the potential air pollution problems more serious. Moreover, the site's proximity to the airport made it necessary to secure special permission from the Federal Aviation Administration to build a high stack. Nevertheless, Edison felt it was worth the risks; adding a unit to an existing site was preferable to developing a new site, partly for economic reasons. Also, residents near an existing plant would be less likely to protest — less likely to feel they were being "invaded."

Of the available sites, Edison's plants as Edgar and New-Boston had generated considerable local objections over air pollution. Everett, on the other hand, where the Mystic plant was located, was a lower-middle-class, heavily industrial community that seemed eager for the added tax base. A new 650 MW oil-fired unit was therefore added right in the center of the metropolitan area, without any significant protest from environmental regulators or from the surrounding community.[51] The importance of

external circumstances is striking when one considers the
LADWP's parallel experience with adding a fossil-fuel unit in an
urban setting. The Scattergood 3 unit, even in its original design,
had lower NO_x and SO_x emissions than the Mystic 7 unit.

The same sensitivity to potential opposition — as opposed to
environmental concern — is reflected in the decision to locate a
nuclear unit at Plymouth, outside Edison's own service area. Sites
within the service area, either north or south of the city, were obvious alternatives. But they were generally located in wealthy and
influential areas, which could be expected to object strenuously
to such a project. Also, a nuclear unit cannot be located too close
to a major population center. Plymouth was an old Yankee town
— not particularly prosperous, and likely to appreciate the substantial real-estate tax gains. At the same time, it was close
enough to accomplish one of Tom Galligan's major purposes —
namely, to show his customers that Edison was trying to control
costs by using a new — and apparently cheap — form of energy.

As a result of the choice, however, a well-known piece of coastline was converted into a nuclear plant site. "They will shoot me
when they find I sold Rocky Point," the owner said at the time.
But Edison had calculated correctly: the prospect of jobs and tax
revenues led to general local approval. Edison gained further
local favor by developing the area around the plant for fishing,
picnicking, and other recreational purposes. A plan to build an
exposition hall and public information center was dropped as too
expensive. Allowing the public to use the plant site was a more
subtle — and no less effective — way to make the case that nuclear
power can be made safe and environmentally acceptable.[52] (See
Figure 27.)

As it turned out, the major critical response to the plant came
not from Plymouth, but from academics in Cambridge fifty miles
away. The Union of Concerned Scientists turned its attention
from air pollution control to nuclear safety. Rather than opposing Edison through mass demonstrations, the group engaged in
sophisticated regulatory challenges. In 1973 they filed a motion
with the Atomic Energy Commission, seeking to block the Pilgrim plant's operating license. The commission ruled out most of
the group's objections, but did consider their argument that the
plant's emergency core cooling system was inadequate. Ultimately, the operating license was granted, but the Union of Concerned Scientists later involved Edison in other hearings that the
company found very costly.

In 1974, with oil prices newly risen and customers up in arms, a

Figure 27. The Pilgrim nuclear plant. The parking area for the shorefront public-use area is clearly visible at the lower left center, just below the station's discharge canal. Courtesy of Boston Edison.

routine inspection and refueling turned into an outage of more than six months, forcing the company to use far more expensive alternative sources of power. The Union of Concerned Scientists contributed to the delay in getting the plant back on line. To Edison's surprise, the group demanded — and won — an AEC hearing on the acceptability of some new fuel bundles the company was installing. The new fuel bundles were made up of sixty-four fuel rods in an eight-by-eight design, instead of the seven-by-seven design that had been in use. The critics claimed that the new system might reduce the effectiveness of the emergency core cooling system, in the event the primary cooling system failed. The company could not simply scrap the new fuel bundles and reuse the old ones, however, because some of the seven-by-seven bundles had developed leaks due to poor manufacturing, and because others had been damaged in the course of removal.[53]

Company engineers were dismayed. They believed that the new scheme was safer than the old one, and it was already in use at other plants. Still, the Atomic Energy Commission agreed to the last-minute request for a hearing. While the hearings were in progress, the company discovered another problem at the plant which, by itself, constituted cause for a shutdown. Sonic inspection of a weld connecting the main cooling pipes to the reactor vessel seemed to reveal a crack. Further tests ultimately showed that the fault was not in the weld but in the calibration of the testing equipment. (This mistake apparently contributed to the decision to reorganize the nuclear side of the company in 1975.) But while the weld was being examined, Edison had allowed the AEC hearing to continue without pressing for a rapid conclusion.[54] The hearings lasted four months, and although the company's position prevailed at the hearings and during later court challenges, the delay was extremely costly for the company.

Edison has long had plans to build a second unit — and perhaps even a third — at the Pilgrim site, but at the end of 1979 Edison still had not obtained a construction permit to begin building the second unit, which it had planned to have on line that year. Regulatory requirements have grown enormously since Pilgrim 1 was planned and built. This time, the company had to do extensive seismological studies of a sort that had not previously been required. The controversy over nuclear power is now acute in Edison's service area, and as with most other utilities the future of its nuclear capacity expansion program is unclear.

Boston Edison's history is less dramatic than that of some of the other companies in this study. Unlike the public companies or

PG&E, it has never been the focus of major political or commercial struggles. Edison grew slowly and steadily, ultimately becoming Boston's sole electric utility. Its subsequent growth has been determined by the region's modest increases in electricity demand —increases that were small enough to be met with occasional, modestly sized projects. Edison dealt with an understaffed state rate-review agency whose membership was influenced by political patronage. As long as technical progress allowed rates to stay level (as it did), the company was left in relative peace. Top management neither had nor needed tight control over the organization. Those who had worked their way up to middle-level managerial positions ran their units with a fairly free hand.

Beginning in the mid-1960s, circumstances made Edison for the first time an object of political interest. The nationwide environmental movement found articulate and energetic advocates in Boston's intellectual community. The issues they raised made good campaign material for state and local politicians. Somewhat later, under the influence of rising oil prices, climbing utility rates, and economic recession, public attention focused on the rate issue.

Edison's first responses typified the decentralization of its former structure. Different groups within the company responded in various ways, and with varying degrees of success. The lawyers, for example, handled the Sudbury transmission-line routing controversy badly. Individual engineers and plant operators, working on their own, pursued several possible solutions to the particulate and sulfur emissions problems. No coherent system-wide approach was developed.

The impetus for change came partly from the unsatisfactory results of these activities. There were also broader social forces at work, mirroring broad changes in the city as a whole. Old patterns broke down. New men rose to middle- and upper-level managerial positions who were less concerned with friendship and ethnicity and more concerned with ability and performance. Top managers—beginning with Tom Dignan and continuing with Charles Avila and Tom Galligan—sought to maintain closer touch with day-to-day affairs and to deepen and strengthen their control. Structural change and extensive diagonal mobility have been critical to these developments. The new management at Edison is noticeably more efficient, more cost-conscious, and more aware of public opinion than past administrations have been.

The demands of the outside world have not been consistent

enough or strong enough to dictate a uniform company policy of responsiveness to environmental concerns. In some areas, like transmission-line planning, Boston Edison has learned a great deal from past experience and has developed considerable sensitivity to local concerns. It was relatively late in focusing on air pollution problems, but it did innovative scrubber development work when the matter became important to the company. Because of shifting external expectations, however, it later dropped the project. Edison's situation does not force it to be proenvironmental in all circumstances, and it does not behave this way. It is responsive, but in ways that reflect the logic of its own particular situation.

10

Explaining Environmental Decisions

After the rich and intricate detail of the cases, what have we learned that is generalizable? What pattern of inter- and intra-company variation in environmental decisions emerges from the profusion of facts, anecdotes, and personalities? What determines the behavior of organizations and how can we ensure that they pay adequate attention to social values such as environmental protection?

The utilities in this study certainly did not base their environmental decisions simply on what was required. Instead, they responded in various ways, sometimes doing what they had to, while in other cases they violated standards or refused to comply with regulations. The Los Angeles Department of Water and Power, for instance, began constructing a new power plant without obtaining the necessary construction permit.

Most surprisingly, some utilities developed a conscious strategy of going beyond what was required. They exhibited the behavior we have described as positively responsive, making improvements in their environmental practices not simply to meet existing standards but in anticipation of future regulations and public expectations. Instead of resisting regulations, they worked hard to comply, developing innovative technological solutions when necessary. In some cases, these utilities have actually approached regulators to suggest new guidelines and regulations that would apply to their own activities.

Although such actions did not contribute to earnings in the short run, they were not undertaken without regard to the organizations' self-interest. Such behavior generally occurred when managers feared that angering the public would in the long run lead to serious adverse consequences for the organization. It most often occurred where local attitudes strongly favored environmental protection and where organized groups actively worked to change company behavior in that direction. Responsiveness was particularly likely when utilities felt that their very survival and growth might be threatened by such popular reaction. Thus, the initiatives taken by these utilities were not entirely voluntary; their actions were a response to the pressures they faced.

Of the six companies in our study, Ontario Hydro and Pacific Gas and Electric most clearly pursued such a strategy. Both operate in relatively affluent areas where environmental protection is highly valued, and where the institutional structure makes it relatively easy for those with environmental concerns to impose sanctions on the organization. They are the companies most subject to fundamental threats in response to poor performance, since they can be disciplined either through the expansion of public power in the latter case or direct government control in the former. Remarks such as "we have to walk on eggs," "we stand for election every year," and "the people keep us in office" display the vulnerability felt by PG&E's managers. Perhaps as a result, members of both organizations ascribe strategic value to a policy of anticipating citizen demands and giving the public the kind of service it wants. Consider, for example, Hydro's decision to install precipitators at its oil-fired Lennox plant despite assurances from regulatory officials that they would not be required. Consider, also, Hydro's ongoing development of new procedures for public consultation over the siting of all new power plants and transmission lines, often without specific directives from the government to do so. Similarly, PG&E publicly committed itself to control NO_x emissions at its Moss Landing plant, invited environmentalists to participate in the siting of a new nuclear plant, and encouraged the Public Utility Commission to establish statewide regulations fixing a percentage of revenue available each year for the undergrounding of distribution lines.

In contrast, Boston Edison and the Los Angeles Department of Water and Power have pursued a mixed policy. Neither utility has faced the same kinds of threats to its independence as PG&E or Hydro, and neither has adopted a general stance of positive responsiveness. Yet in areas where these companies have experienced repeated problems, they have formulated responsive policies. Boston Edison's efforts in the 1970s to consult with affected localities about proposed transmission lines and the DWP's consultations with local officials in Kern County about its projected nuclear plant are two such examples. Both examples show how organizations evolve in the direction of greater responsiveness, as they move from a situation of limited constraints to one of greater demands. Contrast these examples with the LADWP's experience with Scattergood 3 on the one hand, and Boston Edison's battle over the first Sudbury transmission line on the other.

The Southern Company is an unusual case. It has not faced severe environmental pressures, yet rather than remaining inattentive to outside concerns, the company has developed a capacity to deal flexibly with the pressures it does face. In a number of specific areas, it has shown real resourcefulness in finding means to comply with pollution control rules.

Ironically, our cases show that private companies may sometimes be more responsive to public demands than government-owned utilities. The Tennessee Valley Authority, the largest publicly owned utility in the country, in some instances simply refused to obey state air pollution regulations, although it did some of the earliest research on air pollution in the industry. President Carter's appointment of David Freeman to the TVA board of directors and subsequently to its chairmanship appears to have altered its behavior (illustrating that externally imposed changes are ultimately possible). But until the late 1960s TVA's policies were far less responsive than, say, PG&E's or even Southern's. Whether a company behaves responsively, then, depends not only on its ownership, but on a number of more specific features of the situation.

In general, we expect both public and private corporations to become more responsive as social and regulatory pressures increase in scope and intensity. All the organizations in our study tended to evolve in this way. Confronted with growing pressures, they had to become responsive in order to retain some degree of control over their own fate. In a sense, they became responsive in order to avoid becoming obsolete.

A recent statement by the president of the Ford Motor Company, Philip Caldwell, indicates that companies outside the utility industry are becoming increasingly aware of the logic behind such an approach. "We can no longer merely respond to government pressures," Caldwell said. "We will have to anticipate public concerns for the 1980s, for the 1990s, and even for the twenty-first century."[1]

Positive responsiveness is, in large part, a result of conscious *strategy* to anticipate future demands in making current decisions. But there are a number of *structural* features of an organization that accompany and support such a policy: a strong role for outside-oriented personnel and groups in areas such as public relations, law, and environmental affairs; the presence of diverse outlooks in the organization and mechanisms for taking those views seriously when making decisions; and promotional policies that motivate mid-level managers to implement the new approaches energetically. Such structural features not only enable a company to respond positively to environmental pressures; they also improve its capacity to respond to normal business demands as well.

These structural features aid an organization in *noticing* external pressures, *planning* and *deciding* to undertake adequate responses, and *implementing* these responses effectively. Outside-oriented groups, for instance, are clearly necessary for perceiving what the external world is demanding and they often serve as important internal advocates of responsive policies as well. Diverse outlooks are important to developing creative solutions to difficult problems, and to ensuring that the plans that are chosen take into account a variety of viewpoints. Strong top-management control is needed to ensure that plans are reliably implemented.

The most responsive organizations in our study, Hydro and PG&E, generally possessed these characteristics, and all the organizations tended to develop them as they came under increasing pressure. On the other hand, the failure to respond positively to external demands was often associated with a lack of these characteristics. Yet no utility we studied was either perfectly responsive or perfectly unresponsive, whatever its general strategy and structure. Despite certain patterns of historical continuity, the specific policies these companies followed depended too much on the particular views of individual managers and on the shifting strength and ambitions of various groups within the organization for this to be the case. Thus, although PG&E generally adopted a policy of trying to accommodate and co-opt opposing groups, its top managers persisted in trying to find coastal sites for nuclear plants because of their opposition to use of scarce inland water for cooling purposes. And although the Southern Company has not generally been proenvironmental in its policies, its sophisticated research group pioneered in the development of solvent refined coal — an innovative approach to controlling SO_2 emissions.

Such anomalies are possible because external constraints typically leave a company considerable room to maneuver, as we have repeatedly seen. Thus, internal characteristics can have considerable impact on what is done. In order to understand the details of company actions, we need to understand both the external circumstances an organization confronts and the internal factors that affect the organization's response to these circumstances.

The Determinants of Externally Imposed Consequences

Why do some pollution control agencies set more stringent standards than others, and enforce those standards more vigorously? Why did the Los Angeles Air Pollution Control District have an energetic program of roving inspectors seeking out violations when in Boston the state authorities had only one monitoring site? Why did PG&E confront severe limits on its NO_x discharges at Moss Landing while TVA was able to operate plants with enormously greater environmental impact? Why did the Southern Company feel unable to pursue an all-nuclear strategy while Ontario Hydro felt free to make a major commitment to a risky new nuclear technology?

In Chapter 2 we argued that outsiders who want to alter an organization's behavior have to compare the costs to themselves of trying to do so with the likelihood that they will achieve results they desire. What determines how people view these costs and benefits and hence what decisions they make?

One important element in such a decision is the magnitude and seriousness of the environmental harm that is occurring and that might be diminished by public action. Perhaps surprisingly, in the cases we explored, the regulatory system was less arbitrary and capricious than its critics sometimes suggest.[2] Reacting to public pressures, the regulatory system does appear to impose requirements that bear some (crude and imperfect) relationship to public perceptions of the harm being done.

These public perceptions appear to be related to (1) the actual harm being done, (2) the ease with which the public can perceive that harm, (3) the extent to which cultural norms and widespread public attitudes focus attention on the issue, (4) the clarity of scientific evidence concerning the harm in question, and (5) the presence or absence of someone who had reason to call attention to the issue.

Consider, for example, the public concern that confronted PG&E's attempts to build nuclear plants at Bodega, Nipomo, and Point Arena. The San Andreas fault runs along the northern California coastline, and as a result earthquakes are more of a hazard in that region than in, say, Plymouth, Massachusetts, where Boston Edison's Pilgrim plant is located. The cases suggest that awareness of this fault and the nuclear safety implications were sufficiently widespread to have affected what occurred. People in northern California (as well as the AEC) believed that this was an especially hazardous region, and were provoked by that perception to be very cautious about construction of nuclear plants on such sites.

Nuclear plant siting is not the only example in which the actual condition of natural systems and processes—a potential determinant of external consequences—has played a major role. By all current standards and measures, air pollution is especially serious in Los Angeles compared to other cities in our study. Inland mountain ranges trap certain pollutants in the face of the prevailing westerly winds. The frequent sunshine then converts these pollutants into severe photochemical smog. In Boston, the same westerly winds blow much of the region's air pollution out to sea. One reason why air pollution regulations in Los Angeles have been so strict and so rigidly enforced is that citizens there know that the problem is serious. Similarly, more people are affected by air pollution in an urban center like Toronto than in a rural location like Paradise, Kentucky. This helps explain why many in Ontario took Hydro's air pollution more seriously than those in the Tennessee Valley viewed TVA's emissions.

Not all serious problems are equally evident, however. Our cases suggest that public action to alter company behavior was more likely (and that it was easier for outsiders to mobilize) when the issue was immediately obvious. In the early 1960s everyone in Los Angeles knew that the smog problem was getting worse—all you had to do was go outside. It became an easy and attractive political issue. Everyone in the San Francisco Bay area can tell when visibility diminishes because the hills east of the bay are obscured, thus providing an obvious reference mark (like the San Gabriel Mountains near Los Angeles). In Boston, in contrast, long-distance visibility is hard to gauge since there is nothing in the distance to see. Surely the "yellow cloud" at Moss Landing made the protest there more vigorous than would have been the case if the NO_x had been totally invisible. Similarly, in the battle over the Bodega Bay nuclear plant, protesters released balloons with labels reading "This might be a radioactive emission from the proposed power plant"—an action calculated to make the danger they saw more visible to the general public. Most land-use (siting and routing) questions we studied were quite visible in this sense, which may help explain why popular concern over these issues was a problem for almost all our companies. In contrast, there was less public protest over hard-to-perceive problems like thermal pollution.

However, what is "serious" or even "self-evident" depends to some extent upon the observer's conceptual system. There is a great deal of evidence in our cases for the role of mind set in problem definition. When the plans for Bodega started, the issue of nuclear power plant siting was not a salient one in northern California. There was relatively little public comment at the first hearings over the site. By the time PG&E got to Mendocino, public opinion and attention had shifted, and so had the kinds of external consequences the utility confronted. An especially interesting reflection of this phenomenon was Boston Edison's decision not to replace existing towers on a particular transmission line with fewer, and more pleasing, single-pole structures. Edison's managers reasoned that since the poles would be in new locations, they would call more attention to the whole issue. When TVA started strip-mining coal in western Kentucky, this practice was perceived by the public as a hopeful step that would enhance much-desired regional development. Only later did it become redefined as an environmental problem.

The evolution of such general cultural perceptions, and of the changing reactions they caused, accounts for the essential dilemma faced by the organizations in our study.[3] Decision rules and strategies adapted to one set of public attitudes and expectations became obsolete, forcing companies to learn and develop new ways of behaving. They also had to contend with very varied, even conflicting, outside attitudes. How should these companies have gone about balancing public concern over environmental harm with concern over rates and costs? Whose definition of the problem should they have used?

Our cases contain some suggestions about the social factors that can shape public attitudes. First, they confirm the notion — verified by a number of other studies — that concern with environmental protection rises with increased income and education.[4] The people of northern California are more affluent than the people of the Tennessee Valley. Their behavior reveals that they are more concerned with controlling pollution and less with encouraging industrial development. Standards are tighter in the San Francisco Bay area than they are in Knoxville or Birmingham. These differences also reflect broad regional variations in culture and values that clearly have affected different companies to varying degrees. The Sierra Club is more influential in PG&E's service area than in Boston Edison's, reflecting a wide variety of social forces such as ethnicity, class, and the attitudes of those who have chosen to move to those regions. Even within regions, differences in income sometimes have a noticeable effect on public behavior. Relatively affluent towns like Woodside, California, and Sudbury, Massachusetts, have been leaders in pressing for undergrounding of transmission and distribution lines.[5] All told, the influence of socioeconomic factors on environmental preferences, and of those preferences on environmental outcomes, means that to a certain extent people get the kinds of environmental regulation that they want — or that they feel they can afford.

The cases also suggest that changing scientific and technical information helped provoke and crystallize public reaction in some cases. In Los Angeles, public opposition to additional fossil-fuel power plants increased when the key role of NO_x in smog conditions was clarified. Evidence that the smoke plumes of Ontario Hydro's generating plants were linked to ambient SO_2 readings under some conditions likewise encouraged additional public action.

Accumulating evidence not only encourages outside activists, but influences regulators and those inside the regulated organizations. All parties find it harder to defend inaction to themselves, to outsiders, to the courts, and to other agencies when all agree that there is a problem. Conversely, when TVA was unable to discover clear evidence of adverse impacts of sulfur emissions, it was encouraged in its refusal to install tighter control measures.

The attention focused on each problem, the cases suggest, is also a matter of who has what incentive to put a particular problem on the public agenda. A great deal may depend on whether or not some agency, individual, or organization chooses to act as the entrepreneur in the situation. No one at PG&E denies the role of David Pesonen of the Sierra Club in the Bodega Head controversy. People at Boston Edison likewise recognize the role of the Union of Concerned Scientists in some of the utility's legal battles. We have seen how a number of public-agency entrepreneurs have also had an impact. The cooling requirements at PG&E's Pittsburg 7 unit reflect the efforts of at least two such regulatory officials, each of whom had something to gain by calling attention to the problem. Conversely, an energetic DPU member engineered a compromise in a Boston Edison transmission-line dispute. Since the regulatory system has its own frictions and costs of operation, someone who takes the initiative — for personal, ideological, or bureaucratic reasons — can influence just how the process operates in a given instance.

It is clear that "the little individual," to use Buckminster Fuller's phrase, can do a great deal to alter environmental outcomes by mobilizing public opinion, launching effective legal actions, or introducing innovative solutions to difficult problems. Our case studies offer considerable encouragement to those who would like to believe that action by individuals or by small, organized groups can make a difference—even in the face of large bureaucracies.

It is also apparent that, driven by such factors as the development of new knowledge, dramatic events, and so on, broad cycles of media and public attention tend to occur. In a society that treats news as entertainment, the media have a continuing incentive to focus on the new and the current, and to give less time to issues that have become less interesting, if no less important, because they have become familiar. Press attention in the early phases of a controversy was critical in many cases in stimulating outsiders to initiate tougher regulatory action—whether it was the description of the "whisky brown" plume printed in the *Boston Globe*, the editorials of the local paper in Monterey near Moss Landing, or the extensive press coverage of Pollution Probe in Toronto.

We have thus far been considering what it is that determines public perceptions of the magnitude of environmental harm, and therefore perceptions of the potential benefits of successful regulatory action. We hypothesized that the initiation of regulatory action by outsiders would depend also on how costly they found it to impose sanctions on target organizations, and on the magnitude of the sanctions they were able to deploy. Our case studies suggest that two features of the regulatory system are important in determining the costs to outsiders of successful mobilization. These are the technical expertise and resources of the regulatory agencies—which influence agency capacity—and the extent to which the political system gives those agencies reason to act.

In at least one state we have explored, outside consultants had to be hired (by the Environmental Protection Agency) to draw up the state's air pollution control implementation plan because state personnel lacked the relevant expertise. When the utilities protested the plan, the agency was hard pressed to defend it. Similarly, in Massachusetts, low expenditures for monitoring and a lack of technical sophistication among inspection personnel made it difficult for outsiders to use state agencies to control Edison's operating practices. In several states during the period we studied, patronage played a significant role in state government. Budgets were small, salaries low, and agencies had little expertise. This undermined an agency's effectiveness and aggressiveness, and made it all the more difficult for outsiders to use that agency to change corporate behavior.[6] The California Energy Commission, with its large staff and extensive funding, has been better able to influence utility decision making than its relatively anemic Massachusetts counterpart.

To some extent these features of regulatory agencies reflected the larger political system, which determined their budgets, powers, leadership, and so forth. Some agencies were closely tied to this larger system. When outside concern was widespread, they therefore tended to respond with more aggressive action. For example, when a Los Angeles county supervisor was defeated for reelection for being too "soft" on smog, the new board — which controlled the county's Air Pollution Control District — drastically increased antipollution efforts. This linkage can work both ways. When political pressure for pollution control diminished in Florida, so did the assiduousness of the state's air pollution control authorities.

It is important to note that regulatory institutions are not fixed, that they can change in response to increasing or decreasing public concern. New agencies can be set up, such as the Coastal Zone Commission in California, and existing agencies can be given new powers, as was the Ontario Energy Review Board when Hydro's rates were placed under it jurisdiction.

This flexibility of regulatory institutions is consistent with a larger point. Immediate regulatory sanctions are not the only kind of threat that outsiders can hold over an organization like a utility. Instead, noncompliance or poor environmental practice can sometimes result in penalties going beyond those immediately available to regulators. When this is the case, outsiders have a significant source of leverage over an organization. This makes citizen protest more attractive precisely because it is more likely to be successful.

At the most extreme, unpopular organizational behavior can result in threats to the organization's survival, or at least its growth. Such threats are very powerful, since they affect all members of the organization, and can thus overcome weaknesses in its internal incentive system. Pacific Gas & Electric's response to the threat of municipal takeovers is an example of this phenomenon. Faced with this possibility, the company has been very mindful both of cost control and of environmentalists' concerns — and it has worked harder to accomplish these ends than it would have, had it been faced only with public-utility rate regulation and compliance orders from environmental agencies.

On other occasions, the consequence of unresponsive behavior may not be a threat to survival, but simply the likelihood that the regulations will become more severe, making resistance counter-productive. This concern prompted the Southern Company to demand some land-reclamation effort on the part of its strip-mine coal suppliers. Similarly, Boston Edison — encountering renewed plume visibility problems when it switched back to higher-sulfur oil — knew it had to reduce these problems or face a possible retightening of the regulations. The president of the company made sure the problem was dealt with.[7]

Public ownership is one avenue of control that goes beyond immediate regulatory action. Direct ownership is sometimes assumed to be such a powerful method of external control that public companies have sometimes been exempted from regulatory requirements. As we have seen, however, public ownership is not a guarantee of responsiveness.

The distinctive feature of a public enterprise is that the government typically has some general (and specific) executive authority over the organization.[8] This includes the authority to appoint board members and senior executives, the power to determine budgets, and even the right to approve specific projects and actions. The heads of public enterprises are seldom chief executives in the pure sense; like most public-sector managers (except elected chief executives like mayors, governors, and the president) they work within a larger hierarchical structure.

In practice, government control over public enterprises has significant limits. In any organization, including government, superiors do not have perfect control over subordinates. From this point of view, the boards that managed the three public companies we studied were not very effective mechanisms for controlling the behavior of these organizations. Only when an insider was chairman (for example, Wagner at TVA) did they play a significant management role. And in these cases the parent government was still left with the problem of how to control the board. In most other instances board members have simply not had the time, the expertise, or the authority to keep the long-service professionals in the ranks from going their own way. As outsiders, board members have often been perceived as not sharing the organization's traditional values and goals. Unfamiliar with the people they manage, they are often treated as annoyances to be tolerated — or, if need by, isolated by those they nominally supervise.[9] Boards can sometimes be used to transmit orders

from the larger political system—disputes over board membership in Los Angeles in the 1930s and 1940s indicated this. But as
mechanisms through which outsiders can influence an organization, their manipulability and effectiveness will be highly variable.

The manager of a public company (or of any other government
unit, for that matter) may also have organized constituency support. This can make it more costly for an elected chief executive
to try to discipline and control the company. TVA, for example,
worked with the representatives from its region to get Congress to
pass legislation (later vetoed) that would have provided federal
subsidies for its pollution control spending. Political superiors
also may find the discharge or resignation of a senior manager an
embarrassing admission of failure, and may find it difficult to
replace him given civil service restrictions, salary limits, and so
forth. This also strengthens the manager's position. In sum, it is
not hard to understand the difficulties President Kennedy had in
trying unsuccessfully to get TVA to change the location of a proposed power plant, or the difficulties the Los Angeles City Council had in getting the DWP to renegotiate the Navajo plant contracts. In a different political environment and organizational
context, Hydro seems noticeably more responsive to its line superiors, at least on some issues. Yet even here, concerns over the
company's system expansion policies were not translated into an
immediate organizational response.

Perhaps out of recognition that such executive authority is
likely to be imperfect, the public companies we studied were subject to a variety of other specific controls. The Ontario government in effect controls major investment by Hydro and approves
all borrowing. The Los Angeles City Council approves DWP rates
and contracts. Yet these agencies have also on occasion been exempt from regulatory requirements that apply to private companies. Until recently, Hydro and TVA were not subject to rate
review mechanisms, and TVA had long been exempt from state
pollution control laws; even the LADWP was initially exempt
from LAAPCD jurisdiction. From our cases, it seems quite clear
that public organizations that are exempted from formal regulatory controls cannot be counted on to achieve the same ends on
their own initiative. Such exemptions should be granted only with
the greatest of care.

Even where public companies are subject to such controls,
some critics have argued that they are likely to be harder to regulate than private companies because they have superior political

savvy, more access to top policy makers, and so on. This argument implies that public companies will be less responsive — or at least less easily coerced — than their private counterparts.[10]

Our cases do not support such a generalization. The range of behavior we observed in the public and private sectors was very broad. The extent to which any company was responsive — both on given issues and as a matter of strategy — was similarly varied. So was the extent to which regulatory and political institutions facilitated or restricted control by outsiders. The mere fact of public or private ownership by itself does not tell us very much about the kind of behavior to expect. This is simply because such a classification does not tell us enough about those internal and external features of an organization and its situation that shape its behavior.[11]

In the area of rates, there does at first seem to be an obvious difference between public and private companies: all the public companies in our study tended to sell power at rates substantially below those of neighboring private utilities. Yet all also enjoyed tax and financing advantages, such as property tax exemptions, the ability to issue tax-free bonds at favorable rates, and exemptions from other state and federal corporate taxes. Given these differences in financial circumstances, public companies could be less efficient managerially and still charge lower rates.

Public power does appear to have helped hold down the costs of power in a different way, however — among both public and private utilities. The existence of alternatives provides a disciplining force for organizations in both sectors. The competition is not always healthy — as, for instance, when public or private companies invest substantial resources in political campaigning. Yet the cases do suggest that the existence of an alternative helps provide just the sort of credible threat to survival that keeps managers and their organizations working hard.

The relationship between the geographic scope of a public organization and the scope of the government that controls it seems to be one important determinant of the costs of imposing penalties on the organization. When these closely match, and when most citizens of the political unit are affected by the enterprise, the company's behavior is more likely to become a focus of political attention. The existing political parties are more likely to take an interest in its activities. This makes it easier for outsiders to act because they have a ready-made vehicle for expressing their concerns.

Ontario Hydro, for example, serves its entire province. Its decisions have consequently been of continuing concern to the governing Conservative Party, especially since the opposition always stands ready to make an issue of Hydro's behavior. In contrast, TVA serves only a small part of the nation. Political action to change its behavior can be very costly. Most members of Congress have little stake in TVA's choices, unless an issue takes on national symbolic value (for example, the Dixon-Yates controversy). Hence, it is quite difficult for someone concerned with the utility's behavior—even another federal agency or the president himself—to mobilize the sort of national coalition that would be required to constrain it.

On the other hand, when a company serves an area larger than its supervising government's jurisdiction, various citizens will face quite different costs in influencing the organization. As might be expected, those who faced lower costs tended to have a larger impact. The Los Angeles Department of Water and Power has participated in the construction of several large and controversial coal-fired power plants outside Los Angeles, while it has won architectural awards for substation landscaping within the city.

So far, we have been considering the factors influencing the costs and benefits to outsiders of imposing their views on an organization. But one other external factor must be considered—namely, the costs to the organization itself of complying with outside demands. LADWP found it easier to comply with clean-fuel regulations than did TVA, for example, because regional fuel-price variations made the latter heavily dependent on coal instead of oil or natural gas. One reason TVA resisted scrubbers so hard was because of the costs of installing them on a large, and often old, generating system. Resource availability and technology, which determine these costs, were thus clearly relevant.

Our cases also show that technological possibilities and costs were quite uncertain, especially with regard to new devices and approaches. Prototype units often malfunctioned or behaved in surprising ways. Examples are the slagging problems in the boilers at TVA's Cumberland plant, Southern's problems with pressurized boilers, and PG&E's problems with the Pittsburg 7 spray modules. Companies constantly had to decide how far they were willing to try to push new technology and what risks they would take. Their knowledge of these possibilities was hardly systematic, as the history of NO_x control at Scattergood 3 indicates.

Not every organization was or perceived itself to be tightly constrained by cost, as Hydro's investment in CANDU and the LADWP's underground substations suggest. Cost-consciousness was thus in part a matter of regulatory constraint and the larger strategic picture. What appeared to be cheap or expensive to each organization depended heavily on their expectations, which changed over time. Decision rules and standard operating procedures adjusted to new circumstances; what had once appeared to be an enormous and inappropriate burden could begin to seem normal and routine. Particulate controls are a good example. Once upon a time, several utilities in our study controlled particulates with crude mechanical collectors simply in order to protect equipment within the plant. Now most take for granted the need for high-efficiency precipitators designed to keep down emissions under virtually all operating conditions. Such costs are now planned for, and routinely incorporated into, engineering decision rules. Up to a point, they no longer seem unreasonable, unexpected, or impossible to bear, whereas twenty years ago they would clearly have been seen as all three.

Strategy, Structure, and Organizational Behavior

The clear impact of externally determined consequences on the actions of these organizations should not lead us to misread the evidence. Variations in external consequences do not explain why the Southern Company was more willing and able to locate low-sulfur coal than TVA, nor Southern's initiatives in developing solvent refining. External considerations were relevant to PG&E's effort to avoid regulatory confrontation at Pittsburg 7, just as they were in the LADWP's choice to force a confrontation over Scattergood 3. But in neither case was the chosen option the only one available, or even necessarily the one most likely to succeed.

External consequences are also insufficient to explain Boston Edison's scrubber research and the innovative tower design on the Plymouth-Holbrook line. The same can be said of many other examples: Ontario Hydro's pursuit of CANDU, TVA's policy of pioneering larger-sized generating units, and PG&E's initiative in proposing a statewide undergrounding policy. In none of these cases did the companies simply "do what they had to." The world was too imperfectly coercive for that.

All the characteristics of reality discussed in Chapter 2 were repeatedly evident in our studies: multidimensionality, ambiguity, uncertainty, novelty, and so on. The companies we studied could not be sure what the consequences of any action would be. The technology was often uncertain and the behavior of other actors in the system was not fully predictable. The LADWP could not be sure whether the APCD would back down on Scattergood 3. Southern could not predict to what extent various state agencies and the EPA might be persuaded to change their rules in response to the company's efforts. Was Boston Edison legally prevented from building a transmission line through Sudbury or not? What would it have taken for PG&E to convince the AEC to accept the Point Arena site, and, prior to further studies, what was the likelihood that persuasive evidence could be found? Novelty only exacerbated this unpredictability. How would a new agency like the Coastal Zone Commission behave? What effect would increased public concern over energy prices have on state regulatory authorities?

The consequences of any one decision were very complex and difficult to analyze. When Robert Gerdes had to decide what PG&E would do about the cloud at Moss Landing, he had to worry about such matters as costs, technical possibilities, local community relations, setting a precedent for other counties, and internal morale. Boston Edison's choices about transmission lines, TVA's decisions on strip-mine reclamation requirements, and Hydro's attempt to use Canadian generator manufacturers were fraught with similar complexities.

Multidimensional, uncertain outcomes can only be compared, even in theory, by using some set of preferences in order to evaluate alternative results.[12] The notion that there is one best, objectively optimal strategy is in general not defensible, or indeed even conceptually definable, apart from someone's preferences. There is no objective or scientific basis on which TVA's management could evaluate lower prices in comparison to organizational growth, or in comparison to preserving eastern Kentucky coal land from despoliation.

In the real world, moreover, these problems are far too subtle and complex to be solved by formal mathematical analysis. Instead, the companies approached them by relying on habit, in what can perhaps be best characterized as a "strategy-governed" manner. Coal purchasing at TVA, like everything else, was oriented to minimizing the costs of power. TVA played the spot market and fostered price competition to bring down these costs. It was not about to look for the kind of long-term, high-cost arrangements that allowed Southern to obtain low-sulfur coal.

The top management at PG&E, in contrast, tried very hard to avoid public-relations or regulatory difficulties. The lawyers who wanted to challenge the testimony of federal Fish and Wildlife officials over the Pittsburg 7 cooling system did not do so; compromise and compliance were assiduously pursued. One option after another was developed and proposed in order to get the project approved. To characterize such behavior as entirely the result of external coercion is to ignore the role of creativity and judgment, of strategy setting and behavior shaping, that management is paid for.

Many additional examples could be cited: TVA's operational control plans, Hydro's citizen-participation exercises on transmission-line routing, the 800-kilovolt line from Los Angeles to Bonneville, and so on. All were strategic, internally determined choices. In no case was the response "required" by "external constraints," on pain of death and disaster. Indeed, some of these policies were pursued in the face of substantial externally imposed difficulties.

Organizational *strategy* then, is one important guide to an organization's choices in the face of external constraints. Different organizations have different priorities—different goals they are determined to reach, different situations they judge intolerable, different courses of action that they routinely follow. These priorities and reactions—shaped by the historical experience of the organization and the particular views and inclinations of its top managers—become incorporated in the thinking of the organization's members and in the structures it develops for day-to-day decision making.

Thus, Pacific Gas and Electric, threatened throughout its history by governmental infringements of its territory, has adopted a strategy of seeking to co-opt its critics, so that they will not become hostile voters in ownership referendums. Ontario Hydro, established to reduce provincial dependence on United States energy resources, has responded by emphasizing system reliability, system expansion, and self-sufficient technologies. Having successfully justified its right to exist on the basis of its low costs, TVA has continued to emphasize low rates with missionary zeal. And the Southern Company, a network of state companies, still maintains a political style that emphasizes getting acquainted with regulators in each state. In each case, historical precedents going back to the company's founding days have played a strong role in shaping today's decisions.

However important external circumstances are, we should not emphasize their causal role unduly. In part, what is important about them is to be found in the responses that powerful managers have made to them: it is from their choices that history's lessons have been formed. Thus, Pacific Gas and Electric's attitude toward its critics was shaped by Robert Gerdes, who played an influential role in the company from the 1930s until the 1970. TVA's commitment to low costs reflects the leadership of David Lilienthal, one of its first directors, and of G. O. Wessenauer, who managed the company's power affairs from the early 1940s until 1970. And Southern's sensitivity to local politics seems due in no small part to the concern of Thomas Martin, the system's godfather.

In addition to strategy, however, organizational *structure* plays a strong role in determining how choices are made. Task assignments, the size and composition of functional groups, the communication channels, and the control and incentive system all affect corporate choices.

Strategy and structure are closely interdependent. As Alfred Chandler has emphasized, structural changes are often made to implement changes in strategy.[13] To cope with public-power threats, PG&E expanded its legal staff; to expedite new plant construction, Ontario Hydro established a project management system in engineering. But as Joseph Bower has stressed, structural features tend to have behavioral consequences.[14] TVA's Division of Health and Safety, originally established to deal with problems like malaria, pioneered in the development of "operational" controls for sulfur dioxide; Southern's research department made the company a leader in experimentation with solvent coal refining.

The relationship between strategy and structure is both elastic and reciprocal. In successful organizations the two are complementary, in part because a range of strategies is typically compatible with a given structure, just as various structures can support the same strategy. When the two conflict, change can occur in either direction. But in the short run, the existing structure tends to influence behavior so that we need to take a closer look at the internal factors that influence an organization's choices.

The preferences of top managers — particularly those top managers with strong influence — are among the most important of these internal factors. The cases clearly show that in some circumstances the top managers of these organizations had the kinds of controls and loyalty that allowed them to impose their will on the notice-plan-decide-implement cycle. When this occurred, their organizations occasionally exhibited apparently inconsistent behavior from issue to issue, depending on the views of their leaders. For example, PG&E generally tried to avoid confrontations with environmental regulators, yet management's desire to avoid using scarce inland water for cooling nuclear plants led to a series of epic nuclear plant siting battles. Similarly, Harold Smith's desire for independence from United States power led Hydro to cooperate more with public pressure about transmission-line routing or air pollution control than with efforts to limit its overall expansion program.

Even where managers did not have the strongest possible control, persistence, personal expertise, and formal authority on occasion allowed them to have a major impact. Charles Avila at Boston Edison, for instance, hired different architect/engineers and built a new generating plant for less than $90 per kilowatt, versus $140 for the company's previous unit—even though the operators said it couldn't be done. Managers also controlled the decisions that they themselves made. Floyd Goss at LADWP, for example, was able to reverse his own previously announced strategy and build a fossil-fuel unit within the Los Angeles basin because he personally made major investment decisions.

The fact that managers have some discretion does not mean they are free of externally imposed consequences. Robert Gerdes could commit PG&E's formidable resources to the battle over the Mendocino site. But he could not force the Geological Survey or the AEC to accept the proposal. For all of Harold Smith's commitment to CANDU, Hydro ultimately was forced to defer construction of some planned nuclear plants. Yet given the organizational discretion we have described, the personal views of powerful or influential members can be crucial. And this power and influence typically flowed from both the individual's personal characteristics and his position within the organization's structure.

On the other hand, internal structures can create situations that limit top management's discretion. Aubrey Wagner had great difficulty getting TVA to clean up its Kingston plant. Top-management concern was not sufficient to determine an organization's behavior when this management had only weak controls and when subordinates were deeply committed to other points of view.

This last example raises a key question. What features of an organization allow top management to impose its will successfully? Why was Robert Gerdes at PG&E more effective in getting his engineers to clean up NO_x emissions at Moss Landing than was Aubrey Wagner in inducing his to install precipitators?

One part of the explanation is the different roles managers played in promotion decisions well down the bureaucratic ladder. A "deep" control system convinces those at lower levels that pleasing top management is important, thus weakening the potentially competing incentives offered to them by middle managers, group loyalty, or whatever. In contrast, when personnel decisions are decentralized, as they were for many years at TVA, it became much more difficult for the top to influence either the planning or the implementation process. There was very little Wagner could do about the slowness with which an acceptable precipitator or upgrading program was prepared. Strict civil service systems may be even more troublesome in this regard. Promotion-by-exam and elaborate procedural safeguards against any discipline do not encourage managerial control. Under these circumstances, what incentives do employees have to work hard or well?

Deep control systems are not easy to operate in the best of circumstances. Managers may not in fact be able to know or learn enough about the performance and capabilities of all the relevant candidates for many different positions. Even those who have grown up in the organization will have only limited knowledge, which then may be reflected in a tendency to choose those whom they know and trust. With the best of intentions, fortuitous contacts between the top and the middle can have a strong influence on promotions. As a result, in companies with strong control systems, many believe that direct and often accidental acquaintance with top management can be critical to success. Career histories in PG&E and Boston Edison suggest that there is some basis for this viewpoint. Those who advance are often perceived as having been "lucky" or "in the right place at the right time" by others in the company.

For these reasons, especially in large organizations, top management was heavily dependent on the conscientiousness and energy of middle management for accomplishing its goals. Top managers could not do everything, track all decisions, distribute all rewards by themselves. They required effective incentives or personal loyalty, or both, with respect to the "barons" of the organization. Otherwise, as Harold Smith and G. O. Wessenauer demonstrated, those in the "middle" could dominate not only their own groups, but the behavior of the organization as a whole when their group played a key role in that activity.

Central to being able to offer incentives to such "barons" was the existence of a general management structure large enough to offer positions for these individuals to aspire to.[15] What incentives could Wagner offer to Wessenauer? In contrast, there were many possibilities opened to a vice-president of engineering at a company like PG&E. It also helped, especially at top level, if management was willing to redefine the exact set of slots available to suit the talents of the individuals available. In this regard, the private companies in our study were more flexible than their public counterparts. At PG&E, Southern, and Edison in recent years the set of vice-presidential-level jobs has been revised with some frequency. In the process, group leaders were offered the lure that room could and would be made for them at the top if they performed appropriately. Out of such positions a general management *team* could be formed, reducing the burden placed on a single top manager to establish system policy.

Because of the limited control available to any top manager, personally loyal subordinates, with compatible perspectives, could be critical.[16] We noted several companies where there were such relationships. At Hydro, key engineering jobs have gone to Bill Morrison and Lorne McConnell, men who were involved in the development of CANDU along with Harold Smith and who appear to be loyal to him. At PG&E, lawyers and civil engineers in senior positions each have a network of colleagues throughout the organization whom they can count on. And at Southern, president Alvin Vogtle strengthened his control over engineering decisions, and advance planning in general, by putting a group of outsiders with compatible perspectives—Clyde Lilly, Bill Lalor, Bill Reed, and Bill Harrison—in command at Southern Services.

Such practices can easily be perceived as performance-discouraging cronyism unless top management selects people who are capable, and who are seen as deserving by those further down in the organization. It also must be clear that ample advancement opportunities remain for those who are not old friends but who are equally able and willing.

How is top management to break down group loyalties and foster a broader identification with the organization as a whole among its middle-management team? One of the most interesting mechanisms for achieving such broader perspectives is to encourage "diagonal" mobility, where people are promoted to head units or activities for which they have not been trained and in which they have not previously worked. An organization that relies on "straight-ahead" advancement is more likely to produce unit heads with a strong identification with their unit and a belief in the value of its particular past functions. Unit members have a strong incentive to foster the unit's bureaucratic interests, in order to enhance its growth and their own career prospects. In contrast, diagonal mobility helps create different incentives and provides different experiences more conducive to a "company-oriented" view.[17] The rising manager becomes familiar with multiple perspectives, and perhaps comes to accept policies and procedures as means and not ends. Such personnel patterns have been characteristic of PG&E and of Hydro's Engineering Branch, and have become far more frequent in Boston Edison in recent years.

These patterns tend to reinforce a more open-minded management style. Group leaders who have come from elsewhere know they are not the best technical experts in their area. They have to act less authoritatively. As conduits for ideas and suggestions, and as participants in corporate decision making, they are not constantly able to impose their own strong technical commitments (prejudices).

Diagonal mobility could have an adverse impact on the ability of managers to exercise technical control over their own groups. In the absence of conscientious subordinates, it could be difficult for inexpert supervisors to know whether or not what they are told is accurate. Ironically, top managers were the most expert in the areas in which they had worked. In these same areas they also often had the most loyalty from subordinates, and hence the least need to exercise control over them.

Managers who were technically competent exercised on some occasions overly detailed supervision, stifling initiative and slowing the pace of decision making. We encountered one case of a chief electrical engineer who insisted on signing all the drawings personally to check for correctness — creating a serious bottleneck. There is a fine line between appropriate control and a counterproductive refusal to give up former responsibilities when one moves to a higher position.

The cases make it quite clear that even the most forceful managers, with the most loyal and well-controlled subordinates, are heavily dependent on the organization they manage for noticing, planning, and implementing. The way the organization functions clearly depends on the set of groups and individuals within it. In the long run, group characteristics themselves evolve in response to changing external circumstances and internal dynamics. Yet, in the short run, we have repeatedly seen the importance of group characteristics such as size, expertise, and access to top management in determining what occurs.

The cases amply confirm the argument that a group must either *do the work* or *influence those who do the work* in order to have an impact on organizational behavior. If a group participates in the process, its views will be significant; otherwise, they may be ignored. Consider the differential participation in planning and decision making of power plant operators, who generally advocate building more reliable plants. These differences help explain why Hydro's plants did not have the same level of reliability as, say, those built by Boston Edison. The operators in Hydro reported to regional managers concerned mainly with marketing. Outside the Engineering Branch, they were cut off from the design process. In contrast, Boston Edison's engineering group was not large, and much design work was done outside. The operators were numerous and well represented at senior levels in the company. With aggressive, independent leadership, the operators were able to have a major impact on plant design.

The *length*, *directness*, and *accuracy* of communication channels also play a major role in a group's ability to have an impact. Operators at TVA were so far down in the Office of Power that they could not get a hearing on some critical design issues; TVA's fossil-fuel plants also turned out to be relatively unreliable. Reporting through intermediaries who disagreed with them, the operators' views were not vigorously advocated. In contrast, Government Affairs at PG&E (as represented by Kenneth Diercks) often had direct access to the very top of the company and a clear ability to get a hearing. Some in the company see this access as clearly related to certain key decisions.

The cases also suggest that a group's *size* and its *compatibility* with top management are related to its impact on decisions. Size helps ensure that a group has the resources available to do extra work — especially in a crisis. The compatibility of its views with top management's perspectives makes it more likely that it will be asked to do that work. These phenomena were clearly reflected, for example, in the major role the PG&E Law Department has played in corporate planning and in implementing certain kinds of decisions — which helps explain the company's flexible, negotiation-oriented stance. In contrast, the small legal group at the LADWP has had relatively little impact. The problems raised by its limited resources are compounded by the fact that in certain areas its loyalties are ambiguous, since its members work directly for the city attorney. Boston Edison's legal group is small, whereas its public-relations group is large and headed by individuals trusted by top management — thus giving the latter group substantial influence.

In these matters, the aggressiveness of group leaders and the coherence and unity of the groups they led clearly increased their ability to carry out a consistent policy when they did the work or to impose their will on others. The story of Wessenauer and the Office of Power at TVA is a long series of examples that confirm this principle, as is the role of Harold Smith at Hydro, and that of the leaders of plant operations at Edison. The cases confirm that in certain decision situations, stubbornness, energy, aggressiveness, personality, and respect from others will tend to swing the process. Other participants will get tired, be intimidated or convinced, not care so deeply, or have other pressing business. Thus, these stories imply that structure alone does not tell all about an organization's strategy. There is an important element that can only be explained in terms of interpersonal influence and personality — phenomena that are much less systematic from a scientific perspective.

Even some of the most forceful players we have seen have been overruled on occasion, however. In some cases there was a clear role of *expertise* in such decisions.[18] One recalls O.M. Derryberry holding up the picture of the lung at the TVA board meeting and invoking his medical expertise on the side of pollution control. Similarly, in Edison's fight over the Sudbury transmission line, the matter became defined as a legal one and the lawyers insisted on their predominant role.

This observation suggests an interesting corollary — namely, that effective control by the top is enhanced when it is not dependent on any one group for all planning and suggestions. Having multiple and overlapping centers of expertise allows the top to choose among a variety of suggestions. Conversely, being in a monopoly position, where a particular group always does certain work, generally strengthens the role of this group. Thus, the influence of the engineering people at Southern Company Services was limited by the existence of centers of engineering expertise in the operating companies. These could take different positions on design issues related to operational concerns like cooling tower fill material, and pressurized versus balanced draft boilers.

We have also seen repeatedly how a group's positions are influenced by the training and responsibilities of its members. Having been run by engineers with a special interest in transmission problems, the LADWP, with relatively small generating units, has twice constructed the nation's longest and highest-voltage transmission line. PG&E, where civil engineers play a major role, has more hydro power than other comparable companies and throughout the 1950s and 1960s built noticeably smaller fossil-fuel generation units than other companies its size, such as TVA. And surely the scientific background of Southern's research group, together with its access to top management, has been critical to the development of that company's solvent-refined coal research program.

The role of groups also reveals some clear examples of the way in which structural changes can lead to strategic initiatives. The research and environment group at Southern appears to have surprised management by the vigor of its entrepreneurial efforts. Harold Smith apparently did not expect the "Amenities Committee" to recommend spending so much on more attractive transmission towers. And at PG&E at one point, the top management was described by one observer as "stunned" by the recommendations of a task force charged with planning new generating capacity. In each case, a new bureaucratic entity (a permanent unit or committee), once established, began to do more than anticipated.

Like individual managers, groups both respond to and are constrained by external consequences. TVA's Office of Power could delay planning new particulate controls, but eventually it had to go along with meeting externally imposed standards. Conversely, Southern's fuel group was apparently more than willing to search the globe for low-sulfur coal. But the need and opportunity to do so were the result of actions by air pollution control authorities.

Group influence takes on special characteristics in an organization with weak controls and substantial delegation and decentralization. In such a context, those who do the work may shape events more than those who have influence with the top, because the top itself has such little power. A lack of coherence and consistency may be evident in such an organization's behavior. Different perspectives and decision rules will be brought to bear on different decisions.

Thus at the LADWP the architects believed it appropriate to respond to the neighborhood's aesthetic concerns, and they exercised their technical skills in designing attractive substations. In contrast, the transmission-line engineers often designed cost-minimizing, straight line routes, provoking much public protest in the process. Similarly, in the 1960s the mechanical engineers at Boston Edison pushed ahead with scrubber research, while the general counsel engaged the company in a fight over transmission lines. Initiatives from some groups got TVA started on plume monitoring and scrubber research, whereas other parts of the organization simultaneously opposed pollution control requirements.

Given the tasks that utilities perform, organizations with weak controls and strong groups still find it necessary to ensure some internal coordination. This tends to produce intergroup bargaining in which the power of one unit to impose costs on another is critical. In such a context, an apparent monopoly of relevant expertise can give a group a veto position. As a result, any group that wants to prevent others from obtaining control must ensure that no one else obtains such a monopoly. This can be done by building parallel skills or by threatening to use outside suppliers, both of which the TVA Office of Power did on occasion. It built up its own air pollution expertise so as not to be overly dependent on Health and Safety. It threatened to go outside the company for engineering services. This helped give it enough leverage to impose some coherence on organizational strategy.

Whether an organization's policy was determined by strong top management, or by bargaining among groups in the context of a weak control system, the cases suggest an interesting tendency to produce "extreme" outcomes. In a two-party electoral system, compromise and middle-of-the-road positions are typical outcomes.[19] In organizations, in contrast, often one group wins and the others lose. Top managers with strong controls have less reason than elected political leaders to try to please everyone. In contrast, with weak controls, different issues will be decided by different groups, often with distinct and well-developed viewpoints. Both these situations help produce sharply defined choices.

Thus, TVA's early precipitators were underdesigned not by a little but by a lot—whereas its new coal-fired generating units were repeatedly the largest in the world. Boston Edison's early plants reflected a set of decisions designed to make them easier to operate. Certain Hydro plants, in contrast, have forced outage rates that are twice the North American average. There are many other examples in the cases: Hydro's commitment to CANDU; the LADWP's transmission lines; TVA's decision to go all nuclear; the large change in Edison's approach to transmission-line siting.

This generalization puts some of the internal contrasts in company policy in a larger context. When top management at PG&E wanted a course of action that responded to external complaints, the organization could produce a strong commitment to cleanup, as over NO_x at Moss Landing. But when top management stuck to a strategy in the face of protest, the organization was equally energetic in its resistance to change, as at Bodega Head or Mendocino. In both cases, strong controls led to "extreme" outcomes.

Interestingly, it is harder to find such examples for the Southern Company, in part because its collegial decision processes produce bargaining situations that resemble normal political dynamics. This, in turn, leads to compromise choices.

In summary, the cases reveal that some of the apparent intra-company inconsistency in behavior reflects the particular commitments of top management under circumstances where strong controls and loyal subordinates allow top management to impose its will on the organization. Management involvement in personnel decisions down the line and patterns of diagonal mobility help reinforce such control and loyalty. In other cases, weak controls and the impact of varied group perspectives account for such inconsistency. Groups that are large, expert, and that are trusted by top management wind up doing the work in an organization — or influencing those who do the work — and thus have an impact on what occurs. Structure aside, there is also a substantial role for powerful personalities to influence the process of organizational decision making. The result of all these "aggregation processes" is often an "extreme outcome" — a commitment by the organization to one or another well-differentiated strategy.

The Evolution of Organizational Structure

What determines the structure of an organization in the long run? To what extent is it a chosen solution to implementing the organization's strategic objectives and to what extent does current structure influence future evolutionary directions in a less planned manner? In particular, what are the structural prerequisites of positively responsive behavior, and under what circumstances will they tend to develop?

An organization's structure is itself an implicit problem-solving strategy. It provides one answer to the problem of how to organize the firm's human resources. Like any decision rule it tends to have a certain longevity; otherwise, it would not be serving its function, which is to avoid the costs involved in continually reorganizing the members to deal with each new problem. Given the role of habits of mind in all decision making, the burden of proof tends to be on those who would change established practices.

Such continuity reflects structural as well as intellectual processes. Those to whom the current structure gives status and influence tend to try to maintain it. Given such support for the status quo, maladaptive features of an organization can persist as long as some disaster does not occur.[20] Without a major crisis as a focal point, an interesting proposal for a long range planning unit at PG&E, for example, took years to implement.

Given such dynamics, some of the organization's structural features may reflect circumstances at the time of the organization's founding. TVA still struggles with a pattern of decentralization that has its origins in the disagreements of the original board members more than forty years ago. At Southern, the use of outside law firms as corporate counsels and as a source of chief executives reflects a pattern established by Tom Martin when he helped found the Alabama Power Company. At the LADWP electrical engineers have run the power system since it was a scheme in the mind of young Ezra Scattergood.

Yet change does occur. As new demands are made on the organization, some groups grow and flourish. We would argue that many of the same factors that affect task assignments in the short run also influence the evolution of group structure in the long run. Similar processes are at work. Indeed, they are literally the same processes, when growth comes gradually through a series of task-assignment decisions.

Influences on such growth may include the perceived competence of a group and its leader, aggressiveness, the possession of apparently relevant expertise, trust by the top, and compatibility between a group's perspectives and top management's strategic objectives. Having been brought in by Tom Black, Robert Gerdes was able to lead PG&E's lawyers to a major role in the company at a time when the threat of public power made their negotiation and litigation skills seem especially relevant. Similarly, under the leadership of Wessenauer and Kampmaier, the Office of Power at TVA came into prominence after World War II; it organized the breakneck expansion of the power system at a time when chairman Herbert Vogel was quite unsympathetic to nonpower activities.

Groups can grow even if they lack exceptional leaders when they are part of top management's plan for responding to new circumstances. The Southern Company's services and engineering affiliate, Southern Company Services, appears to be going through a steady and carefully designed expansion in influence as it is enlarged to handle the rapid growth and increasingly complex technical needs of the four-state system. The evolution of the Concept Group at Hydro (now a series of units) reflects a similar pattern. So does the process by which TVA's top management progressively expanded the bureaucratic basis of the agency's air quality program as external demands for action in this area increased.

When there is competition for the new role among several groups, not all of them will be successful. PG&E's environmental group could not seem to find any policy-making role left for it to fill, given what other outside-oriented groups had already taken on. And Hydro's lawyers saw little that they could contribute to regulatory relations given the Concept Department's responsibilities in this area.

Even in a hierarchical organization, where top management must ratify structural changes, the initiative for change may come from further down. For example, the director of Hydro's public-relations activities interested the Engineering Branch in involving his people in the planning process, as demands for public participation in that process grew. He increased his group's responsibility, influence, and size as a result.

Given the role of such internal initiatives in structural and hence behavioral change, an organization's response to external pressure may depend on whether or not there are internal groups who will seize the opportunity such pressure affords to try to grow in size and influence. TVA built high stacks very early under the influence of the diffusion modeling and monitoring of its Division of Health and Safety. The Division pushed air pollution activities at a time when decreased dam building meant that its malaria-control functions were diminishing. Hydro's Research Division, in contrast, had other secure and expanding activities and never took the initiative in developing an ambitious air quality monitoring program.

All these changes in internal arrangements involved disruption, protests, concern from members, and the need for top management to expend time and effort. Because small changes have lower costs than big ones, there was a tendency to accomplish large changes through a series of intermediary moves. Sometimes this was by conscious design and sometimes large changes were resisted until small ones proved inadequate. The increased scope of the Engineering Branch at Hydro occurred step by step, as did its structural transformation. The same can be said for the reorganization of fossil-fuel and nuclear operations at Boston Edison.

Small changes can be easy to implement, especially when they involve only a few people, so that they can be made even in the absence of a major problem. The reshuffling of vice-president-level tasks and slots in the three private companies in recent years took place without a provoking "crisis."

Deciding when a problem was sufficiently serious to warrant costly action depended in part upon the strategy of the organization and the goals of its leaders. That is, it depended on what people cared about.[21] To Ontario Hydro, buying power or fuel outside its system — especially from the United States — was a major problem because of its commitment to national and provincial energy independence. In contrast TVA and the LADWP happily brought power from other systems when it was cheap, Southern bought coal from South Africa, and PG&E tried desperately to buy natural gas from Canada. For them such purchases were not a problem because energy independence was not an organizational goal.

Since management has sometimes been responsible for the current strategy and structure, it may take very clear evidence before it is convinced that it has made a mistake and that a genuine problem has arisen. PG&E's persistence on coastal nuclear sites, the LADWP's difficulties with Scattergood, and Edison's delays with its first Sudbury line are all examples of this insensitivity.

As a result, major changes in structure and policy often involved a change in top management.[22] This may be the only way, in practice, to change the way in which problems are analyzed and resolved. Some suggested, for example, that PG&E's withdrawal from Bodega was facilitated by a change of chief executives. Phillips, Mulloy, and now Winnard are credited with providing new directions at the LADWP. Without the commitments of their predecessors, new managers may find it easier to decide that changes in direction are necessary. The processes by which chief executives are chosen, therefore, may play a major role in determining how an organization evolves. On the other hand, in an organization with a weak control system, changing the chief executive might not affect outcomes very much, unless the new team is able to develop the leadership and control previously lacking.

In most of the cases we have considered, top managers were chosen by their predecessors. Ironically, the cases suggest that people may be able to perceive the kind of leadership that new situations require, even when they are not able to offer it themselves. Floyd Goss (who made the Scattergood decision) chose John Mulloy at the LADWP. Tom Dignan of Boston Edison chose Charles Avila and Tom Galligan, his two successors.

Companies vary substantially in their recruitment practices. Some are much more willing and able than others to bring in people at senior levels. In some companies, promising young men are moved around and "groomed," as Tom Galligan apparently was at Boston Edison. In others, the next president tends to be a senior vice-president a few years younger than his retired (or deceased) predecessor. Clearly, the pace of organizational change will be influenced by such practices. Indeed, in several cases in the public companies we studied, new top managers were not picked by their predecessors but came in from outside at the behest of political superiors or a politically chosen board. And in such cases (Winnard at the LADWP, Herbert Vogel and now David Freeman at TVA), significant policy changes followed.

The existing structure also influences the succession process through its impact on the availability of senior executives with various skills and perspectives. Thus, it seems likely that for the next decade or two, PG&E will be led by a combination of lawyers and civil engineers.

When an organization is in trouble, greater attention is paid to the succession problem and, hence, a better job is done in making such a choice. Better people are attracted to more challenging jobs. Paradoxically, therefore, difficulty and conflict can raise the quality of the pool of candidates that an organization can draw upon for its top managers. A number of those we talked to commented on the fact that it had once been very hard to attract talented younger people to the utility industry. But recent controversy had the side benefit of making the business seem more interesting to potential candidates.

The cases also suggest that for several reasons, once an organization has experienced structural change, it is likely to continue to do so. The development of the Concept Group at Hydro suggests one explanation for this pattern — namely, the relationship between change and the presence of strong top management. What other source of initiative is there to overcome the resistance to change? This means that once change occurs, it is likely to occur again. Change itself indicates that someone in the organization (in Hydro's case, Harold Smith) has the power to impose change and the will to pay the costs that change involves. Note, too, that by creating a more fluid structure, management may be increasing its power by increasing its ability to reward middle managers.

Once structural change occurs it becomes easier to do it again; the process becomes familiar and less threatening. Everyone at PG&E, for example, is used to realignments among management. In addition, the costs are lower after the first experience, since people are likely to be less attached to the new arrangements simply because they have not existed for so long. Thus, change tends to become self-perpetuating.

The extent to which any one structural change is associated

with further structural changes also reflects the fact that management tends to develop a "meta" strategy for dealing with various kinds of crises. When outcomes are unsatisfactory, a manager can do many different things: move existing people around, bring in new people from outside, create *ad hoc* groups or task forces, issue new policy directives, alter personnel practices, or change the organization's structure. The decision rules that evolve to guide such choices tend to reflect and be reflected in past experience. In some companies, like PG&E, reorganization is an accepted technique for dealing with certain kinds of situations. In others, ingrained traditions, weak control systems, and strong groups make managers unable or unwilling to think about changing organizational structure.

When the external world allows an organization to do almost anything and still survive and grow, there is little incentive on anyone's part to produce coordinated and effective behavior. Integration and strong controls require hard work. The rewards (both to leaders and members) of such work may not be evident when there is no threat of organizational failure. Indeed, several organizations in our study have, for long periods of time, functioned in contexts that permitted this kind of lax internal control.

Recent events and pressures have brought another evolutionary swing to all these organizations, however. New managers and new structures are stimulating noticeably different behavior as they evolve steadily in a "responsive" direction, in terms of both strategy and structure. We need to examine in more detail what such a structure involves, and when and how it develops—an important question in the context of our overall inquiry.

11

Managing the Responsive Organization

It is certainly in society's interest to have positively responsive organizations; but under what circumstances is it in the interests of a manager and an organization to be positively responsive?[1] How can such an organization be created?

Many of the internal characteristics that facilitate responsive behavior are in fact characteristic of any well-managed organization, regardless of its strategy. This leads to an interesting conclusion. A society that wants to be able to influence the behavior of its organizations has an interest, at a minimum, in having them well managed. Well-managed organizations are easier to regulate because they are more aware of outside consequences and calculate more carefully. Their behavior is more predictable and it can be influenced by well-fashioned incentives. They are better able to solve difficult problems and to alter their own behavior when they decide to do so. What leads a manager to create the kind of well-managed organization that behaves in a responsive manner?

Choice of a Strategy

Many policies are possible for a regulated organization. These range from active resistance to active cooperation. Having chosen to resist, a company can either confront an agency directly, or try to go around it through the courts or the political process. It can try to influence the early stages — before and during legislation — or wait until rules are being written, or even until its own particular case comes up.

Continued and consistent resistance, an obvious option, may be very costly in terms of time, effort, and money. Where there is strong political support for regulation, relaxation of the rules may be unlikely. Resistance may only provoke even stronger standards. By developing a reputation as a "bad guy," a firm risks other repercussions.

A firm then may logically decide to comply. But why should it consider going even further — doing more than is required, taking some initiative, or complying in a situation where it could plausibly argue that "circumstances" prevent it? In other words, why should an organization be "positively responsive"? Doing so obviously does not allow an organization to escape the costs and burdens of satisfying external demands. What it may do, however, is help an organization escape even more severe demands or disruptive requirements that may otherwise develop.

What the organization gains is *control*—control over the *timing*, the *extent*, and the *nature* of these requirements. All these steps, if nothing else, reduce future uncertainties. Requirements can be clarified before planning is well advanced. Unforeseen regulatory roadblocks are then less likely to arise. Several companies in our study were able to proceed smoothly with their plans by explicitly offering some early concessions, even suggesting new regulations. By doing so, they resolved open issues and preempted moves to set stricter limits on their activities.[2]

Such strategies can be successful because there are limits to bureaucratic and political energy. Also, dramatic issues make it easier to arouse public concern. Hence, it may be hard for regulators and proregulation interest groups to tighten "pretty good" rules that have already been established — especially when regulatees have been cooperative and have taken some initiative in putting those rules into place. Indeed, they may consciously choose not even to try, but rather to use their limited resources elsewhere. In contrast, when a firm actively resists all attempts at regulation, it can provoke more stringent standards than those that compromise would have produced. Would Boston Edison have had to put the entire Sudbury line underground and would TVA now face stringent SO_2 limits if each had been more responsive on these issues? One notes that Edison has worked hard to clean the smoke plume from Mystic 7 — perhaps more than legally required — to ensure that it does not attract attention which could again lead to tighter requirements.

PG&E accomplished these ends when it initiated a Public Utilities Commission regulation requiring it to make 2 percent of its revenues from each community available for undergrounding existing distribution lines, and setting standards for new underground lines. It reduced the likelihood that unexpected controversies would arise over proposed distribution lines. It set a tolerable limit—far less than 100 percent—on the number of new lines that would have to be put underground. It also forced the question of *where* undergrounding would take place to be determined by the communities involved, avoiding the potentially troublesome process of deciding itself how to distribute money for such activities.

Our studies suggest that many internal features of organizations tend to bias them against the strategy of responding positively to regulatory requirements. Managers whose life and work would be changed by complying tend to find reasons for not doing so. One executive at TVA, explaining his opposition to stack gas scrubbing systems that would produce a sulfuric acid by-product, said, "I am not in the chemical business and I don't want to be." Since it is hard to know what policy will prove to be best, arguments against cooperation can be effective, especially since they will often be vigorously advanced.[3]

Companies also engage in optimistic self-deception. Having decided that they do not want to comply, they find it easy to convince themselves that the regulation in question is unwise and inappropriate. As ackowleged experts on at least part of the problem, they tend to assume that they will be able to persuade new and inexperienced regulatory bodies to accept their views—if only these bodies are willing to be "objective" and "professional." Such self-confidence, however, often fails to take into account the ambiguity of evidence and inference that characterizes many regulatory decisions. It does not recognize that regulators are very different kinds of people, with different incentives and different perspectives, who may not see the issue in the same way the regulatee does.

What is it about a situation that should make an organization seriously consider being positively responsive? The cases suggest that the nature of regulatory institutions and their resources is one relevant concern. The more technically knowledgeable regulators are, the more resources they have, and the easier it is for them procedurally to impose sanctions, the less attractive companies will find it not to comply. Conversely, consider the incentives in a situation like that of Boston Edison, whose air quality violations for years brought routine reprimands; only after heated public protest did the matter wind up in court, where it was settled by a promise to comply. There is little incentive for an organization to be responsive if the weakness of a regulatory agency confronts it with such a situation.

The capacity of other agencies to retaliate outside the issue in question is also relevant. This clearly can raise the costs of poor public relations — or so PG&E repeatedly calculated. In this connection, the degree of public support for the regulation is extremely important, in part because this helps determine how regulators react to the organization's strategy.

A sensible regulatee tries to consider likely regulatory reaction in advance, as PG&E did in calculating whether to oppose the Bay Area Air Pollution Control District over building cooling towers at Pittsburg 7. Actively resisting a regulation is likely to be successful only if the regulators can accept defeat. If they feel that their jobs might be in jeopardy for failing to be tough — as did members of the LAAPCD during the Scattergood episode — they cannot afford to give in. The cases suggest that the very fact that an issue has become of enough public concern to become the focus of regulation should be a warning to regulatees of the potential costs of noncooperation. All that may be produced is a bit of delay and some poor publicity.

On the other hand, the cases also illustrate some of the disadvantages of responsiveness. The opposition may be encouraged to ask for more. PG&E perceived that the more it promised to do with NO_x control at Moss Landing, the more it was required to do. Certainly there have been successful efforts to convince state agencies to change their rules — noticeably the Southern Company's experience in Georgia and Alabama and the more recent relaxation of sulfur-content rules in Massachusetts. The latter may be more a matter of broad swings in popular opinion over time, but the former was clearly the product of company policy to try to communicate to the states the company's view that the regulations were inappropriate.

A responsive strategy is thus particularly attractive to those who face regulators who are backed by considerable public and political support. This suggests that Hydro should have thought more carefully about taking on the provincial government over capacity expansion, just as PG&E should have been less sure about its ability to convince the AEC and the Geological Survey before pushing ahead with Mendocino. In both cases, political sentiment was against the organizations in question.

When opposing an agency or contesting a legislative effort, the companies in our study found it wise to take an apparently flexible posture. "We agree with your goals but not with your specific methods in this case" was often more effective than a "stone wall" response. It seldom made sense, in the cases we considered, for a regulated organization to try to back the regulatory agency into a public corner.

So far we have been discussing responsiveness on an issue-by-issue basis. Our larger concern is with the evolution of organizations that have a generalized capacity and willingness to behave in this way. Several features of the social and political system make it likely that an organization that responds positively to outside pressure on one issue will have reason to do so more broadly. The possibility of retaliation (through rate controls, for example, or expanding competing systems) is likely to have similar implications across a wide range of issues. Also, the social, political, and economic features of a region that lead to strong public reaction on one issue are likely to foster strong reactions on others. Hence, the same logic that gives a company like PG&E reason to be responsive on any one question implies a reason to follow that approach more generally.

It might seem that managers should try to decide case-by-case if being positively responsive is the most advantageous tactic. Unfortunately, such idealized flexibility may be neither possible nor desirable—for all the reasons that organizations exist, and exist with stable strategies and structures. The whole value of ongoing organizational arrangements is that they do not have to be reconsidered issue by issue. The gains from reshaping the organization's structure for each problem are usually not worth the costs of doing so. Strategies and decision rules exist to avoid the costs of thinking through each problem; their basis is that these costs in the long run will not be worth their benefits.

Since every set of strategies and structures has substantive implications, a manager must decide what conceptual and organizational preconceptions and assumptions to embrace. Our argument is simply that being able and willing to respond positively to changing external pressures will often be in the best interests of the manager and the organization. In a rapidly changing world, it behooves a manager to try to adopt a strategy and structure that allow for flexible and creative responses, and that in the process avoid making himself and his organization obsolete. The irony is that by creating an organization that has the capacity to respond to changing external pressures, one not only makes responsiveness *possible*, but also more *likely*.

In many ways the argument is similar to the argument in favor of an appropriate structural basis for concern with marketing in a commercial company. Having someone in charge of marketing (with resources, access to top management, and so on) makes it more likely that the firm will take an aggressive approach to its marketing problems. For a firm with marketing problems, this may well be an acceptable price to pay for better average performance over time, even if it means that the firm sometimes spends too much on marketing. Similarly, for a firm in an industry based on technical progress, a strong research group that leads the company occasionally to go overboard may be the best organizational solution to the problem of staying technologically competitive. For many managers, the same logic applies to dealing with and responding to regulatory requirements.

Managing for Responsiveness

What can a manager do to develop a responsive organization? The cases suggest several structural features that promote such behavior. Possessing *all* these features is neither necessary nor sufficient for positive responsiveness. The relationship between behavior and structure is too elastic for this to be the case. Individual personalities and ideas have too much impact on organizational outcomes. Yet for an organization to be capable of responding positively to demanding circumstances, most of these features are probably essential.

If managers want to follow a responsive approach, the organization must be capable of noticing changes in the larger world. Its planning and decision making must be capable of producing flexible and creative responses. Such an organization needs diverse viewpoints effectively integrated into its decision-making process. Outside-oriented groups, such as those concerned with public relations, environmental affairs, and law, have an especially important role to play in responsive organizations. Without such viewpoints, the organization will not be sufficiently sensitive to the outside world or capable of developing new and innovative approaches. Furthermore, once such ideas are generated and adopted, they must be effectively implemented.

The cases suggest that one important feature necessary for systematic positive responsiveness is the presence of a strong leader who tolerates—even encourages—dissent. Acting creatively in anticipation of future consequences means acting even in the absence of strong short-run sanctions. Choosing such a policy requires someone to consider the long-range interests of the organization as a whole. This means someone who is broadly acquainted with the organization and its circumstances, who is not tied to any particular function or internal interest, and who is knowledgeable about larger social trends. Usually only someone at or close to the top of the organization can fulfill this role.

Strong leadership is required to get the members of an organization to accept the costs of change and the new ideas that change requires.[4] It is usually not possible to replace a large number of experienced people quickly. A manager must often work with the personnel available. It will be necessary, therefore, to reinterpret the organization's strategy and historic commitments in light of new circumstances, and to win acceptance of that view among the organization's members.

There is an enormous literature on human behavior in organizations that deals with the use of leadership and influence to get members to alter their thinking about problems. It would be impossible to either recapitulate or reinvent this literature here. The cases we have reviewed, however, suggest a few interesting points about this process.

First, the cases confirm our theoretical discussion of the complexity and inconsistency of an individual's values, maxims, and decision rules. Consider the LADWP engineer who said, "We give very high-quality service, perhaps higher than people are willing to pay for." A manager who thought that this engineer was overdesigning could try to shift the emphasis in his thinking from quality to the need to respond to citizen preferences. Similarly, a TVA manager who wanted to devote more attention to environmental problems could evoke the agency's mission of developing "all" the resources of the valley, including its air resources. "Low-cost power" could then be characterized as a means to an end, not the end itself; top management could argue to the faithful that this goal was inappropriate in certain instances, without asking them to give up a deeply felt conviction.

Second, the cases clearly show that influence can be — and in some cases must be — earned. New leaders from outside must prove themselves. Someone with obvious skills, a knowledge of the organization's problems, and a commitment to its continued growth and survival will find it much easier to get cooperation from its members. Otherwise, when an outsider tries to rationalize new approaches on the basis of old slogans, it may be seen as obvious treason by long-service personnel, who know that *they* are the ones genuinely faithful to the organization's historic role. Thus, defending the organization against outside enemies and establishing a rapport with those inside are very helpful in winning the support of veteran employees. The experiences of the various outsiders at the Southern Company, compared to those of the early outside managers at Boston Edison, demonstrate this point.

In the last chapter we noted the importance of a strong control

system and loyal subordinates in implementing responsive policies, and we discussed some of the structural preconditions of
these. The cases also showed the role of formal accountability in
enhancing top management's ability to shape what was done.
The tasks utilities confront do not make decentralization to "profit center" management possible in most cases. Nevertheless, several companies experimented with task-based as opposed to dis-
cipline-based organizational forms in order to increase accountability and provide more relevant incentives. At Hydro, for example, top management was not satisfied that engineering
groups were making the right kind of priority decisions when
there were several projects competing for design resources. This
in turn led to a project manager/project team approach, so that
at least responsibilities for keeping to schedules were clearly
focused.

Within such constraints there is evidence in the case studies for
the value of performance indexes in eliciting superior implementation. Given the demands on top management's time, the routine monitoring of certain activities was a valuable aid in keeping
track of their performance. TVA, for example, found it advantageous to begin collecting and reporting data on the environmental performance of generating plants (dirty stacks) to counterbal-
ance the pressure on operators for cost containment.

Of course, relevant data were not always easy to collect. Sometimes this was because the parameters one would like to have —
like the lifetime costs of a new plant — were difficult to calculate
in advance and not discoverable until many years had passed.
Sometimes it was because diffuse responsibility — as in the choice
of the spray cooling system at Pittsburg 7 — made it hard to determine where the critical responsibility lay. Sometimes it was because the people who had the data did not rush to report on
themselves, which was why TVA turned emissions monitoring
over to an "internal policeman" as opposed to relying on plant
operators. Still, the cases suggest that since performance judgments will be made anyway, managers who went to the trouble to
get some data were often in a better position than those who had
none at all.

Since strong leaders with strong control systems can easily discourage dissent, they must be especially careful not to do so.
Otherwise, they cut themselves off from the information and perceptions of those further down in the organization. Such problems are avoided by a leader who is sufficiently secure, broad-
minded, and flexible to tolerate and even encourage subordinates

to disagree and present new ideas. No senior managers in our cases were perfect in this regard, although Harold Smith does have a reputation for enjoying a good argument (at least on certain issues). When the top discourages dissent, management may persist in a poorly designed strategy—such as one that will lead to a collision with regulatory authorities—without being warned of the problem until the impending disaster actually occurs. PG&E's coastal nuclear plant siting efforts, for example, may reflect this dynamic.

Managers who try to foster new ideas and policies will frequently have to deal with innovative suggestions. They may find themselves less able to judge the quality of an idea than they would have if the organization had limited itself to more familiar and well-understood options. A manager in an innovative organization must therefore be strong enough to trust subordinates and be able to rely on their technical judgment. An individual's psychological makeup and personal relationships with other managers can greatly affect his ability to do this. The most effective managers we met were open, aware individuals who did not rely on formal authority or intimidation in interpersonal relations.[5] Note, however, that such leadership does not relate exclusively to positively responsive strategies; it is valuable—even essential—for any organization in the face of trying circumstances.

Another structural feature that our cases suggest is helpful to a responsive organization is the development of an articulated, explicit strategy. Such a strategy plays a number of roles. It facilitates strong leadership. The imperfections in all incentive systems mean that rewards and punishments cannot guide subordinates with the necessary subtlety; an explicit statement of goals and tactics is required. Middle managers who would like to please their superiors find it difficult to know what to do unless they are guided by an articulated strategy. At PG&E many in the company understood Robert Gerdes' view about the need for overall responsiveness. This helped shape many decisions up and down the line, even on the part of those who disagreed with this approach.

A well-articulated strategy—perhaps surprisingly—also facilitates the process of strategic change. If an organization is to question and readjust its assumptions and tactics over time, it helps to be aware of them. At PG&E those who believe that top management goes too far to avoid regulatory confrontations are at least able to pose the issue clearly, because top management has made its strategy explicit. Similarly, at Boston Edison, Charles Avila's insistence on minimum capital cost for the New Boston generating units posed sharply for his successors the question of whether or not to pay more for increased operating reliability at Mystic 7.

To be sure, an explicit strategy can hinder change if it is specific and well defended (like the minimization of capital costs at TVA). Such a strategy can be quite successful (as was TVA's for thirty years), but only if the situation the organization confronts does not change significantly.

Strategic reconsideration is seldom easy, intellectually or psychologically. When outcomes are unsatisfactory, it may be hard to know if the organization has been trying to do something sensible but has done it badly, or has set out to do the wrong thing. Was PG&E wise to try to build a nuclear plant at Point Arena after the Bodega Head controversy? Was the LADWP right to try to build a nuclear plant in Kern County after problems in Tulare County? Were the cooling modules at Pittsburg 7 a good idea badly implemented, or a bad idea forced by an overly accommodating strategy? Was TVA's resistance to scrubbers a sound defense of the public interest or a knee-jerk strategic response bound to bring pressure on the organization? At what point does a company's inability to implement a strategy become a critical weakness in the strategy itself? It seems clear that much of the difficult-to-quantify "art" of management involves making such judgments and carrying out the alterations in strategy that they imply.

On the other hand, such decisions are not always intellectually difficult (at least with the benefit of hindsight). Many in Boston Edison now claim to have believed at the time that its strategy of confrontation with local towns over the Sudbury transmission line was inappropriate. Yet when the structural conditions that facilitate reconsideration are not present, even disaster may not be enough to provoke rethinking.

The process of strategic reconsideration takes time and effort. In all the companies we studied, there was some tendency for top management to focus on the most urgent matters and to complain of not having enough time for longer-run problems. Often there were many urgent matters, especially as external pressures increased. Just when the need for strategic thinking was greatest, managers found it most difficult to do.

Surmounting this difficulty means either creating a distinct group that has the responsibility for long-range planning and strategy development, or finding some way for top management to devote more time to the task. If senior executives are to have time for larger questiᴏns, top managemet must be expanded and more routine decisions must be delegated to middle managers. The structural reforms of Task Force Hydro and the creation of a "corporate office" appear to be an explicit response to this problem. Especially since subordinates may be reluctant to criticize top management, a multiperson management team may be the only way to develop adequate self-critical capacity.

To alleviate this problem our cases suggest that there may be some value in trying to institutionalize the process of strategic rethinking. It is helpful for the chief executive to be challenged, provoked, and stimulated to new thinking in a context in which he can change his views without undermining his authority. A collegial group of managers who have a reasonable level of mutual trust and respect seems quite important. Both Southern and Boston Edison appear to have benefited from meetings of groups such as this. Some of the companies we have studied have used management retreats — although more for communicating than for developing strategy. For other managers, personal assistants or the board of directors will serve the function of sounding board and critic. A formal strategic planning cycle — common in industry but not in our cases — is another device. Such capacity for reexamination is valuable, regardless of how cooperative the organization decides to be with regard to specific regulatory requirements.

Many of the situations in the companies we studied were quite novel. New problems were continually being identified, and new regulatory relationships established. Given the important role of well-worn habits of mind in all thinking, those organizations that were most creative and flexible often were structured to bring diverse perspectives into their planning and decision making. Consider the gadfly role that a lone meteorologist has played in the midst of Hydro's systems operations group. Similarly, Boston Edison's innovative approach to the tower design and routing of the Plymouth-Holbrook line was the result of continued work by mechanical and electrical engineers, public-relations people, and an outside architectural consultant. Only an organization with diverse members would have generated the diverse solutions that PG&E used in solving the cooling problems of the Pittsburg 7 unit.

People who have not grown up in the organization can be especially valuable because they are able to perceive and reconsider what for insiders are unquestioned assumptions and approaches. The unusual grant-winning entrepreneurship of the ex-academics in Southern Company Services was critical to the company's research efforts on solvent refining. Similarly, Kenneth Diercks' unusual background was critical to PG&E's efforts to work with environmental groups in choosing a nuclear power plant site.

Without such viewpoints, an organization's innovations are likely to be compatible with the predilections of existing groups. The LADWP's transmission-line engineers built ever longer and higher voltage transmission lines. TVA's designers built ever larger plants. Southern's fuel group looked across the globe for low-sulfur coal. All these accomplishments were an extension of disciplinary traditions and prior practices. And they served to defend and justify the adequacy of the sponsoring group's approach to the organization's activities.

Diversity by itself, however, will not necessarily lead to positive responsiveness unless one or more of the major participants in the process are oriented to the outside world. Someone has to know and care about what is happening outside and be able to deal with outsiders when the situation requires. As a general rule, in fact, the size and role of outside-oriented staff groups tend to increase as external pressures become more severe. In part, this process reflects the role of apparently relevant competence in task assignments. When the environmentalists are demonstrating, or regulators are issuing orders, or the state legislature is in an uproar, the organization tries to find a specialist capable of dealing with the problem. Who this turns out to be depends on the prior history and development of the organization, and on which group puts itself forward most visibly. It could be the lawyers, public-relations people, a special environmental group, or whatever. But it is usually not the design engineers or plant operators or personnel managers—who can claim no experience in such matters.

Outside-oriented groups, our cases suggest, tend to support compromise rather than confrontation, for several reasons. First, group members must continually deal with outsiders. For them, outside disapproval and poor public relations have high personal costs. Second, such contact tends to increase their awareness of, and sympathy for, the other fellow's perspective. Given the inconsistency of everyone's own norms and maxims, if you talk to someone long enough, his or her perspective may begin to seem quite persuasive in certain respects. Third, such groups are often asked to persuade outsiders to change their behavior. But to do so, compromise is often necessary. To have access to and influence with those outsiders, the groups that deal with them typically must be able to deliver something in return. So, like ambassadors who come to reflect the perspective of the country they reside in, or the personnel officer who internally advocates large wage packages, those on the interface transmit external pressures and signals into the organization. Fourth, perhaps because of the roles their members tend to play, the professional training and norms of certain professions are more oriented toward compromise than others. Not everyone is trained to understand the other fellow's perspective and to perceive that he (or both of you) could be "right" in a certain situation. Of course, not all lawyers are more flexible than all engineers, and not all public-relations people are more in favor of compromise than all production managers. But one can see tendencies and patterns nonetheless. Indeed, top management itself, which often has extensive contact with the larger world and which is therefore subject to many of these same pressures and processes, often advocates compromise in internal councils for precisely these reasons.

This tendency of internal structure to readjust in a way that favors compromise in the face of rising outside pressures, along with rational calculation by members of the organization, helps make such external pressure effective.

A manager who wants to be able to respond to changing and demanding circumstances is well advised to consider whether there is enough diversity, unconventionality, and outside orientation in his organization. Consider, for example, how the wide array of outside-oriented groups at PG&E contributed to that company's environmental responsiveness. In addition to a strong Law Department, the company has significant units in public relations, government and community affairs, and environmental affairs. In contrast, in the past the LADWP's lack of strong outside-oriented units appears to have hampered its ability to identify external concerns and deal effectively with them.

The evidence we have reviewed is not unambiguous. The relationship of structure to behavior is not simple. Hydro's initial responsiveness was achieved without outside-oriented groups playing a key role. The lawyers have had little input, and Harold Smith has opposed the formation of a separate environmental affairs department. However, the attitude of the engineers themselves — their interest in identifying public concerns and responding to them — has largely compensated for this. And community-affairs specialists from the Public Relations Division have recently been integrated into the Engineering Branch. On the other hand, the lack of diversity in perspectives may have reduced Hydro's sensitivity to public concerns in some nonenvironmental areas, such as finance.

From the viewpoint of a manager, creating a well-situated

group of outside-oriented professionals is a step with substantive implications. Most of the other prerequisites for a positively responsive organization are helpful, whatever strategic posture the organization assumes. But no structure is entirely neutral with respect to its strategic implications. Increasing the role of outside-oriented groups increases the risks of overreacting to external pressures. Such risks have to be balanced against those of ignorance and an inability to relate to changing circumstances, which can result from the failure to make such adjustments.

Having diverse and outside-oriented people is not enough. The cases suggest that creativity and willingness to change requires some internal dynamism of the sort that sharply-defined and inflexible task assignments tend to reduce. Creating a monopoly of various areas of expertise in well-defined bureaucratic units weakens management control and limits innovation by restricting the set of perspectives from which any one problem is approached. In contrast, an overlapping and shifting division of tasks — although it appears less neat on the organization chart — provides multiple sources of plans and strategic suggestions. It also can engender competition that can be a useful incentive for both creativity and thoroughness. In PG&E, for example, the daring proposal to involve environmental groups in power plant siting at Diablo Canyon may not have emerged from a more orderly set of task assignments. Such flexibility in assignments also helps by keeping individuals aware of a wider set of concerns and problems, inhibiting the growth of narrow, well-defined units with well-formulated common assumptions.

A manager has to watch out for the possibility that certain perspectives are not well represented in the decision-making arena because of a weak organizational basis or because of the way communications are organized. Recognizing this possibility, TVA's top management strengthened the Air Quality Branch in the 1950s, around the time of the Kingston controversy, so that it could more effectively monitor actual air pollution control performance.

All our companies encountered serious problems with a functionally based hierarchical system as they tried to respond to rapid external change. The interdependency of divisions often became so great that coordination and integration of activities across units, at levels well below the top, were required.[6]

The common response to this problem in our cases has been to create some sort of crosscutting integrative unit: the Boston Edison air pollution committee, task force Thermal '78 at PG&E, the

Concept Department at Hydro, the Nuclear Projects Office at the LADWP. At least five different approaches to this problem were observed:

a permanent integrating (planning) unit

a semipermanent project team

a permanent intergroup team

an *ad hoc* committee or task force

a formal or informal top-management group

None of these techniques was fully satisfactory. Permanent integrating units avoid duplicative staff work and create people who are specialists in the role of being generalists — that is, integrators. Such lower-level integrating groups (like the Concept Department at Hydro), unlike top management itself, were more likely to hear criticism or dissenting views — precisely because they did not have so much power over others. On the other hand, this tended to give one group a monopoly over key functions, which would risk loss of top-management control if the group in question overly limited the options available. The organization's performance comes to depend heavily on the attitudes and abilities of those in pivotal integrator roles.

Simply creating an integrating group does not mean, however, that it will pay attention to, and incorporate, an appropriate variety of viewpoints. Because these tasks are so critical, they are often assigned to those with the personal confidence of top management. One PG&E task force, for example, had an engineer and a public-affairs person as chairman and vice-chairman, apparently in a desire to "balance" its perspectives.

Delegation of the integrating function appears to have been successful only where top management had developed and communicated a clear strategic plan, and where it was willing to give subordinates authority to act on the basis of that plan. If everyone knows that the entire matter will be reargued before top management, lower-level integrating efforts take on elements of a charade. Temporary committees and task forces are especially problematic in this regard. In our cases, the members of these groups usually had primary loyalties and responsibilities elsewhere, which sometimes meant that it was not in their interests to work hard on the project. Furthermore, such groups were often established to try to sidestep interunit conflicts. "Since Division A and Division B both think they ought to be given the job, let's set up a joint committee to do it — and ask people from C and D while we're at it." In such circumstances, the activities of the committee will seem pointless and will not attract real effort.

Thus, the top must clearly want to delegate conflict resolution and must be willing to abide by the decisions that such a process produces, if anyone is to take it seriously.

If top management disagrees with a recommendation on a major matter, rejecting it is one way to educate subordinates in the nuances of top-management views. But if this happens to more than a small fraction of such recommendations, the system is not doing its job, which is to relieve top management of the need to review everything in detail.

We have seen that top management can, and often does, play a critical integrative role. Such a role requires the same sort of top-management structure that facilitates strategic reconsideration. This is what long-range planning, at the most general level, is really about. Task Force Hydro clearly recognized this need, and thus suggested the establishment of a new corporate office. In all three of our private companies, the top-management group is fairly large and relatively capable of performing integrative functions. Yet in the public companies, resources generally have been more limited. TVA, with its small top management, has had to rely on bargaining among subordinate units to carry out much of the integrative function. This clearly limits the capacity of the top (or, indeed, almost anyone) to act as a focus for systematic policy change. In Hydro the situation in the past has been similar.

On the basis of their research, some writers have concluded that extensive top-management involvement in decision making is not characteristic of organizations dealing with complex, rapidly changing circumstances.[7] These writers have reported that a well-defined hierarchy and a highly involved top management are more prevalent in organizations operating in stable, low-stress environments. Those operating in more demanding environments tend to be much more decentralized, they find, and rely on various integrating devices to coordinate activity. The argument is essentially that the top cannot know enough or respond fast enough to make the decisions, given the layers of hierarchy and the many rapidly changing problems.

These findings are not consistent with our own case studies: strong controls and the direct involvement of top managers were characteristic of our most responsive organizations. And under pressure, these utilities have tended to evolve in the direction of a greater role for top management in critical decision making. One possible explanation of these different views is that, by some definitions, electric utilities—even those that are operating in fairly stressful environments—confront only relatively simple choices. Often utilities face only one crisis at a time, so that a fair degree of centralization does not lead to the same level of managerial overload that would occur in an organization that confronted more decisions. After all, electric utilities do not have to worry much about their "product line" or their competition. The main decisions are about *how* to produce the product, and even these are limited. And in a crisis we did see a tendency for hierarchy to break down—as Roberts Gerdes found himself talking directly to Kenneth Diercks. On the other hand, strong control from the top may not be incompatible with development of lower-level integrating mechanisms, so that delegation produces neither decentralization nor much in the way of discretion lower down, since basic policies are clearly specified in an explicit, articulated strategy. (The functioning of Hydro's Concept Department appears to demonstrate this point.) Certainly, our cases do not support the view that top-management control becomes less important—even if less detailed—as external demands increase.

Implications for Public Management

Public managers often face problems equal to, if not more difficult than, those faced by their private counterparts. Yet they frequently have had fewer management tools at their disposal. Weak top-management structures, weak control systems, strong organizational ideologies, and limited outside-oriented staff are among the handicaps they have faced.

All the public organizations we studied had relatively few general-management positions (except Hydro, *after* its recent reorganization). Compare, for example, PG&E and TVA in this regard. There are several possible explanations for this pattern: fear of criticism for creating too many high-paying jobs in a public entity; traditional public-sector organization patterns; the notion that the organization's tasks are merely technical and hence required little policy or strategy input; the desire to control costs. For whatever reason, the result typically has been to overload and hence lessen the effective control of the chief executive. This pattern also reduces the advancement opportunities available to middle-management "barons," making them more difficult to control. Having only a few general-management slots deprives top management of a collegial group that shares an organization-wide perspective, and that can foster integration, long-range planning, and strategic reexamination. To make matters worse, top managers in public companies have often had relatively low levels of personal staff support. Although some private companies, too, were deficient in this respect, the lack of such staff is especially serious to a manager who is trying to do too much.

Nor did the boards that managed the three public companies effectively supplement these managerial deficiencies. Although some of the individuals who have served as chairman of the board have played a key managerial role — especially at TVA — many other board members have been less expert and were selected for a variety of political reasons.

Weak control systems also seem to be more prevalent in the public sector. Civil service systems, such as the one at the LADWP, can be quite inimical to top-management control. Even an agency with adequate general management may have problems developing and implementing plans when advancement depends more on test scores than on job performance. Naturally, every system has some slack and can be manipulated by a shrewd manager to some degree; a determined top manager, with a certain number of non-civil service or high-level jobs available, can certainly *improve* performance concerns within a civil service organization (as Louis Winnard of the LADWP is demonstrating). But such a system can still limit choices and absorb scarce managerial time and attention.

Eliminating high-level entry compounds this problem. It is not surprising that the LADWP has had to rely heavily on assistance from outsiders in solving difficult problems. Keeping political appointees out of the work force — the main justification for civil service systems — may be important in maintaining the effectiveness of an organization. But a significant part of this benefit may then simply be lost in a promotion system that places little emphasis on job performance.

In general, there appears to be less systematic management development in public companies than in private ones. There is less movement of promising young managers from one area of the company to another to gain broader experience and perspectives. This makes it difficult for top management to assemble the sort of loyal and diverse middle-management team, with broad views of its responsibilities, that is critical to a responsive organization.

Part of the reason for this lack of management development is that, with limited resources and background, the top management in some public companies lacked the time, internal power, and knowledge of subordinates necessary to involve themselves deeply in the promotion process. Emphasis on the technical nature of the organization's tasks and on a pattern of "straight-ahead" advancement — with technical expertise rather than management ability as the key criterion for promotion — only adds to the difficulties.

Effective middle managers, at least within Hydro and TVA, did have control *within* their parts of the organization. With this decentralization, the perspectives of one group and its leaders came to dominate company policy, and the problems of top management were increased. In some cases, not even middle managers appeared to have effective control.

The top managers' difficulties in asserting control are compounded by the fact that public companies typically have multiple, conflicting, and difficult-to-measure objectives. How is top management at TVA to know if its designers and operators are striking the right balance between pollution control and cost control? This difficulty in monitoring and evaluating performance is used to justify civil service personnel systems, and weakens whatever performance-based controls managers do try to introduce.

With weak top management and weak controls, an organization may well lack the internal cohesion needed to survive. Under these circumstances, however, a strong, specific ideology can provide this cohesion (assuming that the environment is not changing too rapidly). The historical evolution of all three public companies has reflected this pattern. To survive and grow in an often hostile environment, they have had to be persuasive in developing and articulating their mission. Because their ideology has helped these organizations to defend themselves, it has tended to become a significant factor in the mental equipment of their members.

Conditions at the organization's founding can leave a surprisingly durable impression. TVA continues to see itself as the low-cost-power yardstick that Franklin Roosevelt envisioned. Ontario Hydro still puts a high priority on Adam Beck's goal of reducing Ontario's dependence on the United States for energy. With low turnover and little hiring from outside at upper levels, senior executives of public companies have often spent their entire life in the organization, exposed to its socializing pressures. Moreover, public organizations may attract as employees people who feel some commitment to its ideology, so that they are predisposed to that process. Indeed, such loyalty can easily become a criterion for promotion.

Highly specific, well-entrenched ideologies can greatly weaken top management's ability to change organizational behavior.

And characteristics such as expertise, apparent loyalty to the organization, and personal contact with key people, which help managers exercise leadership in such circumstances, are precisely those that public managers often lack.

Finally, we found that nonengineering personnel and outside-oriented groups played a smaller role in public companies than in private ones. With less contact with capital markets and, until recently, fewer regulatory demands, public companies may have had less need for a legal and financial staff. Although this may be changing (TVA's legal department has been growing by leaps and bounds in the past few years), public companies have fewer nonengineers both generally and in top management. Also, the presumption that the main issues facing the companies are technical can work against giving a strong role to nonengineers.

Historically, the current situation is anomalous. The public companies we studied were often led by politicians or lawyers during their early years. Engineers have tended to come into prominence only in the post-World War II period. In part, this may be because a community consensus emerged, giving the organization certain narrow functions, and public reaction against "socialism" makes expansion of these functions unlikely. The engineers' own professional perspectives have led them to emphasize the "nonpolitical" nature of their decision making. Once the underlying consensus dissolves (as it has recently over environmental and rate issues), the company and its management tend to become repoliticized. The sort of people in key positions is likely to change accordingly.

This conforms to our general view that as the external pressures on a company grow, it will make internal changes to accommodate itself to these pressures. We have seen a major strengthening of top management at Hydro, new and more aggressive leadership at the Los Angeles Department of Water and Power, and some efforts to break down divisional loyalties at TVA with the appointment of several outsiders to senior posts.

Like the private companies in our study, the public organizations have evolved in the direction of greater responsiveness as they have come under increasing pressure. The point remains, however, that public companies tend to possess fewer and weaker management tools than private firms, which hampers their managers' efforts to respond effectively to trying circumstances.

To keep this discussion of management tools in perspective, it should be noted that in some cases environmentally sensitive policies were generated by group decision rules in the context of a weak control system (the careful substation landscaping at the LADWP, for example). Yet such outcomes can be more a matter of coincidence or of the long-run adaptation of an organization to a stable environment. Whichever the case, such mechanisms will not produce continuing change in the face of continually changing public priorities.

We noted initially that it is theoretically possible for an organization to overreact — even from society's viewpoint — to short-run fads in public attention and priorities. In our case studies, however, there is little sign of this problem. Organization members with a strong professional identification seem to be quick to reject outside concerns — even where these have some scientific basis — in favor of their own perceptions and conditioning. Especially on technical subjects, outsiders are easily dismissed as incompetent, or labeled as destructive self-promoters who want only the attention of the media.

There is no one right way to run all possible organizations in all possible circumstances. There may be many ways to accomplish most functional goals, and these goals themselves may conflict. Both the outside world and many characteristics of the organization itself will and should influence the organization's strategy and structure. These include the skills and interests of its chief executive, the people he has available, his relationship to them, and so forth. The implication is that, insofar as they can be created at all, innovative and positively responsive organizations can be created in various ways.

Nevertheless, our cases suggest that responsive, innovative organizations tend to have strong leaders who encourage a certain amount of questioning and dissent. At any one time these leaders effectively articulate a clear but flexible strategy which they are prepared to revise as conditions warrant. Responsive organizations typically include people with diverse backgrounds, and allow a significant role for groups and individuals whose perspectives and mindsets predispose them to flexibility in dealing with the outside world. However organized, there will be effective mechanisms and procedures for expressing and integrating these diverse perspectives.

Achieving and maintaining control over a large complex organization is not easy. Time limits imply that the ultimate job of a top manager is *not* to make all decisions himself. Activities must be organized so that the need to deal with detail is limited to emergencies. Doing this requires selecting, training, and advancing executives whose perceptions, judgment, and energy can be relied upon. This means that people chosen for key posts, especially middle managers, will often be personally loyal to top management and have compatible perspectives. Such people will also identify with the fate of the organization, and not with specific functions, methods, or approaches. The control system will be strong and deep, and mobility patterns so established that members will have reason to put forth their best efforts.

Most of the characteristics of a responsive organization should be of interest to any manager, regardless of strategic orientation. Every manager should want the capacity to develop and implement effective and creative plans that satisfy changing external circumstances. The only structural characteristic we have discussed with clear, substantive, strategic implications is the role for outside-oriented groups. And there the dilemma is simple: creating the capacity to know about and relate to the outside world tends to move the organization toward responsive compromise.

An organization like this will not always respond positively to public concern, even though it might tend to do so on average. It will, however, be well managed, with the capacity to react intelligently to its opportunities. This is about all that society can hope for or expect.

12

Implications for Regulators

In the cases we have reviewed, regulators consistently found themselves in a difficult position. Often it was quite unclear exactly what the link was between the harm they were trying to prevent and the behavior they were trying to regulate. Aubrey Wagner never tired of criticizing the SO_2 standard, for example. Feasibility and costs were in dispute for a wide variety of control techniques, including precipitators, scrubbers, cooling towers, undergrounding, and earthquake protection of nuclear plants.

In part, this was because many of the regulatory programs that agencies were charged with enforcing were relatively recent developments. Even where the regulatory authority was of longer standing — like the Atomic Energy Commission's jurisdiction over nuclear plants or the role of the Los Angeles Air Pollution Control District — the agencies frequently had to grapple with rapidly evolving scientific and technical information that only exacerbated their uncertainty.

The legislation on which agencies had to rely was often vague and unhelpful. A Congress eager to act despite the lack of data often chose ambiguity as a solution to the problems of coalition building.[1] The states faced similar problems. When Boston Edison applied for a variance to the state's air pollution control regulations, it had to demonstrate that such a move was "in the public interest." The water pollution control legislation that led to the cooling problems at Pittsburg 7 provided for making streams "safe for fish, shellfish, and wildlife." What, operationally, does "the public interest" or "safe" mean in such contexts?

Since the agencies were new, they were often understaffed and inexperienced. Many of the people with the relevant knowledge worked for the regulated firms — as these firms were the first to declare. In addition, agency powers were often quite limited. State agencies frequently had to involve the state attorney general and the courts before they could impose sanctions. One state agency had to contend with other state agencies and with counterpart federal or local entities. And there was always the possibility that the legislature or the governor might intervene.

Imperfect understanding made it difficult to justify not only the general rules but also their application to specific cases. For example, the Nuclear Regulatory Commission and its predecessor, the Atomic Energy Commission, had to decide repeatedly whether the geological evidence on a nuclear site was sufficient, and whether a proposed design was adequate in light of these conditions. Yet no one could say for sure what various data implied for the likelihood of earthquakes of different magnitudes. This only makes it harder to convince the regulated firm of the appropriateness of what it is being asked to do. Such uncertainty allows—indeed almost requires—some bargaining over requirements on a case-by-case basis.

In addition there were some great technical complexities that would have taxed even the most expert of regulators. When the consequences of any action are uncertain, there is always an issue of how large a safety margin should be built into regulatory requirements. Even if it were possible to determine the probabilities of various-sized earthquakes, an agency would still have to decide how unlikely and serious a contingency to allow for. How bad do you assume the meteorology will be, for example, when determining if a proposed plant's emissions will lead to a violation of ambient air quality standards?[2]

Given their limited manpower and technical expertise, as well as the limits of scientific knowledge, regulatory agencies in our case studies were faced with trade-offs between what was easy to monitor and what was relevant. For example, the health effects from particulate air pollution appear to depend primarily on the amount of material that is small enough to be trapped in the lungs.[3] However, the ambient air quality standards focus only on total particulate levels and much enforcement is focused on plume opacity—which is still less relevant but which is readily measured and observed.

The construction of something large—a power plant, a transmission line, or a major piece of pollution control equipment— is the act that is easiest for a regulator to "notice." When the LADWP proceeded with Scattergood 3 without APCD approval, the latter had no doubt about what was occurring. In contrast, overseeing the operation of a facility is much more difficult. Reliable continuous monitoring devices for keeping track of operational outputs are often unavailable. In such cases, agencies were only able to notice violations and invoke sanctions when the consequences of improper operation were easily apparent (for example, the cloud at Moss Landing, visible smoke plumes and acid smut in Boston).

Even in those instances where operations were monitorable, compliance was much easier to enforce when there were control measures available that did not require careful operation for their effectiveness. Control devices vary widely in this regard, from precipitators whose effectiveness is quite sensitive to operating practices, to less sensitive cooling towers and high smokestacks whose effectiveness is relatively independent of operator actions. Similarly, some inputs, like the sulfur content of oil, are relatively easy to observe and control, whereas the sulfur content of coal is much more difficult to regulate. The former is a manufactured and relatively homogeneous commodity whose processing stages are carefully documented, whereas the latter is surprisingly variable—even when it comes from a single mine. Even where violations are detected, imposing sanctions may require lengthy procedures that deplete the agencies' limited resources.

All this leads to a certain amount of explicit or implicit bargaining between regulators and regulatees.[4] Because a source can impose costs on regulators by threatening uncooperative behavior, a regulatee may be able to extract some concessions in exchange for promises of compliance. As with most law enforcement, only if voluntary compliance is widespread will the costs of enforcing environmental regulations be small enough so that violators are likely to be caught. Otherwise, evasion becomes common and the probability of being caught is low. Then even those who would like to obey may feel unable to do so for competitive reasons. And the moral credibility of the requirement is steadily eroded.

The relative power of the participants in this bargaining process is affected by who has to take the initiative in the situation, thereby using up their own scarce resources. Regulatory bodies that had to issue permits before something could be done found it far easier to stop some action or activity than those who had to intervene to change ongoing activities. In the former situation, inactivity itself was an effective control. The LADWP, when faced with permit requirements on substations, went to great lengths to improve its facilities aesthetically.

Given our limited knowledge of environmental effects, the location of the burden of proof also was decisive in some cases.

How is one to prove the absence of harm or risk? PG&E found itself in exactly this situation when it had to convince the Atomic Energy Commission that certain proposed plant sites were seismographically acceptable. Conversely, Ontario air pollution control authorities had to demonstrate that Ontario Hydro's plants in the Toronto area were a serious pollution source, and then get the utility to alter its behavior.

The sanctions available to regulators also shaped what happened. In some cases, the only penalty a company confronted for violating the rules was the need to sign an agreement to come into compliance in the future. Boston Edison repeatedly violated air pollution rules until it faced court action. The affair was settled when the utility agreed to corrective measures. As in other enforcement contexts, the lack of penalties for first offenders, or "first-instance sanctions," meant that a company faced relatively little incentive to comply until it was caught and forced to do so. One reason TVA long ignored state air pollution control authorities was simply because they had no power to impose sanctions on the utility. Similarly, it agreed to put cooling towers on its nuclear plants only when the Atomic Energy Commission threatened not to license the facility.

Even before the rules are written, regulators may agree to sit down with regulatees to call on their expertise and negotiate a mutually acceptable program; PG&E and the Bay Area Pollution Control District did just that on the retrofit of NO_x control measures on old boilers. This is one way to engender the voluntary cooperation that is essential for successful regulation.

In deciding how to proceed, the regulatory body usually could not simply give in to the wishes of those it regulated—although there were cases where that happened. Instead, the legislative entrepreneurs who had developed the program often took an interest in its implementation. Given such interest, the members of a regulatory body may be under pressure to produce results that will justify continued or even increased funding. Also, the possibility of appeal to the courts or to higher political authority is not one-sided. In our cases, the environmentalists were often eagerly awaiting a chance to pursue such appeals if they found it necessary. As with any other organization, the actions of regulatory bodies are often influenced not only by their external incentives, but also by their internal structure—that is, by such factors as their control systems and the political ambitions, personal commitments, and professional pride of their members. In our study we saw a wide range of regulatory behavior, depending on the particular circumstances.

Any one set of forces—such as political pressures—could also point in different directions, depending on circumstances. A governor in the midst of a campaign tightened Massachusetts fuel sulfur-content limits. An ambitious county supervisor tightened ambient NO_x limits in Monterey, California. In Florida, where initially there was widespread support for strong environmental regulations, the governor told his environmental commission, "Don't worry about anyone backdooring you." On the other hand, the Alabama Air Pollution Control Agency apparently faced possible organizational and budgetary retaliation if it did not sit down and bargain with Alabama Power over its SO_2 regulations, especially since the company had ties with the governor as a result of its efforts to bring new business to the state. The recent legislative relaxation of fuel sulfur-content standards in Massachusetts and delays on strict air pollution control deadlines in Florida reflect the potential impact of changes in such factors. On the other hand, where outcomes are publicly visible, and those being regulated are concerned about adverse public reaction, the fear of unfavorable publicity may be enough to induce companies to change their behavior.

Concessions to the regulated are not necessarily bad public policy, especially if they strengthen voluntary compliance and avoid political and legal confrontations. It is possible for a program to be seriously undermined by this process, but this is not inevitable. The key question is how far these concessions take the regulatory program away from its goals—and whether any other approach could produce better results.

Increasing Outside Pressures

Where institutional arrangements were reasonably open, company policies not infrequently proved to be flexible in the face of organized protest. These changes were not typically the work of thousands, or the result of decades of activity. Small numbers of people with skill, luck, and determination have, in the space of a few months, often had a major impact on events. For instance, less than a year after Ontario's Pollution Probe began to take an interest in the environmental policies of Ontario Hydro, the utility decided to switch one of its two Toronto plants from coal to natural gas, in part because of the pressure it had received from this group.

The influence of citizen groups stems in part from the fact that all concerned in the regulatory process may find it very difficult to assess the true nature of popular opinion—a particularly telling example of the way in which uncertainty and limited information can create ambiguous contraints and consequences. This in turn adds greatly to the leverage of small organized interest groups. Since regulators, politicians, and polluters hear very little from the public directly, they are prone to put considerable weight on those expressions of public opinion they do hear. They assume, perhaps correctly, that for every active citizen they see, there are numerous others who share the same viewpoint.[5]

A small group of committed activists also has power because everyone knows that they are willing to take the time and energy to *organize* supporters in order to impose costs on those who ignore them. Even where only a passionate minority cares about an issue, this can be enough to swing an election, if people will actually vote on the basis of that one issue. Just as many politicians try to avoid offending the small but well-organized gun lobby, PG&E has had to be concerned about environmentalists providing a swing vote in referenda on municipalization.

Although regulated companies will undoubtedly be unhappy at the prospect, a dispassionate reading of our cases suggests that a number of regulatory agencies could have achieved their objectives more effectively it they had done a better job in building public support for their programs. In the period we considered, this was not a perceived agency need in many instances. There appeared to be more than enough environmentalists—even from the viewpoint of the regulatory authority—involved in the process on their own initiative. On the other hand, air pollution agencies dealing with TVA and the Southern Company appear to have been isolated and unsupported at times. And this situation is becoming more common as public opinion swings away from environmental concerns.

Agencies in such a situation have to worry not only about attracting short-run attention to their activities and keeping the constituencies that support them informed and involved, but also about building a longer-run base of support. Most agencies, for example, have avoided publicizing enforcement actions. Perhaps they were concerned about maintaining good relations with regulatees and facilitating voluntary compliance. Yet a little publicity —like the housewives with their pollution-damaged linens at a public hearing in Boston—can be very effective in getting the attention of a recalcitrant source. PG&E's attention was certainly attracted at Moss Landing by a public parade in which local officials participated. At a minimum, agencies concerned about their own situation should do a better job of keeping legislators informed about what they are doing and why. Otherwise, legislative reversals of regulations, which we saw in several cases, are liable to become more common. In addition, regulatory bodies should consider greater use of classic public-relations techniques — ranging from personal contact with key constituency groups to providing speakers to school groups—in order to get their perspective disseminated as widely as possible.

In deciding what sort of stance to take, and hence what sort of groups to try to encourage and seek support from, regulators face difficult choices. An agency often cannot satisfy everyone who might agree with its objectives. There is no simple division between those who are "pro" and those who are "anti" environmental protection. An environmental agency will confront some groups who care about added recreation facilities, some who want to preserve wilderness areas, and some who are concerned about health effects. Thus, the agency will have to choose and articulate its own strategy, its own definition of the problems it confronts, and the objectives it pursues.

Such citizen concern appears to be most effective, however, when those who are regulated have something to lose from noncompliance beyond the sanctions available to the regulatory agency. Regulatees appear likely to be more cooperative if institutional arrangements make serious nonregulatory penalties easier for outsiders to impose. This is especially so when organizations feel that their *survival* (or perhaps merely continued growth and prosperity) could be threatened. Behind every encounter with regulatory authorities, for example, PG&E had to fear renewed efforts to expand public power in its service area. Even if survival is not threatened, the possibility of retaliation elsewhere (for example, on rates) or the threat of still stricter regulation in the area in question can help focus the attention of the target organization.

Insecurity, however, will not necessarily produce more environmental protection. Rather, it will increase sensitivity to public opinion, whatever that may be. TVA's opposition to environmental spending on the grounds that it would raise rates is the most obvious example. Boston Edison, too, has occasionally seen positive public-relations value in opposing environmental regulations on cost grounds.

Regulatory officials may have little power to increase a utility's insecurity or to make the nonregulatory consequences of noncompliance more severe or more likely. There are things others can do in this regard, however. For instance, the ease with which municipalities can take over the distribution of power seems to have a significant effect on the responsiveness of private companies. A variety of steps — including changing the legal process by which takeovers can be decided upon, providing wholesale supplies of public power, and requiring private firms to transmit public power at reasonable rates — would increase the disciplinary effectiveness of this option. If Boston Edison had faced the same kind of municipalization threats as did PG&E, it seems unlikely that it would have persisted in its decade-long fight over the Sudbury transmission line. Public companies, too, should be insecure. Whatever mechanisms make municipal ownership possible should also be allowed to operate in reverse, to convert poorly functioning public systems to private ones.

Working with the Regulatory Process

How can regulators increase the effectiveness of the regulatory process itself? Our studies have shown that regulated firms are not pure incentive-oriented profit maximizers. To varying extents, managers are sensitive — albeit within financial limits — to not harming the public and to doing "the right thing." It is not even easy to prove that this is a poor long-run strategy from the perspective of narrow institutional self-interest. As a result, regulatees who believe that the regulations they face lack scientific support and promise dubious social benefits are less likely to respond positively and comply voluntarily. Thus, regulators find their job easier if the requirements they establish are clearly justified and cost-effective — a situation that is socially desirable as well.

Convincing regulatees of this is not easy, however, especially since data often are inadequate. The mindsets, prior commitments, and circumstances of those being regulated are likely to call attention to the reasons for resisting proposed constraints. Thus, there is a strong likelihood that those being regulated will react with hostility to the stringent and imperfectly justified regulations that the political system tends to produce. Advocates of the regulations often respond by saying that no one would have done anything without being pushed, that the regulatees are self-serving in their objections, and that everybody will become used to the idea eventually. Indeed, our cases lend some support to this view: what companies consider "normal" and "reasonable" pollution control *has* changed greatly in the last fifteen years.

Responding to regulatees' opposition by trying to impose draconian programs has obvious disadvantages. When such programs cannot be enforced and promise more than they can deliver, the public becomes disillusioned and regulatees are alienated. Our cases suggest that strong regulatory pressures generally bring about more responsive behavior in the long run. However, if a regulatory agency provokes a crisis, even a normally flexible organization can become quite rigid and may delay the ultimate resolution of a regulatory problem. As Richard Neustadt has pointed out, crises are not a good time for learning.[6] Pressed to resolve their problems quickly, organization members often fall back on traditional strategies. Then they stick to them stubbornly, becoming convinced in the process that their opponents must eventually recognize that their demands are "unreasonable." This can be seen, for example, in the opposition of the town of Woodside to PG&E's transmission line, and in Florida's attempt to impose strict SO_2 limits — neither of which were successful. It is possible for regulators to be too severe, limiting their ability to accomplish their own objectives.

These problems were particularly acute when regulators pursued the strategy of "technology forcing" — that is, of imposing requirements that could not be met without significant technical progress. The difficulties are obvious. How is the regulator to know what really is possible and how is he to enforce the rule once it is promulgated? Interestingly enough, our cases show several instances where this strategy was employed.[7] PG&E at one point came very close to building a new generating plant based on coal gasification, a technology still in the developmental stage for use at the proposed scale. Edison worked hard, and early, on a scrubber system for Mystic, despite the disapproval that other utility presidents expressed to Tom Galligan. Southern has played a similar role in solvent refined coal. PG&E's efforts to control NO_x at Moss Landing are yet another example.

Economists sometimes assert that companies will simply not comply with such requirements — that they will, if necessary, take an inaccurately pessimistic view of what is possible. One utility engineer told us privately that the utilities have called disproportionate attention to the early experimental failure of stack gas scrubbers, to downplay the actual feasibility of installing such equipment. We also saw, however, outside suppliers of technology playing a major role in facilitating compliance (KVB at Scattergood, the spray module manufacturer at Pittsburg 7).

On the other hand, there are also real difficulties in proceeding too fast. Much engineering is experimental, done on a cut-and-try basis, so that the faults discovered in the first of a set of machines are only corrected in later models. Hence, severe regulatory pressure can even be counterproductive, as regulatees become technologically conservative in order to avoid the uncertainties and possible time lag inherent in larger advances.

The cases suggest that when regulatory requirements are stringent without being outrageous, real incentive is provided for internal structural change in the regulated organization. Some of the organizations in our study showed remarkable ingenuity in developing new technologies when they had the structural capacity to innovate and when this seemed necessary to avoid a future crisis. The most striking example of this appears to be Ontario Hydro. Having exhausted most of its unused hydroelectric resources in the 1950s, Hydro played a major role, along with the Canadian federal government, in creating the CANDU technology which could use unenriched, domestically mined uranium.

Although no simple rules of behavior can be drawn from our cases, on balance the evidence is that defensible and cost-effective standards — effectively enforced — provide the best long-run basis for regulatory efforts. Among other things, they allow the agency to proceed vigorously to enforce what it has required. Its members then have the added security of being able to believe in what they are asking for, and can be less concerned about judicial reversal. And by making better social policy, agencies stand a better chance of persuading people to cooperate.

Such advice, unfortunately, is not very specific, especially in light of technological uncertainties. When deciding how hard to push those it regulates, an agency must balance many considerations: political circumstances, the harm involved, the potential economic cost, popular support, industry attitudes, and so forth. These are all relevant to the calculation of what standards to set and how to interpret them in specific cases.

We do have to recognize that setting standards and requirements includes elements of judgment and value — a balancing of competing risks. We saw in our cases how the Environmental Protection Agency opposed high stacks and intermittent controls to achieve ambient SO_2 standards, despite the clear cost advantages of these control methods. It did so on the grounds that too little was known about the fate of the sulfur once it entered the atmosphere. And recent evidence on the long-distance transport of sulfate compounds — which suggests that midwestern sources add appreciably to the pollution burdens of Atlantic-coast cities — indicates that there was some basis for this concern.[8]

Since there are likely to be disagreements as to how to strike such balances, regulators should take steps to communicate the rationale behind their actions — especially to regulatees. Regulators need to get across how the evidence *could* be interpreted in a way that justifies what they propose. They need to point out that there are costs and risks involved in not acting as well as acting. Hence, even with poor data, significant expenditures may be appropriate, though not every measure can be justified in this way.

Frankly acknowledging the ambiguity of the evidence on which regulations are based may not always fit well with the black and white portrayal of the issues that is often used to mobilize action politically.[9] The more subtle approach, however, is likely to gain better public understanding of and support for regulation in the long run. Indeed, it is hard to see how a democratic system of regulation can produce outcomes more "rational" than those for which there is such public support.

With regard to the regulatory process we have also seen that the ease of monitoring and the ease of imposing sanctions both affected company behavior — just as we would expect they would. Such incentives do not fully determine behavior, but nevertheless have some significant impact. This suggests that agencies should give extensive thought to improving the enforceability of their regulations. There are reasons for not trying to control what one cannot measure. There are also reasons for trying to lower the costs to the agency for imposing penalties on violators, so that it is not afraid of using up its own resources in the sanctioning process. In this connection the cases give indirect support to the so-called Connecticut Plan of noncompliance penalties.[10] According to this plan, the size of a fine depends on the costs the company saves by not complying, and the fine is imposed by a simple administrative procedure. What is attractive about the idea is not so much the notion that it removes the economic gains of noncompliance — which is its rationale — but that it is simple, defensible, and mechanical in its operation. Had such a system been in place, Boston Edison might well have moved sooner to do something about the pollution coming from its Edgar and South Boston plants.

Such a scheme would facilitate the efforts of groups within the regulated organizations to encourage the compliance process, since they would then have an excuse for action. Once fines were imposed, internal groups such as law, finance, and public affairs — not to mention top management — would likely be drawn into the process. In discussing the problems of getting another part of his organization to act, one utility lawyer told us, "It's easier if you can tell them that they *have* to do it because that's the law."

Exercising Influence within Target Organizations

Given that much of a company's behavior rests on a balance among its internal perspectives, regulators need to consider what they can do to use and strengthen potential allies within the organizations they regulate. How can they foster the structural conditions for more responsive behavior? The key is understanding the internal structure of the organizations they deal with. This can help them communicate effectively with those inside who are likely to be sympathetic, and perhaps even alter the company's balance of internal perspectives. There are at least three kinds of tactics for doing this.

Reverse Lobbying. To ensure that their viewpoint is properly recognized, regulators can try systematically to educate and persuade regulatees—corporate lobbying in reverse. Large companies normally make it their business to maintain contact with regulatory agencies and legislative committees. Regulators should consider comparable practices. Developing a rapport with potentially sympathetic and influential members of regulated companies offers several benefits. It can provide regulators with a clearer channel into, and perhaps even an advocate within, planning and decision-making processes.

Regulators may be uncomfortable about initiating contacts with members of the firms they are regulating because it may create the appearance that they are "making deals behind closed doors." We saw just such an accusation against PG&E in the Bodega Head controversy. Nevertheless, there is clear value to this sort of communication between agencies and companies—at least for the larger regulatees—so that some balancing of risks and benefits is necessary. In some cases, making it known publicly beforehand that the agency will and does meet informally with regulatees and citizen groups, and keeping an open list of such contacts, could at least avoid the appearance of inappropriate secrecy.

Regulators should want to know those members of an organization who have an impact on company policy, and who at the same time have perspectives and responsibilities that make them sympathetic with, or at least understanding of, the regulators' concern. Jim Leyden, vice-president for public relations at Bos-

ton Edison; Bill Morison, director of design and development at
Hydro; and Bill Harrison, vice-president for research at the
Southern Company are three examples of such influential managers who could be especially helpful to environmental regulators. Talking informally with a few company members about
various past decisions should bring the role of these people quickly
to light.

Through such contacts, regulators can ensure that influential
company officials truly understand the agency's intentions and
position and that top managers know what their own organization is actually doing. Such a strategy would be especially important if those who normally handled relations with the regulatory
agency lacked the power or the initiative to bring about changes
in company policy.

The Scattergood 3 incident in Los Angeles illustrates the general need for closer relations between companies and regulators.
The DWP failed to assess accurately the position of the Air Pollution Control District, and its communications with the control
agency were sporadic. The agency, too, could have done a better
job of finding out what was happening at the DWP during the
long silences that were a feature of their relationship. It should
have discovered that the utility did not realize that a permit
would not be forthcoming. It should have made sure that senior
managers in the DWP—and the city government—understood
the seriousness of the developing confrontation. A legal confrontation with the Department of Water and Power caused the
agency much trouble that better communications might have
avoided.

In contrast, the history of the DWP's Kern County plant demonstrates how outside agencies can use careful, well-placed communication to help shape an organization's behavior. The Kern
County planning board was eager to attract added tax base. A
staff member took responsibility for developing public support
for the plant. He encouraged the utility to communicate with
appropriate members of the affected communities. This enabled
the project to move ahead in a manner that local leaders found
acceptable.

Required Contacts with the Outside. There are a number of
procedural devices that can provide outside agencies and groups
with channels into an organization; these include publicly circulated and evaluated impact statements, and public hearings.
Such procedures can have several effects. They help educate outsiders by providing them with information, analysis, and argu-

ments not otherwise available. They can provoke modifications of individual projects. And, with regard to the regulated organization, they can effect significant changes in its internal structure.

By exposing organizational members to new and possibly unfamiliar perspectives, such processes can make them more aware of and sensitive to outsiders' views. Like most people, organization members do not enjoy being publicly criticized. Also, they are likely to be concerned with the costs their organization might suffer if it were to anger the public. This makes it unlikely that members will remain completely unmoved in the face of direct contact with outside critics at public hearings. We have noted how Louis Winnard, the new general manager of the Los Angeles Department of Water and Power, seems to be taking advantage of this dynamic. His warning to DWP personnel that they should be prepared to testify publicly on their recommendations is bound to make them think harder about the likely public response to their proposals.

By forcing members to adapt to new demands and situations, such processes can facilitate the development of new mindsets and decision rules. A number of observers commented that many engineers had difficulty initially in preparing environmental impact statements because "they weren't used to thinking that way." With time, however, they have become more accustomed to identifying and weighing environmental costs and benefits at an early stage of a project.

Environmental review requirements can lead to new structural features. As a result of the National Environmental Policy Act of 1969 and subsequent state legislation, many companies established new departments or expanded old groups to coordinate the process of preparing and revising environmental impact statements. These departments ranged from editorial and public-information units to research staffs that were created or enlarged to conduct the scientific studies needed to satisfy the Act, or at least to supervise the outside contractors who did the work. In several ways, then, these requirements created new internal groups and internal environmental advocates. Such developments, in turn, have had an impact beyond the specific changes made in any particular project immediately under review.

Public hearings and reviews tend to increase the role of existing outside-oriented groups such as public relations. When such processes are required, the engineers in an organization often agree that it is wise to consult with experts on external opinion before making final plans. In the process, the balance of group perspectives in the corporate policy-making process can be altered.

Effecting Internal Changes Directly. Regulators can also bring about changes within an organization by requiring them as part of the regulatory program. Consider, for example, the Nuclear Regulatory Commission's requirements that companies with nuclear power plants have satisfactory quality assurance and internal safety review mechanisms. Another example is the requirement that recipients of federal contracts and grants develop acceptable affirmative action procedures. In some cases, towns must have certain qualified personnel (licensed sewage treatment plant operators, for example) in order to be eligible for federal money.

There are many structural features of potential interest to a regulator, including personnel practices, promotion criteria, reporting and review mechanisms, training programs, use of consultants, and task assignments of various groups. A regulator who could ask for anything might wish that a company would improve its environmental affairs department by, say, improving its scientific quality in certain areas, getting a new and more senior manager, having the department take responsibility for collecting information on the day-to-day operation of the company's pollution control equipment, and having the department manager report directly to the executive vice-president.

Although not all these actions are appropriate or possible subjects for formal regulatory specification, some could, in fact, be influenced by public agencies. Apart from explicit rules, regulators could impose some of these requirements as part of a settlement in an enforcement proceeding. Often such proceedings end with the offender's filing a compliance plan that promises a set of actions to remedy existing problems. Shifting monitoring responsibility within the company might be appropriately discussed in such a context. An agency may have even more detailed impact when regulation is joined to the use of the contract mechanism, especially if a research and development effort is involved. Approval of key personnel, of project organization, and of evaluating, monitoring, and reporting requirements are routine parts of major federal contracts. The lure of government money to demonstrate a new technology, for example, can give the government significant leverage — provided the contracting and regulating agencies coordinate their activities (which, unfortunately, they generally do not).

Where these mechanisms are not usable, regulators can try informal bargaining. Since much judgment and discretion is involved in regulatory matters, officials could try to extract internal changes as the price for being more understanding about a regulatee's problems. This is likely to be much less satisfactory than more formal approaches. Explicit, open agreements do increase the accountability of the regulators through the political process, and do protect regulatees against the arbitrary abuse of discretion. On the other hand, a sensible and honest regulator's willingness to accept a proposal may well depend on his view of the capacity and energy of those who will manage the effort. It is hard to say that he should ignore such features of the situation, and that he should not explain his views to the regulated organization.

Although likely to be resented by some top executives, these measures can lead to changes in an organization that can be beneficial from a manager's point of view. For example, regulators might push for changes that management itself would favor, if the latter were aware of the situation. Outside pressure can also be helpful to a manager in overcoming internal opposition to structural changes, allowing him to blame the regulators for something he wanted to do anyway but avoided for internal political reasons. Given the impact of structure on behavior, regulators might well be willing to take more initiative and run more risks in this regard than they usually have in the past.

Regulators who want to be more effective have several options. The reasonableness of what they ask, the ease with which they can monitor behavior and enforce penalties, public support for the regulatory program, and the existence of channels through which concerned citizens can impose costs on a recalcitrant organization are all potential levers for improving regulatory effectiveness. Within the limits of their existing knowledge, tools, and public support, agencies can also influence the companies they are regulating through informal contacts and measures designed to affect the internal organizations of these companies. Regulators who want to do better generally can. They confront obstacles and problems, but they are no more "perfectly coerced" than those they regulate.

Despite the discretion organizations do have, regulators and regulatees alike respond to the larger world if this larger world is insistent enough. Certainly, there is no one-to-one correspondence between public expectations and the behavior of a utility or regulator. Individuals all along the way—both inside and outside these organizations—make choices that have their own independent bearing on events. Yet, in the final analysis, people can and do influence the choices of power. Organizations can be responsive, but only when this is what public expectations and efforts warrant and require.

Epilogue: Personal Responsibility and the Environment

We found that the environmental policies of different companies could in part be explained without reference to the individual values or personal commitments of their managers. When community concerns were substantial and when effective outside institutions existed, the long-run self-interest or organizations motivated them to take heed of their environmental impacts. The accounts that managers gave us of their organizations' decisions also fit this pattern. Rarely did we hear managers say that they had decided to institute pollution controls because they personally had come to feel that old policies were wrong; rather they said that social expectations had changed, so that old practices were no longer acceptable.

No doubt some managers perceived that the new policies were "right." Perhaps they were secretly glad that circumstances had forced them to act this way, but kept these feelings hidden because they lacked the solid justification that corporate self-interest offers in contemporary American culture. It is clear, however, that proenvironmental policies were motivated to a great extent by calculations of what would foster the survival of the organization.

This picture of managerial motivation leads us to rely primarily, or even entirely, on external pressures and incentives to alter the behavior of an organization. Given that this can be done in some measure, is this a bad situation to be in? Perhaps we should be relieved to know that organizations are indeed capable of reshaping themselves when pressed to do so.

Yet many of the same reasons that make it desirable to have organizations respond positively—to protect the environment without having to be coerced in detail—also make it desirable to have organizations that take some initiative on such matters even before publicly imposed sanctions and incentives are put into place. If they did take such initiative, there would be even less need to invest resources in policing corporate behavior, and there would be less danger that problems would go uncontrolled because the public attention and social resources needed to deal with them were lacking. Managerial action motivated by a range of social concerns would be particularly valuable in curbing undesirable activities at an early stage, *before* their effects became severe enough to provoke a public outcry. Managers might be expected to notice some problems earlier than the public at large simply because these problems are closely connected to their activities. Perhaps a desire to be responsible for minimizing a business's social side-effects could enable a manager to pay attention to early but obvious warning signs.

But can we reasonably expect managers to be aware of the need for change before society has defined their actions as a problem? Aren't we, in this way, saying that we expect managers to be more sensitive to their own shortcomings than we are to ours? In terms of the discussion of human problem solving presented in Chapter 2, it may seem that this is expecting too much. Managers confront a large array of problems: production problems, investment questions, financial uncertainties, personnel needs, and so on. Because time is short, they typically solve these problems as best they can, relying on previously acquired strategies, axioms, maxims, and rules of thumb. It is unlikely that such strategies will be systematically revised as long as they appear to be functioning adequately. This makes it unlikely that "new" or "small" problems, or potential problems, will be given much attention when they are not yet subject to public concern and do not have an obvious impact on corporate profits. Small problems ignored today *may* have very unfortunate consequences in the future. But it is difficult to know which stitch in time will save nine.

Traditional normative and positive theories of the firm also argue against an assumption of social responsibility by managers. In these theories the manager is seen as the trustee of the shareholders' interests. Pursuing other objectives is a betrayal of their interests and may jeopardize the survival of the firm. If competitors do not make the same social investments, their costs will be lower and their products will be cheaper. Within an ideal market system, a company maximizes society's welfare by pursuing its own economic interests — that is, by producing what people want in the most efficient manner possible. Making corrections to compensate for imperfections in the market is the government's responsibility, not the manager's. After all, it is argued, what right does the individual manager have to impose on the organization his or her ideosyncratic tastes in social policy?

The difficulty with this argument is that most large firms today have significant discretion. A modest additional expenditure on pollution control, or an added effort to reduce discrimination in hiring or improve product safety, will seldom have a significant impact on a firm's survival and growth even if some of its competitors do not exactly follow suit. And economists since the 1930s have pointed out that whatever the moral obligations of managers to shareholders, the former do have significant autonomy.

There is substantial evidence that managers in fact use their autonomy to pursue organizational ends other than strict profit-maximization. Such ends may include higher executive salaries, organizational growth, and fewer administrative problems, as well as "altruistic" objectives on occasion. On balance, will society be better off if managers consult their own moral sensibilities when they make such discretionary choices? We believe the answer is "yes."

There are, as well, psychological and philosophic problems in asking managers to suppress their own moral values. Why should society consider it acceptable for managers to pursue selfish objectives like wealth and power, and yet also tell them not to pay any attention to other goals they might value? What do such expectations do to them as individuals and as citizens?

There is some recent evidence (not confirmed by our interviews) that the best and the brightest of young managers are dissatisfied with traditional conceptions of loyalty to the corporate interest and of the firm's social responsibility. Psychologist Michael Maccoby reports in *The Gamesman* that the most innovative and sophisticated managers of today possess a yearning, admittedly ill-defined, to reach out beyond their own and their company's ambitions and find some way to use their managerial talents to contribute to society.[1] Louis Banks, former managing editor of *Fortune* and now a professor at the Massachusetts Institute of Technology's Sloan School of Management, writes that older managers are confused by the insistence of young people in their company on pursuing other goals in addition to their own and the corporation's success. These goals include activities outside the company—such as spending time with one's family, supporting the career of one's spouse, and developing roots in one community—and corporate goals other than money-making. It is not that these young managers are unwilling to work or to see their company succeed; they have other concerns as well. Banks quotes one as saying, "We are what we make of ourselves. When we compromise our code of ethics, our integrity, we steal from society. Each theft results in less worth stealing, as well as a belief that what is left isn't worth saving." Another stated, "I feel that a company must be positioned between two dynamic continuums: social demands and company operating demands, and there must be continual reevaluation of the fit. When the fit has become static and nonresponsive, my association with the company will become a personal embarrassment, and my performance and loyalty will start to shake."[2]

This suggests to us, as well as to Banks, that, along with society's changing expectations of the corporation, today's young managers have expectations to which the corporation must respond. This is not surprising, in view of the fact that the corporation's young managers are part of the same society that is expecting more from the corporation. Moreover, society's concern with the quality of the environment, and young managers' concern with the possibility of self-expression in their work, both reflect an increasing abundance which allows people to devote their attention to the fulfillment of nonmaterial (or traditionally unpriced) values.

We have argued that, regardless of managers' interests in maximizing the welfare of their own organization, society has put demands on these organizations that have forced them to evolve in the direction of greater positive responsiveness. There is in our view of organizations, however, room for the exercise of personal responsibility, not only in the pursuit of individual self-interest, but also in furthering the interests in society as a whole.

Notes

1. Statement of the Problem

1. We are indebted to Graham Allison for his advice on this point.

2. Support for these propositions is given in the cases that follow. Additional evidence is provided by Marc J. Roberts and Susan O. Farrell, "The Political Economy of Implementation: The Clean Air Act and Stationary Sources," in Ann F. Friedlaender, ed., *Approaches to Controlling Air Pollution* (Cambridge, Mass.: MIT Press, 1978), pp. 152-181; and Penny Feldman and Marc J. Roberts, "Magic Bullets or Seven Card Stud: Implementing Health Care Regulations," in Richard Gordon, ed., *Issues in Health Care Regulation* (New York: McGraw-Hill, 1980), pp. 66-109.

3. Anthony Downs, "The Political Economy of Improving Our Environment," in Downs et al., *The Political Economy of Environmental Control* (Berkeley: Institute of Business and Economic Research, University of California, 1972).

4. This use, we believe, closely follows the meaning of the term in ordinary speech. It implies, however, that the adequacy of an explanation depends on the knowledge, beliefs, and purposes of its recipient. For further discussion of these points (on which there is a very large literature in the philosophy of history and the philosophy of science), see Marc J. Roberts, "On the Nature and Condition of Social Science," *Daedalus*, Summer 1974, pp. 47-64.

5. We can predict things we cannot control, as when Phoenicians predicted the tides; explain things we cannot predict, as when we prepare a safety report on an airplane crash; and even control some things we cannot explain, as when plants were selectively bred before the development of genetics. For a full discussion, see Roberts, "On the Nature and Condition of Social Science," pp. 47-64.

6. This view implies a relatively complete rejection of Milton Friedman's classic argument that the "assumptions" of a model — that is, its description of underlying structure — are simply logically irrelevant mnemonics for remembering the implied predictions. In his view, separate "applications theorems" must be developed to indicate where each "pattern" or "theory" holds, since the congruencies between the "assumptions" and reality cannot be used in this way. This seems plainly counter to common practice, as well as to common sense. See Milton Friedman, "The Methodology of Positive Economics," in his *Essays in*

Positive Economics (Chicago: University of Chicago Press, 1953), pp. 3-43.

7. For a similar view, see Herbert A. Simon, "Problems of Methodology — Discussion," *American Economic Review* 53 (May 1963): 229-231.

8. However, it is possible to measure at least some of the variables we have considered and to test them statistically.

9. This is in at least partial contrast to many classic works in organization theory, from Max Weber to more recent authors such as James March, Herbert Simon, Anthony Downs, and Gordon Tullock. See, for example, Anthony Downs, *Inside Bureaucracy* (Boston: Little, Brown, 1967); James G. March and Herbert A. Simon, *Organizations* (New York: John Wiley, 1958); and Gordon Tullock, *The Politics of Bureaucracy* (Washington, D.C.: Public Affairs Press, 1965). For Weber's discussion, see Max Weber, *Essays in Sociology*, ed. Hans H. Gerth and C. Wright Mills (New York: Oxford University Press, 1958), ch. 8. We will not even try to generalize about all large business firms, unlike Robert A. Gordon, *Business Leadership in the Large Corporation* (Berkeley: University of California Press, 1966), or Adolf A. Berle and Gardiner C. Means, *The Modern Corporation and Private Property* (New York: Harcourt, Brace & World, 1932).

10. The traditional hierarchical view goes back at least to Max Weber, whereas the "participative" model has been used by, among others, Richard M. Cyert and James G. March, *A Behavioral Theory of the Firm* (Englewood Cliffs, N.J.: Prentice-Hall, 1963), ch. 4.

11. From this viewpoint, therefore, we need not decide in general terms whether decision making in organizations is "analytical" or "cybernetic" or "cognitive"; see this question as posed by John D. Steinbruner in *The Cybernetic Theory of Decision* (Princeton, N.J.: Princeton University Press, 1974). Nor do we have to adopt one or the other of the models presented in Graham Allison, *The Essence of Decision* (Boston: Little, Brown, 1971). Each of the models these authors offer is a possible basis for understanding a particular situation. The question is which of them, singly or in combination, accounts for what has occurred. For example, Allison regards the rational interests of the organization and its internal bureaucratic politics as alternative explanations. The important factor in any particular case, however, is the motivation behind the behavior of key members of the organization.

12. Our work is thus very much in the spirit of the so-called "contingency theory" of organizations, from a descriptive as well as a prescriptive point of view. The key work on this theory is Paul R. Lawrence and Jay W. Lorsch, *Organization and Environment* (Homewood, Ill.: Richard D. Irwin, 1969).

13. See, for example, Carl G. Hempel, *Aspects of Scientific Explanation* (New York: Basic Books, 1965). Hempel focuses on what he believes to be the role of so-called "covering laws," which seem invariably to be of this form.

14. For a more extensive discussion of this point, see Roberts, "On the Nature and Condition of Social Science," pp. 47-64.

15. Thus, in mathematical terms, the relationship we are looking for is a "functional" one: it deals with the function relating a set of independent variables to a dependent variable, and describes how this function itself varies under different circumstances.

16. We are indebted to James Duesenberry for this point.

2. A Framework for Explaining the Behavior of Organizations

1. This contrasts with much of the sociological literature, which focuses on why and how organizations exist. See, for example, Amitai Etzioni, *A Comparative Analysis of Complex Organizations*, rev. ed. (New York: Free Press, 1975).

2. An earlier version of these concepts was given in Marc J. Roberts, "A Framework for Explaining the Behavior of Resource Allocating Organizations," Harvard Institute of Economic Research, Discussion Paper no. 264 (Cambridge, Mass., 1972).

3. Roberts, "On the Nature and Condition of Social Science," pp. 47-64.

4. See Kenneth Arrow, *The Limits of Organization* (New York: W. W. Norton, 1974); Marc J. Roberts, "On Time," *Quarterly Journal of Economics* 4 (November 1937): 386-405; and Oliver Williamson, "The Vertical Integration of Production," *American Economic Review* 61 (May 1971): 112-123.

5. See, for example, Ronald Coase, "The Nature of the Firm," *Economica* 4 (November 1937): 386-405; and Williamson, "The Vertical Integration of Production."

6. For example, Parsons suggests that organizations often have to socialize employees to value the kinds of rewards the organization can offer. See Talcott Parsons, "The Motivation of Economic Activities," *Canadian Journal of Economics and Political Science* 6 (May 1940): 187-202, reprinted in Parsons, *Essays in Sociological Theory*, rev. ed. (New York: Free Press, 1954). Clearly, this sort of process cannot be easily or rapidly reversed.

7. In noting the potential advantages of hierarchical organizations, we are not contending that, historically, large industrial enterprises were created only to attain these benefits — an issue of legitimate scholarly debate. Marxist writer Stephen Marglin, for example, in his essay, "What Do Bosses Do?" Harvard Institute of Economic Research, Discussion Paper no. 222 (Cambridge, Mass., 1971), contends that large hierarchical firms were developed to control and exploit labor — for the sake of the owners. Rather than exploring here whether hierarchy and specialization are always beneficial, and to what degree, we are simply contending that a system of stable relationships among technical specialists and "specialists" in general coordination does solve certain problems that arise in human cooperation, regardless of the motives of those creating the organization, or the nature of ownership and control relations in the larger society.

8. See Herbert A. Simon, *The Sciences of the Artificial* (Cambridge, Mass.: MIT Press, 1963) for a discussion of this problem of "decomposability," which economists also consider when they talk about the viability of "suboptimization" — that is, solving various component parts of the overall problem separately.

9. Herbert A. Simon, "Problems of Methodology — Discussion," *American Economic Review* 53 (May 1963): 229-231.

10. A classic discussion of this point is R. Duncan Luce and Howard Raiffa, *Games and Decisions* (New York: John Wiley, 1957).

11. This point has been emphasized by Nicholas Georgescu-Roegen in

Analytical Economics (Cambridge, Mass.: Harvard University Press, 1966), pp. 83-91.

12. Oddly enough, many economic models of firm behavior in economics do not allow for such learning. Firms are presumed to assume that the specific decision, or at least the decision rule, used by the other firms in the industry will remain stable. See the classic discussion in William Fellner, *Competition among the Few* (New York: Knopf, 1949).

13. James G. March and Herbert A. Simon, *Organizations* (New York: John Wiley, 1958); also Chester I. Barnard, *The Functions of the Executive* (Cambridge, Mass.: Harvard University Press, 1938).

14. Thus, we are arguing that actual thought processes are a complex mixture of routine responses and attempts at analyses, where the latter are likely to be highly imperfect because of limits on our cognitive capacities. They are, therefore, a mixture of all three types of thinking, as presented in John D. Steinbruner, *The Cybernetic Theory of Decision* (Princeton, N.J.: Princeton University Press, 1974).

15. One of the best-known expositions of this point is to be found in Thomas Kuhn, *The Structure of Scientific Revolutions*, 2d ed. (Chicago: University of Chicago Press, 1970), but it has been made by many other authors. See, for example, Stephen Toulmin, *Human Understanding*, vol. 1 (Princeton, N.J.: Princeton University Press, 1972).

16. E. H. Gombrich, in *Art and Illusion* (New York: Pantheon, 1961), argues that similar sets of assumptions govern activities such as painting, where they are reflected in the visual conventions that make up style.

17. Thus, "values" in the sense of unproved and unprovable statements about what is desirable are logically prior to "facts" in the sense of propositions about the world, because the latter can only be defended on the basis of the former. The reverse is not true, however: no collection of "facts" can establish a "value." The naturalistic fallacy is a fallacy.

18. Most microeconomic models, for example, have this peculiar dual status. They are models of how people should behave, on certain assumptions, and proposed descriptions of how they do behave. See, for example, Edwin Mansfield, *Microeconomics* (New York: W. W. Norton, 1970).

19. This viewpoint is decidedly different from that presented in Kuhn's classic, *The Structure of Scientific Revolutions*, in which disagreeing scientists are portrayed as either sharing or not sharing a defining "paradigm" that includes all critical assumptions. In our view there can be more or less "revolutionary" changes in science, depending on the extent to which there are shared fundamental assumptions (if any) that could serve as the basis for constructing mutually acceptable arguments.

20. Readers familiar with the sociological literature will wonder whether we mean to include only those outputs that serve as apparent goals for the organization, or also those that serve what Merton calls "latent" functions—the implicit and unintended purposes an entity serves in the social order. See Robert K. Merton, "Manifest and Latent Functions," in his *On Theoretical Sociology* (New York: Free Press, 1967). Our answer, which is consistent with our approach, is that we want to focus on outputs that are valued by those inside and

outside the organization, and whose production affects organizational outcomes. In Merton's own example of "latent" functions—the social work role of the urban political machine—the favors he describes as "latent" clearly were perceived as valuable by both insiders and outsiders and therefore fit well into our framework. Such outputs may be partially unconscious (for example, patients' desires for doctors to deliver magical reassurance), but they are still relevant to our analysis if changes in outputs (for example, a doctor's failure to prescribe placebos) will in turn influence the way in which the outside world reacts.

21. The second and third categories that follow are those typically taken into account in most theories of the firm, in the form of "factor market" and "product market" conditions. See, for example, the review in Frederic M. Scherer, *Industrial Market Structure and Economic Performance* (Chicago: Rand McNally, 1970), ch. 5.

22. The only economics work we are aware of that takes a similar view is a brief note by Zvi Griliches, in which he points out that the notion of what is technically possible cannot be precisely defined in a "yes-no" fashion. See his "Comment," in *The Rate and Direction of Inventive Activity*, A Conference of the Universities-National Bureau Committee for Economic Research (Princeton, N.J.: Princeton University Press, 1962), pp. 346-353.

23. The uncertainty in such penalties makes it difficult to draw the "penalty function" that relates consequences to company actions. See Marc J. Roberts, "Environmental Protection: The Complexities of Real Policy Choice," in Neil A. Swainson, ed., *Managing the Water Environment* (Vancouver: University of British Columbia Press, 1976).

24. Marc J. Roberts and Susan O. Farrell, "The Political Economy of Implementation," in Ann F. Friendlaender, ed., *Approaches to Controlling Air Pollution* (Cambridge, Mass.: MIT Press, 1978); Penny Feldman and Marc J. Roberts, "Magic Bullets or Seven Card Stud: Implementing Health Care Regulations," in Richard Gordon, ed., *Issues in Health Care Regulation* (New York: McGraw-Hill, 1980), pp. 66-109.

25. "Payoff functions" are a generalization of the more limited notion of "penalty functions" mentioned in note 23 above.

26. See Ralph L. Keeney and Howard Raiffa, *Decisions with Multiple Objectives* (New York: John Wiley, 1976).

27. The term "structure," in the sense used here, is based on Alfred D. Chandler, *Strategy and Structure* (Cambridge, Mass.: Harvard University Press, 1962), although his use includes some of what we distinguish as the "control system." The term as it appears here is now widely used in the managing literature. See, for example, Joseph L. Bower, *Managing the Resource Allocation Process* (Boston: Harvard Graduate School of Business Administration, Division of Research, 1970).

28. Barnard, *The Functions of the Executive*, pp. 136-137; Michel Crozier, *The Bureaucratic Phenomenon* (Chicago: University of Chicago Press, 1964), p. 164.

29. This point is discussed repeatedly by Kenneth R. Andrews in *The Concepts of Corporate Strategy* (Homewood, Ill.: Dow Jones-Irwin, 1971), especially pp. 1, 16-17, 191. The classic discussion of the problem of integration in

the business context is Paul R. Lawrence and Jay W. Lorsch, *Organization and Environment* (Homewood, Ill.: Richard D. Irwin, 1969). See also Gordon Tullock, *The Politics of Bureaucracy* (Washington, D.C.: Public Affairs Press, 1965), pp. 181-186; and Anthony Downs, *Inside Bureaucracy* (Boston: Little, Brown, 1967), pp. 148, 183-190.

30. Indeed, as Richard E. Neustadt argues in *Alliance Politics* (New York: Columbia University Press, 1970), a crisis is preeminently a time when a manager is forced to rely on his theories, prejudices, and beliefs because there is no time to acquire and analyze new data.

31. The term "control" or "control system" goes back at least to Barnard's classic, *The Functions of the Executive*, and has since been widely used in similar ways by many writers.

32. See Downs, *Inside Bureaucracy*, pp. 59-80.

33. See Tullock's discussion of the "imperial" bureaucracy of the British Colonial Office, which depends for its "coordinating principle essentially on the relevant ruling group having gone to the same schools thirty years past" (Tullock, *The Politics of Bureaucracy*, p. 173).

34. There are many stories about such problems from Soviet experience — for example, the practice of rewarding managers on tonnage output has resulted in very overweight machines. See Joseph S. Berliner, *Factory and Manager in the U.S.S.R.* (Cambridge, Mass.: Harvard University Press, 1957).

35. That is, in a strong control system the contingent probability distributions of rewards and punishments for various actions have noticeably different expected values and reasonably small variances. High variance, in contrast, implies a relatively *arbitrary* system.

36. See Thomas C. Schelling, "Command and Control," in James W. McKie, ed., *Social Responsibility and the Business Predicament* (Washington, D.C.: The Brookings Institution, 1974), especially pp. 85-88. He argues that, because chief executives may not be able to enforce directives on social responsibility deep in the organization, it may sometimes be advantageous for the government to impose these requirements directly.

37. This does not mean, however, that such "jumpers" have no incentive to perform well in their current responsibilities, since doing a good job can be the best basis for such a jump. This is in contrast to Downs, *Inside Bureaucracy*, p. 95.

38. Michael E. Hunt, "Competition in the Major Home Appliance Industry, 1960-1970" (Ph.D. diss., Harvard University, 1972), discusses how one major firm found it necessary to fund long-range research and development centrally, because division managers would not use divisional funds to support research projects that had payoffs beyond the managers' expected tenure.

39. Robert W. Ackerman, "How Companies Respond to Social Demand," *Harvard Business Review* 51 (July/August 1973): 88-98.

40. When organization growth is antithetical to survival or would undermine the positions of key actors, we should not necessarily expect growth. See Marc Tipermas, "Jurisdictionalism: Politics of Executive Reorganizations" (Ph.D. diss., Harvard University, 1976). See also Matthew Holden, "Imperialism in Bureaucracy," *American Political Science Review* 60 (December 1966): 943-951.

41. See, for example, Crozier, *The Bureaucratic Phenomenon*, on the personalities and attitudes of various managerial groups in a series of French industrial plants. See also Lawrence and Lorsch, *Organization and Environment*, p. 153.

42. James Q. Wilson, *Varieties of Police Behavior* (Cambridge, Mass.: Harvard University Press, 1968).

43. For a classic study of the role of professional training in shaping an organization, see Herbert Kaufman, *The Forest Ranger* (Baltimore: Johns Hopkins Press, 1960).

44. We first encountered this argument in a seminar given by Professor Guido Calabresi of Yale Law School.

45. Talcott Parsons in particular emphasizes the importance of role identification, as opposed to incentives, in eliciting active cooperation of members in an organization.

46. Philip Selznick, *Leadership in Administration* (New York: Harper & Row, 1957), pp. 105-106, discusses the joint importance of recruitment and indoctrination, whereas Barnard sees "leadership" as the most important "function of the executive."

47. See Andrews, *The Concepts of Corporate Strategy*, for a discussion of various meanings of the term.

48. Similar problems are encountered in anthropology, where myths and legends used to explain social and cultural phenomena may diverge substantially from current reality. One interesting example is E. E. Evans-Pritchard, *The Neuer* (Oxford: Clarendon Press, 1940).

49. The cases that follow provide examples of both kinds of situations.

50. We are indebted to Richard Neustadt for this point.

51. Selznick, *Leadership in Administration*, p. 93. The classic work on groups is George C. Homans, *The Human Group* (New York: Harcourt, Brace & World, 1950).

52. Despite various "cybernetic theories," it is clear that people and, hence, organizations are not just reactive (see Steinbruner, *The Cybernetic Theory of Decision*). They can anticipate changes in their circumstances and act on their own initiative. In this case, Simon's work is suggestive, given his notion that when goals are easily achieved, definitions of what is "satisfactory" will adjust upward, touching off a review of behavior. See Herbert A. Simon, "A Behavioral Model of Rational Choice," *Quarterly Journal of Economics* 69 (February 1955): 99-118.

53. For a less explicit analysis along similar lines, see James G. March, "The Business Firm as a Political Coalition," *Journal of Politics* 24 (November 1962): 662-678; and N. E. Long, "The Administrative Organization as a Political System," in Sidney Mailick and Edward H. van Ness, eds., *Concepts and Issues in Administrative Behavior* (Englewood Cliffs, N.J.: Prentice-Hall, 1972), pp. 101-121. A similar perspective is offered by Charles Perrow, "The Analysis of Goals in Complex Organizations," *American Sociological Review* 26 (December 1961): 854-865.

54. Thus, with reference to our earlier discussion in note 19 above, we cannot say that they either "do" or "do not" share "a paradigm." They are in an intermediary position.

55. Amitai Etzioni, "Control," in James G. March, ed., *Handbook of Organizations* (Chicago: Rand McNally, 1965), pp. 655-657; Tullock, *The Politics of Bureaucracy*, p. 132.

56. See Tullock, *The Politics of Bureaucracy*, pp. 206-209.

57. Jeffrey L. Pressman and Aaron B. Wildavsky, *Implementation* (Berkeley: University of California Press, 1973).

58. On this point, see Richard M. Cyert and James G. March, *A Behavioral Theory of the Firm* (Englewood Cliffs, N.J.: Prentice-Hall, 1963), pp. 120-121. They stress that a firm will try simple changes before it will consider anything as complex as changing organizational structure.

59. See Arrow, *The Limits of Organization*, pp. 58-59.

60. Neustadt, *Alliance Politics*, pp. 65-69, 119, 128.

61. Chris Argyris and Donald A. Schön, *Organizational Learning: A Theory of Action Perspective* (Reading, Mass.: Addison-Wesley, 1978).

62. Thus the question becomes: How fundamental a change in perceptions is the organization willing to consider? Will it entertain new ways to make and sell existing products, a movement into completely new lines of business, its own transformation into a syndicalist cooperative, or its evolution into a monastic order?

63. Bower, *Managing the Resource Allocation Process*.

64. Chandler, *Strategy and Structure*.

65. After all, no one "chooses" what genetic variations to experiment with in evolution.

3. A Primer on Electric Utility Operations

1. The discussion that follows is necessarily very brief. Readers who would like to pursue these issues in more detail might want to consult Joseph Priest, *Energy for a Technological Society*, 2d ed. (Reading, Mass.: Addison-Wesley, 1970), for an easy-to-read, nontechnical discussion; or Richard C. Bailie, *Energy Conversion Engineering* (Reading, Mass.: Addison-Wesley, 1978), which covers similar material but from an engineering viewpoint, using a good deal of formal mathematics. Those interested in a detailed discussion of some aspects of generating technology might want to consult *Steam, Its Generation and Use* (New York: Babcock and Wilcox, 1972). Produced by a leading boiler manufacturer, it has numerous, clear diagrams and photographs of various fossil-fuel and nuclear plants, control equipment, and so forth. Anthony V. Nero, Jr., *A Guidebook to Nuclear Reactors* (Berkeley: University of California Press, 1979), is relatively thorough without being very technical. A wide-ranging and well-selected group of recent papers can be found in M. Granger Morgan, ed., *Energy and Man* (New York: I.E.E.E. Press, 1975).

2. The sources listed in the previous note all treat environmental issues to some extent. Another helpful work is Richard Wilson and William J. Jones, *Energy, Ecology and the Environment* (New York: Academic Press, 1974). Two recent broad surveys of national energy problems contain useful discussions of environmental effects: Sam H. Schurr et al., *Energy in America's Future* (Baltimore: Johns Hopkins Press, 1979), especially pt. IV, pp. 343-397; and Hans H.

Landsberg et al., *Energy: The Next Twenty Years* (Cambridge, Mass.: Ballinger, 1979), especially chs. 10-12, pp. 327-465.

3. Much of the pioneering work on the diffusion of power plant emissions (air pollution) was done at TVA. Two of the most relevant of the many papers that the group at TVA published on these matters are: S. B. Carpenter et al., "Principal Plume Dispersion Models: T.V.A. Power Plants," *Journal of the Air Pollution Control Association* 21, no. 8 (August 1971): 491-495; and T. L. Montgomery et al., "A Simplified Technique Used to Evaluate Atmospheric Dispersion of Emissions from Large Power Plants," *Journal of the Air Pollution Control Association* 23, no. 5 (May 1973): 388-394. See also Bailie, *Energy Conversion Engineering*, pp. 403-413.

4. Wilson and Jones, *Energy, Ecology and the Environment*, pp. 200-222; and Council on Environmental Quality, *Environmental Quality: 1977*, eighth annual report (Washington, D.C.: Government Printing Office, 1977), pp. 151-168. One major recent and controversial study is Lester B. Love and Eugene P. Seskin, *Air Pollution and Human Health* (Baltimore: Johns Hopkins Press, 1977). There has been even less work done on nonhuman effects. One interesting recent study is Richard M. Adams et al., *Methods Development for Assessing Air Pollution Control Benefits*, vol. III: *A Preliminary Assessment of Air Pollution Damages for Selected Crops within Southern California*, Office of Health and Ecological Effects, U.S. Environmental Protection Agency, EPA-600/5-79-DO1C (Washington, D.C., 1979). The study shows that losses vary greatly depending on crop sensitivity and on the local area's level of air pollution (see table 6.2, p. 82). See also *Air Pollution across Natural Boundaries: The Impact on the Environment of Sulfur in Air and Precipitation*, Royal Ministries for Foreign Affairs and Agriculture, Stockholm, 1971.

5. Although TVA has perhaps been subject to the most controversy, due to varying ecological conditions the most difficult land reclamation problems arise in the arid western states, areas in which the Los Angeles Department of Water and Power is part owner of some large, coal-fired generating capacity, as we discuss below. See James E. Rowe, ed., *Coal Surface Mining: Impacts of Reclamation* (Boulder, Colo.: Westview Press, 1979).

6. The one alternative source that might make some significant medium-run contribution is solar power. See Schurr et al., *Energy in America's Future*, pp. 306-342; Landsberg et al., *Energy: The Next Twenty Years*, ch. 13, pp. 467-507; and Priest, *Energy for a Technological Society*, chs. 11 and 12, pp. 262-307. Among our companies, PG&E has taken the lead in geothermal development at the Geysers site. Both PG&E and TVA have also undertaken some significant efforts to encourage customer conservation in recent years, which is not a source of power but does lower the need to build new facilities.

7. See Edison Electric Institute, *Statistical Year Book of the Electric Utility Industry for 1978* (Washington, D.C.: Edison Electric Institute, 1979), table 8S, p. 15, for sales data for 1958-1978. Even more recent data can be found in *Electrical World*, January 15, 1980, p. 14.

8. There is still substantial disagreement about how best to represent and allow for such uncertainties, and as to the implications for guessing wrong. Compare Michael L. Telson, "The Economics of Alternative Levels of Reliabil-

ity for Electric Power Generation Systems," *Bell Journal of Economics* 6, no. 2 (Autumn 1975): 679-694, with Edward G. Cazalet et al., *Costs and Benefits of Over/Under Capacity in Electric Power System Planning* (Palo Alto, Calif.: Electric Power Research Institute, 1978). This has become a critical issue, especially for the California utilities in our study. See California Energy Resources Conservation and Development Commission, *Electricity Forecasting and Planning*, vol. II, especially ch. 5, staff-proposed preliminary report, Sacramento, Calif., September 24, 1976.

9. This phenomenon is called the "Averch-Johnson effect" after the authors of the paper that first argued this point about investment in general, not just pollution control capital. See Harvey Averch and Leland L. Johnson, "Behavior of the Firm under Regulatory Constraint," *American Economic Review* 52, no. 6 (December 1962): 1052-1069.

10. Paul Joskow, "Inflation and Environmental Concern: Structural Change in the Process of Public Utility Price Regulation," *Journal of Law and Economics* 17, no. 2 (October 1974): 291-327.

11. Federal Power Commission, Bureau of Power, *Annual Summary of Cost and Quality of Steam Electric Plant Fuels, 1975* (Washington, D.C.: Government Printing Office, 1976).

12. Schurr et al., *Energy in America's Future*, pp. 256-268.

13. Charles Komanoff, *Power Plant Performance* (New York: Council on Economic Priorities, 1976), pp. 94-95.

14. Nero, *A Guidebook to Nuclear Reactors*, pp. 109-119; also Hugh C. McIntyre, "Natural-Uranium Heavy-Water Reactors," *Scientific American* 233 (October 1975): 17.

15. On precipitators generally, see "An Electrostatic Precipitator Systems Study," final report to the National Air Pollution Control Administration, Southern Research Institute, Birmingham, Ala., October 30, 1970. A very detailed survey of the field is also offered by U.S. Environmental Protection Agency, *Control Techniques for Particulate Air Pollutants*, Office of Air Programs, Research Triangle Park, N.C., January 1969. On the effects of sulfur on collection efficiency, see Roger G. Ramsdell, Jr., and Charles F. Soutar, "Anti-Pollution Program of Consolidated Edison Company of New York," paper presented to the Environmental Engineering Conference of the American Society of Civil Engineers, Chattanooga, Tennessee, May 13-17, 1968, especially fig. 7. See also "Are Precipitators Dead?" *Electrical World*, August 1, 1971; and William G. Henke, "The New 'Hot' Electrostatic Precipitator," *Combustion*, October 1970, pp. 50-54.

16. Sulfur Oxide Control Technology Assessment Panel, Federal Interagency Committee for Evaluation of State Air Implementation Plans, *Projected Utilization of Stack Gas Cleaning Systems by Steam-Electric Plants* (Springfield, Va.: National Technical Information Service, 1973). See also Paul H. Weaver, "Behind the Great Scrubber Fracas," *Fortune*, February 1975, pp. 106-114.

17. Richard B. Stewart and James E. Krier, *Environmental Law and Policy* (Indianapolis: Bobbs-Merrill, 1978), pp. 402-404.

18. Ibid., ch. 8, pp. 733-808.

19. Lettie McSpadden Wenner, *One Environment under Law* (Pacific

Palisades, Calif.: Goodyear Publishing Co., 1976), pp. 51-103. On the amount of discretion left to the states, see Marc J. Roberts and Susan O. Farrell, "The Political Economy of Implementation: The Clean Air Act and Stationary Sources," in Ann F. Friedlaender, ed., *Approaches to Controlling Air Pollution* (Cambridge, Mass.: MIT Press, 1978).

20. Landsberg et al., *Energy*, pp. 378-381. Also Council on Environmental Quality, *Environmental Quality: 1979*, tenth annual report (Washington, D.C.: Government Printing Office, 1979), pp. 58-61.

21. Stewart and Krier, *Environmental Law*, pp. 994-996.

4. The Tennessee Valley Authority

1. Tennessee Valley Authority (hereafter abbreviated "TVA"), *Power Annual Report*, 1975, p. 30. On TVA's varied functions, see any annual report, or founding legislation, 48 Stat. 58 (1933), 16 U.S. Code no. 831 (1958).

2. TVA, *Power Annual Report*, 1975, pp. 1, 21. See Aaron B. Wildavsky, "TVA and Power Politics," *American Political Science Review* 55 (September 1961): 579, on transition to steam plants.

3. TVA, "Questions Raised Concerning TVA's Power Program at Hearings before the House Subcommittee on Public Works Appropriation—May 1973." On regional discontent, see Deborah Shapley, "TVA Today: Former Reformers in an Era of Expensive Electricity," *Science* 19 (November 1976): 814-815.

4. TVA's origins are described in many books and articles about the agency. For a good account in a basic text on the agency, see E. Herman Pritchett, *The Tennessee Valley Authority: A Study in Public Administration* (Chapel Hill, N.C.: University of North Carolina Press, 1943), ch. 1.

5. Martha Derthick, with the assistance of Gary Bombardier, *Between State and Nation: Regional Organizations in the United States* (Washington, D.C.: Brookings Institution, 1974), ch. 2. See also Thomas K. McCraw, *Morgan vs. Lilienthal: The Feud within the TVA* (Chicago: Loyola University Press, 1970); and Thomas K. McCraw, *TVA and the Power Fight, 1933-39* (Philadelphia: Lippincott, 1971).

6. Rexford G. Tugwell and E. C. Banfield, "Grass Roots Democracy—Myth or Reality," *Public Administration Review* 10 (Winter 1950): 47-55; Edward Cowan, "Today TVA Is Assailed as Threat to Environment," *New York Times*, August 5, 1973, pp. 1, 43.

7. 48 Stat. 58 (1933), 16 U.S. Code no. 831 (1958).

8. Marguerite Owen, *The Tennessee Valley Authority* (New York: Praeger, 1973), p. 183.

9. Cowan, "Today TVA Is Assailed," p. 43.

10. Pritchett, *Tennessee Valley Authority*, pp. 57-65, 105; McCraw, *TVA and the Power Fight*, particularly ch. 7.

11. Wildavsky, "TVA and Power Politics," pp. 579-580.

12. Wildavsky, "TVA and Power Politics," pp. 580-587; and Aaron Wildavsky, *Dixon-Yates: A Study in Power Politics* (New Haven, Conn.: Yale University Press, 1962). Emmett John Hughes, *The Ordeal of Power: A Political*

Memoir of the Eisenhower Years (New York: Atheneum, 1963), p. 152, quotes Eisenhower as saying, "By God, if we could ever do it before we leave here, I'd like to see us *sell* the whole thing [TVA], but I suppose we can't go that far."

13. Wildavsky, "TVA and Power Politics," pp. 587-588; Roscoe C. Martin, "The Tennessee Valley Authority: A Study of Federal Control," *Law and Contemporary Problems* 22 (Summer 1957): 374-376; and John Ed Pearce, "The Creeping Conservatism of TVA," *The Reporter* 26 (January 4, 1962): 32.

14. Wildavsky, "TVA and Power Politics," p. 587; U.S. Congress, Committee on Appropriations, *Public Works Appropriations for 1956* (Washington, D.C.: Government Printing Office, 1955), pp. 331-351.

15. Wildavsky, "TVA and Power Politics," pp. 587-588. See also *Congressional Quarterly*, August 21, 1959, p. 1138; and *Congressional Quarterly Almanac* 15 (1959): 261-265.

16. Arnold R. Jones, "The Financing of TVA," *Law and Contemporary Problems* 26 (Autumn 1961): 730-731. (Jones was a director of TVA.) On congressional view of power budget, see exchange between Aubrey Wagner and U.S. Representative Joe L. Evins in U.S. House of Representatives, Committee on Appropriations, Subcommittee on Public Works, *Hearings: Public Works for Water, Pollution Control, and Power Development and Atomic Energy Commission Appropriation, 1971* (Washington, D.C.: Government Printing Office, 1970), pt. 4, p. 157.

17. TVA, *Annual Report*, 1972, p. 13.

18. Transcript of hearings before the Alabama Air Pollution Control Commission on relaxation of SO_2 standards, May 1973.

19. Interviews with TVA personnel, September 1973.

20. See Bruce Rogers, "Public Policy and Pollution Abatement: TVA and Strip Mining" (Ph.D. diss., Indiana University, 1973), pp. 21-22, 325. See also "3 Ecological Groups Sue T.V.A. on Strip-Mine Coal," *New York Times*, March 3, 1971.

21. Bureau of National Affairs, *Environment Reporter—Current Developments*, June 11, 1976, p. 221.

22. Bureau of National Affairs, *Environment Reporter—Current Developments*, July 22, 1977, p. 444, on suits; August 12, 1977, p. 570, on Clean Air Act Amendments.

23. TVA, *Environmental Statement: Policies Relating to Sources of Coal Used by the Tennessee Valley Authority for Electric Power Generation*, December 6, 1971.

24. In FDR's words, TVA was to be "a corporation clothed with the power of government but possessed of the flexibility and initiative of a private enterprise" (Pritchett, *Tennessee Valley Authority*, p. 222). On structural features, see Martin, "The Tennessee Valley Authority," pp. 356-357; and Pritchett, *Tennessee Valley Authority*, pp. 249-262. On efforts to place TVA in the Department of the Interior, see *The Journals of David Lilienthal*, vol. 1, *The TVA Years* (New York: Harper & Row, 1964), pp. 125-138, 150.

25. Pearce, "The Creeping Conservatism of TVA," p. 34. Owen, *The Tennessee Valley Authority*, p. 55, presents this episode as less of a confrontation. Owen states that "TVA did not construe the letter as a directive. Respect-

fully, the arguments presented were rebutted, and, without protest from the President, the plant was located where the Board determined it should be placed to provide electricity to consumers of the region at the 'lowest possible rates' as the Act directs."

26. Interview with former U.S. Public Health Service official, August 22, 1974.

27. In June 1974 the EPA-TVA Task Force made a report entitled *Preliminary Assessment of Alternative Sulfur Oxide Control Strategies for TVA Steam Plants.* In late 1976 the EPA issued notices of violation in response to TVA's continued failure to meet the SO_2 emission standards. This was apparently not effective in changing TVA's behavior, and in July 1977 the EPA joined Alabama, Kentucky, and a number of environmental groups in legal challenges to TVA. The out-of-court settlement to this suit is the basis for TVA's current control program. See *Environment Reporter—Current Developments* 7, no. 42 (February 18, 1977): 1611; vol. 7, no. 47 (March 25, 1977): 1795-1796; vol. 8, no. 12 (July 22, 1977): 444-445; vol. 9, no. 33 (December 15, 1978): 1451-1452.

28. Contending that its heat discharges are not causing ecological harm, TVA has not installed cooling towers at any of its coal-fired plants other than at Paradise (where once-through cooling was causing a "fish fry," according to one Kentucky official). A few others are apparently violating state standards. S. L. Jones, director of the Water Quality Control Division of the Tennessee Department of Public Health, said in 1975 that there was a good possibility that TVA was violating state thermal standards at three of its Tennessee plants. He added, however, that he didn't think any serious harm was being done at these sites. On the decision to install cooling towers at nuclear plants, see TVA Press Release, "Cooling Towers Planned for TVA Sequoyah Plant," September 17, 1973.

29. Shapley, "TVA Today," pp. 816-817.

30. TVA, *Organization Bulletin* 1 (January 1, 1973): 1.

31. Pritchett, *The Tennessee Valley Authority,* pp. 151-166, 186-216.

32. Owen, *The Tennessee Valley Authority,* app. B, pp. 260-261.

33. "From the beginning the policy of the general manager's office was decentralization and delegation of authority. Considering the wide range of activities in which TVA was engaged, such a policy was practically inevitable. For no one man could have been found with the capacity to direct the dam construction program, fertilizer research, agricultural development, power production and marketing, and so on. These are all fields for specialists and the true role of the general manager in such a situation is to act as a coordinator of specialists" (Pritchett, *The Tennessee Valley Authority,* p. 166; and interviews with TVA officials, September 1973).

34. Interview with former chairman Aubrey Wagner, December 12, 1973.

35. Ibid.

36. In interviews on July 21, 1976, and September 17, 1973, respectively, former general manager Louis J. Van Mol and assistant director of personnel John S. Bynon noted that the heads of Offices and Divisions are encouraged to work out their differences before going to the general manager and the board. Van Mol noted that the Office and Division heads were working under time lim-

its prescribed by the general manager.

37. G. O. Wessenauer came to TVA in 1935 and served as manager of power from 1944 to 1970; R. H. Kampmeier joined TVA's power engineering staff in 1933 and served as assistant manager of power from 1950 to 1968.

38. Interview with Fred Thomas, September 20, 1973.

39. Of course, internal structure alone does not explain the accommodating strategies of the TVA Divisions outside the Office of Power. These Divisions, too, were aware of external concern with keeping rates low, particularly after 1967, when rates started to rise. The point is, however, that there was a strong internal group reinforcing this message and making it highly advantageous for a Division to develop a strategy that would fit in with the overall "low-cost power" objective.

40. Thomas C. Schelling, *The Strategy of Conflict* (New York: Oxford University Press, 1973), pp. 22-28.

41. Although most board chairmen have been insiders, many other directors have come from outside the organization.

42. Bruce Rogers, "TVA and Strip Mining," pp. 225-232, 249-252, 277-279. On Smith's background, interview with Smith, May 1, 1975.

43. Aubrey Wagner started with TVA in 1934 as a navigation engineer. In 1951 he became assistant general manager. In 1954 he succeeded John Oliver as general manager when Oliver resigned following the appointment of Herbert Vogel as chairman. Wagner is widely credited with having "held TVA together" during the stressful years of Vogel's chairmanship. In 1961 President Kennedy appointed Wagner as a director, and in 1962, following Vogel's departure, Wagner was made chairman. In 1977 he announced that he would not ask to be reappointed when his term ended in 1978.

44. Interview with Robert Betts, director of personnel, September 17, 1973.

45. Ibid. Rapid organizational growth in the last few years has increased opportunities for upward mobility.

46. Interview with Jim Durrell, chief, financial planning staff, August 6, 1974.

47. Interview with TVA official, December 1973.

48. Interview with Aubrey Wagner, December 12, 1973.

49. Robert Betts, in an interview on September 17, 1973, noted the tendency to hire at low levels.

50. Based on review of TVA career biographies. Interestingly, within the Office of Power, there have been some recent attempts to engage in management development by moving promising managers among Divisions and bringing them into the Manager's Office for one-year stays.

51. Interviews with Robert Betts, September 17, 1973, and March 3, 1974.

52. Interview with Aubrey Wagner, December 12, 1973.

53. Interview with Frank Gartrell, September 19, 1973.

54. Interview with John Bynon, assistant director of personnel, September 17, 1973.

55. Interview with Fred Thomas, describing O. M. Derryberry, September 20, 1973.

56. Interview with Frank Gartrell, September 19, 1973.

57. Interview with Gerald McGlamery, assistant director, Stack Gas Emissions Studies Staff, September 20, 1973.

58. Pritchett, *Tennessee Valley Authority*, pp. 269, 282-283.

59. Two general managers came from Personnel, one from Budget, one from Budget and Personnel, and one from Law. Wagner is an exception, having been head of Navigation Planning before becoming assistant general manager.

60. Lynn Seeber to authors, March 11, 1976. Seeber's three outside appointments were the only ones made during the period 1966-1976, when a total of thirty-five Division director positions were filled.

61. Interview with Robert Betts, September 17, 1973.

62. Ibid.

63. Interview with Lynn Seeber, December 14, 1973.

64. Interview with Aubrey Wagner, December 12, 1973. But in an interview on February 25, 1975, former general manager John Oliver told a revealing story about Wessenauer's "toughness." On one occasion, Wessenauer and representatives from some other, conservation-oriented Divisions were in Oliver's office trying to settle an issue between them. All the parties made their cases, but the other Divisions had not done their homework as well as the Office of Power. Oliver said he was going to write a memo favoring Power's position. Late that afternoon, Wessenauer came into Oliver's office and expressed concern over the fact that the other Divisions hadn't made the best case they could. As Oliver recalls, he said, "I don't know how to handle these things except to make the best case I can. And the other guys should make the best case they can." Feeling that the matter may not have been decided on the merits, he recommended that Oliver consider the matter further before issuing a decision — advice that Oliver accepted.

65. Watson has since been succeeded by a new manager of power. Interview with Aubrey Wagner, December 12, 1973.

66. Interview with Fred Thomas, September 20, 1973.

67. Martin, "The Tennessee Valley Authority," pp. 369-379; and Tennessee Valley Authority, Division of Health and Safety, *Annual Report*, 1968, pp. 1-4.

68. Tennessee Valley Authority, Division of Health and Safety, *Annual Report*, 1958, p. 20.

69. J. A. Hudson and Joseph Greco, "Pollution, Precipitators, Problems, and Plans (TVA's Particulate Emission Compliance Program)," Paper delivered at American Power Conference, April 29-May 1, 1974, pp. 1, 2; Fred W. Thomas, "TVA's Air Quality Management Program," *Proceedings of the American Society of Civil Engineers, Power Division Journal*, March 1969, p. 137; also, internal memorandums between J. F. Ferris, who oversaw Health and Safety, and C. E. Blee, chief engineer, during planning of Johnsonville; and Tennessee Valley Authority, *The Johnsonville Steam Plant* (Knoxville, Tenn., 1958), Technical Report No. 31.

70. Fred Thomas to authors, May 26, 1976. General manager John Oliver established the multidivisional committee in a memorandum dated May 12, 1953; Project Authorizations nos. 594, 594-1, and 594-2 set out scope of work.

71. The initial Project Authorization, no. 594, explicitly stated that air quality work would be discontinued unless air pollution problems were shown to exist. The Division of Health and Safety's annual reports for 1952-1954 and 1957 discuss evidence of air pollution damage around Johnsonville and Kingston.

72. On Johnsonville, see Division of Health and Safety, *Annual Report*, 1953, p. 16; *Annual Report*, 1954, p. 20; and Fred Thomas, "TVA's Air Management Program," pp. 133, 137. On interest in higher stacks, see notes on conference with Moyer D. Thomas, consultant, March 6, 1971, in TVA files; on stack heights of subsequent plants, see Division of Health and Safety, "Review of Air Pollution Control—TVA Steam Plants," June 1967, p. 13.

73. See note 71.

74. Division of Health and Safety, "Review of Air Pollution Control," pp. 8-11.

75. Thomas, "TVA's Air Management Program," p. 137.

76. Interview with Frank Gartrell, September 19, 1973; executive order involved was no. 11282, issued May 28, 1966.

77. Interviews with TVA officials, September 1973 and May 1975.

78. Interview with T. L. Montgomery, at the time chief of the Air Quality Branch, now environmental scientist in the Division of Environmental Planning, September 20, 1973.

79. Fred Thomas to authors, May 26, 1976; annual reports of the Office of Health and Environmental Sciences, 1970, and Division of Environmental Planning, 1973.

80. See, for instance, TVA, Division of Environmental Planning and Division of Power Resource Planning, "Technical Presentation on TVA's Program for Meeting Ambient SO_2 Standards," September 14, 1973.

81. Tennessee Valley Authority, Division of Power Resource Planning, Kingston Steam Plant, "Installation of Tall Stacks—Summary of Alternatives and Environmental Impacts," July 1973, p. 9.

82. TVA is planning to use low-sulfur coal from the Southeast to meet state SO_2 standards at its Shawnee and Johnsonville plants. E. C. Hill, for twelve years a member of TVA's coal-purchasing department and now an independent broker, said in an interview in 1975 that TVA had, up to that time, discouraged offers of low-sulfur coal by its evident unwillingness to pay a premium price for it.

83. On compliance plan, see TVA press release, "Background Information—Air Quality Plan," July 27, 1978. On opposition of distributors, interview with TVA official, February 1980.

84. Hudson and Greco, "Pollution, Precipitators, Problems and Plans," pp. 1-3, on use of collectors. No strong dissent emerged in our interviews or in documents from that time.

85. Interviews with Aubrey Wagner, September 18, 1973, and Fred Thomas, September 20, 1973.

86. Interview with Fred Thomas, September 20, 1973.

87. Pen-and-ink chart provided by TVA to authors; Hudson and Greco, "Pollution, Precipitators, Problems and Plans," p. 11; interview with TVA operator, March 1976.

88. Interviews with Frank Gartrell, Fred Thomas, and Aubrey Wagner, September and December 1973. On decision to omit particulate controls, see Tennessee Valley Authority, "TVA's Paradise Steam Station, Planning, Design and Construction Highlights," Paper delivered at American Power Conference, Chicago, March 1961, p. 21.

89. TVA, Division of Health and Safety, "Review of Air Pollution Control," pp. 22-24.

90. Interviews with Frank Gartrell, May 8, 1975, and G. O. Wessenauer, May 6, 1975.

91. TVA Division of Health and Safety, "Review of Air Pollution Control," pp. 14-18, 22-25.

92. Interview with Aubrey Wagner, July 25, 1975.

93. Notes, charts, and commentary supplied to the authors by Aubrey Wagner.

94. TVA press release, January 24, 1973.

95. Interview with Larry Montgomery, September 20, 1973.

96. Environmental requirements seem to have contributed substantially to the Law Division's growth. Although the Division was very active early in TVA's life, it later shrank dramatically. Since the late 1960s, a large number of lawyers have been added to deal with environmental matters.

97. George Kimmons to authors, August 8, 1975.

98. Pen-and ink chart provided by TVA to authors shows many precipitators falling short of designed efficiencies. A partial list includes:

Plant	Design Efficiency (%)	Actual Efficiency (%)
Allen	90	70
Bull Run	99	81-97
Kingston	95	90
Paradise	98	95
Gallatin	95	90-92
Widows Creek	90	50-70

99. Interview with TVA design engineer, December 1973.

100. Ibid.

101. Interview with TVA operator, March 1976.

102. Ibid.

103. Ibid.

104. Both types of units are now made by American manufacturers. The distinguishing feature of the "European" approach, offered by several firms, is that it does not rely on freely suspended wires (which tend to break) to provide one pole of the electrostatic field. J. Albert Hudson, Statement to Tennessee Air Pollution Control Board, Nashville, June 18, 1974, p. 6; Hudson and Greco, "Pollution, Precipitators, Problems and Plans," pp. 13-14.

105. Pearce, "The Creeping Conservatism of TVA," p. 32.

106. TVA, *Power Annual Report*, 1975, p. 38.

107. National attention was first directed to TVA's involvement in strip mining by a 1962 *Atlantic Monthly* article by Harry M. Caudill, a dedicated critic of strip mining and a native of Kentucky. See Harry M. Caudill, "The

Rape of the Appalachians," *Atlantic Monthly* 209 (April 1962): 37-42. By 1965 awareness of TVA's involvement in strip mining had become more widespread. Articles about TVA's practices appeared that year in the *New York Times* and the *Washington Daily News.*

108. Rogers, "Public Policy and Pollution Abatement," pp. 52-86. Rogers' thorough doctoral thesis is the source of most of our information about the evolution of TVA's policies on strip mining.

109. Ibid., pp. 104-111.

110. Ibid., pp. 104-106, 116, on initial efforts to deny responsibility; pp. 160-205, on efforts to encourage state action; and pp. 206-237 on decision to insert reclamation requirements in coal-purchasing contracts.

111. Ibid., p. 243. General Accounting Office report was entitled, "Opportunities for Improvements in Reclaiming Strip Mined Lands under Coal Purchase Contracts, TVA," August 9, 1972.

112. Rogers, "Public Policy and Pollution Abatement," pp. 249-252, 277-279.

113. Ibid., p. 422.

114. TVA, *Power Annual Report*, 1973, pp. 10-11.

115. Interview with Lynn Seeber, December 14, 1973.

5. The Pacific Gas and Electric Company

1. Detailed material on PG&E's early history can be found in Charles M. Coleman, *PG&E of California: The Centennial Story of Pacific Gas & Electric Company, 1852-1952* (New York: McGraw-Hill, 1952). For a shorter sketch, see "PG&E," *Fortune* 20 (September 1939): 33 ff.

2. PG&E, "Outlook for 1974," and *Annual Report*, 1974. See also Charles Komanoff et al., *The Price of Power: Electric Utilities and the Environment* (Council on Economic Priorities, 1972), pp. k-1 to k-3, for a general discussion of PG&E's operating characteristics and political environment. In a more recent evaluation, PG&E appears as the least polluting utility. See Ronald H. White, *The Price of Power, Update: Electric Utilities and the Environment* (New York: Council on Economic Priorities, 1977).

3. In the largest "absorption" in its history, PG&E bought these interests for 1,825,000 shares of PG&E common stock, giving North American a 17.2 percent voting interest. There was some suspicion in the Securities and Exchange Commission and elsewhere that there was thus more to Black's appointment than met the eye. See "PG&E," *Fortune*, pp. 33; and Coleman, *PG&E of California*, passim.

4. "PG&E," *Fortune.*

5. For many years, PG&E bought and transmitted the city's surplus power in violation of the statute, since San Francisco lacked its own transmission facilities. In 1945, after extended litigation, a complex interchange arrangement was worked out whereby a number of specific customers—who had formerly bought Hetch Hetchy power from PG&E—now bought it from San Francisco but continued to receive it over the PG&E grid. This arrangement has changed the situation very little, since for transmitting this power PG&E re-

ceives payments essentially equal to the markup it used to make on the Hetch Hetchy power before selling it. These events are recounted in Joe S. Bain, Richard E. Caves, and Howard Margolis, *Northern California's Water Industry: The Comparative Efficiency of Public Enterprise in Developing a Scarce Natural Resource* (Baltimore: Johns Hopkins Press, 1966). For a detailed account of PG&E's role in opposing public power in the 1920s, see Federal Trade Commission, *Utility Corporations*, U.S. Senate Document 92, pt. 10-16, 70th Congress, First Session (Washington, D.C.: Government Printing Office, 1930). See also "PG&E," *Fortune.*

6. Mary Montgomery and Marion Clawson, *History of Legislation and Policy Formation of the Central Valley Project* (Berkeley: U.S. Department of Agriculture, Bureau of Agricultural Economy, 1946).

7. Montgomery and Clawson, *History of Legislation*; Bain, Caves, and Margolis, *Northern California's Water Industry.*

8. PG&E, "Electric Service Area—History and Operations," in *Report on Operations of the Electric Department*, pp. 2-2 to 2-3 (document submitted to California Public Utilities Commission with application no. 54279 for rate increase).

9. The history of these lines as well as the motives of the private power industry in preventing federal domination are outlined in some detail in PG&E, "Pacific Intertie," n.d.

10. Interview with Bill Johns, then PG&E assistant general counsel, January 29, 1974.

11. One such recent petition in Berkeley, for example, was defeated on a referendum ballot by 85 percent of the voters. Interviews with Kenneth Diercks, PG&E Office of Government and Public Affairs, March 6, 1974; and Robert Gerdes, chairman of the executive committee, April 2, 1974.

12. Interview with Kenneth Diercks, March 6, 1974.

13. Interview with John Sproul, then vice-president for gas supply, March 14, 1974.

14. Various managers expressed these views, including Frederick Mielke, then vice-president and assistant to the chairman of the board, interviewed April 2, 1974.

15. Interview with Robert Gerdes, April 2, 1974.

16. Interview with Wally Allen, director of environmental quality, March 22, 1974.

17. Interviews with Bill Johns, January 29, 1974, and Jack LaRue, then marketing manager of the San Jose Division, March 7, 1974.

18. See Bay Area Air Pollution Control District, "Laws Establishing and Affecting the Bay Area Air Pollution Control District," n.d., and "Fact Sheet," n.d.

19. See California Public Utilities Commission, *Annual Report*, 1973-74, pp. 7-8; and "PG&E," *Fortune.*

20. Interview with Thomas Graff, western regional counsel for the Environmental Defense Fund, February 14, 1974.

21. For additional information on the workings of the Energy Commission, see ch. 8.

22. Interview with Stanley T. Skinner, treasurer, and Gordon R. Smith, financial analyst, March 14, 1974. See also PG&E, "Distribution of Common and Preferred Stock Ownership by Class of Investor, December 31, 1972," in *General Report and Allocations of Common Properties and Expenses* (document submitted to Public Utilities Commission in application for a rate increase).

23. "PG&E," *Fortune*; "Growth Power on the Pacific," *Business Week*, September 2, 1967, pp. 44-46.

24. Interviews with various senior executives, March/April 1974.

25. See also "Growth Power on the Pacific," *Business Week*; and PG&E pamphlets, "Energy Story," n.d., and "Nuclear Power at Humboldt Bay," n.d.

26. See "PG&E Unveils Plans to Build Super System," PG&E News Bureau, February 27, 1963.

27. See *Wall Street Journal*, April 13, 1977, p. 16; May 23, 1977, p. 7; and August 26, 1977, for accounts of continuing difficulties over Diablo.

28. See Bay Area Air Pollution Control District, "Air Pollution and the San Francisco Bay Area," n.d.

29. See California Air Resources Board, "California Air Basins," December 1975); and "Air Pollution Control in California—1976."

30. Interview with Robert MacKnight, director of engineering, South Coast Air Quality Management District, August 22, 1977. See also *Los Angeles Times*, February 16, 1977.

31. These include a vice-president for public relations, an Office of Governmental and Public Affairs, an Office of Environmental Quality, a director of quality assurance, and a vice-president and general counsel. See PG&E organization chart.

32. Interviews with Bill Johns, January 29, 1974; and Fred Searls, then vice-president and general counsel, January 25, 1974.

33. Interview with Bill Johns, January 29, 1974.

34. Interview with Robert Gerdes, April 2, 1974.

35. Interview with Fred Searls, January 25, 1974.

36. Interviews with Bill Johns and John Sproul, March 14, 1974.

37. Interview with Bill Johns, January 29 and March 20, 1974.

38. Interview with senior PG&E manager, March/April 1974.

39. Interviews with Ellis B. Langley, vice-president for division operations, March 20, 1974; and Richard K. Miller, vice-president for personnel and general services, March 22, 1974.

40. Interview with John Bonner, former president and chief operating officer, April 3, 1974.

41. Interview with John Bonner, April 3, 1974; interview with Ellis Langley, March 20, 1974.

42. See, for example, curriculum vitae for Richard Miller, and for Joseph Y. DeYoung, vice-president for commercial operations. The importance of the Divisions in executive training was also mentioned in interviews with Ellis Langley, March 20, 1974; and Richard Miller, March 22, 1974.

43. Interviews with various members of the environmental quality staff.

44. Interview with Barton Shackelford, then vice-president for planning

and research, March 6, 1974. Since Shackelford's promotion to senior vice-president, this position has been filled by Nolan Daines, former manager of the Land Department.

45. Interviews with various PG&E personnel, March/April 1974.

46. Interview with PG&E staff member, March/April 1974.

47. Interviews with Richard Miller, March 22, 1974; and John Sproul, March 14, 1974.

48. Interview with John Bonner, April 3, 1974. The fact that top executives have come up through the ranks is borne out by their curriculum vitae. Several, in fact, began with the company thirty or more years ago as laborers, mail boys, elevator operators, clerks, or plant assistants. John Bonner's curriculum vitae shows that he began with the company in 1937 as assistant hydrographer.

49. Interviews with John Sproul, March 14, 1974; Richard Miller, March 22, 1974; and Frederick Mielke, April 2, 1974.

50. Interviews with Fred Searls and Bill Johns, January 25, 1974; and Kenneth Diercks, March 18, 1974.

51. Interview with Richard H. Peterson, then vice-chairman of the board, March 27 and April 3, 1974. Fouraker, as discussed by Paul R. Lawrence and Jay W. Lorsch in *Organization and Environment* (Homewood, Ill.: Richard D. Irwin, 1969), suggests that external threats generally bring about centralization in organizational decision making.

52. Interview with PG&E staff member, March/April 1974.

53. Interview with Ellis Langley, March 20, 1974.

54. Interview with PG&E employee, March/April 1974.

55. Interview with PG&E source, March/April 1974.

56. Interviews with PG&E sources, March/April 1974.

57. Recently, however, PG&E has appointed an outside attorney, Mason Willrich, as vice-president for corporate planning to try to deal with some of these problems.

58. Interview with PG&E source, March/April 1974.

59. See PG&E, *Annual Report*, 1975. Of the sixteen board members in 1975, three were bankers, two were financial consultants, six were businessmen, one was a conservationist (Doris Leonard), and four were PG&E executives.

60. Interview with PG&E source, March/April 1974.

61. Interview with Fred Searls, January 25, 1974.

62. Interview with PG&E source, March/April 1974.

63. Interview with Frederick Mielke, April 2, 1974.

64. Interviews with PG&E sources, March/April 1974.

65. This and following information on undergrounding policies is compiled from interviews with Fred Searls and Bill Johns, January 25, 1974; Bill Johns, January 29 and March 20, 1974; John C. Morrissey, associate general counsel, March 21, 1974; Richard Peterson, March 27 and April 3, 1974; and John Sproul, March 14, 1974. See also PG&E, "Proposed Testimony of Witnesses, September 1965 — Aesthetics and Economics" (document submitted to the PUC as part of undergrounding proposal).

66. PG&E, "Proposed Testimony of Witnesses, September 1965."

67. Ibid.

68. Communication from Richard Peterson, July 5, 1979.

69. See Komanoff et al., *The Price of Power*, p. k-2.

70. These figures have been taken from PG&E's pamphlet, "Mighty Moss," n.d. See also Komanoff et al., *The Price of Power*, pp. k-21 to k-23.

The following discussion of the Moss Landing NO_x problem is derived from interviews with Paul Matthews and Elmer Johnson, Steam Generation, March 11, 1974; John Bonner, April 3, 1974; John Sproul, March 14, 1974; and Wally Allen, March 22, 1974.

71. Interview with Robert Gerdes, April 2, 1974.

72. Interview with PG&E source, March/April 1974.

73. Interview with Robert Gerdes, April 2, 1974.

74. The discussion of the Pittsburg 7 cooling system is derived from interviews with Frederick Mielke, April 2, 1974; Kenneth Diercks, March 6 and 18, 1974; Elmer Hall, March 18, 1974; and Bill Johns, January 29 and March 20, 1974.

75. Still later, a formal state thermal policy was passed, but Pittsburg 7 was then grandfathered in, exempting it from added requirements.

76. For a general discussion of nuclear siting difficulties, see Komanoff et al., *The Price of Power*, pp. k-3 to k-5.

77. PG&E's troubles at Bodega Head have attracted considerable public attention. See, for example, Komanoff et al., *The Price of Power*, p. k-3. See also David E. Pesonen, "A Visit to the Atomic Park," (series of articles reprinted from the *Sebastopol Times* as part of a contribution toward a People's Park at Bodega Head), and S. Prakesh Sethi, "Pacific Gas and Electric Company, San Francisco: Attempt to Construct a Nuclear Power Plant at Bodega Bay," in S. Prakesh Sethi, *Up against the Corporate Wall* (Englewood Cliffs, N.J.: Prentice-Hall, 1971).

78. Quoted in Sethi, "Pacific Gas and Electric Company," p. 2.

79. Sethi, "Pacific Gas and Electric Company," and Pesonen, "Visit to the Atomic Park," p. 3.

80. Interviews with Kenneth Diercks, March 6 and 18, 1974; and Fred Searls, January 25, 1974. Sutherland's involvement is also noted in Sethi, "Pacific Gas and Electric Company," p. 2, and Pesonen, "Visit to the Atomic Park," p. 3.

81. Interview with Kenneth Diercks, March 6 and 18, 1974; Pesonen, "Visit to the Atomic Park," pp. 8, 9; and Sethi, "Pacific Gas and Electric Company," p. 3.

82. Pesonen, "Visit to the Atomic Park," pp. 13-15; interview with John Morrissey, March 21, 1974.

83. Sethi, "Pacific Gas and Electric Company," p. 10; Pesonen, "Visit to the Atomic Park," p. 31.

84. Sethi, "Pacific Gas and Electric Company," pp. 5-6, 13-14.

85. Pesonen, "Visit to the Atomic Park," pp. 17, 20-22; Sethi, "Pacific Gas and Electric Company," pp. 14-16.

86. Sethi, "Pacific Gas and Electric Company," pp. 16-17. Interview with Kenneth Diercks, March 6 and 18, 1974.

87. Sethi, "Pacific Gas and Electric Company," p. 17; interviews with John Morrissey, March 21, 1974; and Fred Searls, January 25, 1974.

88. Sethi, "Pacific Gas and Electric Company," pp. 17-18.

89. Sethi, "Pacific Gas and Electric Company," pp. 18-19; and *Wall Street Journal*, November 2, 1964, p. 7 (quoted in Sethi). Interviews with John Morrissey, March 21, 1974; Fred Searls, January 25, 1974; and Ferdinand Mautz, vice-president for engineering, March 6 and April 1, 1974.

90. This was certainly true of the Bodega project. See, for example, Pesonen, "A Visit to the Atomic Park," p. 23; and interview with Fred Searls, January 25, 1974.

91. See Pesonen, "A Visit to the Atomic Park," p. 9; and Sethi, "Pacific Gas and Electric Company," pp. 7-8, 11.

92. Interview with Eli Silver, marine geologist, United States Geological Survey, September 27, 1974. When Humboldt Bay closed recently for refueling, the Nuclear Regulatory Commission staff refused to allow the plant to reopen unless modifications were made in its seismic design. PG&E, however, disputes the agency's claim that changes made are unsatisfactory. See *Wall Street Journal*, August 8, 1977, p. 24.

93. This is evident, for example, in David Pesonen's articles. The point was also made by Kenneth Diercks, March 6 and 18, 1974.

94. This was indicated in an interview with Fred Searls, January 25, 1974.

95. Interviews with Kenneth Diercks, March 6 and 18, 1974; and Bill Johns, January 29 and March 20, 1974.

96. Interviews with Kenneth Diercks, March 6 and 18, 1974; Robert Gerdes, April 2, 1974.

97. Interviews with PG&E sources, March/April 1974.

98. Interview with PG&E source, March/April 1974.

99. For an account of this controversy in the Sierra Club, see *New York Times*, March 14, 1969, p. 20.

100. See *Wall Street Journal*, April 13, 1977, p. 16, and August 26, 1977, p. 19.

101. Interviews with Ferdinand Mautz, March 6 and April 1, 1974; Kenneth Diercks, March 6 and 18, 1974; and Elmer Hall, chief siting engineer, March 18 and 20, 1974.

102. David Pesonen, "Power at Point Arena" (Sierra Club, July 1972). Also interviews with Ferdinand Mautz, March 6 and April 1, 1974; Kenneth Diercks, March 6 and 18, 1974; Elmer Hall, March 18 and 20, 1974; and Fred Searls, January 25, 1974.

103. Interview with Eli Silver, September 27, 1974. Silver told us that since most faulting on the California coast is in a northwest direction, the obvious place to look for pertinent data is along a northwest line through the reactor site. PG&E, however, focused on northwest lines *west* of the site, and only on lines perpendicular to the coast through the site (a much less likely direction of faulting). Once PG&E submitted more data, Silver thought there *was* evidence of seismic activity in the appropriate area. PG&E, however, has always taken the view that the data were insignificant, and it explicitly withdrew its application without prejudice to the possibility of reapplying at a later date.

104. Interviews with Kenneth Diercks, March 6 and 18, 1974; John Bonner, April 3, 1974. See also PG&E, *Annual Report*, 1972.

105. Interview with Bill Johns, January 29 and March 20, 1974.

106. Interviews with Kenneth Diercks, March 6 and 18, 1974; Elmer Hall, March 18 and 20, 1974; and Robert Gerdes, April 2, 1974.

6. Ontario Hydro

1. Ontario Hydro, *Annual Report*, 1974, pp. 5-6. A few areas of the province receive their power from other utilities.

2. Merrill Denison, *The People's Power: The History of Ontario Hydro* (Toronto: McClelland & Stewart, 1960), p. 52 and ch. 8. Denison is the source of most of our information on Hydro's early history.

3. Ibid.

4. Task Force Hydro, *Hydro in Ontario: Financial Policy and Rates: Report 4*, April 1973, pp. 70-71.

5. Denison, *The People's Power*, pp. 46, 147, 205, and 215. Sanford F. Borins suggested to us the importance of party politics to Ontario Hydro's situation.

6. Province of Ontario, The Power Corporation Act, R.S.O. 1970, ch. 354, as amended by 1972, c.l.s. 73, and 1973, ch. 57 (March 1974), pt. I, sections 3, 24, and 54.

7. On consultations, see interviews with George Gathercole, April 24, 1974, and with others in Hydro during 1974.

8. See for example W. G. Friedmann and J. F. Garner, eds., *Government Enterprise, A Comparative Study* (New York: Columbia University Press, 1970), especially pp. 30-43, 79-87; David Coombes, *State Enterprise: Business or Politics?* (London: Allen and Unwin, 1971), pp. 86-122.

9. Solandt Commission, *Closing the Generation Gap*, March 1974, pp. 1-17.

10. Canadian Royal Commission on Electric Power Planning (Porter Commission), *Report 1*, May 1976.

11. Ontario Hydro, *Annual Report*, 1975, p. 4. Also, correspondence from Robert B. Taylor, chairman of Ontario Hydro, to Dennis R. Timbrell, minister of energy, Ontario, 11 February 1976; and interviews with David Robinson, Route and Site Selection Division, April 1, 1975, and February 19, 1976, on approvals for new facilities.

12. Task Force Hydro, *Hydro in Ontario: A Future Role and Place: Report 1*, p. 37.

13. Task Force Hydro, *A Future Role and Place*, pp. 50-51; Robert Williamson, "Steel Man to Succeed Gathercole," *Toronto Globe & Mail*, February 15, 1974, p. 1.

14. Task Force Hydro, *Hydro in Ontario: An Approach to Organization: Report 2*, pp. 36-37; Ontario Hydro, *Annual Report*, 1974, pp. 2-3, 5.

15. Task Force Hydro, *A Future Role and Place*, p. 21.

16. Interview with Wayne Roddick, Canadian (federal) Department of Environment, on Ontario's early concern with pollution problems, Winter 1975.

17. Interview with Brian Kelley, former member, Pollution Probe, April 22, 1974. See also Pollution Probe files.

18. Solandt Commission, *Closing the Generation Gap*, pp. 1-17.

19. On development of the St. Lawrence, see Denison, *The People's Power*, pp. 246, 256. Two good sources on history and nature of CANDU technology are Task Force Hydro, *Nuclear Power in Ontario: Report 3*, 1973, and Hugh C. McIntyre, "Natural-Uranium Heavy-Water Reactors," *Scientific American* 233 (October 1975): 17-27. CANDU reactors are able to use unenriched uranium as fuel because, as a moderator, heavy water is very efficient; it captures relatively few neutrons released during the fissioning of uranium atoms, permitting a chain reaction to occur even with natural uranium, which has a relatively low concentration of fissionable U_{235} atoms. Although heavy water is expensive—and the plants needed to produce it require a large capital investment—the CANDU technology eliminates the need for fuel enrichment; both financially and technically this is a good trade for the Canadians, who have expertise in producing heavy water but not in fuel enrichment.

Another distinctive feature of CANDU is the use of many individual pressure tubes, rather than one single pressure vessel, to contain the nuclear reaction. This makes continuous refueling of the reactor possible, whereas U.S.-style reactors must be completely shut down for refueling. The individual pressure-tube design has safety advantages as well, since less of the highly radioactive "used" fuel builds up in the core at one time or is collected in one pressure unit, and the heavy-water moderator serves as a supplementary cooling source in the event of a loss of coolant.

20. Interviews with Harold A. Smith, vice president for engineering and operations, Ontario Hydro, November 30, 1973, and May 17, 1976. As of late 1975, after about four years of service, Pickering units 1 and 2 were operating at a capacity factor of 80 percent and unit 4 had achieved a record capacity factor of 93 percent, giving the plant one of the best operating records in the world, despite problems which reduced unit 3's factor to 65 percent.

21. Letter from P. G. Campbell, general manager for design and construction, Ontario Hydro, to authors, April 5, 1976. Information on Lakeview outages from Ontario Hydro, *System Expansion Program* (document submitted to the Ontario Energy Board), vol. 3 (December 19, 1973), suppl. 3.1-4, p. 1. Power cuts to "interruptible" users were far below interruptions allowed in contracts, but in 1968 and 1969 they were greatly in excess of other years, and Hydro feared it might have to cut delivery to regular customers. M. V. Spence, production engineer, Ontario Hydro, July 29, 1976.

22. Ontario Hydro, in reviewing this chapter, stated that no decision was reached to ignore power loans from U.S. utilities in planning capacity reserves. However, in Ontario Hydro, *System Expansion Program*, vol. 3, pp. 21, 27-28, the utility stated that it did not purchase power on a firm, contract basis from U.S. utilities, and, in addition, that although it had depended during the 1960s on the possibility of importing power on an emergency basis, "it will not be a factor in planning for the period 1977-1982."

The 30 percent reserve margin that Hydro began aiming for was not significantly out of line with reserves maintained by some neighboring utilities with similar characteristics, according to Ontario Energy Board consultant G. W. Clayton in his *1974 Review of Ontario Hydro*, vol. 1, pp. 5.57-62. However, this margin is far higher than that maintained by some of the other utilities in our study, who appear to be more cost-conscious. The Southern Company's reserves are far lower, and Pacific Gas and Electric, a system not unlike Hydro in size and type of capacity, aims for around 12-15 percent reserves. Hydro has, in the last few years, reset its reserve target at 25 percent.

23. Task Force Hydro, *Financial Policy and Rates*, pp. 70-71.

24. McIntyre, "Natural-Uranium Heavy-Water Reactors, p. 19.

25. Ontario Energy Board, Report to the Minister of Energy, *Ontario Hydro—Power System Expansion Program and Financial Policies*, August 1974, p. 73; W. Darcy McKeough, Treasurer of Ontario, to R. B. Taylor, chairman, Ontario Hydro, January 22, 1976.

26. Interview with Ontario government official, March 1976. Ontario Hydro, *Annual Report*, 1974, p. 13; *Annual Report*, 1975, p. 2.

27. Interview with William G. Morison, director, Design and Development Division, Ontario Hydro, November 27, 1973.

28. McIntyre, "Natural-Uranium Heavy-Water Reactors," pp. 22-23; and career information on Harold A. Smith supplied by Ontario Hydro.

29. Hydro's previous chairman, George Gathercole, was economic adviser to the Ontario government before becoming vice-chairman and then chairman of Hydro. A number of other members were self-employed professionals who served on their local municipal utility commissions.

30. Interview with Hydro president D. J. Gordon, April 24, 1974.

31. Interview with Harold A. Smith, November 26, 1973.

32. Interview with member of Hydro's Division of Law, November 1973.

33. Interview with Harold Smith, May 14, 1976. Smith, who appointed Campbell, stressed that he did not appoint Campbell solely to put a construction man over both Construction and Design; rather, Campbell seemed best for the job.

34. Interview with Harold Smith, November 26, 1973.

35. Ibid.

36. Ibid. Also see Smith's memorandum to the Commission, "Organization of the Construction and Engineering Division," May 5, 1965.

37. Interview with Harold Smith and Pat Cambell, November 26, 1973. Letter from Pat Campbell to authors, April 5, 1976. Also, announcement issued by directors of generation projects and station projects on reorganization to take effect June 19, 1969.

38. Interview with Harold Smith, November 26, 1973.

39. Interview with former thermal operations manager, July 7, 1975.

40. Interview with Arthur Hill, now director of the Route and Site Selection Division, Ontario Hydro, November 27, 1973.

41. Ibid. See also Arthur Hill, "Reliability and Maintainability Activities: Utility Application" (paper delivered at Canadian Nuclear Association Symposium on Reliability and Maintainability, September 1973); and J. Kraznodebski, Generation Projects Division, Ontario Hydro, "Application of Reliability and Maintainability in Nuclear Power Stations" (paper delivered at Reliability

Engineering Conference for the Electric Power Industry, February 1974).

42. Ontario Hydro, *System Expansion Program*, vol. 3, suppl. 3, 1-4, p. 1.

43. Interview with thermal operations manager, July 7, 1975.

44. In particular, operators' objections to prototypes were ignored.

45. Interview with Arthur Hill, April 2, 1975.

46. Interview with thermal operations manager, July 7, 1975.

47. Interview with J. W. James, former manager, Energy and Environment Department, June 28, 1976. James was killed in an airplane crash in September 1976 while taking part in investigations for the Royal Commission on Electric Power Planning in Northern Ontario.

48. Interview with J. W. James, June 28, 1976. Also, correspondence from W. R. Effer, section head in the Department of Energy and Environment, to authors.

49. Interview with Douglas Harrison, Chemical Research Department, Ontario Hydro, July 18, 1975.

50. In an interview on May 17, 1976, Harold Smith noted that the Research Division has acted as a service unit, performing work requested or likely to be requested by other groups in the organization, and commented that he has not wanted the Research Division to be an "environmental policeman."

51. Interview with public-relations official, Ontario Hydro, April 1974.

52. Interview with Harold Smith, November 26, 1973.

53. Interviews with Harold Smith, November 30, 1973, and January 24, 1977.

54. Interview with Harold Smith, November 30, 1973.

55. Task Force Hydro, *A Future Role and Place*, p. 34.

56. W. Darcy McKeough, Provincial treasurer, to Hydro chairman R. B. Taylor, January 22, 1976.

57. Interview with J. W. James, former manager of Energy and Environment Department, April 24, 1974.

58. Ibid.

59. Interview with E. F. O'Keefe, senior approvals engineer, Air Quality Branch, Ministry of Environment, Ontario, April 23, 1974.

60. Figures provided by R. G. Swift, Enquiry and Research Services, Public Relations Division, Ontario Hydro, in letter of November 20, 1973.

61. Interviews with spokesmen for Detroit Edison, Commonwealth Edison, and Consolidated Edison, September and October, 1975.

62. Solandt Commission, *Closing the Generation Gap*, pp. 1-17.

63. On Lennox withdrawal, see Solandt Commission, *Transmission: A Public Inquiry into the Transmission of Power between Lennox and Oshawa*, April 1975, p. 12. On Bradley-Georgetown withdrawal, see Environmental Hearing Board, *Ontario Hydro Bradley-Georgetown 500 kv Transmission Line Right of Way*, December 1975, p. iii; and interview with David Robinson, community affairs specialist, Route and Site Selection Division, Ontario Hydro, April 1, 1975.

64. Interview with David Robinson, April 1, 1975.

65. Ibid. See also public information packets provided by Ontario Hydro

concerning the Lennox-Oshawa and Bradley-Georgetown transmission lines.

66. Solandt Commission, *Transmission*; and Environmental Hearing Board, *Ontario Hydro Bradley-Georgetown Line.*

67. Interviews with David Robinson, June 28, 1976, and March 1, 1977.

68. Ibid.

69. Interview with Douglas Harrison, Chemical Research Department, Research Division, Ontario Hydro, July 18, 1975.

70. Interview with William G. Morison, now director of the Design and Development Division, Ontario Hydro, November 27, 1973.

71. Ontario Ministry of Environment, Proposed Guidelines for Thermal Stations (n.d.); and interview with Arthur Hill, former head of Concept Department, April 2, 1975.

72. Interview with Douglas Harrison, July 18, 1975.

73. Ibid.

74. Interview with C. H. Clark, manager, Chemical Research Department, March 1976.

75. Interview with D. K. A. Gillies, manager, Environmental Protection, Central Thermal Services, Ontario Hydro, April 1, 1975.

76. Interview with Harold Smith, May 17, 1975.

77. Interview with Douglas Harrison, July 18, 1975.

78. Ministry of Environment, Water Resources Branch, Position Paper on Power Plant Cooling (draft), p. 15.

7. The Southern Company

1. There also are some other entities—for example, a company that owns one particular plant and is in turn jointly owned by two operating subsidiaries—but they can be ignored for our purposes. A fifth operating company, South Carolina Power Company, was also part of the original system. Paul H. Rigby and Warren I. Cikins describe Southern's interconnected operations in some depth in their case study on the Alabama Power Company, *A Public Utility Plans for Expansion* (Birmingham: University of Alabama, School of Commerce and Business Administration, Bureau of Business Research, December 1956), pp. 9-10, 28-32.

2. Historical information on the Southern Company system was obtained primarily from histories written by company executives, including Thomas W. Martin, *Forty Years of Alabama Power Company, 1911-1951* (New York: Newcomen Society in North America, 1952); Thomas W. Martin, *The Story of Electricity in Alabama* (Birmingham, 1952); Harllee Branch, *Alabama Power Company and the Southern Company* (New York: Newcomen Society in North America, 1967); Harllee Branch, *Georgia and the Georgia Power Company: A Century of Free Enterprise* (New York: Newcomen Society in North America, 1957); and Jack Watson, *Electric Power and People Power: The Story of Mississippi Power Company* (New York: Newcomen Society in North America, 1969).

3. Southern Company, *Annual Report*, 1950; *Annual Report*, 1977, p. 2.

4. On the Commonwealth and Southern years, see George Bush, *Future Builders: The Story of Michigan's Consumers Power Company* (New York: McGraw-Hill, 1973). Also, interview with Sherwood Lawrence, director of Power Engineering, Southern Company Service, April 2, 1975, on functioning of service company during those years.

5. Southern had another scrape with TVA in the 1950s, when Southern president Eugene Yates and Middle South Utilities chairman Edgar Dixon proposed, at the Eisenhower administration's invitation, the soon famous "Dixon-Yates" plan to supply power to TVA's customers in Memphis, Tennessee, through a contract with the Atomic Energy Commission. After considerable controversy, Memphis built its own plant (which it soon leased to TVA). See Aaron Wildavsky, *Dixon-Yates: A Study in Power Politics* (New Haven, Conn.: Yale University Press, 1962); Martin, *The Story of Electricity*, pp. 107-113; also C. Herman Pritchett, *The Tennessee Valley Authority: A Study in Public Administration* (Chapel Hill: University of North Carolina Press, 1943), ch. 3; and Bush, *Future Builders*, pp. 343-347, on TVA fight with Commonwealth and Southern.

6. Martin, *The Story of Electricity*, p. 32; on rate cuts, see Alabama Power Company, *Annual Report*, 1937, p. 6; and Georgia Power Company, *Annual Report*, 1939, p. 9. On Willkie's attitude on rates, see Bush, *Future Builders*, pp. 299-300.

7. See Martin, *The Story of Electricity*, pp. 94-97, 116-120, on industrial development departments, and pp. 131-135 on founding of Southern Research Institute.

8. Bush, *Future Builders*, p. 350. On Commonwealth and Southern's financial practices, see Bush, *Future Builders*, pp. 270-271; and Thomas K. McCraw, *TVA and the Power Fight, 1933-39* (Philadelphia: Lippincott, 1971), pp. 50-51. Bush provides further background on the public utility investigations on pp. 265-279.

9. Bush, *Future Builders*, pp. 352-354 and 357-358; and Moody's Public Utility Manual, 1976, p. 1475, on dissolution of Commonwealth and Southern and formation of the Southern Company. The Southern Company's annual report for 1949 describes the formation of Southern Services.

10. Average personal income per capita in the South rose from $1,707 in 1960 to $3,369 in 1970, to $5,198 in 1975 — only 13.5 percent below the national average. Figures from Albert W. Niemi, Jr., University of Georgia, presented in *Time* 108, no. 13 (September 27, 1976): 73.

11. Interview with John Farley, manager of environmental licensing, Southern Company Services, May 8, 1974.

12. Interview with Bob Collom, chief, Air Quality Section, Georgia Department of Natural Resources, February 1974; *Rules and Regulations for Air Quality Control*, Georgia Department of Natural Resources, September 1973, pp. 215-217.

13. Natural Resources Defense Council v. EPA, U.S. Court of Appeals, Fifth Circuit, decision reported in *Environment Reporter—Cases*, March 1, 1974. On EPA review, see Air Programs Office, Environmental Protection Agency, Region IV, Atlanta, Georgia, Evaluation of the Georgia Control Strat-

egy, June 21, 1974. In a later decision, the Fifth Circuit Court ruled that EPA had acted acceptably in approving Georgia Power's tall stacks. Only *future* reliance on tall stacks was prohibited, it said; disallowing stacks built in the past would unfairly penalize good faith compliance efforts by the company.

14. Interview with James W. Cooper, director, Division of Air Pollution Control, Alabama Air Pollution Control Commission, August 19, 1974. EPA guidelines are set out in "Requirements for Preparation, Adoption, and Submittal of Implementation Plans, 42 CFR pt. 420, published in *Federal Register* 36, no. 158 (August 14, 1971): 15486-506, especially 15490.

15. Interviews with James Cooper, August 19, 1974, and with John Farley, manager of Environmental Licensing, Southern Company Services, May 8, 1974. Figures provided by Cooper show that, on the basis of EPA's C.R.S. model, the following maximum 24-hour average concentrations of SO_2 (measured in micrograms per cubic meter) would occur around Alabama Power Company plants, if coal with the maximum sulfur content permitted by the regulations were burned:

Plant	Lbs/million Btu allowed	Max. 24-hr. concentration, $\mu g/m^3$	+ Background
Barry	1.2	61	120
Chickasaw	1.2	80	120
Gadsden	4.0	173	75
Greene	4.0	237	25
Gaston	4.0	122	25
Gorgas	4.0	198	25

These figures are well within the 24-hour primary ambient standard of 365 $\mu g/m^3$. However, it is widely accepted that the C.R.S. model with which these figures were derived is not precise and may be in error by a factor of 2. See Joseph Tikvart and Connally Mears, "Applications of the Single Source (CRSTER) Model to Power Plants: A Summary," in U.S. Environmental Protection Agency, *Proceedings of the Conference on Environmental Modeling and Simulation*, Cincinnati, Ohio, April 19-22, 1976, p. 703. Hence, 24-hour, average concentrations at Gadsden could reach 346 $\mu g/m^3$; at Greene County, 474 $\mu g/m^3$; and at Gorgas, 396 $\mu g/m^3$, very close to or greater than the primary ambient standard. These concentrations are possible even with the new, taller stacks that Alabama Power Company built after the initial SO_2 standards were adopted. Without these taller stacks, Alabama Power Company would almost certainly violate ambient standards under the new SO_2 emission standards set by the state agency.

16. See transcript of hearings before Alabama Air Pollution Control Commission, April 18, 1973. On prior role of environmentalists, interview with James Cooper, executive director of the commission, August 19, 1974.

17. Interview with David Levin, June 1975. Mike Toner, of the *Miami Post-Herald*, provided information on clean-air groups in Florida, and Terry Cole, of the Florida Department of Environmental Regulation, supplied information on environmentalists' involvement in variance hearings, in interviews in June 1975.

18. In interviews in May and June 1975, several individuals identified the various factors involved in the modification of Florida's regulations: William Burch, EPA, Region IV, Atlanta; Mike Toner, *Miami Post-Herald*; John Craig, formerly senior research engineer at Southern Company Services, and now director of environmental affairs at El Paso National Gas; and Terry Cole, Florida Department of Environmental Regulation. (Cole asserted that public support for environmental regulations had *not* declined, but agreed that the utilities had mounted a strong campaign against the standards.)

19. Interview with Victor Belba, inspector for the Georgia Department of Natural Resources, July 28, 1976.

20. Federal Power Commission, Steam Electric Plant Air and Water Quality Control Data (for year ended 1971), Summary Report, June 1974.

21. Southern Company, *Annual Report*, 1971, p. 2; *Annual Report*, 1972, p. 11; *Annual Report*, 1974, p. 12.

22. Recently, a candidate for the Georgia rate commission was elected handily, on the basis of a pledge that he would not grant any rate increase to Georgia Power Company during his six-year term.

23. Interviews with Dewitt Rogers, *Atlanta Constitution*; Neil Herrin, Georgia Power Project; Robert Scherer, president, Georgia Power Company; and Joseph Farley, president, Alabama Power Company, June 1975. See also Southern Company, *Annual Report*, 1974, p. 27; *Annual Report*, 1962, p. 11.

24. These arrangements also allayed antitrust action against the system by the U.S. Justice Department. Southern Company, *Annual Report*, 1974, p. 27; also annual reports for 1962, 1965, 1966.

25. Southern Company, *Annual Report*, 1975, pp. 32-33. Rigby and Cikins, *A Public Utility Plans for Expansion*, pp. 8-9, on executive committee.

26. Interview with Alvin Vogtle, president, Southern Company, July 9, 1975.

27. Interview with Joseph Farley, president, Alabama Power Company, August 20, 1974.

28. Interviews with Joseph Farley, August 20, 1974, and Robert Scherer, May 9, 1974.

29. Interviews with Eason Balch, May 6, 1974, and January 31, 1977.

30. Interview with Alvin Vogtle, July 9, 1975.

31. Southern Company, "A New Look for the Southern Electric System," describes the new policy on corporate image; see advertisement in *Wall Street Journal*, March 1, 1978, p. 8.

32. Interview with John Farley, manager of Environmental Licensing at Southern Company Services, March 29, 1975.

33. Rigby and Cikins, *A Public Utility Plans for Expansion*, pp. 52-53.

34. Interview with James Ludwig, vice-president for fuels, Southern Company Services, August 21, 1974.

35. Southern Company, "Focus: The Environmental Side of Research and Development," n.d.

36. This concern with Southern Company Services' power came through as an undercurrent in our discussions with operating company personnel and was reflected in comments such as, "Sometimes they [Southern Company Ser-

vices] act as if this were one system."

37. Interview with William Reed, president of Southern Company Services, May 7, 1974.

38. For instance, in an interview in August 1974 one operating company engineer mentioned that if identical units are used at a plant, savings that might be achieved by sharing certain equipment, like control rooms and cranes, might not be possible. But then he noted that at his company's newest plant there was considerable sharing of equipment among units.

39. Interview with Alvin Vogtle, July 9, 1975.

40. Interview with William Harrison, senior vice-president, Southern Company Services, May 7, 1974.

41. Interview with Alvin Vogtle, July 9, 1975.

42. Interview with Joseph Farley, president, Alabama Power Company, August 20, 1974.

43. Interview with Roy Krotzer, May 8, 1974.

44. Ibid.

45. Interview with William Reed, president, Southern Company Services, May 7, 1974.

46. Interview with a Southern Company Services engineer, Spring 1974.

47. Ironically, another company that used wood fill had a disastrous and costly cooling-tower fire shortly after this decision was made. The "fill" is formed into a series of grid-like structures within the tower, which serve to disperse and diffuse the water so that it cools faster. Interview with Alvin Vogtle, July 9, 1975.

48. Interview with Joseph Farley, August 20, 1974.

49. Southern faces higher interest rates and greater difficulties in raising capital than TVA. Interviews with William Reed, May 7, 1974, and February 17, 1977. Reed stressed that the system is *not* antinuclear and would pursue a more ambitious nuclear program if it could afford one.

50. Interview with Dwayne Summar, vice-president for public relations, Southern Company Services, August 23, 1974. In the Energy Supply and Environmental Coordination Act of 1974 and the 1977 Clean Air Act amendments, Congress stood firmly by its policy of stringent emission standards for new power plants.

51. Interview with James Ludwig, on divestiture of company-owned mines and concern about limiting capital obligations, August 21, 1974.

52. Interview with James Ludwig, August 21, 1974.

53. Ibid.

54. Interview with Dwayne Summar, August 23, 1974.

55. The United Mine Workers expressed concern over the fact that the South African miners worked under contracts that required them to live in crowded barracks, separated from their families, for months at a time, subject to criminal penalties for breaking work rules or leaving their jobs, and earned wages of $3 a day or less. See Don Stillman, "UMWA Launches Battle to Stop South African Coal Imports," in *United Mine Workers Journal*, June 1-15, 1974, pp. 7-13; also, Ed Townsend, "UMW Seeks to Ban South African Coal," in *Christian Science Monitor*, August 22, 1974. Southern Company personnel,

in conversations with the authors in 1974 and 1975, rejected the notion that the South African miners worked under "slave labor" conditions and contended that the miners were well-paid by South African standards. In official statements, the company emphasized its need for the South African coal to meet environmental requirements and dismissed concern about the impact of its purchases on racial policies in South Africa, stating that the system companies "of course have no control over operating practices of any of their suppliers, and this relatively small purchase surely could have no effect on policies in South Africa, nor would the withholding of such a purchase" (Southern Company release, "South African Coal: The Other Side of the Story," p. 2).

56. Stillman, "UMW Launches Battle." Also UMWA and Attorney General of Alabama to Commissioner of Customs, Motion to Withhold Release of Merchandise, August 16, 1974; accompanying statement includes legal discussion of evidence that the miners are working under "slave labor" conditions. On shareholder resolution, see "Southern Co. Criticized on South Africal Coal," *United Mine Workers Journal*, June 1-15, 1975, pp. 1, 7-9.

57. Don Stillman, "Customs Refuses Bar on South African Coal," *United Mine Workers Journal*, February 16-28, 1975, p. 5; "Southern Co. Criticized on South African Coal;" correspondence from James Ludwig to authors, January 26, 1977.

58. "U.S. Bureau of Mines figures indicate that Alabama has 2,045,500,000 tons of deep minable low-sulfur coal and 33,000,000 of strippable low-sulfur coal. Most of it is within 200 miles of the power plants that plan to burn the coal imported from South Africa" (Stillman, "Customs Refuses Bar on South African Coal").

59. Appendix to brief field by UMWA and Attorney General of Alabama with Motion to Customs Commission to Withhold Release of South African Coal.

60. Interview with James Ludwig, December 3, 1974. Low-sulfur utility coal, purchased under long-term contracts, was worth about $30-$40 in the Southeast in 1976, according to a letter from James Ludwig to authors, January 26, 1977. Southern paid about $27 a ton for the metallurgical-quality, deep-mine coal purchased in Alabama for the Miller plant, and the South African coal cost $30 per ton *delivered.*

61. Interview with Dwayne Summar, August 23, 1974. Summar and John Vezeau, Southern Company Services' Birmingham public-relations supervisor, state that establishing the public-relations office in Birmingham was not related to the difficulties experienced over the South African coal purchases, but was done to distribute the work load more rationally, and particularly to focus on relations within the Southern system.

62. In buying the coal, the company stated that a new Bantu Labor Act passed in South Africa, in part through the efforts of the company's own lawyers, meant that "slave labor and penal sanctions" did not exist in the mines, a point the company worked to get across to local groups.

63. Out of the initial work with the three prototypes has come EPA funding for a full-scale demonstration of one of these technologies at another utility site. The vendor of that process has devised an improvement based on less ex-

pensive reactants, and contracts currently are being completed to reactivate that system at Plant Scholz. The second process has been abandoned by the same vendor in favor of a completely new, extremely promising process, which is simpler and less expensive than the original prototype. Evaluation studies on its are now nearing completion at Plant Scholz. Work on the third process was discontinued at Plant Scholz, but a major outgrowth of the work was a larger-scale demonstration of a portion of the process at a facility in Germany. Interviews with William Harrison, May 7, 1974, and John Craig, formerly senior research engineer at Southern Company Services, now director of environmental affairs for El Paso Natural Gas, May 8, 1974, and May 1, 1975, and correspondence from Harrison to authors, February 20, 1979.

64. Interview with William Harrison, May 7, 1974. "Southern Company Terms Test of Special Coal a Success," *Wall Street Journal*, July 20, 1977, p 8; "Sweet Smell of Success' (advertisement), *Wall Street Journal*, March 1, 1978.

65. Interview with John Craig, May 1, 1975.

66. Ibid.

67. Table contained in memorandum to William Reed from Sherwood Lawrence, April 30, 1974, released to the authors. Also Charles Komanoff et al., *The Price of Power* (New York: Council on Economic Priorities, 1972), pp. N-8 to N-45. On Gadsen plant, interview with John Farley, May 6, 1974.

68. Interview with Sherwood Lawrence, August 20, 1974.

69. Interviews with Sherwood Lawrence, August 20, 1974, and Tom Byerley, manager of Environmental Affairs, Georgia Power Company, August 23, 1974. According to Byerley, Bob Causey, Georgia Power's manager of production, pushed for more precipitator sectionalization in the early 1960s, but Plant Bowen whose first unit came on line in 1971, was the first to have adequate sectionalization.

70. Many of the stacks were well under 200 feet high prior to 1965; see Federal Power Commission, Steam Electric Plant Air and Water Quality Control Data. On start of move to higher stacks, interview with Southern Company Services engineer, May 1974, and interview with Tom Byerley on monitoring program, August 23, 1974.

71. Interview with Southern Company Services engineer, May 1974.

72. Interview with Roy Krotzer, manager, Engineering Services, Alabama Power Company, August 20, 1974.

73. Interview with James Ludwig, December 3, 1974.

8. The Los Angeles Department of Water and Power

Note: At the request of the Department of Water and Power, no personnel below the very top level are identified by name either in the text or the notes.

1. For this and following information on the history of the Los Angeles Department of Water and Power, see Vincent Ostrom, *Water and Politics: A Study of Water Policies and Administration in the Development of Los Angeles* (Los Angeles: Haynes Foundation, 1953), pp. 27-77. A chronological outline of the essential facts is also provided in LADWP, *Water and Power Facts and Figures to 1975-6*, pp. 7-70. See also LADWP, *From Pueblo to Metropolis: Water Is the Story of Los Angeles*, n.d.

2. The story of the aqueduct has been grossly simplified here. For a more detailed account, see Ostrom, *Water and Politics*, pp. 9-16; and LADWP, *Water and Power Facts and Figures*, pp. 12-13.

3. See Ostrom, *Water and Politics*, pp. 61-63 and 116-143 for a more complete account of the battles over Owens Valley water.

4. See Ostrom, *Water and Politics*, pp. 78-85 for a description of the nature and practices of the "Power Machine," and pp. 73-77 for an account of its destruction.

5. Ibid., p. 102; and LADWP, *Water and Power Facts and Figures*, p. 21.

6. Interview with retired general manager Robert V. Phillips, February 25, 1977.

7. The contrast between this atmosphere of the 1950s and that of the late 1960s and early 1970s was emphasized especially by Robert Phillips, interview of February 25, 1977, and by chief electrical engineer James Mulloy, interview of February 22, 1977.

8. *Charter of the City of Los Angeles*, section 229, subsection 5. These formal and informal relations with the board were also described by Ostrom, *Water and Politics*, pp. 63-75 and 97-103 and in interviews with LADWP general manager Louis H. Winnard and James Mulloy, February 22, 1977, and with Robert Phillips, February 25, 1977.

9. Correspondence to authors from general manager's office.

10. *Charter of the City of Los Angeles*, section 229, subsection 5. See also Ostrom, *Water and Politics*, pp. 109-111. The absence of city council authority over budgetary matters was confirmed in an interview with LADWP Financial Office staff, February 23, 1977.

11. Interview with Robert Phillips, February 25, 1977.

12. Interviews with James Mulloy, February 22, 1977, and Robert Phillips, February 25, 1977.

13. Interview with retired chief electrical engineer Floyd Goss, May 28, 1974.

14. Telephone interview with *Los Angeles Times* staff reporter Larry Pryor, July 6, 1973; interview with Robert Phillips, February 25, 1977.

15. For general accounts of the origins and early achievements of the Los Angeles County Air Pollution Control District, see *1974 Profile of Air Pollution Control* (Los Angeles: LAAPCD, 1974); A. J. Haagen-Smit, "The Control of Air Pollution," *Scientific American* 210 (January 1964): 25-31; Remi Nadeau, *Los Angeles: From Mission to Modern City* (New York: Longmans, Green, 1960), pp. 284-291; and Morris Neiburger, "Smog Today and Smog Tomorrow," *Nation* 201 (December 6, 1965): 432-435.

16. *1974 Profile of Air Pollution Control*; and *APCD Reports*, February 1955, September 1955, and March 1956.

17. *APCD Reports*, July 1956; interviews with LADWP Air Quality staff, May 23, 1974, and with APCD engineer John Danielson, June 25, 1974. See also "Southern California Edison," in Charles Komanoff et al., *The Price of Power: Electric Utilities and the Environment* (New York: Council On Economic Priorities, 1972), for a discussion of Edison's record on pollution control. See also Ronald H. White, *The Price of Power, Update: Electric Utilities and the Envi-*

ronment (New York: Council on Economic Priorities, 1977).

18. *APCD Reports*, April 1960, April 1961, and February 1964. Also *1974 Profile of Air Pollution Control*. Burning low-sulfur oil not only limited SO_2 emissions but so reduced visible plume opacity that variances were no longer required.

19. See "Southern California Edison," in Komanoff et al., *The Price of Power*.

20. Telephone interview with Jack Nevitt, APCD Enforcement Division, July 9, 1973; interview with John Danielson, June 25, 1974; and interview with LADWP Air Quality staff, May 23, 1974.

21. See especially LADWP, *From Pueblo to Metropolis* and *Water and Power Facts and Figures*, for this and following information on the DWP's plant expansion.

22. LADWP, *Water and Power Facts and Figures*.

23. Interview with Floyd Goss, May 28, 1974. See also, *APCD Reports*, January 1965, December 1966, and April 1967.

24. See LADWP, "Pacific Intertie," n.d.

25. For the LADWP's account of the controversy surrounding this project, see its pamphlet, "Energy Crisis" (n.d.).

26. For an account of environmentalists' response to the Kaiparowitz, Intermountain, and similar desert projects, see G. Christian Hill, "A Replay of Kaiparowitz?" in the *Wall Street Journal*, October 20, 1977.

27. These changes were emphasized especially by James Mulloy, in an interview on February 22, 1977, and by Robert Phillips, interview of February 25, 1977.

According to LADWP, *Water and Power Facts and Figures*, p. 86, the DWP did not raise rates *at all* until 1956. Subsequently, there were *no* increases (but there was one reduction) between 1959 and 1970. Since 1970, however, the DWP has raised rates no less than five times.

28. Interview with Robert Phillips, February 25, 1977.

29. Interview with LADWP Financial Office staff, February 23, 1977.

30. Interviews with James Mulloy, February 22, 1977, and with LADWP Financial Office staff, February 22, 1977. See also, City of Los Angeles, *Mayor's Blue Ribbon Committee Report on the DWP Rate Structure*, April 1977.

31. Interview with Robert Phillips, February 25, 1977. Also, *Los Angeles Times*, June 21 and 22, 1973; July 10 and 27, 1973; and September 19 and 21, 1973.

32. Interview with Robert Phillips, February 25, 1977; James Mulloy, February 22, 1977; and with LADWP Financial Office staff, February 23, 1977.

33. Interview with LADWP Financial Office Staff, February 23, 1977.

34. Telephone interview with Robert Phillips, June 6, 1977. See also, "Voter Information Pamphlet for the General Municipal Election, Tuesday, May 31, 1977," compiled by city clerk Rex E. Layton, pp. 83-86.

35. See especially *Los Angeles Times*, November 16 and 22, 1973; and December 10 and 13, 1973. The whole conservation program proved a bit embarrassing. Between the ensuing favorable year for hydroelectric generation in the Pacific Northwest and the success of the conservation program, the DWP

ended up with a surplus of imported oil — and not enough storage tanks to put it in.

36. That Winnard was the first outsider brought in as general manager since Morris is verified by LADWP, *Water and Power Facts and Figures*. The mayor's role was suggested to the authors in a confidential interview, and the DWP's official position was put forth in correspondence from the general manager's office.

37. Margaret Gerteis and Stephen R. Thomas, "Politics of Air Pollution Control in Southern California" (unpublished materials prepared for Executive Programs in Health Policy and Management, Harvard School of Public Health, October 1977). See also *Los Angeles Times*, July 3, 1976. County supervisors sought unsuccessfully in 1975 to forestall this state-mandated reorganization by forming a federation of the pollution control districts of San Bernardino, Riverside, Orange, and Los Angeles. This interim arrangement was known as the Southern California Air Pollution Control District.

38. Gerteis and Thomas, "Politics of Air Pollution Control in Southern California." See also State of California, Health and Safety Code, Division 26, Mulford-Carrell Air Resources Act. Also, Southern California Air Pollution Control District, "New Source Review Rules, Rule 213, Adopted October 8, 1976, by Air Resources Board"; and *Los Angeles Times*, October 9, 1976, and February 16, 1977.

39. See State of California, Coastal Zone Conservation Act of 1972 (Public Resources Code, subparagraphs 27000-27650).

40. See State of California, Environmental Quality Act of 1970 (Public Resources Code, subparagraphs 21000-21174). Interviews with LADWP Engineer of environmental coordination, February 22, 1977, and with James Mulloy, February 22, 1977.

41. See LADWP organization chart. The recent reorganizations of general manager Louis Winnard have changed this structure somewhat.

42. Interview with Louis Winnard, February 22, 1977.

43. Most of this information on civil service, promotional, and hiring procedures at LADWP is based on interviews with the LADWP director of industrial relations, February 23, 1977, and by telephone on April 1, 1977. Some details were also provided in interviews with LADWP Water Quality staff, May 22, 1974; Civil and Structural Design staff, May 22, 1974; and the engineer of environmental coordination, May 21, 1974.

44. Telephone interview with LADWP director of industrial relations, April 1, 1977. Personnel cutbacks have, however, added to the workload, and hence to the overtime — especially of technical personnel. The high overtime pay of some employees has attracted attention.

45. Interview with LADWP Transmission Line Design staff engineer, May 23, 1974. There is some indication that this is changing. However, the DWP agrees that "there is no hard and fast rule as to what must be taken to the immediate supervisor."

46. LADWP Civil and Structural Design staff, in interview of May 22, 1974, attested to their freedom to be creative. Interview with LADWP Resource Planning personnel, May 21, 1974, offered similar evidence.

47. Interview with Floyd Goss, May 28, 1974.

48. This was acknowledged in interviews with Louis Winnard and James Mulloy, February 22, 1977; and with LADWP legislative representative, February 23, 1977.

49. Interview with engineer of environmental coordination, May 21, 1974.

50. Information regarding Mulloy's advancement has been derived from LADWP, *Water and Power Facts and Figures*, and from Mulloy's curriculum vitae.

51. The changes in Phillips' style of management are attested in interviews with LADWP Financial Office staff, February 23, 1977, and with Robert Phillips, February 25, 1977.

52. Information on Winnard's background and on the changes he has brought about is based mostly on an interview of February 22, 1977, and on his curriculum vitae. Also helpful were interviews with James Mulloy, February 22, 1977, and with the director of industrial relations, February 23, 1977; and a telephone interview with Public Affairs Office staff on January 17, 1977.

53. Interview with LADWP Financial Office staff, February 23, 1977, provided information on new budgeting procedures.

54. Interview with LADWP Air Quality staff and Office of Environmental Coordination staff, February 22, 1977.

55. Interview with engineer of environmental coordination, February 22, 1977.

56. Interview with Louis Winnard, February 22, 1977.

57. Interviews with James Mulloy, February 22, 1977; with director of industrial relations, February 23, 1977; and with Louis Winnard, February 22, 1977.

58. Interview with Louis Winnard, February 22, 1977.

59. Interviews with director of industrial relations, May 29, 1974, and with engineer of environmental coordination, May 21, 1974; telephone interview with director of industrial relations, April 1, 1977.

60. The Department of Water and Power disagrees with this analysis, arguing that the its participation in joint projects reflects the merits of this approach, not the backgrounds of the DWP's personnel. Our view is that the causality is mixed—different approaches appear more or less advantageous, depending on one's background.

61. Interview with Floyd Goss, May 28, 1974; interviews with System Planning staff, May 21, 1974, and with Transmission Line Design staff, May 23, 1974.

62. Floyd Goss to Marc Roberts, February 17, 1977.

63. Interview with Floyd Goss, May 28, 1974.

64. LADWP, *Management Bulletin* 481 (February 28, 1967).

65. Correspondence from general manager's office.

66. Interviews with engineer of environmental coordination, May 21, 1974, and February 22, 1977; with Water Quality staff, May 22, 1974; with Station Electrical Design staff, May 23, 1974; and with Air Quality staff, February 22, 1977.

67. *Los Angeles Times*, January 1 and August 2, 1972; interviews with Public Affairs Office staff, May 29, 1974.

68. Goss was responding to the criticisms of the DWP's advertising campaigns that emerged at the time of the Scattergood affair. The trial judge at the time declared that as a publicly owned utility, the DWP had no need to "boost its sales." See "Los Angeles Water and Power vs. LAAPCD," in Bureau of National Affairs, *Environment Reporter—Cases*, vol. 1, p. 1612.

69. Interviews with Public Affairs Office staff, May 29, 1974, and telephone interview January 17, 1977; interview with Water Quality staff, May 22, 1974.

70. LADWP, *Water and Power Facts and Figures*.

71. Interview with LADWP legislative representative, February 22, 1977, provided information for this and following material about that office.

72. Interview with Robert Phillips, February 25, 1977; and interview with Masamori Kojima, mayor's liaison, June 25, 1974.

73. Interviews with Louis Winnard and James Mulloy, February 22, 1977.

74. Interview with LADWP legislative representative, February 23, 1977.

75. Interview with engineer of environmental coordination, February 22, 1977.

76. Interview with LADWP legislative representative, February 23, 1977.

77. Interview with Ralph G. Wesson, Office of the City Attorney, May 21, 1974; interviews with the engineer of environmental coordination, May 21, 1974, and February 22, 1977.

78. Interview with Robert Phillips, February 25, 1977.

79. Interview with engineer of environmental coordination, February 22, 1977.

80. Robert Phillips, interview of February 25, 1977, commented on the necessary limitations of the board.

81. Interview with James Mulloy, February 22, 1977.

82. Interview with Floyd Goss, May 28, 1974.

83. Interview with Floyd Goss, May 28, 1974. Similar comments were made by LADWP engineer of steam generation, interview of May 28, 1974; Civil and Structural Design staff, May 22, 1974; Transmission Line Design staff, May 23, 1974; and Station Electrical Design staff, May 23, 1974.

84. Interview with LADWP Civil and Structural Design staff, May 22, 1974.

85. Interview with Floyd Goss, May 28, 1974; interview with Transmission Line Design Staff, May 23, 1974.

86. Interviews with Transmission Line Design staff, May 23, 1974, and with Water Quality staff, May 22, 1974.

87. Interview with Transmission Line Design staff, May 23, 1974.

88. Ibid.

89. Ibid.

90. For more specific discussions of Los Angeles' smog problem, see Lester Lees et al., *Smog: A Report to the People* (Pasadena, Calif.: California Institute of Technology, Environmental Quality Laboratory, 1972); and Haagen-

Smit, "The Control of Air Pollution," pp. 25-31.

91. See Neiburger, "Smog Today and Smog Tomorrow," pp. 432-435; Nadeau, *Los Angeles: From Mission to Modern City*, pp. 284-291; and California Air Resources Board, "Chronology of Air Pollution Control."

92. Interview with Floyd Goss, May 28, 1974.

93. Except as otherwise noted, the following discussion of the Scattergood controversy is derived from "Los Angeles Water and Power vs. LAAPCD," *Environment Reporter—Cases*, vol. 1, pp. 1580-1612, and from a chronology of communications between the two provided us by the LADWP. This account draws strongly on interviews with LADWP Air Quality staff, May 25, 1974, and with Floyd Goss, May 28, 1974.

94. The reader will recall that the APCD had routinely denied Southern California Edison and the DWP permits on the basis of plume opacity; they had regularly obtained variances from the Hearing Board.

95. Interview with Floyd Goss, May 28, 1974.

96. Interview with LADWP Mechanical Design staff members, May 22, 1974.

97. This view was expressed in interviews both with James Mulloy and with Air Quality staff, February 22, 1977.

98. *Los Angeles Times*, February 19, 1971; and interviews with Robert L. Chass, former air pollution control officer, June 24, 1974; Ralph Wesson, May 21, 1974; LADWP Mechanical Design staff, May 22, 1974; LADWP engineer of steam generation, May 28, 1974; and telephone interview with Jack Nevitt, LAAPCD Enforcement Division, July 9, 1973.

99. Interviews with LADWP Air Quality staff, May 23, 1974; Robert Chass, June 24, 1974; and Jack Nevitt, July 9, 1973.

100. See Gerteis and Thomas, "Politics of Air Pollution Control in Southern California"; LADWP, "Final Environmental Impact Report for the Operation of Scattergood Steam Plant, Unit 3, with Fuel Oil"; interviews with engineer of environmental coordination and Air Quality staff, February 22, 1977.

101. "Los Angeles Water and Power vs. Los Angeles APCD," *Environment Reporter—Cases*, vol. 1, pp. 1580-1612.

102. Interviews with Robert Chass and with William B. Krenz, assistant director of engineering, LAAPCD, June 24, 1974.

103. Interview with Air Quality staff, May 23, 1974.

104. Interview with Robert Chass, June 24, 1974.

105. "Los Angeles Water and Power vs. Los Angeles APCD," *Environment Reporter—Cases*, vol. 1, pp. 1580-1612.

106. Ibid.

107. Ibid.

108. Ostrom, *Water and Politics*, p. 102; interview with Floyd Goss, May 28, 1974.

109. Interview with Floyd Goss, May 28, 1974.

110. Interview with Floyd Goss, May 28, 1974. Telephone interview with *Los Angeles Times* staff reporter Larry Pryor, July 6, 1973; interview with LADWP nuclear project manager, May 28, 1974.

111. *Los Angeles Times*, August 1 and 2, 1972; interviews with LADWP

Water Quality staff, May 22, 1974; Resource Planning staff, May 21, 1974; nuclear project manager, May 28, 1974; telephone interview with Larry Pryor, July 6, 1973.

112. Interviews with LADWP Public Affairs staff, May 29, 1974; Resource Planning staff, May 21, 1974; nuclear project manager, May 28, 1974; Masamori Kojima, mayor's liaison, June 25, 1974.

113. Interview with nuclear project manager, May 28, 1974.

114. Interviews with nuclear project manager, February 23, 1977, and May 23, 1974.

115. See *Los Angeles Times*, March 10 and 14, 1978; LADWP news release, March 13, 1978; telephone interview with Office of Environmental Coordination staff, March 17, 1978.

116. See LADWP pamphlet, "Mohave," n.d. Additional information was provided by Floyd Goss in interview of May 28, 1974.

117. See Lawrence A. McHugh, "Four Corners Power Complex: Pollution on the Reservation," *Indiana Law Journal* 47 (Summer 1978): 603-610, for background on environmental controversies.

118. Interview with LADWP Resource Planning staff, May 21, 1974.

119. See *Los Angeles Times* editorials, June 22, 1973, and September 21, 1973.

120. Interview with Robert Phillips, February 25, 1977. See also *Los Angeles Times*, June 21, 1973; July 10 and 27, 1973; and September 19, 1973.

9. Boston Edison

1. Our primary source of information on Boston Edison's early history is James V. Toner, *The Boston Edison Story, 1886-1951: 65 Years of Service* (New York: Newcomen Society in North America, 1951).

2. Frank Farnsworth, Jr., "Some Aspects of the Development of the Electric Utility Industry in New England, 1924-49" (Ph.D. diss., Harvard University, 1952).

3. William E. Leuchtenburg, *Flood Control Politics: The Connecticut River Valley Problem, 1927-50* (Cambridge, Mass.: Harvard University Press, 1953), is a good source of information on the history of efforts, ultimately fruitless, to develop the Connecticut River Valley for power. Essentially, the states— apparently under the influence of the private utility companies—blocked federal initiatives to develop the Connecticut Valley. In addition, although he was at times interested in extending the TVA example to other river valleys, Franklin Roosevelt ultimately decided not to pursue the idea.

4. William D. Shipman, *An Inquiry into the High Cost of Electricity in New England* (Middletown, Conn.: Wesleyan University Press, 1962), is a good discussion of this question. Shipman argues that New England utilities, for various reasons, have typically been too small to take adequate advantage of economies of scale.

5. Interview with Charles Avila, former president and chairman of Boston Edison, August 14, 1975. "Although there were a few highly trained engineers during the company's early rapid-growth years, leadership then required

backgrounds of financing, corporate law, and accounting, whereas large numbers of employees were operatives or in clerical and record-keeping activities," Avila said.

6. Earl Latham and George Goodwin, Jr., *Massachusetts Politics* (Medford, Mass.: Tufts University Civic Education Center, 1960).

7. Interviews with former DPU commissioners William Cowan, April 10, 1975, and Barbara Hassenfell, April 10, 1975, and with then-current commissioner Eunice Howe, April 11, 1975. Interviews conducted by Susan Catler.

8. This account of Edison's rate history is taken from clippings in the *Boston Globe* archives. See Leuchtenburg, *Flood Control Politics*, for discussion of talk of forming a Connecticut Valley Authority.

9. Interview with Donald Newton, Braintree Power and Light Department, November 7, 1979.

10. *Boston Globe*, January 8, 1969; "Boston Edison," Harvard Business School, case study no. 9-371-076, 1970, p. 11.

11. Interview with a state legislator and a staff member of the Department of Public Health.

12. James Toner, "The Boston Edison Story."

13. Interviews with Boston Edison employees, August 1974.

14. Interviews with Charles Avila, August 14, 1975, and William Irving, October 11, 1974. Irving was at the time an engineering manager at Edison and is now managing director of the Jacksonville Electric Authority.

15. Correspondence from Francis Staszesky, now president of Boston Edison, to authors, March 12, 1979.

16. Interview with Thomas Galligan, chairman of Boston Edison, August 22, 1974.

17. Interview with Charles Avila, August 14, 1975.

18. Interview with Thomas Galligan, August 22, 1974.

19. Interview with James Lydon, senior vice-president for corporate communications, August 14, 1974.

20. Correspondence from Francis Staszesky to authors, March 12, 1979.

21. Interview with Boston Edison executive, August 1974.

22. Interview with Charles Avila, August 14, 1975.

23. Interestingly, Lydon has a background in engineering, and began his Edison career as an engineer.

24. Interview with Thomas Galligan, August 22, 1974.

25. Interview with John Desmond, assistant general counsel, Boston Edison, August 13, 1974.

26. Interview with William Irving, October 11, 1974. Irving was the first head of the new environmental group and left Edison to become managing director of the Jacksonville Electric Authority. Creating the Environmental Affairs Department gave Edison's top management a suitable place to move Irving, who had been a deputy superintendent of engineering. This is a good example of how organizational changes can serve both strategic and personnel-development aims.

27. Francis Staszesky to authors, March 12, 1979.

28. Interview with J. Edward Howard, Spring 1976. Howard became

vice-president for nuclear engineering and operations.

29. Interview with Charles Avila, August 14, 1975.

30. Interview with Charles Dolloff, Environmental Affairs Department, August 14, 1974.

31. Francis Staszesky to authors, March 12, 1979.

32. Interviews with Charles Dolloff, August 14, 1974, and Frank Lee, now manager of Environmental Affairs Department, August 1973. Dolloff stated that concern about the precipitators catching fire was a major reason for not using them when the switch was made to oil.

33. Interview with Francis Staszesky, August 14, 1974, on installation of monitors, and on the effect of the Thanksgiving 1966 inversion on the company's thinking. See also "Boston Edison," Harvard Business School case study, pp. 8-9.

34. Interview with Francis Staszesky, August 14, 1974, and Boston Edison engineer, Summer 1974.

35. *Boston Globe*, January 8, 1969. "Boston Edison," Harvard Business School case study, p. 11, makes reference to three other enforcement actions for similar fallout problems.

36. Interview with Charles Dolloff, August 14, 1974.

37. Interview with William Irving, October 11, 1974.

38. Ibid.

39. "Boston Edison," Harvard Business School case study, pp. 21-26.

40. Interviews with Department of Public Health staff members, June 1974. Boston Edison chairman Thomas Galligan reports that he spoke with both Mayor White and Governor Sargent around the time the regulations were established; both told him that the prevailing political climate would make it difficult for them to oppose strong air pollution standards.

41. See Stone and Webster Engineering Corporation, "Air Quality Analysis," Boston, August 29, 1969. In a critique of the Stone and Webster study, the Union of Concerned Scientists argued that although Boston Edison's *annual* contribution to ambient SO_2 levels might be low, the company's metropolitan plants regularly caused *hourly* standards to be exceeded, and would probably continue to do so if 2.2 percent sulfur fuel were burned on a normal basis. See Union of Concerned Scientists, "An Analysis of the Sulfur Dioxide Pollution Levels due to the Mystic, New-Boston, and L St. Power Plants of the Boston Edison Company," September 29, 1970.

The U.S. Environmental Protection Agency, too, remained skeptical about fuel switching in an area like Boston, where there are many pollution sources. Although fuel switching might make sense where there was a single, isolated source, it made less sense in a multisource situation, EPA staff felt, since it is much harder then to correlate the emissions from individual sources with the general ground-level concentration of SO_2. Interview with Peter Haggerty, regional EPA office, July 2, 1974.

42. Interviews with top managers and the company's annual reports indicate that Boston Edison took the viewpoint that it had a responsibility to defend its consumers' interests against unnecessary costs, even if the public were pressuring for these added costs. As the company's 1969 *Annual Report* stated, "As

advancing technology makes it ever harder to keep the public informed, it becomes our crucial responsibility to try ever harder to do so. There is one basic principle we would wish above all to convey: It is in the public interest and in our corporate interest to act *as the public would act* if it had complete information about our business" (italics added).

43. Interview with Thomas Galligan, Spring 1976.

44. Interviews with Thomas Galligan and William Irving, Spring 1976.

45. Much of our information came from *Boston Globe* archives and interviews with Sudbury selectman John E. Taft and consultant Alexander Kusko, July 8, 1974, who advised the town of Sudbury during the fight over this transmission line.

46. Interview with James Lydon, senior vice-president for corporate communications, August 14, 1974.

47. Interviews with John E. Taft and Alexander Kusko, July 8, 1974.

48. Interview with James Lydon, August 14, 1974.

49. Interview with a Boston Edison engineer.

50. Ibid.

51. Interview with James Lydon, August 14, 1974, on corporate judgment that "public acceptance of the Mystic site was relatively good compared to other sites like Edgar." Before building the new unit, the company agreed to a "nondegradation" plan with state regulatory authorities. Under the plan, Edison agreed to install a scrubber on the unit or, alternatively, to install a precipitator on the unit and burn .3 percent sulfur oil in units 1-3 and operate them only 500 hours a year. Edison officials acknowledge that, even with these measures, more SO_2 would be emitted from the plant with the new unit in operation; it was expected, however, that ambient SO_2 levels in the immediate vicinity of the plant would not increase. Interview with William Irving, Spring 1976.

52. Interviews with Charles Avila, August 14, 1975, and James Lydon, August 14, 1974.

53. Interview with J. Edward Howard, August 22, 1974.

54. Ibid.

10. Explaining Environmental Decisions

1. "Panel Is Named in Ford Study," *Boston Globe*, November 3, 1979.

2. There is a large academic literature which is critical of regulation. Some of the best-known works in this area are George J. Stigler, "The Theory of Economic Regulation," *Bell Journal of Economics and Management Science 2*, no. 1 (Spring 1971): 3-21; Charles L. Schultze, *The Public Use of Private Interest* (Washington, D.C.: The Brookings Institution, 1977); Allen V. Kneese and Charles L. Schultze, *Pollution, Prices and Public Policy* (Washington, D.C.: The Brookings Institution, 1975). See also Roger G. Noll, *Reforming Regulation* (Washington, D.C.: The Brookings Institution, 1971), and Commission on Law and the Economy, American Bar Association, *Federal Regulation: Roads to Reform* (Washington, D.C.: American Bar Association, 1978).

3. A classic discussion of the "issue attention cycle" is Anthony Downs, "The Political Economy of Improving Our Environment," in Downs et al., *The*

Political Economy of Environmental Control (Berkeley: University of California, Institute of Business and Economic Research, 1972).

4. See, for example, H. G. Fredrickson and H. Magnus, "Comparing Attitudes toward Pollution in Syracuse," *Water Resources Research* 14 (October 1968): 877-889; R. C. Lucas, "Wilderness Perception and Use—The Example of the Boundary Waters Canoe Area," *Natural Resources Journal* 3 (January 1964): 394-411; W. R. D. Sewell and I. Burton, *Perceptions and Attitudes in Resource Management*, Department of Energy, Policy Research and Coordinating Branch, Resource Paper no. 2 (Ottawa: Queens Printer, 1971).

5. This is in keeping with studies of local politics in other problem areas such as housing. See, for example, J. Clarence Davies, *Neighborhood Groups and Urban Renewal* (New York: Columbia University Press, 1966), and Langley C. Keyes, *The Rehabilitation Planning Game* (Cambridge, Mass.: MIT Press, 1969).

6. These variations were also observable in states not considered in this study. See Marc J. Roberts and Susan O. Farrell, "The Political Economy of Implementation: The Clean Air Act and Stationary Sources," in Ann F. Friendlaender, ed., *Approaches to Controlling Air Pollution* (Cambridge, Mass.: MIT Press, 1978).

7. For a more general discussion of the circumstances under which self-regulation tends to occur, see R. E. Caves and M. J. Roberts, *Regulating the Product* (Cambridge, Mass.: Ballinger, 1975).

8. There is a very large literature, especially outside the United States, about the question of how to relate public enterprises to the general government and whether or not these entities should be run on purely "business" principles. Some useful sources are David Coombes, *State Enterprise: Business or Politics* (London: Allen and Unwin, 1971); W. G. Friedmann and J. F. Garner, eds., *Government Enterprise: A Comparative Study* (New York: Columbia University Press, 1970); Lloyd D. Musolf, *Public Ownership and Accountability: The Canadian Experience* (Cambridge, Mass.: Harvard University Press, 1959); and Richard Pryke, *Public Enterprise in Practice* (New York: St. Martin's Press, 1971).

9. Notice that many of these same problems also plague politically appointed agency managers (for example, cabinet and subcabinet officers) when they face dealing with well-entrenched agency staffs.

10. J. Q. Wilson and P. Rachel, "Can the Government Regulate Itself?" *The Public Interest*, Winter 1977, pp. 3-14.

11. Indeed, we did not even observe some of the more important forms of public ownership, such as a government merely holding a stock interest in what is normally a privately organized company. See, for example, M. V. Posner and S. J. Woolf, *Italian Public Enterprise* (Cambridge, Mass.: Harvard University Press, 1967); C. A. Ashley and R. G. H. Smails, *Canadian Crown Corporations* (Toronto: Macmillan, 1965); and Douglas V. Verney, *Public Enterprise in Sweden* (Liverpool: Liverpool University Press, 1959).

12. Ralph L. Keeney and Howard Raiffa, *Decisions with Multiple Objectives* (New York: John Wiley, 1976).

13. Alfred D. Chandler, *Strategy and Structure* (Cambridge, Mass.: Har-

vard University Press, 1962).

14. Joseph Bower, *Managing the Resource Allocation Process* (Boston: Harvard Graduate School of Business Administration, Division of Research, 1970).

15. Gordon Tullock, *the Politics of Bureaucracy* (Washington, D.C.: Public Affairs Press, 1965), pp. 113-120.

16. Note that most economic models do not take such phenomena as loyalty into account. Only future rewards motivate. The impact of the past, and the loyalty, sympathy, and so on it might engender, are all assumed to be of negligible importance.

17. Talcott Parsons, "The Problem of Controlled Institutional Change," *Psychiatry* 8, no. 1 (February 1945): 79-101, reprinted in Parsons, *Essays in Sociological Theory* (New York: Free Press, 1954).

18. Paul R. Lawrence and Jay W. Lorsch, *Organization and Environment* (Homewood, Ill.: Richard D. Irwin, 1969), pp. 64-65.

19. Gordon Tullock, *Toward a Mathematics of Politics* (Ann Arbor: University of Michigan Press, 1967).

20. Philip Selznick, *Leadership in Administration* (New York: Harper & Row, 1957), p. 144; also, William H. Starbuck, "Organizational Growth and Development," in James G. March, ed., *Handbook of Organizations* (Chicago: Rand McNally, 1965), pp. 481-482.

21. James G. March and Herbert A. Simon, *Organizations* (New York: John Wiley, 1958).

22. Kenneth Arrow, *The Limits of Organization* (New York: W. W. Norton, 1974), pp. 58-59.

23. Anthony Downs, *Inside Bureaucracy* (Boston: Little, Brown, 1967), pp. 228-230.

11. Managing the Responsive Organization

1. The answer to this question has been disputed. See Anthony Downs, *Inside Bureaucracy* (Boston: Little, Brown, 1967), p. 197.

2. Reduction of uncertainty is often of major concern to management. See R. E. Caves, "Uncertainty, Market Structure and Performance," in J. W. Markham and G. F. Papanek, eds., *Industrial Organization and Economic Development* (Boston: Houghton Mifflin, 1970).

3. Graham Allison, *The Essence of Decision* (Boston: Little, Brown, 1971), p. 162.

4. Chester I. Barnard, *The Functions of the Executive* (Cambridge, Mass.: Harvard University Press, 1938), pp. 166, 174, 280; and Talcott Parsons, "The Problem of Controlled Institutional Change," *Psychiatry* 8, no. 1 (February 1945): 79-101, reprinted in Parsons, *Essays in Sociological Theory* (New York: Free Press, 1954), pp. 242-243.

5. In this sense they embody, at least to some extent, some of the interpersonal characteristics that Argyris and Schön argued facilitate organizational change. See Chris Argyris and Donald A. Schön, *Organizational Learning: A*

Theory of Action Perspective (Reading, Mass.: Addison-Wesley, 1978).

6. The classic discussion of this problem is Paul R. Lawrence and Jay W. Lorsch, *Organization and Environment* (Homewood. Ill.: Richard D. Irwin, 1969).

7. See Jay R. Galbraith, "Organization Design: An Information Processing View," in Paul R. Lawrence and Jay W. Lorsch, eds., *Organization Planning: Cases and Concepts* (Homewood, Ill.: Richard D. Irwin, 1972), for a report on studies done in the early to middle 1960s by Burns and Stalker, Woodward, Harvey, Hall, and Lawrence and Lorsch.

12. Implications for Regulators

1. This is a quite general phenomenon apart from the environmental arena. See, for example, R. H. Binstock and Martin A. Levin, "The Political Dilemmas of Intervention Policies," in R. H. Binstock and E. Shanas, eds., *Handbook of Aging and the Social Sciences* (New York: Van Nostrand Reinhold, 1976).

2. Many regulations are written to allow a specified *frequency* of violation when in fact any given policy produces a *probability* of violation. The question of what probability is implied by the observed frequency of violations will typically be a vexatious question of statistical inference.

3. U.S. Council on Environmental Quality, *Environmental Quality, 1978*, ninth annual report (Washington, D.C.: Government Printing Office, 1978), p. 3.

4. Matthew Holden, "Pollution Control as a Bargaining Process: An Essay on Regulatory Decision Making," Cornell University Water Resources Center, Publication no. 9, October 1966.

5. Politicians are not the only ones who confront such a dilemma and react in this way. So do television networks, who tend to pay great attention to even small samples of viewer response.

6. Richard E. Neustadt, *Alliance Politics* (New York: Columbia University Press, 1970).

7. Donald N. Dewees, "The Costs and Technology of Pollution Abatement," in Ann F. Friedlaender, ed., *Approaches to Controlling Air Pollution* (Cambridge, Mass.: MIT Press, 1978), especially pp. 317-323. Dewees argues that similar progress has been "forced" with regard to automobile air pollution control.

8. U.S. Department of Health, Education, and Welfare, "Report of the Committee on Health and Environmental Effects of Increased Coal Utilization" (Washington, D.C.: Government Printing Office, 1977).

9. See Helen Ingram, "The Political Rationality of Innovation: The Clean Air Act Amendments of 1970," in Ann F. Friedlaender, ed., *Approaches to Controlling Air Pollution* (Cambridge, Mass.: MIT Press, 1978).

10. Connecticut Enforcement Project, *Economic Law Enforcement*, vol. 1: *Overview* (Hartford, Conn.: Department of Environmental Protection, 1975).

Epilogue

1. Michael Maccoby, *The Gamesman: The New Corporate Leaders* (New York: Simon & Schuster, 1977).

2. Louis Banks, "Here Come the Individualists," *Harvard Magazine* 80, no. 1 (September/October 1977): 24-29.

Index

Acid rain, *see* Air pollution

Aesthetic issues, 46, 55, 125, 143, 250, 271-272, 273, 315, 347; smoke visibility, 146, 148, 190, 192, 379. *See also* Transmission systems

Agricultural and fertilizer development: TVA and, 64, 67-68, 79, 94, 98

Air pollution, 6, 23; health effects of, 48-49, 58, 94, 96, 97, 98, 213, 378; weather conditions and, 48, 59, 98, 99, 129, 199, 292, 307, 310, 328; smog, 48, 125, 129, 145, 250-251, 273, 292, 328, 332; acid rain and acid smut, 49, 59, 308, 309, 379; monitoring of, 96-97, 99, 187, 198-200, 307, 310, 327, 331, 351, 362, 368, 378-379, 387, 391. *See also* Ash (particulate) emissions; Fossil-fuel technology; Nitrogen oxides (NO_x); Sulfur dioxide/sulfate (SO_2/SO_x) emissions

Air Pollution Control Districts/agencies, 61; of Alabama, 73, 209, 210-211, 213, 220, 358, 381; of Bay Area, 126, 148-150, 358, 380; of Florida, 212-213, 230, 381; of Los Angeles, 250-252, 254, 258, 273-278, 327, 332, 334, 338, 377, 378, 389; of Boston, 309, 310, 327

Air pollution regulations and control, 49, 60-61, 386; in Los Angeles area (and LADWP), 60, 243, 250-254, 267, 273-278, 282, 292, 328, 330; TVA and, 63, 64, 73-78 *passim*, 82, 83, 95-117 *passim*, 214, 325, 347, 348, 362, 368, 380; in Bay Area (and PG&E), 125, 126, 129-130, 146-150, 190, 328, 329; Canadian, 171, 173, 187, 192, 197-201, 341, 380; Southern Company and, 210-214, 230-242, 358; Boston Edison and, 291-294,

301-312, 318, 322, 328, 357, 377, 380, 387. *See also* Legislation

Alabama, 65-74 *passim*, 88, 98, 103, 231, 286. *See also* Air Pollution Control Districts/agencies

Alabama Power Company, 204-211 *passim*, 215, 218, 223-229 *passim*, 233, 239, 287, 350, 381. *See also* Southern Company

Alameda, California, 122

Antitrust actions, 123, 159, 208

Argyris, Chris, 43

Army Corps of Engineers, U.S., 70, 149, 152

Ash (particulate) emissions, 48, 102, 108, 129, 146, 192, 227, 306-308, 378; control of, 57-61 *passim*, 96, 103-112 *passim*, 193, 226-227, 239, 240, 321, 337, 347; and salt drift, 149-150

Ashwander v. *TVA*, 69

Askew, Reuben, 212

Atkinson (Georgia) plant, 239

Atomic Energy Commission, *see* Nuclear Regulatory Commission

Avila, Charles, 289, 298-301 *passim*, 305, 321, 341, 352, 363

Balch, Eason, 219

Banks, Louis, 396, 397

Barton, Alan, 229

Bay Area, *see* San Francisco and Bay Area

Beck, Adam, 163, 245, 373

Betts, Robert, 91

Biggs, California, 122

Black, James, 121, 122-123, 128, 133, 137, 139, 161, 287, 350

Blackouts, *see* Generation cutbacks

447